D. H. Lawrence: The Man Who Lived

Papers Delivered at the D. H. Lawrence Conference

at Southern Illinois University, Carbondale   April 1979

Edited by Robert B. Partlow. Jr. and Harry T. Moore

Southern Illinois University Press   Carbondale and Edwardsville

Permission to quote from the works of D. H. Lawrence by the estate of D. H. Lawrence, the estate of Mrs. Frieda Lawrence Ravagli, and Laurence Pollinger, Ltd., as published in the titles listed below, is gratefully acknowledged.

Black Sparrow Press: Gerald M. Lacy, ed., The Escaped Cock, 1973.
Cambridge University Press: Letter of 25(?) January 1928 from D. H. Lawrence to Catherine Carswell.
William Heinemann, Ltd.: Lady Chatterley's Lover, 1961; Mornings in Mexico and Etruscan Places, 1956; "The Novel," in Sex, Literature and Censorship, 1955; Phoenix: The Posthumous Papers of D. H. Lawrence, 1936; The Rainbow, 1955; Sea and Sardinia, 1956; Sons and Lovers, 1958; Studies in Classic American Literature, 1964; and Twilight in Italy, 1956.
New American Library: Lady Chatterley's Lover, 1959, 1962.
Random House, Inc.: St. Mawr and The Man Who Died, 1959.
The Viking Press, Inc.: Etruscan Places, 1968; John Thomas and Lady Jane, 1973; Phoenix, 1936; The Rainbow, 1955; Sons and Lovers, 1958; Studies in Classic American Literature, 1964; and Women in Love, 1960. Harry T. Moore, ed., The Collected Letters of D. H. Lawrence, 1962; Vivian de Sola Pinto and Warren Roberts, eds., The Complete Poems of D. H. Lawrence, 1971; and Warren Roberts and Harry T. Moore, eds., Phoenix II: Uncollected, Unpublished, and Other Prose Works by D. H. Lawrence, 1968.
Yale University Library: Letter of 25(?) January 1928 from D. H. Lawrence to Catherine Carswell.

Permission to quote from the sources listed below is also gratefully acknowledged.

Faber and Faber Limited: Philip Larkin, High Windows, 1974.
Farrar, Straus & Giroux, Inc.: Philip Larkin, High Windows, 1974.
Harper & Row Publishers, Inc.: Denis Donoghue, "'Till the Fight Is Finished': D. H. Lawrence in His Letters," in D. H. Lawrence: Novelist, Poet, Prophet, edited by Stephen Spender, 1973; lines 43-61 from "Crow's Account of the Battle" in Ted Hughes, Crow. Copyright c 1971 by Ted Hughes. Reprinted by permission of Harper & Row Publishers, Inc.
Ted Hughes, "Existential Song." By permission of the author.
New Directions Publishing Corporation: Denise Levertov, The Poet in the World, 1973; Francisco Garcia Lorca and Donald M. Allen, eds., The Selected Poems of Federico Garcia Lorca, 1955; William Carlos Williams, Selected Poems, 1963.

Library of Congress Cataloging in Publication Data

International D. H. Lawrence Conference: Lawrence Today, Southern Illinois University in Carbondale, 1979.
    D. H. Lawrence, the man who lived.

    Includes bibliographical references and index.
    1. Lawrence, David Herbert, 1885-1930--Criticism and interpretation--Congresses. I. Partlow, Robert B. II. Moore, Harry T. III. Illinois. Southern Illinois University, Carbondale. IV. Title.
PR6023.A93Z63196   823'.912   80-15262
ISBN 0-8093-0981-5

Contents

Foreword

The idea of holding the "International D. H. Lawrence Conference: Lawrence Today" at Southern Illinois University in Carbondale in April 1979 was first suggested by Professor Robert B. Partlow, Jr., editor of the Dickens Studies Annual and chairman of the Department of English. When he mentioned the possibility of this conference to me, I said it was an excellent idea, but explained that, because of other pressing commitments, I could act only in a somewhat distant advisory capacity: I could suggest the names of some Lawrence critics as well as some possible topics and would be happy to present a paper myself, but could do no more. With industry and astuteness--and I will accept no disclaimers of modesty from him--Dr. Partlow went to work at once on the project, which he brilliantly organized, first of all obtaining a suitable grant from the National Endowment for the Humanities and then inviting participants. Besides this, he made arrangements for lodging, transportation, and meals, and of course organized the program.

The Conference was an enormous success, and fortunately we have in this volume the lectures that were delivered as well as the panel papers. In addition to the various important scholars who took a direct part in the proceedings, we had visitors from as far away as Jamaica, Portugal, and Japan. One of the most distinguished guests was Mr. Gerald Pollinger of London, director of the Laurence Pollinger Authors' Agency and executor of the Lawrence Estate. We were also pleased to have Mr. Michael Black, Publisher of the Cambridge University Press, under whose sponsorship Lawrence's entire writings are being reprinted in textual editions; many of the editors of these volumes, from both Great Britain and the United States, also attended, and this volume presents some of their assessments of the progress of the project. In addition to the veteran Lawrence scholars who took part in the project--such as Mark Spilka, Ernest Tedlock, George Zytaruk, James C. Cowan, L. D. Clark and others--the program here included a number of younger Lawrence commentators who greatly helped to illuminate the proceedings, making this book altogether one of the

few truly fine critical and expository volumes on the man whom so
many major critics now regard as the outstanding English writer of
this century.

The Southern Illinois University Press is proud to be bringing
out this book in commemoration of the fiftieth anniversay of his
death. The papers included show how forcefully he still lives.

Harry T. Moore

Carbondale, Illinois
April, 1980

[Note: In commemoration of the Lawrence death anniversary, a film
has been made of my Lawrence biography, Priest of Love, to be released at the time this book appears in the winter of 1980. The film
is directed and produced by Christopher Miles and Andrew Donally,
featuring Ian McKellen, Janet Suzman, Ava Gardner, John Gielgud,
Maurizio Merli, with Sarah Miles in a cameo appearance. The book
has been filmed in Mexico, England, and Italy.]

Preface

During the Spring Semester of 1978 a small informal committee of
English professors asked me, as chairman of the department, what we
should do to acknowledge publicly our respect for, and admiration of,
the most eminent of our colleagues on his retirement from full-time
teaching. This was one of my chairmanly duties I could accept enthu-
siastically, since I too had known and esteemed Research Professor
Harry T. Moore for the more than twenty years we had both served in
the department. During that time he had produced an enviable list of
books and articles, continuing his work of the preceding twenty-five
years in modern literature, especially concerning himself with D. H.
Lawrence, as you all know. To say that Professor Moore is the doyen
of Lawrence studies is to state a truism.

Professors Ted Boyle and Richard Peterson, themselves productive
scholars of modern literature, the most active members of the committee
during the preliminary planning and the later actual conduct of the
Conference, originally thought in terms of a Festschrift, the time-
honored mode of public praise for a master-scholar and master-teacher.
But, as we considered the usual possibilities for a Festschrift--in-
vited papers by former students, by colleagues in the departments in
which Harry Moore had served, and by those leading Lawrence scholars,
past and present, with whom he had been associated--we became less
than satisfied. It seemed to us that a conventional Festschrift was
not entirely appropriate for a man who had been a pioneer in his field,
a pathbreaker, a visionary in the sense that he was among the first to
see that Lawrence was, and is, a writer of major literary and historical significance. So, what to do?

Noticing that one of Professor Moore's major achievements at
Southern Illinois University was the staging of a successful Lawrence-
Joyce Conference in 1958, the committee decided to ask him if he would
agree to the staging of a Lawrence Conference on campus if, this time,
he did not have to do all the administrative work. To our relief, he
agreed at once and with enthusiasm, probably because we, with less

xi

than Machiavellian subtlety, did not acknowledge that the Conference
was a roundabout means of getting him to accept a Festschrift. Since
as chairman I have comparatively little to do, the committee "elected"
me as director of the project and instructed me to seek out the
necessary funding.

This chore was a good deal less onerous than any of us had expected. The National Endowment for the Humanities accepted the concept
with very little difficulty and made a sizable grant available in sub-
vention of the Conference. The authorities of Southern Illinois University backed the project wholeheartedly. The Dean of the College of
Liberal Arts, Dr. Lon Shelby; the Vice President for Academic Affairs,
Dr. Frank Horton; the Dean of the Graduate School, Dr. John Guyon, and
his entire staff in Research and Projects; and the Dean of Libraries,
Dr. Kenneth Peterson, all coöperated fully, even to the extent of
providing matching funds in a time of financial austerity.

Special thanks for the success of the Conference are also due to
many others: the faculty and graduate students of the Department of
English; members of the staff of Morris Library, who prepared the
exhibit of Lawrence and the catalogue of the letters, editions, por-
traits, paintings, and memorabilia--here special thanks must be
offered to Professor Richard Peterson of the Department of English,
and to Professors Alan Cohn, David Koch, and Kenneth Duckett of the
Library staff; to the Speech Department, and especially Dr. Robert
Fish and his students who acted out a fascinating, original presentation of scenes from Lawrence's novels and short stories; and finally,
but far from last, the administrative staffs of several services on
campus, Transportation, the Student Union, Accounting, Continuing
Education, and the Learning Resources Services. Without the efficient
cooperation of all these people, the Conference could never have
succeeded.

The organizing committee and Professor Moore were responsible
for the structure of the Conference, primarily in the typical scholarly
format of lectures and panel discussions, and the invitation of some
of the leading contemporary authorities in each of the categories
selected. Unfortunately it was not possible to invite papers by all
who have written persuasively about Lawrence in the last twenty or
so years--the committee ruefully apologizes to those who may seem to
have been ignored. But, as the papers which are printed in this volume
demonstrate, we have little reason to feel unhappy about those we did
invite: all are interesting, and several are important contributions
to Lawrence scholarship.

I am not a specialist in modern literature or in Lawrence, rather
in Victorian literature and Charles Dickens, and so I should probably
not make any (possibly ill-founded) comments about the nature of the
scholarship of the papers presented during the Conference, except to
say how impressed I was. I think I did notice, I hope not because of
faulty memory, a significant difference between the Lawrence-Joyce
Conference of 1958 and the Lawrence Conference of 1978. Lawrentians
in 1958 seemed to concentrate on "appreciation" of the man as a person:
biographical details of his relations with people, his travels, his
importance as the last of the Romantics, his "revolutionary" ideas,
the excitement he generated in them--so much so that they appeared as
a band of brothers (and sisters), a clique united defensively to

protect a writer whom they knew to be less than generally acceptable.
Participants in 1978 seemed to me to operate on the premise that there
is no need to defend Lawrence: whether or not one accepts his ideas
in whole or part, he is simply a datum of modern literature. Like
Joyce and Yeats, he is there and scholars and critics must take him
into consideration. So, as with Dickens a critical generation earlier
in the twentieth-century, the task becomes, not to defend Lawrence as
a writer, observer or thinker, but to investigate his artistry and
"philosophy," using all the tools of modern research and criticism.
Most of the papers delivered during the Conference, notably those
dealing with the forthcoming Cambridge editions of the letters and
works, strongly suggest this important shift in scholarship and
criticism.

Since all the participants in the Conference agreed to allow
publication of their work by the Southern Illinois University Press,
we can now print for the use of students of Lawrence the proceedings
of the Lawrence International Conference held in Carbondale 2-5 April
1979, a year before the larger celebrations of Lawrence to be held in
England and in Taos in 1980.

And, with our less than Machiavellian subtlety, the directing
committee did finally produce what amounts to a Festschrift for Harry
Moore. He will not allow us to dedicate the volume to him, nor will
he admit the necessity of such a Festschrift, but I am sure that
Lawrentians throughout the world agree with us that the Conference
and this volume are suitable evidence of our admiration and respect
for a friend and mentor of many years. Floruit.

Carbondale, Illinois   Robert B. Partlow, Jr.
April, 1980

Notes on Contributors

Armin Arnold, a native of Switzerland, professor of German at McGill University and Fellow of the Royal Society of Canada, has written D. H. Lawrence and America as well as a biography of Lawrence in German, and has edited D. H. Lawrence: The Symbolic Meaning. He has also written books on expressionism, Joyce, Shaw, the detective novel, and Dürrenmatt. At present he is working on a book about Georg Kaiser.

Peter H. Balbert, associate professor of English at Wells College, has written D. H. Lawrence and the Psychology of Rhythm and several recent articles on Lawrence. He is completing the manuscript for a book tentatively entitled "The Phallic Imagination."

Michael H. Black, University Publisher of Cambridge University, has written The Literature of Fidelity and Poetic Drama as Mirror of the Will. He is supervising the editing of the complete reprinting of textual editions of Lawrence's works.

Lydia Blanchard, assistant professor of English at Mount Vernon College, has published articles on Lawrence and feminist criticism in The D. H. Lawrence Review, Modern Fiction Studies, and Studies in the Novel. She is now at work on a book dealing with the vision of history in the novels of Lawrence, Orwell, and Mailer.

James T. Boulton, professor and head of the Department of English at the University of Birmingham and Fellow of the Royal Society of Literature, has edited Lawrence in Love and volume 1 of The Letters of D. H. Lawrence, 1901-1913. He is General Editor of the Works and the Letters.

L. D. Clark, professor of English at the University of Arizona, has been awarded several major grants: a Cutting Traveling Fellowship, a Ford Foundation Travel Grant, a Fulbright, and a National Endowment for the Humanities Grant. He has written fiction (The Dove Tree, Is

This Naomi? and Other Stories) and criticism (Dark Night of the Body:
D. H. Lawrence's "The Plumed Serpent," The Minoan Distance: The Symbolism of Travel in D. H. Lawrence), and is currently finishing his
edition of The Plumed Serpent for the Cambridge University Press and
a novel, Cross Timbers.

Laverne Harrell Clark, wife of L. D. Clark, is a free-lance author,
photographer, and lecturer. She has written extensively and published
photographs, especially about southwestern Indian culture, in addition
to her work in fiction and poetry. She is presently engaged in index-
ing more than two thousand photographs of Lawrence's travels in Europe.

James C. Cowan, professor of English at the University of Arkansas,
was president of the D. H. Lawrence Society from 1975 to 1977, president of the South Central MLA in 1978, and has been editor of the
D. H. Lawrence Review since 1968. In addition to writing several articles on Lawrence and Faulkner, he has published D. H. Lawrence's
American Journey. He will soon publish D. H. Lawrence: An Annotated
Bibliography of Writings about Him.

Keith Cushman, associate professor of English at the University of
North Carolina at Greensboro, is the Founding Editor-in-Chief of the
journal of the D. H. Lawrence Society of America. His major work,
apart from many articles on Lawrence, Bellow, Nin, Hardy, Trollope,
Larkin, and Ted Hughes, is D. H. Lawrence at Work: The Emergence of
the "Prussian Officer" Stories. He is continuing to work on the
Prussian Officer Stories.

Emile Delavenay, professeur honoraire at the University of Nice, wrote
D. H. Lawrence: The Man and His Work: The Formative Years: 1885-1919
and Edward Carpenter and D. H. Lawrence. During World War II he broad-
cast for B.B.C. and was one of the founders of the United Nations.

David Farmer, director of Special Collections of the McFarlin Library
of the University of Tulsa, has published numerous articles, edited
Essays in Honor of C. L. Cline, and mounted major exhibitions of
Siegfried Sassoon and Ezra Pound. He is now completing an edition of
Women in Love and volume 5 of the letters of Lawrence, both for the
Cambridge University Press series, a bibliography of Flannery O'Connor,
and a study of John Rollin Ridge and Cherokee attitudes toward the
American Indian.

Sandra M. Gilbert, associate professor of English at the University
of California at Davis, has written Acts of Attention: The Poems of
D. H. Lawrence and a volume of poems entitled In the Fourth World;
she also coauthored The Madwoman in the Attic: The Woman Writer and
the 19th Century Literary Imagination and coedited Shakespeare's
Sisters: Feminist Essays on Woman Poets. She is at work on a sequel
to The Madwoman to be titled No Man's Land and a collection of poems
called Emily's Bread.

Evelyn Hinz, associate professor of English at the University of
Manitoba and editor of Mosaic together with John J. Teunissen,

professor of English at the same university and editor of The Canadian
Review of American Studies, has published many articles, the definitive
edition of Roger Williams's A Key into the Language of America, and
Henry Miller's World of D. H. Lawrence. Professor Hinz, the authorized
biographer of Anaïs Nin, has published three books on that author.

Gerald M. Lacy, professor of English at San Angelo University, Texas,
has traced and catalogued some 6,000 Lawrence letters and is presently
at work preparing volume 6 of the letters of Lawrence for the Cambridge
University Press. He previously issued The Letters of D. H. Lawrence
to Thomas and Adele Seltzer.

Ian S. MacNiven, associate professor at SUNY Maritime College, has
edited A Descriptive Catalogue of the Lawrence Durrell Collection at
Southern Illinois University; coedited with Harry T. Moore, Literary
Lifelines: The Richard Aldington-Lawrence Durrell Correspondence;
and is coeditor of Deus Loci: The Lawrence Durrell Newsletter. He is
now at work on a biography of Kay Boyle and, with Harry T. Moore, an
edition of the correspondence of Richard Aldington and Ezra Pound.

Harry T. Moore, Distinguished Research Professor Emeritus of Southern
Illinois University, Fellow of the Royal Society of Literature, past
president of the College English Association, honorary president of
the D. H. Lawrence Society of America, is a pioneer in Lawrence scholarship, and a still-active stimulus to the exploration of the life and
work of the novelist and poet. A list of Professor Moore's published
biographies, critical articles, lectures, editions, and bibliographies
on various literary subjects would fill several pages.

Gerald Pollinger, director of Laurence Pollinger, Ltd., Authors' Agents,
in London, is the Literary Executor of the estate of Frieda Lawrence
Ravagli. He is a veteran RAF pilot.

John S. Poynter teaches at the People's College of Further Education
in Nottingham and acts as editor of the D. H. Lawrence Society Journal.
His current project is the collection and recording of interviews with
Eastwood residents who remember the young Lawrence.

Warren Roberts, retired professor of English and director of the Humanities Research Center at the University of Texas at Austin, is serving
as General Editor, with James Boulton, of the Cambridge Edition of the
works of Lawrence. He has written Bibliography of D. H. Lawrence, coedited the Complete Poems of D. H. Lawrence, and coauthored D. H.
Lawrence and His World, with Harry T. Moore, with whom he also cocdited
a volume of Lawrence essays, Phoenix II.

Charles L. Ross teaches at the University of Hartford. He has been the
recipient of both a Fulbright and a Guggenheim scholarship. His The
Composition of "The Rainbow" and "Women in Love": A History was published in 1979.

Charles Rossman, associate professor of English at the University of
Texas at Austin, has been a Fulbright lecturer and is on the Editorial

Board of the _D. H. Lawrence Review_ and _Studies in the Novel_. He has
published a number of essays on Lawrence and Joyce and edited a collection of critical essays on Mario Vargas Llosa. He is at work on a
book on Llosa and is editing a volume of critical essays on Carlos
Fuentes.

Keith Sagar, Senior Staff Tutor at the University of Manchester,
has written _The Art of D. H. Lawrence_, _The Art of Ted Hughes_, _D. H.
Lawrence: A Calendar of his Works_, and _The Life of D. H. Lawrence_.
His current projects include _A D. H. Lawrence Handbook_, _D. H. Lawrence:
Life into Art_, and volume 7 of the letters of Lawrence for the Cam-
bridge University Press.

Scott Sanders, associate professor of English at Indiana University,
published _D. H. Lawrence: The World of the Major Novels_ and is completing two novels and a critical volume entitled _The Imagination of
Nature_.

Mark Spilka, professor of English and Comparative Literature at Brown
University, is also editor of _Novel: A Forum on Fiction_. He wrote _The
Love Ethic of D. H. Lawrence_, _Dickens and Kafka_, and _Virginia Woolf's
Quarrel with Grieving_, and edited _D. H. Lawrence: A Collection of
Critical Essays_ and _Toward a Poetics of Fiction_. His work in progress
includes books on Hemingway's quarrel with androgny, Lawrence's quarrel
with tenderness, and new literary quarrels with tenderness.

Michael Squires, professor of English at Virginia Polytechnic Institute
and State University, published _The Pastoral Novel: Studies in George
Eliot, Thomas Hardy, and D. H. Lawrence_, has just completed _The Creation of "Lady Chatterley's Lover,"_ and is working on the Cambridge
Edition of _Lady Chatterley's Lover_.

Ernest Tedlock, Professor of English Emeritus of the University of
New Mexico, is best known for his _The Frieda Lawrence Collection of
D. H. Lawrence Manuscripts_, _D. H. Lawrence: Artist and Rebel_, and
D. H. Lawrence and "Sons and Lovers," but he has also published books
on Dylan Thomas and on Steinbeck, as well as his own poetry. He is
presently working on two novels and a volume of poetry.

George J. Zytaruk, professor of English and president of Nipissing
University College, Canada, is president of the D. H. Lawrence Society
of America. He has published _The Quest for Rananim: D. H. Lawrence's
Letters to S. S. Koteliansky, 1914-1930_, _D. H. Lawrence's Response to
Russian Literature_, and for the _D. H. Lawrence Review_, vol. 12, nos.
1 and 2 (1979), he edited a 238-page masterwork of Lawrence scholarship, "The Collected Letters of Jessie Chambers."

Introduction

Greetings from the D. H. Lawrence Society of America

GEORGE J. ZYTARUK

I am grateful to the sponsors of this Conference for the opportunity to bring you greetings on behalf of the D. H. Lawrence Society of America. This campus is the home of the Honorary President of the Society, and it is, indeed, appropriate that an International Conference on D. H. Lawrence should be taking place where Harry T. Moore has worked so long and so effectively to achieve for Lawrence the understanding and stature that the writer now enjoys.

One of the major aims of the Lawrence Society, as stated in our charter, is "To sponsor meetings, seminars, and conferences dealing with D. H. Lawrence." And it is conceivable that one day the D. H. Lawrence Society, through its own efforts, will organize a comparable scholarly assembly at some equally appropriate site, such as Bandol or Vence in the South of France. Unfortunately, we are still a very small and impecunious body and, for the time being, must cling to that conglomerate of learned societies, the MLA, and hold our meetings during the Christmas Season.

The very idea of a D. H. Lawrence Society no doubt stirs some misgivings in the minds of many literary scholars. And we should not be surprised if the thought of belonging to an organized group of any sort is regarded as somehow incompatible with Lawrence's basic ideas--all that he fought to abolish.

Yet there is, we believe, a legitimate part of his personality and of his thought that is consistent with the Society's desire to link together in some more formal way everyone who shares Lawrence's hopes for mankind. The Prophet of the Midlands was very much concerned with founding a better social order, and his ultimate hope was a society in which people could lead more vital lives.

Despite his failed ventures in this regard, despite the disillusion he experienced in his many Utopian schemes, Lawrence

3

persisted in trying to create a new vision. His enthusiastic hopes
for Rananim, as we know, were dashed, time after time. Indeed, his
dearest partner of greatness, Frieda herself, has recorded that she
never believed in it. And except for Dorothy Brett--the Carswells,
Murry, Lady Ottoline, Russell, Forster, Huxley, Koteliansky, and
Katherine Mansfield, in the end, all rejected his call to set off
in quest of Rananim. Finally, Lawrence was forced to confess:
"That Rananim of ours has sunk out of sight."

The D. H. Lawrence Society has no illusions about changing the
world through founding a new social order. And I want to assure you
that, despite Lawrence's urging, our members are not about to put
on "tight scarlet trousers fitting the leg, gay little orange-
brown jackets and bright green hats" as a first step in "the revolution against dulness."

But is there not in the back of all our minds, of those who
believe that Lawrence still has something vital to say to us, that
somehow the world might be better for his vision? And even if we
cannot apply his ideas directly to bring about immediate social
benefits, a conference such as this, where we can talk at length
about Lawrence and his ideas is a positive effort. Of course, only
as individuals can we finally decide whether our participation here
is beneficial.

I congratulate Southern Illinois University for its initiative
in bringing all of us together and, on behalf of the D. H. Lawrence
Society of America, express the wish that the proceedings will
prove enjoyable and enlightening.

If, in addition, this Conference helps to rekindle even a
faint glimmer that, in a sad and troubled world, a better life is
still possible, I for one will not have to wonder, like T. S. Eliot's
J. Alfred Prufrock, whether this was all worthwhile.

Lawrence's Voice: A Keynote Address

ERNEST TEDLOCK

Thirty years ago a book by me bearing the unprepossessing title
The Frieda Lawrence Collection of D. H. Lawrence Manuscripts: A
Descriptive Bibliography attracted a surprising, to me, amount of
critical attention. Harry T. Moore reviewed it in the Saturday
Review. After expressing some astonishment at the advent of this
newcomer to Lawrence studies, and after arousing my paranoid in-
stincts by challenging my dating of some manuscripts, he gave me a
pretty good sendoff. Anyhow, as you can see, I survived. Only to be
invited to give this keynote address, which I may not survive.

I begin my search for a keynote in my distant past, though in
the present tense. This in the hope of creating more immediacy of
feeling, because the experiences recounted are important to me.

I am seventeen, in my first semester at the University of
Missouri. On a Saturday afternoon, as I walk by a dormitory, I
decide to go in and look for a student who has invited me to visit.
As you would expect on a fine fall Saturday, the lobby seems completely empty. I peer through the shadows, call out, and am about
to flee when over by a window a figure rises up violently from the
couch on which it has been lying. It holds aloft a book in one
hand. It shouts at me, "Have you read The Red Badge of Courage?"
Without waiting for an answer (the question is, of course, rhetori-
cal), the figure subsides, presumably to reread, and I go away in
a state of shock. A few days later I read The Red Badge, and to this
day I sometimes dream of crawling up to a wall, slowly daring to
rise to my knees and look over, there to see, leaned back against
a tree, a skeleton in uniform. He, it, has dug a deep hole with his
heel as he died. If he were to hold up a book and shout at me, the
dream would be complete. The point of my saying this is that writing
and reading are profoundly exciting, moving, hypnotic adventures in
voice, and listening to voice. As Crane, "The trees began softly to
sing a hymn of twilight. The sun sank until slanted bronze rays
struck the forest. There was a lull in the noises of insects as if

5

they had bowed their beaks and were making a devotional pause. There
was silence save for the chanted chorus of the trees. Then, upon
this stillness, there suddenly broke a tremendous clangor of sounds.
A crimson roar came from the distance."[1]

I am in my twenties, living in a dormitory at the University
of Chicago. I am invited by a wonderful man--some of you may have
known him, Fred Millett--to join a group with whom he plans weekly
readings of novels. I go, and (to my shame I confess) I am bored--
by his fine, cultivated voice and manner, and by the book he is
reading aloud to us. I think it was Pride and Prejudice. I am in
one of those amorphous emotional states that can assail a young man.
I am out of my cultural depth. I think only of contemporary love
and lust. And I have never learned to listen. Along about the third
grade my teachers began the insistence on silent reading. We were
not even to move our lips, let alone voice those wonderful complexities of sound and meaning as near to us as Mother Goose. We were,
for the rest of our lives, to go for speed.

I am in my thirties. After a civilian stint with the Air Force
teaching photography, I am an English instructor in the Navy program
at the University of New Mexico. Our department has just received a
grant from the Rockefeller Foundation to do a bibliography of the
Lawrence manuscripts in Frieda Lawrence's possession at Taos. There
has already been some attrition of these manuscripts because of
Frieda's penchant for giving them away. She is like the Texan in a
story she likes to tell. When she admired his shirt, he took it off
and gave it to her on the spot. I am the second candidate to be
interviewed by Frieda. She likes me. Her generosity persists. Ten
months later, when I have finished my task, she leaves me alone
with the manuscripts. "Take one for yourself," she says. I look at
all those pages bearing Lawrence's absolutely beautiful handwriting,
always under perfect control, perfectly clear and fluent. Over there
are the three holograph versions of Lady Chatterley's Lover. I decide
on sanity, and take a mixed typescript-manuscript of an early version
of the essay on Hawthorne. I shall never forget the parting words of
the Foundation representative, who also had to approve of me. He
said, "Don't get stuck on one man."

That is how, one fine fall afternoon, I find myself driving
Frieda up to the ranch above San Cristobal, where the manuscripts
are kept in a huge, rather rusty safe under the porch near the
kitchen. They will now be taken in a large case to her home in the
valley, and I will take a few at a time to my work space in the
University's Harwood Foundation. This is my first visit to the
Kiowa ranch and my first chance to talk to Frieda about her hopes
and plans. She chooses to ride in my old Dodge coupe. Her pride
makes it the equal of a Mercedes. My wife, Agnes, and our two children follow in Angelo Ravagli's car. We settle into the old Lawrence
cabin, where we are very aware of his ambience--the big fireplace
with its rough wooden mantle, the small rooms, the neatness, tidy,
whitewashed, feeling all hand-made.

Next day Frieda asks me over to the chalet-like house Angie
has built for them. I find her engaged in the archetypal activity
of sewing. She brings our talk around to Lady Chatterley's Lover

and the conversations between Clifford and his Cambridge intellectual friends, more overheard than participated in by Constance. I
think, later, how Frieda was not so acquiescent listening to
Lawrence. Now, she asks me what I think Lawrence is up to in those
scenes. It is too early in my life for me to make reference to the
customs of male chauvinism or to the possible limitations of
Lawrence's kind of liberation of women. I mumble something about
the indignity of the unfulfilled woman's having to listen to men
to whom the mind is of greater importance than relationship. I am
really not very clear, but she lets it go.

Back at the cabin I decide to do my homework. I read in
Chapter 4 one account of Connie's situation. It is frequently quoted
by Lawrence scholars who feel they understand Lawrence's message
and may even demonstrate thereby that they are on the right side.
I don't feel particularly holier than they, and I am more interested
in the "voicing," the diction which, as so often in Lawrence's
fiction, depends on the commonplaces, the social euphemisms, the
understatement of people of Connie's background and class. The
ultimate point of my interest is that we really have to listen
attentively to the complexities of tone and diction before we can
say we understand what Lawrence is saying. Maybe here the response
ought to be little more, or less, than a relaxed grimace.

I am in my forties. On a beautiful sunny day in summer I am
sitting in front of the old Lawrence cabin, near the big pine tree
with the tin phoenix nailed to it. (It was David Garnett who once
pointed out that these trees have grown since Lawrence's sojourn,
so that the view is altered.) I am in the company of Robert Creeley,
the poet; Bobbie, his wife, who paints; Bobbie's daughter, about
four, who runs naked in the good air; and their bearded friend, a
painter. Creeley is this summer's holder of the Lawrence fellowship
with residence at the ranch. I, as chairman of the committee that
made the award, have come up from Albuquerque to see how they are
getting along. The fellowship is one of the things that Frieda
wanted to happen at the ranch--she wanted some life up there--and I
have tried to see that her wish is realized. She is buried at the
chapel nearby. In his quiet, nearly inaudible voice, Creeley introduces me to his painter friend, who turns on me that kind of steady,
quizzical gaze that always makes me feel such people must know something I do not. He seems friendly. He asks me what is my connection
with Lawrence. I do not remember my response to this hard question,
probably something to the effect that I teach him. Anyhow, I recall
quite clearly his asking, "But didn't Lawrence say what he had to
say?" This sounds rather like the challenge of a heckler, and, as
Lawrence might have put it with a grin, surely ought to be ignored
by those in charge. I only claim that I have no wish to dilute the
intellectual rigor of Lawrence studies.

Earlier I described the high excitement of the student who had
just finished The Red Badge of Courage; Fred Millett's attempt to
draw us into the civilized and potentially profoundly moving act of
listening to the voice of creative genius; Frieda's interest in what
Lawrence was saying in the passage from Lady Chatterley's Lover,
which is surely qualitatively different from an abstract of his

meaning; and finally the painter's query, "Didn't Lawrence say what he had to say?" If we answer "Yes" to that, then perhaps our attention will be turned more to the nuances of how, to greater appreciation of and pleasure in the inseparability of the meaning from the life in the words--the sense of the being of the man, his vitality, his voice.

This is my keynote: the importance of Lawrence's voice, of listening to what it is communicating, perhaps Lawrence's voice, surely not his voice when he was discussing mundane matters with Frieda (if he ever did), surely not the timbre of his voice (I have read that it was not a very good, resonant voice), maybe not even his tone, the nuances of it as he read aloud. Perhaps one ought to say that it was a voice he imagined, reserved for, and projected into his work. Sometimes this voice uses the voices of others through mimicry and certain effects of bantering and mockery. Very seldom is it the neutral tonelessness of what used to be called expository prose. It teases even while it explains.

In the past few months I have spent a good deal of time catching up, reading the essays and books written by you who are participating in this Conference and by other Lawrence scholars. This especially involved what you published in the sixties and so far in the seventies. I am candid when I tell you that much of your work has given me the pleasure of finding it new and challenging. I cannot refer to it or quote a wide range of it here except to note those studies of voice in Lawrence.

In a recent collection by W. T. Andrews are three commentaries from an older generation of critics: David Garnett, W. H. Auden, and Virginia Woolf. Garnett and Auden clearly have in mind aspects of voice, that is, the way Lawrence sounds, or, if you wish to withhold judgment, the way they think he sounds. Virginia Woolf is more visual, as if Roger Fry were looking over her shoulder.

In a 1936 review of Phoenix: The Posthumous Papers, Garnett calls Lawrence's attitude, hence tone, "saucy," indeed no more than that at times. But all the essays are worth reading and are full of the lively mockery of Lawrence's mind.[2] A spirited, irreverent, perhaps saucy dialogue with the world is what we hear so often from Lawrence. It may be what Garnett once thought a sort of lower-class Cockney attitude, a charge against which Lawrence defended himself by pointing to his deeply religious side.

In "Some Notes on D. H. Lawrence" Auden emphasizes the disarming nature of Lawrence's high spirits even when he is scolding, and the Agape that replaces his anger when he writes of plants and animals, indeed his change of voice.[3]

And Virginia Woolf, getting at a quality in Sons and Lovers that she describes in terms more tactile and visual than descriptive of sound, seems to summarize it as a rapture of being, as in the swinging scene between Paul and Miriam.[4] Here she is into something that might be called the kinesis of style, and we can recall how early Lawrence felt compelled to defend his rhythms. And with rhythm we are directly into effects of voice. There is also in the swinging scene a strongly antiphonal effect in the dialogue. And the rapture is surely audible.

Two commentaries that are relevant to the question of voice
center on the corn harvest scene in The Rainbow: Frank Glover
Smith's book D. H. Lawrence: The Rainbow and Ian Robinson's essay
"D. H. Lawrence and English Prose." Smith makes the telling contrast
between a passage from T. S. Eliot's Four Quartets and the corn harvest scene from The Rainbow, a contrast involving the treatments of
marriage, love, and especially human relationships with the earthly,
what can be called physical oneness with each other and a living
cosmos. Lawrence celebrates the earthly; Eliot denigrates it.[5] The
expression of these values is indeed a matter of voices, and can
and must be heard. Eliot's objective correlative sounds aridly
abstract read with Lawrence's observed and felt kinesis of harvest.
Ian Robinson's essay is one of the more explicit and analytical discussions of Lawrence's prose (as distinguished from his poetry, as
a matter of traditional terminology). While it may seem to end inevitably in commonplace, it is refreshing after the interminable
abstractions of the usual explications of Lawrence's "thought."
Discussing the same harvest scene, Robinson focuses on the question
of rhythm. He suggests that the linkage that produces the rhythms
is achieved not by the subordination of syntax but by the speaking
voice, indeed its tone. This reliance is like that of the 1611 Bible
or of Chaucer. He then makes a truly extravagant claim that Lawrence
took the language further than anyone had before. In a scientific
age he made the creative imagination central to thought.[6]

There are many brief comments on voice and tone running through
recent Lawrence criticism. D. Kenneth Mackenzie notes in his essay
entitled "Ennui and Energy in England, My England" that even in
a passage of expository commentary that is quite explicit there is
a contemplative spirit and an absence of the didactic or censorious.
Another passage has a lightness, followed by a depth that is
resonant.[7]

Keith Alldritt's The Visual Imagination of D. H. Lawrence contains, besides the emphasis announced in the title, a considerable
and insightful discussion of aspects related to what I call voice.
In his discussion of The Rainbow (the three paragraphs beginning
"Away from time, always outside of time!" and ending "There his soul
remained at the apex of the arch, clinched in the timeless ecstasy,
consummated"), Alldritt is concerned with the complexity and intensity of the feeling, and how, as narrator, Lawrence maneuvers. He
details the grammatical structures that give movement to the sentences and provide our sense of the rhythm of the excitement felt
by Will. Alldritt finds a sonority like that of the Creed, and a
touch of chanting or incantation. At the same time, one of Alldritt's
favorite terms is "texture," as if, like so many of us, he finds his
own familiar verbal reality on the printed page.[8]

Ultimately the question of voice and literary form reaches well
into modern philosophy. John and Ann Remsbury in their essay
"Lawrence and Art" introduce the names of Hegel, Merleau-Ponty, and
Wittgenstein. The identification with Wittgenstein is based on a
similarity of moral fervor in insisting on not being misled by
attractive ideas, and the use of the simplest words and phrases.
Both exhibit also intelligence that is clairvoyant and a growing

sanity. While all of this bears ultimately on the question of voice, the Remsburys at one point make the relevance clear by casting an imaginary commentary by Lawrence on the development of modern art since his death, in his bantering tone.[9]

These examples of awareness of Lawrence's voice must seem rather rudimentary. Before I end with my own reflections on the problems for the art of writing that are raised by questions of voice, let me refer to one book in particular, Richard E. Palmer's Hermeneutics: Interpretation Theory in Schleiermacher, Dilthey, Heidegger, and Gadamer (published in 1969 as part of Northwestern University Studies in Phenomenology and Existential Philosophy). While the largest part of the book does not deal with so-called oral interpretation, the hermeneutical view is that all silent readings are oral interpretations in disguise. I would add that the greater the silence, the greater the probability that the nuances have been reduced to the habitual thought pattern of the reader.

My own questions and the responses that follow are far from systematic, but they cover some of the problems that creative writers must, it seems to me, not only think about at times but find crucial to their sense of skill and truthfulness in their craft. My feelings are, at least sometimes, adequate responses to Lawrence's feelings, when I am most aware of listening to him.

First, then, isn't it a rather terrible thing to be able, indeed to be compelled, to make the judgments the voice of this narrator so often makes? Even what seem to be deftly objective accounts of situations are also judgments once we know his position. The voice is that of someone--a persona projected by Lawrence--of someone who knows, who is indeed confident of knowing, sometimes explicitly as in passages on relationship toward the end of such an early story as "Odour of Chrysanthemums." And to know is to bear the burden of knowing, for what is so often known is a trauma, a departure from the norm, an inability to love as in "The Rocking Horse Winner," an immense disaster in relationship. The tone, including the little touches of some characteristic diction grounded in class and cultural attitude, is almost never tragic, in range is sometimes comic, as in "Rawdon's Roof." "I shall kill them with the silent bullets of my work," Lawrence said during the wartime years, thinking of his kinds of enemies. And of course even understatement could render failure and sorrow, and attack their causes.

In naming the tone of Lawrence's voice, those who attend to it sometimes use the term "bantering." Mimicry is an important part of that--a deft use of the habitual exclamations, the verbal ways of handling serious matters without being embarrassed by being thought too serious, or indeed too moral--the clichés and understatement by which those who talk in sophisticated ways manage, and often dispose of, the trouble they see. As we've been saying recently, it is important to be "cool," to "keep one's cool." Such voices never break down into anything resembling the incoherence, or the lesser coherence, of extreme feeling. In many of Lawrence's later stories, the voice talks on and on about situations and their people as if it had gathered with us during some interlude in our day, perhaps at a cafe in the south of France, cocktails more likely

than tea, to gossip, meditate, consider, even in a way confess.
Certainly bantering tends to make all of this more bearable.
    Does it make it more bearable for Lawrence? He voices certain
kinds of situations over and over. Does this repetition indicate a
psychological, spiritual, moral habit? Has he at some point begun
to write by formula? Has the bantering satirist become perversely
addicted to the experience of the anti-life, and less knowing in
an experiential sense of the positive side of his dualism, of what
he can confidently call "life"? When I consider these questions,
my felt answer is that he has been tempted, even threatened, but
that there are signs everywhere of his recovery. Yet I can see how
some surveyors of the whole career might come to misgivings. They
would be those who do not share Lawrence's religious views and his
vitalistic moral transpositions. They could be humanists who believe
that reason and good will can prevail in improving the human condition. They could be Christians ranging from fundamentalist positions
as far as the essential rationalism of Unitarians.
    To affirm our sense of integrity in Lawrence, we have to rely
on our awareness of his voice. To the very last thing he wrote on
his deathbed this voice is wonderfully fresh, creative, and (perhaps
a strange value term to use) courageous. Remarkable eventuality, he
never really lost the faith, the knowledge, the trust in life that
is essential to the vitalist. Clearly, he suffered a great deal.
Though I shy away from the Christian parallels, perhaps it ought to
be said that I know of no appeal for mercy in extremity, and no
repudiation. His move toward tenderness in Lady Chatterley's Lover
a few years before his death takes on special poignance. How much
of that came from his own need? I should think a lot. But when he
speaks, the voice is strong.
    Let me recapitulate my adventure in Lawrence and my arrival
at this emphasis. Frieda Lawrence said that she wanted some life
at the New Mexico ranch, and there is surely an echo in that of
Lawrence. She also said to me, "They'll never tame it, Ted." And
that is true, though they have succeeded in littering parts of it.
David Garnett spoke of the "saucy" side of Lawrence, and "the lively
mockery of his own mind." Auden noted the "strident, hectoring"
quality of the voice at times, and the intrusion of anger and frustration, but loved Lawrence's wonderful high spirits, his agape,
his "joy of vision" equal to the "joy in writing," and the "passionate personal attention" he offered to birds, beasts, and flowers.
Virginia Woolf caught the "rapture of physical being," the kinesis,
life and art as process. Frank Glover Smith compared Lawrence's
celebration, surely an act of voice, of the human, earthly side of
marriage, love, and social relation, with the attitude of his traditional antithesis, T. S. Eliot. Ian Robinson pointed out how in
The Rainbow phrases are connected by "the tone of the speaking
voice," as they are in the 1611 Bible and in Chaucer, and as they
are not in Dryden's grammatical structuring of meaning. Mackenzie
gave us variations of tone in "England, My England." John and Ann
Remsbury compared the use by Wittgenstein and Lawrence of the
simplest words and phrases found in the spoken language and of the
intelligence working through this. Alldritt talked of Lawrence's

maneuverability as narrator, of the responsiveness to feeling, of the sonority, and of the suggestion of chanting, incantation, in The Rainbow.

Such bits as these have made up my keynote. In my experience, the early years of my reading more frequently resulted in the kind of absorption and excitement shown by my example of the reader of The Red Badge of Courage, than the years of attention to texts that could abstract meaning with a certain kind of summary accuracy, but hardly dealt with the matter of voice and feeling. It seems to me now that it is terribly important to go further into this--to listen to our texts again and better. We don't have a very full or attractive vocabulary with which to discuss the matter, and probably never shall. The step from text to any kind of paraphrase or analysis is a delicate thing. We can try improving this. But perhaps we ought simply to read more aloud, and then invite the meaningfulness of the silences.

The Lawrence Estate

GERALD POLLINGER

There are many television programs nowadays which are recorded in front of what is termed a live audience. Subsequently, by use of various recording devices, noises such as applause and laughter are incorporated in the sound track, often giving a totally false impression of the reaction of the audience at the time of the recording. Before many of the programs actually commence, the audience is treated, if that is the right word, to someone who is known in the trade as a "warm-up man," and this apparition occurs whether the program is serious or intended to be humorous. The "warm-up man" has an almost impossible task, for he has to put the audience in the right mood, the right frame of mind, the right sensitivity to that which follows. And after his short-lived moment of glory he disappears to leave the stage and, indeed the audience, to savor and enjoy all that which follows.

I feel rather as a "warm-up man" must feel when he walks onto the stage and faces an audience cold, as it is called. My appearance in front of you will be relatively fleeting and I cannot hope to prepare you for the galaxy of entertainment and erudition which you will experience during the course of the next several days. I cannot hope to emulate the experience or trespass on the intelligence of the speakers who are to follow, for I have not spent long waking hours studying the philosophy of the author we are here to commemorate, nor painstakingly compared manuscripts to discover the minutest change in emphasis or connotation, nor engaged in weeks of research and detection to look for forgotten or temporarily mislaid correspondence.

But what I have done, and what I do is, I believe, to manage the Estate of Frieda Lawrence Ravagli, not only in the way she would have wished, but in the way my father, Laurence Pollinger, would have required of me. And if I have achieved but part of that then I shall count myself as having been both fortunate and successful.

13

Surrounded as I am by so many of my clients and friends--some of whom I have known only by correspondence these past thirty years-- it might seem a little presumptuous for me to venture an explanation of my profession (the second oldest in the world) or to embark upon a brief history. But I am also aware that there are many present who may not know how I spend all my working life, and most of my non-office hours too.

Most authors have agents. It is not a nice word, but "impresario" sounds too much like show-business, so "agent" will have to suffice as a description of my profession. Most authors need agents, although there are a few who like to be involved in the hurly-burly of financial transactions and the thrust and parry of contractual negotiations.

Primarily, however, the task of the author is to write, to compose, to select, to compile, and to edit. Let nobody who has not put pen to paper ever think that the craft is an easy one: it is one of the hardest métiers known to man, and far too little sympathy and praise is given to those who are deserving of these. The author entrusts his work to an agent, who then becomes more than a midwife to the child of the creator's mind and labors. He is, in turn, and not necessarily in order, an advisor, a mentor, a lawyer, a friend, a counsellor, an accountant, and an Indian chief. It is his task to perform a marriage between the author and the publisher, to find the right producer in the right media, and to arrange the contract for the benefit of, and not automatically for the maximum financial benefit of, the person who has given the work into his care. Subsequently he must administer the contracts he has arranged and seek to explore and to exploit other facets of an individual work in other media, in other countries, and in languages other than the original.

The responsibility of the agent to his client does not end with the demise of the author. In a number of cases, particularly when the author has been prolific and a professional, the agent will be appointed either as Literary Executor or as agent for the Estate of the author. In such a way I have the privilege of continuing to act for such literary figures as Lord Byron, Scott Fitzgerald, H. E. Bates, Carl Sandburg, and Theodore Dreiser, to mention only a few whose names are familiar to you.

I will not deal here with the day-to-day activities of an author's agent, but give you three quite different examples of the ways in which he is involved with authors past. For example, it took some six years of constant correspondence and follow-up detective work to ascertain the rights position of each of Edith Wharton's books; subsequently it was possible to embark on a successful publishing program. In a completely different genre, the work of James Blish has to be kept in absolutely apple-pie order, because so many of his stories have appeared in different collections. Finally, when, as chairman of the Science Fiction Club, I address over five thousand people scheduled to attend the world convention in Brighton in August 1980, I shall be able to give them the latest news about Star Trek.

I am particularly proud of arranging the mass-market paperback editions in England of the works of John Cowper Powys. Often acclaimed (after D. H. Lawrence) as the second greatest British novelist, we now have over fifty of his books in print, are about to publish a hitherto unknown novel entitled After My Fashion, and have just arranged for the television series of A Glastonbury Romance.

Deliberately I have said little up to now about D. H. Lawrence, and I have no intention of preëmpting any of the later speakers who have been most closely concerned with his complete correspondence or the exciting forthcoming appearance of all his writings in a corrected definitive form. But I would like to say a little about how I came to be involved with "Bert," as he is always referred to in his birthplace of Eastwood.

Lawrence initially employed James Brand Pinker to act on his behalf, and also for a short while Robert Mountsier in the United States. But he had not forgotten that at the time Sons and Lovers was published he had also been approached by Curtis Brown, and after the First World War he contacted what was then the largest of the literary agencies where in 1920 my father, Laurence Pollinger, was to be his correspondent. The subsequent history of their relationship and of my father's relationship with Frieda until she died in 1956 has been well charted by others and I need not dwell on it here. I will say, however, that when Professor Harry T. Moore suggested, out of kindness to my father's memory, that he exclude from his projected collection of Frieda's letters those in which she had been critical of certain actions, I insisted, as my father would have done, that the letters be published "warts and all," so that history would be accurately portrayed for future readers. My father (L. P. as he was known to all in the office and many outside it) was to all his authors a good and kindly figure, a benign and friendly presence, exuding good humor and exhibiting a shrewdness which rightly earned him a reputation of being the greatest of his profession. But he did not suffer fools gladly (and would have hated that cliché too), as those who tried to take advantage of his clients were swift to discover.

Although L. P. said that I met Lawrence, I confess to being too young at the time to recall any such meeting. But I met Frieda on several occasions after I joined my father's company in 1947 following a voluntary and adventurous era with the Royal Air Force.

As you know, Laurence Pollinger was Literary Executor to both David Herbert and to Frieda, and my name was coupled with his after Frieda's death.

As is well known, after Lawrence died in Vence on 2 March 1930, no will could be found, although Frieda thought it had been sent to Thomas Seltzer in 1925. This was unlikely: had it been sent to anyone at this time, it would have been sent to L. P., and I am certain that he would have kept it safely. Although John Middleton Murry offered to act as Lawrence's Literary Executor, an offer to which Aldous Huxley objected, Frieda directed my father to act as Literary Executor once the Letters of Administration were granted 14 December 1932. (It was in fact L. P. who visited George Lawrence and gave him a check for ₤500 as his share of the value of the Estate. William

Ernest had died in 1901, but the two sisters, Emily and Ada, also
each received Ł500. Bearing in mind that the value of Bert's estate
was only Ł2,438, Frieda's gesture of offering Ł1,500 to the three
relatives was at that time generous, and was so regarded by the
Court.)

Frieda died 11 August 1956 (her seventy-seventh birthday) and
her will, dated 3 November 1955, contained the following clause:
"I, also, herewith, nominate, constitute and appoint Mr. Laurence
Pollinger, Literary Executor, and, in the event of his decease
prior to mine, his successor shall be Pearn-Pollinger-Higham Ltd.,
to deal with all of the matters stemming out of the literary work
of D. H. Lawrence and of my self (Mr. Pollinger, my wonderful agent
who has handled my affairs for the past thirty years, offices at
39-40 Bedford Street, Strand, London, W. C. 2, England)." On
8 March 1969 the two Executors, Angelo Ravagli and Montague Weekley,
appointed my father and myself as joint literary executors, the
survivor to act solely in the event of death or retirement of the
other. When L. P. died in April 1976, the responsibility for managing
the Estate on behalf of the heirs passed to me. And when I die, his
company, Laurence Pollinger Limited, will assume that role.

There are seven current beneficiaries. In England live the
three children of Ernest Weekley: Monty Weekley, Elsa Seaman, and
Barbara Barr. The other four reside in Italy. Two of these, Fabio
and Marco, are the children of the deceased son, Federico, of Angelo
Ravagli, who himself died in February 1975 (and not 1976, as appears
in several publications). The other two beneficiaries are Angelo's
second son, Stefano, and daughter, Magda. The remuneration arising
from Lawrence's works is divided equally among the English and
Italian beneficiaries. At some date in the near future, arrangements
will be made for Elsa Seaman's son, Richard, coupled with Stefano
Ravagli, to be appointed Trustees of the Estate, for at present
Monty Weekley, sadly in failing health, is the only Executor alive
and the only person apart from myself empowered to sign contracts.

Much of my recent work has been in connection with the forthcoming Lawrence Festivals in 1980 and 1985. (May I add that when I
say "my" work I am adopting the Royal singular, since without the
unstinting back-up of all my staff, particularly my assistants
Yvonne Muller and Margaret Pepper, my own efforts would flounder.)
Apart from the Cambridge Edition of Lawrence, I acted as midwife to
the very successful Heinemann/Octopus Omnibus editions, the publisher of which freely admits that without Lawrence the remainder
(including Kafka, Orwell, Greene, and Hemingway) might not have
followed. The Cambridge Edition will be published, less apparatus,
by Heinemann and by Viking, and eventually in other languages also.
The Festival Committee of which I am a member is making many
arrangements for 7-17 May 1980, including an exhibition of the
material owned by George Lazarus, the photographic collection of
Keith Sagar, the stage performance of eight of the plays, and the
screening of all the motion pictures made to date. We are currently
expecting the televising during 1980 of a new version of Sons and
Lovers, The Rainbow, and Not I But the Wind by Frieda Lawrence.
Just possibly there may also be motion pictures ready then of The

<u>Plumed</u> <u>Serpent</u>, <u>The</u> <u>Woman</u> <u>Who</u> <u>Rode</u> <u>Away</u>, <u>The</u> <u>Man</u> <u>Who</u> <u>Died</u>, and
<u>St.</u> <u>Mawr</u>. There may also be television series of <u>Lady</u> <u>Chatterley's</u>
<u>Lover</u> and <u>The</u> <u>Priest</u> <u>of</u> <u>Love</u>, by Harry T. Moore, which will form
with <u>Kangaroo</u> the basis of a documentary biography. As the paintings
would not survive transit to Nottingham, a minor exhibition of water-
colors together with a new book of Lawrence's paintings may be
presented.

And what of the forthcoming books about Lawrence with which we
have been concerned? There are several of these, commencing with
Warren Roberts' revised bibliography, Keith Sagar's Calendar and
<u>Life</u> <u>of</u> <u>Lawrence</u>, and Harry Moore's and Dale S. Montague's <u>The</u>
<u>Correspondence</u> <u>of</u> <u>Frieda</u> <u>Lawrence</u> <u>and</u> <u>Her</u> <u>Circle</u>. These are part of
what has been termed "the Lawrence industry." There are also video-
cassettes of the televised stories, and an authorized artist is
preparing designs as well as a stylized Phoenix logo which is to be
incorporated in what could accurately be described as merchandise,
not least of which will be specially-woven lengths of Nottingham
lace and Wedgwood plates.

During the last year or two, the D. H. Lawrence Society in
England has performed, as just part of its many services, as guides
to visitors transported to Nottingham and Eastwood by special train
and coach, arranged with British Rail and the premier hotel in
Nottingham. The birthplace, in the charge of its curator, Enid
Goodband, is established as a "must" for visitors of all nations,
and these now number thousands each year. The civic authorities have
also cooperated magnificently with both the Society and the Estate
in recognizing--not before time--that Lawrence is one of England's
greatest sons.

Managing Lawrence occupies much of my time, and sometimes there
are complexities and difficulties. This is especially so with motion
picture and television contracts. I never cease to marvel at the
ways lawyers can make complex what is basically so simple.

Many writers of books about Lawrence know me from one angle
only: that of the person who requires them to pay permission fees
for the use of copyright material. We receive about six applications
every day for the use of Lawrence's work, and I know that some
authors resent being asked to pay for using work by another author.
However, I can assure every applicant that, if I am his agent, and
there are several of my clients present, I shall act just as forcefully on his or her behalf when his or her writings become in demand.
My view on this matter is quite clear: I believe that that which an
author has created is his alone, and that should others wish to
benefit from his genius and his industry then it is only right and
proper that he should be recompensesd. My conviction in this matter
holds good for every writer of every kind of prose or poetry. But I
must make clear that I would not perform my function if I did not
want to do so and if I did not think that I was doing something
worthwhile, both for literature and the general public.

During the next few days we shall be hearing from persons who
know much more about Lawrence than I can ever hope to know. My happy
task is to act as his administrator. I hope that I do that properly.

Following, in the order listed below, are the texts of some of the most important legal documents affecting the Lawrence estate.

1. Lawrence's Will.
2. Lawrence's Death Certificate.
3. Frieda Lawrence Ravagli's Will.
4. Frieda Lawrence Ravagli's Death Certificate.
5. Certification of Mrs. Ravagli's Will.
6. Deed Appointing the Literary Executors of the Lawrence Estate.

1. Lawrence's Will

[Extracted from the Principal Probate Registry of the High Court of Justice.]

I, the undersigned do hereby give and bequeath unto my wife Frieda Lawrence all those things real and personal of which I die possessed. [Signed] David Herbert Lawrence, 9 November 1914.

Witnessed by John Middleton Murry and Katherine Mansfield, 9 November 1914.

2. Lawrence's Death Certificate

[Valid Only if Bearing Impressed Court Seal.]

Be it known that David Herbert Lawrence--of the Villa Robermond, Vence A/M, in France--who died there on the 2nd day of March 1930 domiciled in England--made and duly executed his last Will and Testament and did not therein name any Executor.

The Right Honourable Lord Merrivale, the President of the Probate Divorce and Admiralty Division of the said High Court having on the 3rd day of November 1932 by his final decree in an action entitled Lawrence against Lawrence and others pronounced for the force and validity of the said bill.

And be it further known that at the date hereunder written Letters of Administration with the Will as mentioned in Paragraph 2 of the Statement of Claim--of all the Estate which by law devolves to and vests in the personal representative of the deceased were granted by His Majesty's High Court of Justice, at the Principal Probate Registry thereof to Frieda Emma Johanna Maria (in the Will called Frieda) Lawrence, of the above address, Widow the Relict of deceased, the Residuary Legatee named in the said Will--limited until the original Will or a more authentic copy thereof be brought into and left in the said Registry.

Dated the 14th day of December 1932.
Gross Value of Estate, ₤2438.16.5.
Net Value of Personal Estate ₤2438.16.5.
Former Grant (Admon) P. R. dated 5 June 1930.
Revoked.

3. Certification of Death Certificate

I certify that this is a true copy of the Will as contained in Paragraph 2 of the Statement of Claim in an action entitled Lawrence against Lawrence and others the force and validity of which was pronounced for by the final decree of the Right Honourable Lord Merivale the President of the Probate and Admiralty Division of the High Court of Justice on the 3rd day of November 1932 (limited until the original Will or a more authentic copy thereof be brought into and left in said Registry) deposited and proved in this Registry.

Dated this 20th day of August 1968.[Signed, illegible, by the Registrar.]

4. Frieda Lawrence Ravagli's Will

[Valid Only if Bearing Impressed Court seal.]
C. M. Weekley, Executor; Eustace S. Brown, Commissioner for Oaths.

Last Will and Testament
of
Frieda Emma Johanna Maria Lawrence Ravagli

I, Frieda Emma Johanna Maria Lawrence Ravagli, being of sound and disposing mind and memory and mindful of the uncertainties of life, hereby make, publish and declare this, my Last Will and Testament, hereby revoking any and all former Wills, codicils or bequests by me, at any time, made.

First
I direct the payment of my just debts, my funeral expenses and the expenses of my last illness, out of my personal estate, as soon as can conveniently be done.

Second
After the payment of my just debts, my funeral expenses and the expenses of my last illness, I give, devise and bequeath, as follows:

A. The Kiowa Ranch, located at San Cristobal, New Mexico, with "The D. H. Lawrence Shrine," to an organization to be created and sponsored by the University of New Mexico, providing they succeed in making a perpetual D. H. Lawrence Memorial or Foundation.

B. The actual residence of Los Pinos Ranch, situated in El Prado, New Mexico, to my husband, Angelo Ravagli, including all personal property therein.

C. To my sister, Johanna Krug nee von Richthofen, through the Swiss Bank Corporation in Basle, Switzerland, the amount of One Hundred Dollars ($100.00) per month, during her natural life.

D. To Charles Medley of 52 Bedford Square, London, W. C. 1., England, if he be living at the time of my death, the sum of Five Hundred Pounds. [Signed] Frieda Emma Johanna Maria Lawrence Ravagli.

E. All of the rest, residue and remainder of my estate, copyrights of D. H. Lawrence and literary work of the said D. H. Lawrence and myself, shall be divided into two parts:

One part (50%) to my husband, Angelo Ravagli;

One part (50%) shall be equally divided between my three children, namely, Montague C. Weekley, Elsa Seaman and Barbara Barr, all
living in London, England, provided, however, that my son, Montague,
shall receive first, from the part of the two sisters, the sum of
Four Thousand Three Hundred and Sixty-Five Pounds (their father,
when he died, left to Elsa and Barbara, Four Thousand Eight Hundred
and Sixty-Five Pounds, while Montague received only Five Hundred
Pounds). In the event that one or more of my children predecease me,
then, in that event, that child's, or children's share, shall go to
my grandchildren, the issue of that child, or children.

Third

If my husband shall predecease me or shall have died in and as
the result of the same accident or catastrophe that may cause my
death and thus is unable to take under this, my Last Will and Testament, and in such event the entire estate that he would have received,
if he were alive, shall be equally divided between the three children
of my said husband, namely: Stefanino Ravagli, Magda Micaela Ravagli
Gambetta and Federico Ravagli, all living in Italy.

Fourth

I hereby order and direct that I be buried in a rough coffin,
outside of and just below the Lawrence Memorial Chapel, located on
the Kiowa Ranch, pursuant to the reservation heretofore made in connection with the said Ranch, and that my grave be marked with a
wooden cross. I further, order and direct that my executors shall
insert a notice in the Taos paper, after my death, as follows:
[Signed] Frieda Emma Johanna Maria Lawrence Ravagli.
"To my Friends: A last farewell to all my friends thanking them
for all their friendship. Frieda Emma Johanna Maria Lawrence Ravagli."

Fifth

I hereby nominate, constitute and appoint my husband, Angelo
Ravagli, and my son, Montague C. Weekley, to serve as Executor and
Co-Executor, respectively, of this, my last Will and Testament.
I, also, herewith, nominate, constitute and appoint Mr. Lawrence
Pollinger, literary Executor, and, in the event of his decease prior
to mine, his successor shall be Pearn-Pollinger-Higham, Ltd., to deal
with all of the matters stemming out of the literary work of D. H.
Lawrence and of myself (Mr. Pollinger, my wonderful agent who has
handled my affairs for the past thirty years, offices at 39-40 Bedford
Street, Strand, London, W. C. 2, England).
In witness whereof, I have hereunto set my hand and seal, to
this, my Last Will and Testament, consisting of three typewritten
pages, to each of which I have subscribed my name, at Taos, New
Mexico, this 3rd day of November, A. D., 1955. [Signed] Frieda Emma
Johanna Maria Lawrence Ravagli.
Signed, sealed, published and declared by Frieda Emma Johanna
Maria Lawrence Ravagli, as and for her Last Will and Testament,
before us, who at her request, and in her presence, and in the pres-
ence of each other, did hereunto subscribe our names, as attesting
witnesses, at Taos, New Mexico, this 3rd day of November, A. D., 1955.
[Signed] R. Howard Brandenburg, Residing at Taos, New Mexico; [Signed]
Helen M. Kentnor, Residing at Taos, New Mexico.

5. Frieda Lawrence Ravagli's Death Certificate

[In the High Court of Justice, the Principal Probate Registry]

Be it known that Frieda Emma Johanna Marie Lawrence Ravagli of
El Prado Taos County New Mexico in the United States of America
married woman died there on the 11th day of August 1956 domiciled in
the State of New Mexico.

And be it further known that at that date hereunder written the
last Will and Testament (a copy whereof is hereunto annexed) of the
said deceased was proved and registered in the Principal Probate
Registry of the High Court of Justice and that Administration of all
the estate which by law devolves to and vests in the personal representative of the said deceased was granted by the aforesaid Court to
Charles Montague Weekley (in the will called Montague C. Weekley) of
Netteswell House Bethnal Green Museum Bethnal Green London museum
curator son of deceased one of the executors named in the said will
Power reserved to the other executors Lawrence Pollinger being the
liberary executor only

And it is hereby certified that an Inland Revenue affidavit has
been delivered wherein it is shown that the gross value of the said
estate in England (exclusive of what the said deceased may have been
possessed of or entitled to as a trustee and not beneficially)
amounts to £4126.11.10 and that the net value of the estate amounts
to £4126.11.10.

Dated the 16th day of May 1960. [Signed] Comptom Muir, Registrar
Probate Extracted by Sydney Morse & Co., Alder House 1 Alders-
gate Street London E. C. 1.

6. Certification of Mrs. Ravagli's Will

[Valid Only if Bearing Impressed Court Seal]

State of New Mexico
County of Taos

I, Josefa Santistevan, Clerk of the District Court, in and for
said County aforesaid, do hereby certify that the foregoing is a true,
perfect, and complete copy of the Last Will and Testament of Frieda
Emma Johanna Maria Lawrence Ravagli, deceased, together with Letters
Testamentary in the matter of the Estate of Frieda Emma Johanna Maria
Lawrence Ravagli, deceased.

I, further, certify that said Last Will and Testament was duly
admitted to probate in the District Court of Taos County, New Mexico,
agreeable to the laws and usages of the State of New Mexico, and that
said Letters are still in full force and effect.

In testimony whereof, I have hereunto set my hand and affixed
the seal of said Court, at my office, in Taos, New Mexico, this 15th
day of Feb., A. D., 1960 [Signed] Josefa Santistevan, Clerk of the
District Court.

State of New Mexico
County of Taos

I, Fred J. Federici, Judge of the District Court of Taos County,
New Mexico, do hereby certify that Josefa Santistevan, whose name is

and was, at the time of signing and sealing the same, Clerk of the District Court of Taos County aforesaid, and keeper of the Records and Seal thereof, duly appointed and qualified to office; that full faith and credit are and of right ought to be given to all her official acts as such in all Courts of Record and elsewhere; and that her said attestation is in due form of law, and by the proper officer.

Given under my hand and seal this 16 day of Feb., A. D., 1960. [Signed] Fred J. Federici, District Judge.

State of New Mexico
County of Taos

I, Josefa Santistevan, Clerk of the District Court in and for said County in the State aforesaid, do hereby certify that Fred J. Federici, whose genuine signature is appended to the foregoing certificate was, at the time of signing the same, Judge of the District Court of Taos County, of the State of New Mexico, duly commissioned and qualified, that full faith and credit are and of right ought to be given to all his official acts as such, in all Courts of Record and elsewhere.

In testimony whereof, I have hereunto set my hand and affixed the seal of said Court, at my office in Taos, New Mexico, this 14th day of Feb., A. D., 1960. [Signed] Josefa Santistevan, Clerk of the District Court.

7. Deed Appointing the Literary Executors of the Lawrence Estate

This deed is made the 8th day of March, One thousand nine hundred and sixty Nine by Angelo Ravagli of Villa Bernarda Spotorno Prov. Savona, Italy and Montague C. Weekley of Bethnal Green Museum E. 2. in the City of London (hereinafter called "the Trustees")

Whereas the Trustees are the Executors and Trustees of the Will dated the 30th day of November One thousand nine hundred and fifty five of the late Frieda Emma Johanna Maria Lawrence Ravagli (hereinafter called "the Testatrix") Probate of which Will was granted to Montague C. Weekley out of the Principal Registry on the Sixteenth day of May One thousand nine hundred and sixty

And whereas by the said Will the Testatrix appointed Laurence Pollinger predeceasing her his successor should be Pearn Pollinger & Higham Limited

And whereas the said Company no longer exists but the said Laurence Pollinger is now carrying on the business of literary agency as Managing Director of Laurence Pollinger Limited and has continued to act personally as such Literary Executor

And whereas the Trustees are desirous of ensuring that there should be proper continuity of such literary executorship now in consideration of the premises this deed witnesseth that the Trustees hereby appoint Gerald John Pollinger to act jointly with the said Laurence Pollinger during their joint lives or until one or the other of them shall retire and thereafter the Survivor shall act solely as such Literary Executor and finally after the death or retirement of such Survivor the Company Laurence Pollinger Limited shall act as such Literary Executor.

In witness thereof the parties hereto have hereunto set their hands and seals the day and year first above written [Signed] Angelo Ravagli; [Signed] Montague C. Weekley.

Lawrence's Short Stories

The Achievement of *England, My England and Other Stories*

KEITH CUSHMAN

I would like to propose that the England, My England volume, published in 1922, is Lawrence's most outstanding accomplishment as a writer of short stories. This collection includes some of his most striking tales, works characterized by imaginative boldness, aesthetic richness, and formal integrity. Though the England, My England stories were not written to be published together, the individual stories gain a good deal from the company they keep in the volume. Leo Gurko has made a case for the imaginative unity of the three novellas collected in The Ladybird.[1] I would like to perform the same service for the England, My England stories. These stories are much more than a miscellaneous gathering, much more too than the exercises in assorted literary perversity perceived by Kingsley Widmer.[2]

Six of the ten stories are well known and widely anthologized. "The Horse Dealer's Daughter" and "The Blind Man" are among Lawrence's most famous tales, and the title story, "Tickets, Please," "Samson and Delilah," and "Monkey Nuts" have also received much attention. "You Touched Me" is an odd, fascinating preview of The Fox, while "Fanny and Annie" is an appealing treatment of the theme of second best, so prevalent in Lawrence's early career. "Wintry Peacock" deals with a woman's well-founded suspicion that her soldier-husband has fathered an illegitimate child in Belgium. "The Primrose Path" is the story of a young man's response to his scapegrace uncle. Lawrence had sent this story to Edward Garnett in the summer of 1913, but Garnett was unable to place it. Consequently Lawrence used it—the only story in England, My England which had not first appeared in a magazine—to round out his collection. Even though "The Primrose Path" seems something of a left-over, it is very much at home with all the other stories of erotic confusion and entanglement. As was his usual custom, Lawrence revised the magazine verions—most exhaustively "England, My England"—before book publication.

The stories in the Prussian Officer collection and the early
stories collected posthumously in A Modern Lover are rooted in autobiography or at least in the immediate world of Lawrence's childhood
and young manhood. The early stories depend for their effect upon the
sharply realized milieu of countryside, colliery town, and occasionally (as with "The White Stocking") city. The emotional impact of
the finest of the early stories is related to Lawrence's own identification with their materials. "Odour of Chrysanthemums" is the most
obvious example.

Though the emotional richness of the early tales is impressive,
nevertheless Lawrence has made a significant advance in England, My
England, where he does not rely on personal experience in the same
way. His new ability to break loose from his own experience, to
imagine his fictions more freely, is a measure of growing artistic
confidence and maturity. The pleasures of the Prussian Officer collection include intense authorial engagement. In contrast, many of
the England, My England stories are marked by sardonic detachment.

Though a number of Lawrence's finest tales were written and
collected later in his career, the stories collected in The Woman
Who Rode Away and the posthumous The Lovely Lady are much more un-
even in quality, much more likely to suffer from thinness. "The Rocking-Horse Winner" is matched by "Glad Ghosts." "The Man Who Loved
Islands" must co-exist with the nervous satiric attacks on John
Middleton Murry. Nothing in England, My England is as nasty as "None
of That" or as feeble as "The Last Laugh." My case for England, My
England is based in part on the book's high percentage of achieved
success.

The England, My England stories are, appropriately enough, all
about English characters in English settings. All are studies in
the relations between men and women (though with an author like
Lawrence that hardly says anything profound). I will proceed by exploring what I take to be the major unifying elements in the collection. First, the stories of England, My England grow out of the experience of World War I and out of a new sense that the England of
Lawrence's best hopes has become a lost cause. Second, the stories
reveal Lawrence using myth and fairy tale structurally and playing
off established mythical meaning for his own purposes. Following
Sandra Gilbert's excellent example, I will refer to this latter practice as revisionary mythmaking.[3] Third, the stories, unlike many of
the later tales, are nondoctrinaire. Instead they are in the best
sense ambiguous. Finally, for the most part the England, My England
stories are written in a vein of Lawrentian comedy.

The War and England

As few people know any longer, the title of the first story and
of the volume itself is drawn from a patriotic poem by William Ernest
Henley, the late Victorian author of "Invictus." I will quote the
concluding stanza of Henley's poem in order to illustrate the extent
of Lawrence's irony. The vast difference between Lawrence's England
and that of William Ernest Henley underscores the meaning of the
England, My England volume:

> Mother of Ships whose might,
>   England, my England,
> Is the fierce old Sea's delight,
>   England, my own,
> Chosen daughter of the Lord,
> Spouse-in-Chief of the Ancient Sword,
> There's the menace of the Word
>   In the Song on your bugles blown,
>   England--
> Out of heaven on your bugles blown!

All that turn-of-the-century might produced only the catastrophe of World War I.

In a letter of 26 April 1913 Lawrence had said that he wrote because he wanted "folk--English folk--to alter, and have more sense."[4] Such a sentiment can be powerfully felt behind such works as _The Rainbow_, but with the exception of Mabel Pervin and Jack Fergusson in "The Horse Dealer's Daughter," the English men and women of the _England, My England_ stories are beyond the possibility of alteration. Lawrence has imaginatively detached himself from the situation of England, just as in his own life he was then pointing toward America. He seems almost to take delight in observing his characters as they march toward perdition.

In _The Ladybird_ Lawrence says that "the years 1916 and 1917 were the years when the old spirit died for ever in England";[5] he of course refers to the period of the worst carnage on the Western Front. The title story of _England, My England_ directly addresses the death of the old English spirit. In the other stories Lawrence seems content to accept the fact that the old England is no more. He has moved on beyond crisis.

At the same time this volume is nevertheless part of Lawrence's response to the war. The dislocation and breakdown found throughout the collection point to the war's impact. So perhaps does the fact that nearly all the love relationships in the book are battles. "Tickets, Please" illustrates this point especially well, for it concludes with the tram-girls physically assaulting their elusive male supervisor.

"England, My England" itself is the work that is Lawrence's most direct statement _about_ the war. The "Nightmare" chapter of _Kangaroo_ describes England during wartime more vividly and concretely, but in "England, My England" Lawrence makes a concerted attempt to analyze and understand why the war happened to England and why England lacked the spiritual resources to come through intact. Lawrence's story of the failure of the dilettante Egbert is really the story of the failure of his generation and indeed the failure of England. Significantly, the original version of the story was published as early as October 1915. Lawrence revised the story extensively in December 1921, transforming it into a fully considered statement about England and the war.

It is not generally noticed that most of the other _England, My England_ stories are rooted in the English experience of World War I. In both "Tickets, Please" and "Monkey Nuts" the traditional sexual roles have been subverted because the men are off fighting. The

battles between John Thomas Raynor and the tram-girls and between
Miss Stokes and Albert for the affections of Joe are placed in the
context of the dislocations of wartime and its immediate aftermath.
Similarly, Samson comes back to reclaim his Delilah in the first year
of the war, asserting his traditional rights at a time when the
traditional order is visibly disintegrating.

In "The Blind Man" Maurice Pervin is able to live the life of
"sheer immediacy of blood-contact with the substantial world" (CSS,
p. 355)[6] because he has been blinded in Flanders. For all the richness of this life, his blindness is the result of a wound. Maurice's
experience in the trenches has made him less than a whole man. The
war is obviously the occasion for the battle between the sexes in
"Wintry Peacock," for the story revolves around a letter from a Belgian girl in which she claims that she has had a baby by the married
Corporal Alfred Goyte. Hadrian in "You Touched me," like Henry Grenfel
in The Fox, comes home to win one of the unmarried women only after
the war has ended and things can return to normal.

E. W. Tedlock has commented that the England, My England
stories "contain Lawrence's most direct treatment of the war's effect
on life."[7] Only in the title story does Lawrence show us a soldier
fighting in the war and none too convincingly: the machine-gun
Lawrence says Egbert is in charge of actually seems to be an artillery-
piece. But the point is not the war itself. Instead Lawrence uses
details from the war to support his perception of irrevocable change.

Revisionary Mythmaking

The England, My England stories have tight, strong structures.
This is partly because Lawrence is making use of ready-made structures that he finds in myth and fairy tale. In turning away from the
Midlands and his own experience, he discovers rich resources for his
narrative. England, My England is a collection of Lawrentian myths
and fairy tales.

Although he constructs the stories on a foundation of myth and
fairy tale, he subverts the myths and fairy tales he makes use of.
The Lawrentian meaning resonates against the traditional, received
meaning it replaces. This effect--revisionary mythmaking--contrib-
utes to the great vitality of the stories.

"The Blind Man" is a notable case in point. Surely its invocation of the paradox of sight through blindness has both Oedipus and
Lear behind it. Like the Duke of Gloucester, Oedipus sees truly only
when he is blinded. The true perception in both plays is associated
with the light of reason, and Lawrence is having none of that. Instead he finds genuine, enduring value in the darkness. Blindness is
not merely the path back to light. At the same time Lawrence insists
that neither darkness nor light is adequate in itself. It is whole-
ness of being that must be striven for.

"Tickets, Please" is Lawrence's version of the myth of Orpheus
and the maenads. In the myth Orpheus returns to Thrace after his
failure to rescue his beloved Eurydice from the underworld. He encounters some Ciconian women raging as maenads, and they tear him to
pieces. The explanation for their violence varies, but one tradition

has it that each of the women wants him for herself and battles to possess him.

Lawrence transforms the mythical artist and lover into the tram inspector John Thomas Raynor. The tram-girls are Lawrence's maenads, and, true to form, they are angered by John Thomas' male elusiveness. He goes walking with the girls at night, nonchalantly flirts, and refuses to become more than a mysterious "nocturnal presence" (CSS, p. 339). Annie organizes the girls, they corner John Thomas and demand that he choose. When he still refuses, they attack: "She had taken off her belt, and swinging it, she fetched him a sharp blow over the head with the buckle end. He sprang and seized her. But immediately the other girls rushed upon him, pulling and tearing and beating him. Their blood was now thoroughly up" (CSS, p. 343). Lawrence's maenads are appropriately "maddened," and they "giggle wildly" (CSS, p. 344). But Lawrence's Orpheus is not destroyed. Forced to choose, he chooses Annie, and in so doing he conquers her: "Annie let go of him as if he had been a hot coal" (CSS, p. 344). Something is "broken in her" (CSS, p. 345), and the other girls seem similarly dazed.

Both myth and short story express a fear of female sexuality. The power of eros is so intense that it becomes destructive. The exalted love of Orpheus and Eurydice and the unbridled ferocity of the maenads are but two manifestations of the same phenomenon. Lawrence adds a social context to the myth by placing his story in wartime: the women are free to break away from traditional restraint and inhibition because the men are not there to control them. However, Lawrence significantly revises the myth. Though his Orpheus can be battered in body, the power of male sexuality prevents his destruction.

"Samson and Delilah" revises the Biblical story, seemingly in the interest of male ascendancy. Though Lawrence's Delilah has soldiers tie up the Samson who has come to reclaim her, she is unable to shear his locks. Indeed she does not wish to do so: after he frees himself from the loosely tied rope, he discovers to his astonishment that she has left the door unlocked. This Delilah cannot resist the power of Samson's "dark, bright, mindless Cornish eyes" (CSS, p. 412). At story's end he has reclaimed his rightful place in the relationship. She glowers at the fire and shudders while he insinuates his hand between her breasts and talks on. As we shall see, she has "the eyes of some non-human creature" (CSS, p. 413) herself, and the struggle between Samson and Delilah is far from over.

As George Ford has noted,[8] "Fanny and Annie" is a version of the myth of Persephone and Pluto. Fanny, a proud, beautiful lady's maid, returns reluctantly to her home town "to marry her first-love" after her "brilliant and ambitious cousin" (CSS, p. 459) has jilted her. Fanny's return is a descent into the underworld:

> Flame-lurid his face as he turned among the throng
> of flame-lit and dark faces upon the platform. In
> the light of the furnace she caught sight of his
> drifting countenance, like a piece of floating
> fire. . . . His eternal face, flame-lit now! The
> pulse and darkness of red fire from the furnace

> towers in the sky, lighting the desultory,
> industrial crowd on the wayside station,
> lit him and went out (CSS, p. 458).

The cousin could have led Fanny out of the provinces into a larger world. Now she must settle for second best, and even worse, a "red-faced woman" (CSS, p. 467) stands up in chapel and denounces Fanny's old sweetheart, accusing him of being responsible for her daughter's pregnancy.

But Lawrence's Persephone chooses the darkness. If the flames of the industrial town conjure up Hades, there are flames to be found within Fanny herself as she responds to Harry's "physical winsomeness" and his "flesh" that seems "new and lovely to touch" (CSS, p. 466). Though at first she is "inflamed with a sort of fatal despair" (CSS, p. 465), soon enough the only fire is that of physical attraction: "Fanny felt the crisp flames go through her veins as she listened" (CSS, p. 466). With comic deftness Lawrence reveals that Fanny finds Harry more interesting and attractive after the denunciation. She will stick it out and go through with the marriage. This Persephone will be happy to live in the underworld with her working-class Pluto.

John Vickery has observed that "England, My England" makes use of the mythic pattern of the scapegoat.[9] Egbert as scapegoat is expelled first from his family and then from England. Traditionally the community drives out the scapegoat in order to restore itself, but no such restoration is possible in "England, My England." Egbert perishes, and Lawrence seems to feel that England will perish in his wake. The horsemen Egbert sees shortly before his death are associated with the riders of apocalypse.

"The Horse Dealer's Daughter" even sounds like the name of a fairy tale, and Mabel Pervin is a version of Cinderella. She is oppressed by her three brutish brothers, the prescribed number out of fairy tales. She does the dirty work in the household, cleaning up while they sit around and call her "the sulkiest bitch that ever trod" (CSS, p. 446). Mabel has no fairy godmother to transform her into a princess. Instead, she must find her own salvation; her new life must be earned. Paradoxically she can achieve this only after immersing herself in the dark waters of death and destruction. Mabel is rescued from her suicide attempt by no Prince Charming but instead by Jack Fergusson, the country doctor, a man who is also suffering from the sickness unto death.

"The Horse Dealer's Daughter" also makes use of "Sleeping Beauty." Like Sleeping Beauty, Mabel must go through the experience of death in order to be truly brought to life. Fergusson saves her from the dark pond and its "cold, rotten clay" (CSS, p. 450). New life comes not from a magical kiss from the handsome prince but from a ritual immersion in the waters of destruction, followed by a passionate commitment made by a man who does not understand what he is doing.

Lawrence also revises "Sleeping Beauty" in "You Touched Me." Matilda Rockley goes at midnight to her father's bedroom, not realizing that Hadrian is sleeping there instead. Her touch awakens Hadrian, and "the fragile exquisiteness of her caress startled him" (CSS, p. 402). Lawrence reverses the fairy tale, for here it is the prince

who awakens. At that, Hadrian is rather a sorry substitute for Prince
Charming. In "You Touched Me" the power of human contact is quicken-
ing and awakening for both man and woman; both are brought to life.
It must be added that Hadrian and Matilda do not seem destined to
live happily ever after.

Lawrence's use of myth and fairy tale is a topic that demands
full-scale exploration. Persephone and Pluto span his career from
the courtship of the Morels to "Bavarian Gentians." Sleeping Beauty
can be found in Louisa in the early "Daughters of the Vicar"; she is
also very much present in Connie Chatterley. Ultimately Lawrence
would create his own original fairy tales in such stories as "The
Rocking-Horse Winner" and "The Man Who Loved Islands."

In _England, My England_ the inherited stories provide Lawrence
with ready-made structures. More importantly, he subverts traditional
values as he subverts the traditional stories he makes use of. The
England, My England stories have so much vitality partly because of
the way they reverberate against familiar myths and fairy tales.
Lawrence takes considerable delight in his revisionary mythmaking,
in telling the stories of Oedipus, of Orpheus and the maenads, of
Cinderella, of Sleeping Beauty one more time--and telling them his
way.

In Pursuit of Ambiguity

In contrast to many of the stories from Lawrence's later years,
the stories of _England, My England_ are undogmatic and nondoctrinaire.
Though they of course explore some of Lawrence's central beliefs,
they also seem to demonstrate that at this point he felt that such
beliefs could not be maintained with anything like certitude.

Throughout his career Lawrence was a passionate seeker after
absolute truth, even as he doubted the existence of absolute truth.
In the Foreword to _Fantasia of the Unconscious_ he asserted that "art
is utterly dependent on philosophy,"[10] and periodically he produced
works expounding his "metaphysic." However, though Lawrence felt he
needed a basis of belief out of which he could create his fiction and
poetry, the belief he arrived at was rarely more than provisional.

Ursula in _Women in Love_ functions as a counterweight to Birkin,
bringing him back down to earth when he gets too carried away in his
flights of abstract Lawrentian fancy. If Birkin is in some ways a
spokesman for the author, so is Ursula. The shrillness of _The Plumed
Serpent_ reveals Lawrence's difficulty in convincing himself of the
violent mumbo-jumbo he has concocted in that novel, and Kate Leslie
is equally skeptical. Though Lawrence is often criticized for being
dogmatic, he is more apt to be his own best critic whenever he starts
preaching his latest version of the truth.

Many of the _England, My England_ stories seem to dramatize
Lawrentian truths, but these truths tend to disappear when scrutinized
carefully. "The Blind Man" is an excellent case in point. The story is
a brilliant evocation of the rich life of intense, direct contact with
the physical world. Lawrence's artistry is so commanding that he makes
us feel as if we have truly entered Maurice Pervin's sensuous world.
Even so astute a reader as Mark Spilka, impressed by the presentation
of this world, is fooled into believing that Maurice "moves toward

greater fullness of being" in his contact with the feeble Bertie, and E. W. Tedlock actually contends that Maurice and Bertie achieve "essential, vitalistic communion."[11]

Actually the scene of ritual communion only serves to underscore Maurice's extreme isolation. The life of the senses is one-sided and incomplete. Though Maurice is generally happy enough in his new-found darkness, he is also subject to "devastating fits of depression which seemed to lay waste his whole being. It was worse than depression--a black misery" (CSS, p. 347).

The desperately lonely Maurice, cut off and painfully isolated by his blindness, yearns for a relationship with Bertie Reid, the brittle, superficial friend of his wife. "'Touch my eyes, will you?-- touch my scar,'" Maurice asks in the barn, and Bertie, under the blind man's hypnotic spell, must do as he is bid. Maurice is overjoyed and exults over the "new delicate fulfilment of mortal friendship" (CSS, p. 364). But while Maurice croons, "'we shall know each other now,'" Bertie stands "as if in a swoon, unconscious, imprisoned," gazing "mute and terror-struck," "trying by any means to escape" (CSS, p. 364). Maurice feels triumphant only because he is blind and cannot see what has really happened. If the scene of ritual contact attempts to bring the physical and the mental together in living relationship, Lawrence's point seems to be that such a relationship is not easy to accomplish. Lawrence called the ambiguous end of the story "queer and ironical."[12] The story is almost a parody of his lifelong imaginative effort to integrate the powers of darkness and light.

"The Horse Dealer's Daughter" has no irony, and yet it too is open-ended. This story concludes with a moving declaration and commitment of love between Mabel Pervin and Jack Fergusson, her rescuer. The story seems to be a full-fledged embodiment of salvation through the dark mystery of sexuality. Yet there is nothing programmatic-- or even fully resolved--about "The Horse Dealer's Daughter." The reader would like Mabel and Fergusson to be redeemed by their passion, but it is also unmistakable that something dangerous and destructive has been unleashed. Forces have been set in motion which are not controllable. At the end of the story when Fergusson must go back to his office, Mabel worries that the spell of their passionate encounter will be broken. But her fear that he "can't want to love" (CSS, p. 456) her is unfounded. He can't help loving her--if "love" is the right word: "'No, I want you, I want you,' was all he answered, blindly, with that terrible intonation which frightened her" (CSS, p. 457). Notice the association of the power of eros with blindness, which serves to link "The Horse Dealer's Daughter" and "The Blind Man." Indeed Mabel and Maurice even have the same surname, Pervin, which is probably not accidental. Clyde de L. Ryals has described "The Horse Dealer's Daughter" as a "vivid presentation of what Jung calls the rebirth archetype,"[13] and the story does fit that pattern. Yet there is something troubling about Mabel Pervin's rebirth: the story is more ambiguous than a Jungian reading allows.

The unleashing of passion has something of the same effect in "Tickets, Please." The tram-girls get more than they have bargained for, and so does John Thomas. Though victorious, he is battered and bruised. There is only qualified triumph in an exit taken with "his face closed, his head dropped" (<u>CSS</u>, p. 345). The girls, unsettled, upset, and embarrassed, are all "anxious to be off," and they tidy themselves "with mute, stupefied faces" (<u>CSS</u>, p. 346). Lawrence suggests that in the battle of the sexes, ultimately no one can be a winner. The conflict is too basic to be resolvable.

The husband in "Samson and Delilah" seems to regain supremacy over his wife just as John Thomas defeats the tram-girls. Samson has returned to reclaim what is rightfully his and to strip his wife of the power she has enjoyed in his absence. Indeed she is secretly eager for him to restore his dominant role.

Yet "Samson and Delilah" is anything but dogmatic. At the end when he touches "her between her full, warm breasts, quietly," "she started, and seemed to shudder" (<u>CSS</u>, p. 426) as she gazes into the fire, a response so ambiguous that it is almost indecipherable. And "Samson and Delilah" has such an open ending that the story breaks off in mid-sentence:

> "And don't you think I've come back a-begging," he said. "I've more than <u>one</u> thousand pounds to my name, I have. And a bit of a fight for a how-de-do pleases me, that it do. But that doesn't mean as you're going to deny as you're my missis . . ." (<u>CSS</u>, p. 426).

The concluding ellipsis tells us that though Samson seems to be fully in command, the war is not over. He has gained the upper hand over his Delilah, but she has survived and will fight again. She will also win her share of the battles. Instead of dramatizing man's inherent right to dominate woman, the story is only insisting that man and woman must struggle for domination. Widmer simplifies when he argues that Delilah "submits finally to male purpose."[14] Instead of offering sexist dogma, "Samson and Delilah" presents a dialectical process.

The conflict in "Monkey Nuts" leads to the defeat of Miss Stokes. But though the aggressive woman is humiliated, the net result is that the deathly relationship between the unformed, malleable Joe and the emotionally sterile Albert will continue. This is another story in which the battle leads to no victory. Though the soldiers rout Miss Stokes, "they had a weight on their minds, they were afraid" (<u>CSS</u>, p. 378).

In "You Touched Me" Lawrence once again seems to be dramatizing a belief in the primacy of the senses, and once again closer inspection reveals otherwise. The rat-like Hadrian pressures the spinster Matilda into marrying him because she touched him on the brow that fateful night, though by mistake. There is no denying "the fragile exquisiteness of her caress," which "revealed unknown things to him" (<u>CSS</u>, p. 402). Even so, Matilda and her sister's suspicion that he is after their inheritance is not entirely unfounded. For whatever reason, Hadrian will not be denied. The women's dying father sides with Hadrian, seeming "to have a strange desire, quite unreasonable, for revenge upon the women who had surrounded him for so long" (<u>CSS</u>, p. 407). A story which seems to be presenting the power of physical attraction is actually once again illustrating the fundamental hostility between men and women. Matilda at last capitulates, and she and Hadrian are married. The story's conclusion parodies both conventional happy endings and Victorian deathbed scenes. This ending is as "queer and ironical" as the ending of "The Blind Man":

> "Let's look at you, Matilda," [the dying father] said. Then his voice went strange and unrecognisable. "Kiss me," he said.
> She stooped and kissed him. She had never kissed him before, not since she was a tiny child. But she was quiet, very still.
> "Kiss him," the dying man said.
> Obediently, Matilda put forward her mouth and kissed the young husband.
> "That's right! That's right!" murmured the dying man (CSS, p. 410).

And that is all there is. Such grotesqueness hardly speaks for any compelling belief in the positive power of touch.

Though the England, My England stories explore the key Lawrentian themes of this fruitful period, they do not seek to provide the themes with resolution. In the most sardonic stories in the collection-- "The Blind Man," "Tickets, Please," "Monkey Nuts," "You Touched Me," and "Wintry Peacock"--he seems almost to be playing games with his themes. If in Women in Love or The Plumed Serpent he seems to be searching for large answers, in England, My England he is content to rest with ambiguity. Indeed he insists on ambiguity.

Sardonic Comedy

In November 1921 Lawrence complained to Earl Brewster that "if I hadn't my own stories to amuse myself with I should die, chiefly of spleen."[15] He was finishing The Captain's Doll at the time, but the remark related to the England, My England stories as well. Lawrence indeed seems to be having a good time in these stories. There is a kind of creative zest in the way he goes about doing over Oedipus Rex, the myth of Orpheus and the maenads, and the story of Sleeping Beauty after his heart's desire. The best of the stories display a marvelous ease and civilized poise--and a sardonic humor as well. The reversals I have been sketching in this essay are in part comic reversals.

"The Blind Man," "Tickets, Please," "The Primrose Path," "You Touched Me," "Wintry Peacock," "Samson and Delilah," "Monkey Nuts," and "Fanny and Annie" all contain elements of comedy, and with the exception of the warm-hearted "Fannie and Annie," the comedy has an edge. This comedy has little in common with the broadly satiric comedy of "The Christening" or the flippant, jeering manner of The Captain's Doll or, most disastrously, Mr Noon. Comedy in England, My England is much more delicate and deadpa , much more effective too. I am not arguing that the stories are purely comic but rather that comedy is an important, customarily unnoticed ingredient.

I have already touched on the comic dimensions of these stories in speaking about revisionary mythmaking and ambiguity. "The Blind Man" and "You Touched Me" end on utterly sardonic notes. John Thomas' victory in defeat, Joe's and Albert's defeat in victory, the unlocked

door that follows forcible ejection in "Samson and Delilah," and
I should add the sensitive young narrator's confusion and discomfort
as his uncle proceeds down the primrose path: these scenes are not
simply comic, but comic they are. At this point in Lawrence's career
the battle of the sexes is intrinsically a comic spectacle.

The little-known "Wintry Peacock" is decidedly in a comic vein,
and the joke is at the expense of the incompatibility of men and
women. The witch-like Mrs. Goyte asks the young narrator to translate
a letter to her soldier-husband from a Belgian girl who claims he
has fathered her illegitimate child. Though the narrator mistrans-
lates the letter to protect the husband, he cannot allay the wife's
suspicions. At the end of the story he comes across the returned
Alfred Goyte and tells him about his encounter with Mrs. Goyte.
Narrator and soldier instantly form a bond of maleness against the
wife and against the female world.

Laughter resounds all through "Wintry Peacock." Mrs. Goyte
bends "down, doubled with laughter" when the narrator reads an
effusion in the letter about her husband's "beautiful English eyes"
(<u>CSS</u>, p. 383). The husband breaks "into a short laugh," then laughs
"aloud once more," and finally goes "into a loud burst of laughter
that made the still, snow-deserted valley clap again" (<u>CSS</u>, pp. 392,
393) as the narrator explains his efforts at deception. The story
ends with the narrator discovering that the Belgian girl is even
more formidable than the wife and running "down the hill shouting
with laughter" (<u>CSS</u>, p. 393).

Of course all this laughter has a hollow ring to it. The narrator shouts with laughter at the end because he has seen at firsthand how fully men and women are at odds. Mrs. Goyte is criticized
throughout for her willfulness, but her husband is criticized for
letting himself be dominated by women. Nor is the narrator immune
from the laughter, for his behavior with Mrs. Goyte and her husband
implicates him in the games of love and war. Though he is laughing
at the married couple, the joke is that he is laughing at himself as
well. All of which makes the comedy complex and sardonic. The "mis-
ogyny"[16] Kingsley Widmer perceives is present, but Lawrence is critical of the men in the story as well.

Lawrence's use of comedy is a major topic that has never been
adequately explored. Comedy is one of the keynotes of <u>England, My
England</u>. In so many of these stories the attempt to bridge the gap
between man and woman only produces a wider chasm. This failure of
relationship is presented comically. And when all is said and done,
stories entitled "Monkey Nuts," "Tickets, Please," "Fanny and Annie,"
"The Primrose Path," and "You Touched Me" can't be entirely serious.

Conclusion

It can also be argued that many of the <u>England, My England</u>
stories reveal Lawrence's growing need to assert male domination
over women. The volume after all belongs to the period between <u>Women
in Love</u> and the leadership novels, a time when star polarity was en
route to being transformed into male authority. The novellas that
date from this period--<u>The Fox</u>, <u>The Captain's Doll</u>, and especially
<u>The Ladybird</u>--are all concerned with female submission to the male

will. "Tickets, Please," "Monkey Nuts," "Samson and Delilah," "You Touched Me," and "Wintry Peacock" all dramatize the struggle for masculine supremacy and not always appealingly. In this context "The Horse Dealer's Daughter" seems a throwback to Lawrence's earlier efforts to bring the sexes together in passionate harmony.

At least, however, in most of the England, My England stories-- as in Kangaroo later on--Lawrence undercuts the notion of male authority at the same time he attempts to dramatize it. If it is an ideal he is striving for, it is an ideal he does not believe is attainable. As noted, John Thomas Raynor departs with his head bowed as well as bloodied, and Samson's victory is only provisional. The only thing certain is the struggle between man and woman, and in England, My England that struggle is presented with comic detachment.

Though the best stories in England, My England have received their share of critical attention, that attention has always been given to the stories in isolation. I have tried to suggest that the collection deserves to be taken seriously as a book, and I have tried to point out some of the reasons why. The New York Times reviewer said it all as early as November 1922: "By far the greater number of these stories have a subtlety, an evasive quality underlying yet penetrating the texture of the exterior plot. Even when they seem simple, they are in truth intensely complex, composed of innumerable tiny fibres of thought and feeling and instinct, passing into one another by imperceptible degrees."[17]

The Early Short Stories of Lawrence

JOHN S. POYNTER

Lawrence wrote to Edward Garnett on 17 April 1913, "I can only write what I feel pretty strongly about: and that, at present, is the relation between men and women."[1] At the time Lawrence was writing the first draft of The Sisters, which was to involve him deeply in symbolic relationships within an exploration of this theme and which was to manifest itself in The Rainbow and Women in Love. In a similar way The White Peacock, The Trespasser, and Sons and Lovers all illustrate Lawrence's sensitive awareness of the issues involved in the man/woman relationship, though it is only in Sons and Lovers that this theme was, at that time, to be explored to a finality, a finality which was to dictate the path of his later work.

All these early novels are, to a great extent, autobiographical: all three revolve around Lawrence's personal experiences at home in Eastwood in his youth or in his teaching at Croydon. In each one, the woman is seen to get the better of the man. And each novel seems to share a sort of morbid atmosphere, a sense of the "unreal," set within the "real." This "unreal" aspect was, I think, to encompass Lawrence's symbolic explorations and was almost a sense of fantasy. The "real" aspects came from Lawrence's personal observations of the world around him. So the early novels seem to strive to combine adequately these two elements and hence set an experimental paradigm for his future works. But what led up to a successful combination in this respect? And, if such a dichotomous merging was to be successful, how was it initially to be explored by the author?

To answer these questions we must, I believe, consider Lawrence's early short stories. I postulate that these stories, particularly those we are familiar with in The Prussian Officer set, and within stories such as "Love Among the Haystacks," not only allowed Lawrence to experiment with characters, events, and themes he was to use later in his novels, but were an essential prerequisite to the success of his later work. As we progress through these short stories, we find an ever-increasing complexity as the basic ideas are turned over,

constantly re-formed and retested as Lawrence sought a solution to
the problems besetting him at this time.

As these early short stories formed an experimental setting for
Lawrence's characters and relationships, so the early poetry provided
a chance for Lawrence to experiment with his initial exploration of
the symbolic aspects within such relationships: his relationships
with other members of his family, especially his mother, his relationship with Jessie and Louie, and his own relationship with his social
surroundings.

In a way the early stories are much like traditional folktales,
in that they express the "reality" of life in story form, in Lawrence's
case the ongoing life around him: in the colliers' families and their
daily comings and goings, in his own teaching experiences and life
in Croydon, in his home and personal relationships.

The stories themselves can be grouped according to themes. One
of these is Lawrence's relationship with Jessie Chambers, as in "A
Modern Lover," "The Shades of Spring," and "Second Best." Each of
these concerns itself with Lawrence's struggle to come to terms with
this relationship. Each involves a triangular relationship of characters, a girl and two men, one in process of breaking with her and
the other, portrayed as second best, in process of replacing the
first, who has in some way to justify his guilt.

The competition between the two men serves also to illustrate
another of Lawrence's concerns, that of class differences. Brought
up in a working-class home, but where a class gulf existed between
his mother and father and was always evident in the family atmosphere, Lawrence could not help exploring this facet, as in such
stories as "Goose Fair," "A Fragment of Stained Glass," "Her Turn,"
and "Daughters of the Vicar." In these, socially superior women dominate the male who, as a social inferior, is often seen as rather
pathetic. This is particularly true of the collier husband characters
and must, to some extent, reflect Lawrence's view of his father.
"Daughters of the Vicar" looks deeply into class relationships; it
is important because it offers some indication of the working out
of ideas later evidenced in The Rainbow and Women in Love.

Lawrence's Croydon experiences are utilized in the early stories,
most notably in "The Witch à la Mode," which illustrates his involvement with Helen, and in "The Old Adam," in which we see family scenes
within the lodging-house. Lawrence's poetry runs parallel with the
events described, and the well-known "A Baby Running Barefoot" serves
to suggest his continuing exploration of symbolic aspects within his
experimental framework. "The Old Adam" is particularly interesting
for it involves a scene of physical violence, a fight scene. If, as
is usual in these stories, Lawrence makes himself the lead figure,
then he is represented as Severn, the man who has the fight. So, the
question arises, did Lawrence have such a fight in real life? While
I know of no direct evidence of such in Croydon, it is told in Eastwood, by certain contemporaries of Lawrence, that he was involved in
exactly such physical violence with Professor Weekley in Colwick
Woods, Nottingham, while he was still at University College.

The third facet which Lawrence explored in these stories is that
of a "search for self," as it applied to his immediate set of circumstances within his environment. This search concerned Lawrence for

much of his life, but particularly during his early years of writing. As the early stories progress, Lawrence, by placing himself again and again in the role of the lead character, gradually works out his personal solution to life, thus enabling him to justify his present position and past actions.

To summarize, the early stories may be seen as illustrating: (1) Lawrence's personal relationships, particularly with females, Jessie, Louie, Helen, and the complication of his mother; (2) Lawrence's observation of and involvement in the class struggle, again with special reference to male/female relationship and the conflicts this creates; (3) Lawrence's search for an understanding and justification of his own position, his "search for self."

Within these stories Lawrence is able to experiment with these aspects. And paralleling the stories, he explored, in such poems as "Renascence" and "Snap-Dragon," the symbolic meanings of these aspects and provided himself a framework of imagery. The stories accurately depict the everyday life of his community, especially the colliers' lifestyle, and clearly indicate Lawrence's involvement in that life, as for example in the hay-making scenes in "Love Among the Haystacks." In this story Lawrence combines all the themes mentioned earlier.

What was his ultimate goal? Where do these stories, experimental in many ways, eventually lead? I suggest they form a pathway to his first major breakthrough, the production of Sons and Lovers, in which he is able to represent all the aspects of plot, previously experimental in the stories, together with the symbolism explored in the early poetry. In contrast to the partial answers and the falterings of The Trespasser and The White Peacock, Sons and Lovers is successful. Lawrence needed the short stories to achieve his success.

These remarks are not, of course, intended to detract from the value of these early stories. Most readers are able to identify with them, with their folk-tale appeal. And I, coming from Eastwood, find the description of the characters, events, and ways of life vivid and immediate. Lawrence himself thought these early stories were important and successful, for they opened up a way for him to come to terms with himself, to reach an understanding physically and spiritually, and to point toward the completion of Sons and Lovers. Thus, as early as April 1913, he could write to Edward Garnett, "I know I can write bigger stuff than any man in England,"[2] and to A. W. McLead, "It is my best work, by far."[3]

More important still, the early short stories followed by Sons and Lovers allowed Lawrence to break away from his old style, his old life and regime, and to set the path for his future literary career, toward The Rainbow and Women in Love. These and subsequent works, even as late as Lady Chatterley's Lover, owe a legacy to the early short stories.

D. H. Lawrence's Indian Summer

IAN S. MACNIVEN

I am using "Indian Summer" to designate two closely related periods of Lawrence's life and art: his adventures with American Indians and his writings directly influenced by them; and the late flowering of his talent in Italy which produced, paradoxically, some of his most optimistic fiction at a time when his life was clearly ebbing. As John Poynter has suggested, in his short stories Lawrence tested the moods and themes for his novels, and it is where mood and theme mesh in the stories that he is most successful.

When Edwin Muir wrote that Lawrence had "picked up a thread of life," he replied scornfully, "Darn your socks with it, Mr. Muir?"[1] At risk of Lawrence's ghostly displeasure, I shall hang onto one thread which runs through all his work: the figure of the primitive, instinctual man.

The primitive man, by his very nature close to the elemental, took on a new aspect in Lawrence's late fiction, where he was often associated with death, whereas earlier he had been more consistently life-celebrating. His earliest primitive is the relatively gentle miner in his "pit-dirt," but the increasing violence with which Lawrence viewed the inanities of the world made him respond sympathetically to the closed, resentful, violent Amerindians he encountered. During his first American period, Lawrence spoke to Knud Merrild of the need to kill--and he said he would like to start with Mabel Dodge Luhan! He was in this mood when he wrote The Plumed Serpent, his most disturbing novel philosophically and politically. Death and destruction, and eventually resurrection, became the major themes of Lawrence's short fiction as well after 1923.

The other themes of his late short fiction fade by comparison, and many stories are marred by a jeering tone. There is much skimpoling of acquaintances and friends--at least seven of the nineteen late short stories are either playful or deliberately cruel attacks on Murry, the Compton Mackenzies, or the Brewsters. Mabel Dodge Luhan and Dorothy Brett also took their licks in the American stories, but in these it seems to me that Lawrence's anger or amusement at the originals is transcended by his overriding concern with the death-versus-vitalism theme. A lighter theme of the late short stories is the satirically comic view of personal relations in "The Blue Mocca-sins," "Rawdon's Roof," and "Mother and Daughter."

Although his illnesses and disappointments might make him tem-porarily preoccupied with death and violence, resiliency was a vital feature of Lawrence's character, and he seemed always to have expected disillusionment. As he wrote to Earl Brewster on 15 May 1922: "I love trying things and discovering how I hate them."[2] Since rebounding well was one of his traits, the rebirth theme in the fiction written after his near-death in Oaxaca during February of 1925 should not come as a surprise.

Lawrence's fascination with the American Indian did not begin with his arrival at Taos, New Mexico, on 11 September 1922, but goes back to his youthful readings of Cooper and his wartime studies of Mesoamerican Indians. In a letter of 5 November 1921 to Mrs. Luhan, he gives an amusing picture of himself trying to apprehend, like a good primitive, through various sense organs. "I had your letter this afternoon and read it going down to Corso: and smelt the Indian scent, and nibbled the medicine: the last being like licorice root, the scent being a wistful dried herb." The same month Lawrence wrote to Earl Brewster: "The glamour for me is in the West, not in the fulfilled East" [16 Nov 1921].

Glamor may have figured largely in his preconceptions, but, faced with the realities of Amerindian life, Lawrence wrote somewhat plain-tively to Kotelianski a mere seven days after his arrival at Taos: "Mabel Dodge immediately sent me motoring off to an Apache gathering 120 miles away across desert and through canons. Weird to see these Red Indians—the Apaches are not very sympatisch, but their camp, tents, horses, lake—very picturesque" [18 Sep 1922]. Two days later he wrote to E. M. Forster: "These are Red Indians—so different—yet a bit Chinesey. I haven't got the hang of them yet." Lawrence soon felt he had "got the hang" of the Indians: he resolved them into the debased and the pure, those who had given in to the white man, versus those who had maintained their integrity, their reliance on the old gods. Tony Luhan belonged to the former category, and Lawrence was offended because he could fix Mabel Dodge's car.

His actual contact with wild and primitive Indians was apparently fairly slight. On his second trip to Mexico, he wrote to Frieda in England: "Sometimes here in Guadalajara one sees the wild Quichelote Indians, with their bows and arrows and hardly any clothing. They look so queer, like animals from another world, in the Plaza listen-ing to the band" [10 Nov 1923]. The primitive Indian came to represent for Lawrence a being who was masterful but also "remote," "impersonal," "inhuman." In "The Woman Who Rode Away" Lawrence presents this version of the primitive man stripped to the essence of dark power and violence.

"The Woman Who Rode Away" and "Sun" form a complementary pair of stories giving contrasting views on the relationship of woman to man and to the natural elements, specifically the sun and moon. "The Man Who Loved Islands" and The Man Who Died form a corresponding pair dealing with the male psyche, but stressing the complex man. Thus the four stories suggest another set of complementary relationships: female/male, primitive/complex, hot/cold, and, of course, destruction/salvation.

All four tales are escape stories in which the protagonist runs to a fate of his--or her--own choosing. In "The Woman Who Rode Away," Mrs. Lederman escapes from the mechanical world of the failed silver mines and the will-dominance of her Dutch husband, and finds in her sacrifice to the sun a destruction to which she acquiesces: she has long been dead in spirit. In "Sun," Juliet, whose name echoes Shakespeare's "Juliet is the sun," escapes from the Capulet-like materialistic world of New York and her "grey" husband, and is reborn through her communion with the sun. In "The Man Who Loved Islands," Mr. Cathcart escapes from community and human ties to find the cold, snowy negation of self which is the true expression of the death within him. In The Man Who Died, the unnamed Christ figure escapes from his spiritual, messianic, but humanly barren role as religious leader to find integration and fulfillment in the temple of Isis through the ministrations of the sun-priestess: "to touch her was like touching the sun."[3] The pairing is again destruction/salvation, and the point of view of the two pairs of stories is female and male, respectively.

The grouping I have made is not merely arbitrary. While the escape from will-dominance and the vitalistic rebirth of women and men are old themes for Lawrence, the death of civilization which he saw in World War I, and his own shattered health, made him long for a saving rebirth. Lawrence was appalled yet fascinated by the violence of Mexico, and he preferred it to what he saw as the will-driven, mechanistic deathliness of Anglo-American society. The Berkeley-educated Mrs. Lederman is surrounded by death--a dead dog, dead mines, the "thrice-dead little Spanish town"[4]--before she escapes to seek her own physical death at the hands of the Chilchui Indians. In all of Lawrence's fiction which is American in theme, setting, and composition, death is especially prominent. After Lawrence's American orgy of violence he turned again, as though sated, to the gentler theme of rebirth in "Sun," "Glad Ghosts," and The Man Who Died.

Internal ties bind "The Woman Who Rode Away" to the other tales, to "Sun" especially. Mrs. Lederman becomes the bride of the sun in a ceremony which, the Indians hope, will tempt the sun to return to their people. She is identified with the female moon--a complement to the sun-priestess of Isis--and at the hour of her sacrifice she is in the dark cave awaiting the simultaneous striking of the sun's rays and the blow of the poised phallic knife in the hands of the chief priest, "naked and in a state of barbaric ecstacy." The womb-like cave opens high in a cliff-face, and is overhung by a cascade of ice. Mrs. Lederman is naked and held down to receive the knife-thrust, spread-eagled in an exaggerated sexual openness. The old priest faces her--and the sun--in the position of a violator. The date is the shortest day of the year, the beginning of the rebirth of the seasons. For her there will be no rebirth: the white world has lost its mastery, and the moment that the sun enters the cave, Lawrence tells us that "then the old man would strike, and strike home, accomplish the sacrifice and achieve the power."

Like Mrs. Lederman, Juliet in "Sun" is troubled by the "anger and frustration inside her, and her incapacity to feel anything real." However, while the Woman Who Rode Away is characterized as one whose "nerves began to go wrong," one driven by "foolish romanticism more unreal than a girl's," given to "crazy plans" and "madness," Juliet is in full control of her desires, and so we are forced to take her more seriously. Once in Italy, Juliet lies in bed and watches the "naked sun stand up." In a secluded place, she offers her bared bosom to the sun, though she feels a "hard pain against the certain cruelty of having to give herself." This is analogous to the pain the Woman Who Rode Away will feel under the knife, with her body bared to the sun. For Juliet, however, the sun brings not dissolution but a restoration: "She could feel the sun penetrating even into her bones; nay, farther, even into her emotions and her thoughts." Here again the differences between the actions stress the complementary nature of the stories: Mrs. Lederman awaits her death before a setting sun, forcibly held open; Juliet awakens to a rising sun, to her rebirth, and opens herself willingly to a sun high overhead.

The experience of the Woman Who Rode Away is not entirely negative: she does become integrated with the universe, with both the microcosm and the macrocosm. Under the care and drugs of the Indians, she "felt she heard [her] little dog conceive. . . . And another day she could hear the vast sound of the earth going around, like some immense arrow-string booming." In a parallel movement, Juliet is able to reconcile herself to the microcosm of child and husband, as well as to the macrocosm of sun and universe. Unlike Mrs. Lederman, however, she turns toward life.

"The Woman Who Rode Away" is, in both the female element and the death element, a clear complement to The Man Who Died. The Man Who Died awakens from death and is reborn into an integrated spirit-and-body life; Mrs. Lederman is dead in spirit from the beginning, and finally she dies into integration with that spirit-cum-body, God-plus-man state she had both willfully denied and been denied during her existence in white society. When she dies, she will return to the sun/moon, male/female harmony. She is also complementary to the Man Who Died in that she is the passive and accepting woman, while he is the active, erect, life-seeking man. As a symbol of the dissolution of the white man's world, she is in complementary opposition to Juliet in "Sun."

There are other indications of the complementary nature of "The Woman Who Rode Away" and The Man Who Died. Mrs. Lederman's immolation takes place in a cave, and the consummation of the Pan-like rebirth of the Man Who Died occurs in a cave as well, but for Mrs. Lederman the cave is cold, and the sun's rays must pass through ice, while the Man Who Died has a fire provided by the priestess of Isis. Another complementary point is that his wound is finally healed by the massaging of the priestess, while her chest is to be opened after the massaging by the priests. Also, her ministrants see her as sexless, sterile, while the priestess of Isis conceives a child by the Man Who Died. The theme of sterility links Mrs. Lederman to Mr. Cathcart in "The Man Who Loved Islands," since he too finds himself closed in, by snow which covers his door and window just as the ice covers the mouth of the sacrificial cave.

It is significant that Mr. Cathcart's failure to connect is a
failure to control, while Mrs. Lederman loses her sense of life
because no one in her civilized society could control her with the
proper understanding and strength. Juliet's disappointment in "Sun"
is that she has to take on the burden of herself: she cannot go to
the Italian peasant because such a mismatch could only lead to disaster, another version of the disaster Mrs. Lederman meets with the
young cacique. In The Man Who Died, Lawrence resolves the woman's
need for primitive tenderness by placing this virtue in the complex
person of the protagonist. This reintegration of instinctual tenderness with the complex individual places the Man Who Died with Rupert
Birkin, Mark Morier, the narrator of "Glad Ghosts," and Oliver Mellors
in the line-up of Lawrence's spokesmen. Just so, "The Woman Who Rode
Away," "Sun," "The Man Who Loved Islands," and The Man Who Died belong
within the mainstream of Lawrence's best fiction, in which mood and
theme mesh in parallel seriousness.

The Textual Edition of
Lawrence's Works

The Works of D. H. Lawrence: The Cambridge Edition

MICHAEL H. BLACK

The Cambridge University Press expects to publish in 1980, the fiftieth anniversary of Lawrence's death, the first volumes of a complete edition of his works. The Cambridge Edition may fairly claim to be the first edition of the whole canon of a classic modern author, and has a particular interest for a number of reasons.

Scholars have known for a long time that Lawrence is being read in very unsatisfactory texts. But even the ordinary reader may come upon a misprint in his reading and pause over it. The obvious question--if I can see this incorrect reading, how many plausible but incorrect readings am I failing to see?--may then occur to him, and he may feel a justified unease. He does not expect this in a twentieth-century author. We all tend to think that in our own age the processes of first publication and reprinting should secure a text against corruption. But this is not so. It is a reasonable proposition that all important authors of the earlier part of the century now need a proper critical edition. The amount of corruption to be removed will vary. In Lawrence's case it is very great indeed.

The basic reasons for this are five. First, Lawrence was from his very first novel and far into his writing career subject to censorship or bowdlerization, because he was concerned with sexual relations in an era when this was a frightening topic. Sometimes he was consulted about such cuts and asked to collaborate; sometimes very small cuts were made without reference to him. Second, he was in his early works subjected to a different kind of editing by those who thought he was, by Flaubertian standards, "formless." Third, he was sometimes asked to tailor things to fit a particular periodical. These three causes mean that there are considerable portions of excised Lawrence waiting to be put back where they belong; fortunately we still possess many of them. Lawrence accepted some of these changes because from 1912, when he eloped with Frieda Weekley, he could live only by his pen. He needed the money, so he accepted changes as one condition of publication. But this was acquiescence, not approval.

The fourth factor, now becoming clear to us, is that Lawrence was a conscious artist who reworked all his main fictions and poems carefully, sometimes drastically, and went on doing so. Fortunately once more, the drafts or stages often survive in the possession of libraries and collectors, who have been notably generous in making them available to us. This means that an editor can reconstruct the growth of a work in question, showing what was conscious choice on Lawrence's part, and what was imposed on him.

The fifth factor is the history of publication itself. It is not simply that fifty years of reprinting have produced a normal accumu- lation of transmission errors. From very early on Lawrence became a wanderer, dealing with publishers in London and New York from Italy, New Mexico, Australia, or wherever he happened to be. This factor complicates the previous one, as follows. Lawrence would typically produce a holograph manuscript (state 1). This was typed by someone else, who occasionally misread Lawrence's hand. Lawrence would fail to spot all the errors but would have second thoughts and revise, so state 2 is already a complication. Perhaps more than one typescript copy would be made, and these would not incorporate all the changes. One copy might be sent to a publisher in London, the other, via an agent, to another publisher in New York. Lawrence might then see and read proofs. Since he seems rarely to have checked against copy, but never missed a chance to revise, another complicated state is produced. Ultimately the English and American editions appeared, differing from each other in significant respects; but at some intervening stage a publisher (Martin Secker, for instance) might have decided to make a few small silent changes or cuts, for reasons of propriety or because some third party recognized himself in one of the characters and threatened legal action.

This is a composite or ideal case, placing together some of the main factors we have found in operation. It demonstrates that our editors must, as a preliminary to their work, survey all the surviving states of each work, compare them, reconstruct the history of the growth, change, or corruption which they embody, and then state the principle on which that particular work must be edited. This will evidently vary from work to work, depending on the surviving evidence and the particular sequence of changes, but typically it takes the form that one state is to be taken as base-text (we avoid the term "copy-text," with its misleading implications) to be emended to take account of changes in other states.

Already an important editorial principle emerges. Much editorial theory has evolved from work on Elizabethan drama, where an entirely different situation obtains. There are no surviving MSS, only an early printed text or texts, showing variants between copies of one edition or between editions. Here the editor, by examining and collating printed texts, infers a complex process in the early printing-houses and goes on to infer a series of departures from a lost MS. In a sense, the editor is trying to reconstruct that MS, as the author's "final intention."

In Lawrence's case, however, a surprising number of the states before first publication exist, and these are crucial. The first

printing is indeed a departure, in many cases, from his "final intention," but we have also learned to distrust, and not to use, that
phrase. He would go on revising as long as he was allowed to; and the
"intention" that he had reached before publication was then complicated or frustrated in the various ways suggested above. And, unlike
the history of Shakespeare's text, where editions since the eighteenth-
century incorporate a long tradition of often inspired emendation, the
history of Lawrence's text is one of reprinting without authoritative
revision. The publishers concerned have become aware that there is a
problem, but until now there has been no systematic recension, and no
mere reprint has authority or calls for serious examination. The
editor of each of our texts has to go back behind the first printing
to the sources. These do not exist for every text, but they do for a
significant number.

As a consequence, the Cambridge Edition will not list in its
apparatus any variant in later printings simply for the sake of listing such variants--they have no significance. Nor will it list tables
of hyphens or word-breaks in such printings or elsewhere. It will,
however, show the variants between states which demonstrably passed
through Lawrence's hands before publication and variants between
printed editions which he (sometimes in a loose sense) supervised.

This approach to the text will be reflected in other editorial
matters. The introduction to each volume will not provide yet another
critical essay about the work concerned. It will trace in detail the
genesis and development of the text, starting from the relevant point
in Lawrence's life and writing career and carrying the story through
to publication and reception. In a non-trivial sense, the introduction will be factual and will supply the reader with a great deal of
information, much of it new and recovered from the study of the documents, about Lawrence's life, his career as a writer, the actual publication and reviewing of his books. Here it has been invaluable that
we have been simultaneously editing and publishing the Letters, since
they are a very rich source of information about the Works. These
editions are both essential preliminaries to any biography which can
claim to be fully researched or authoritative, and the Press and the
Estate do have it in mind to commission such a Life.

What will be the total effect on the text? Will the ordinary
reader notice it? The answers are: very considerable, and yes. My
composite example above was derived from what we already know about
a number of texts, and some specific details of these can already be
given.

Sons and Lovers. The MS of this novel is in California, and a
facsimile has just been published by the University of California
Press. It reveals what the book was like before the publisher's
reader, Edward Garnett, cut it for publication: it was considerably
longer. These cuts were urged on Lawrence, who agreed to them, largely,
I would contend, because he needed the money that publication would
bring. It might be argued that he accepted the cuts against his will,
and our editor will therefore have to decide whether to restore all of
them or some of them.

The Rainbow. The original edition was banned in 1915, and all
subsequent English editions have been expurgated, though Penguin

reprinted the early American text. But even that text is unsatisfactory because of the multiple errors in transcription from the manuscript and also because (as we discover from the Letters) some censorship was exacted <u>before</u> publication. There are cuts to restore here too.

<u>Women</u> <u>in</u> <u>Love</u> was mutilated in all English editions to meet threats of libel action, and there are again many errors of transmission.

In these three cases the restoration of cuts and the correction of errors will restore Lawrence's greatest and most popular works to their intended form for the first time. Since these are the most-read texts, attention is likely to be fixed on them, but other works have an interesting textual history as well.

<u>Mr.Noon</u>. This is known in an incomplete version: some 140 pages published of a total of 407 actually written. When the whole is published, a virtual new work is added to the canon.

<u>The</u> <u>Poems</u>. Lawrence rewrote his poems more freely than anything else of his. What was a long poem at one stage becomes a short one at another, and <u>vice</u> <u>versa</u>. The task of editing the poems has to be faced all over again and will produce new versions. Cambridge will also produce in supplementary volumes the intermediate draft material, for the use of students and scholars.

<u>The</u> <u>Short</u> <u>Stories</u>. At one point in "The Ladybird" the compositor turned over two sheets of copy at once. The result happened to make sense and nobody noticed. "The Border Line," which Lawrence wrote and had published in a magazine in 1924, was included in his 1928 collection, <u>The</u> <u>Woman</u> <u>Who</u> <u>Rode</u> <u>Away</u>. When he received the proofs for that volume, he discovered that the ending was missing from Secker's typescript. In desperation he made up a new, much shorter ending (four and a half pages in length) for the story, an ending which has been reprinted ever since. The abbreviated ending is artistically inferior to the original, which is hardly surprising as Lawrence warned Secker from Switzerland how hard it would be to capture the atmosphere of Germany again four years later. The Cambridge Edition will revert to Lawrence's original longer version for the ending.

In "The Overtone" some sexually explicit sentences were deleted (see Appendix to this paper).

Lawrence wrote "The Lovely Lady" in 1927 for Lady Cynthia Asquith, who was editing <u>The</u> <u>Black</u> <u>Cap</u>, an anthology of mystery and murder stories. She objected to the absence of a proper ghost and to the length of the original version. Lawrence proceeded to write a shorter version of the story which was published in <u>The</u> <u>Black</u> <u>Cap</u> and subsequently reprinted by Secker in the posthumous collection, <u>The</u> <u>Lovely</u> <u>Lady</u>. It has been reprinted in this version ever since. However, Lawrence's attitude throughout his life to such cuts was that he would always, grudgingly, permit them to be made by editors of periodicals in which the stories originally appeared, in the hope that the full-length version would be used in his next collection of short stories. The Cambridge Edition will restore the story to its original length, which is a third as long again.

<u>The</u> <u>Plumed</u> <u>Serpent</u>. Lawrence fell ill when he had finished the manuscript. He dreaded revising the typescript made from that, and when he did so his efforts were erratic. Hundreds of mistakes made by

the typists--and there were at least three typists--slipped past him,
for, as so often, he corrected from memory, not against the manuscript. The most glaring of these errors are omissions and misreadings
that lead to a change of sense. Dozens of single words are left out,
with a resulting shift in meaning, often considerable. Misreadings
such as sort for rant, experience for expression, last for least,
struggling for straggling, like for light, and many more, bring about
obvious distortions. Most important of all, there are some thirty
omissions, ranging from long phrases to whole paragraphs, that often
change the meaning of whole passages, in which questions sometimes
remain unanswered, or remarks are attributed to the wrong speaker.

Apocalypse. This volume, like some others, will include an
appendix giving some 80 MS pages which Lawrence did not include in
the published version. We shall not incorporate this material in the
text, since this was not Lawrence's intention. But making the unpublished material available will considerably affect understanding of
the text, and readers of Lawrence will find it of great value since
it records his last thoughts about life and religious feeling.
Lawrence was dying when he wrote Apocalypse. He wrote it in longhand
and gave it to a friend to be typed. He was too ill to check carefully and did not see that the typescript left out whole phrases
and misread many words. His well-known habit of repeating words was a
source of much error: the copyist's eye sometimes jumped from the
first use of the word to the second and omitted the phrase between.
The book was set from the defective typescript, and the Italian publisher exercised a final censorship on the now-dead Lawrence by cutting out some derogatory references to Mussolini. These changes and
cuts will be restored.

And so on. We can say already that no text by Lawrence will be
reproduced--can now be reproduced--exactly in the form in which it is
at present read, and that many of the texts will be significantly
different.

The actual labor of this work in editorial man-hours is enormous.
The effect on the texts is the equivalent of removing layers of varnish from a picture. For instance, all house-styling by the original
publishers and printers disappears; all editing by American publishers
removing Briticisms; all the little changes where a nervous publisher
thought Lawrence was being a little "bold" sexually; all misprints in
the early editions, and by definition all misprints in later editions
(see Appendix for some examples). We shall have something as close as
scholarship can make it to what Lawrence wanted.

In many texts, therefore, there will be, as a result of this
labor, hundreds or even thousands of variants. Let us take a representative example. The White Peacock, Lawrence's first novel, seems
to be an entirely innocent work and one would not expect it to have
been affected by these factors, but Lawrence suffered every complication from the very first, and the text has a history, disentangled by
Andrew Robertson, which seems very strange. The MS was rewritten from
a first draft and copied out by several Croydon friends, including
the late Helen Corke. Their hands have to be identified and their
contributions checked for error. This MS was the printer's copy,
and was house-styled by Heinemann, so Lawrence's punctuation was

overridden and has to be restored. Lawrence saw and read galleys,
but did not check against copy. He made some corrections which have
to be incorporated, but missed one or two plausible printing errors,
which have to be corrected. Then an extraordinary thing happened. For
reasons perhaps to do with copyright, the text was set all over again
in the United States, from the corrected galleys presumably. The
American publisher eliminated some Briticisms (e.g., a Bass became a
bottle of beer), corrected some errors, introduced one or two, molded
the type, printed from plates, and sent a duplicate set of plates to
England. These plates were read and corrected in England, so there
are minute variations between the American and English texts. More
important, at the last moment Heinemann felt that some of the gamekeeper story was too "strong" in its language and asked Lawrence to
bowdlerize himself; he did, his first encounter with Mrs. Grundy.
When all this is known and disentangled and a text can be reconstructed,
The White Peacock will have some thousands of variants from the accepted text, and some of them--to our surprise--are interesting and
substantial. We had expected this with the later, major texts, but
not with the very first novel.

Lawrence died in 1930. Works published in his lifetime--or,
rather, the current corrupt texts of them--would have fallen into the
public domain at the end of 1980. Some works were published posthumously; the copyright of these runs until fifty years after first
publication (longer in U.S. law).

Any edition, of course, represents a new copyright. Shakespeare
in a general sense is in the public domain, but the Cambridge Shakespeare on which John Dover Wilson spent forty years of editorial labor,
and the Press many thousands of pounds of investment, is a Cambridge
copyright and can be used or reproduced only by permission. The Cambridge Lawrence represents an interesting departure from the normal
run of scholarly editions in that it is indissolubly linked with the
copyright of the main works themselves. This is implicit in what is
said above: first, the posthumous works are still in copyright; second,
a great deal of hitherto unpublished material is now to be published
(and unpublished work is the perpetual copyright of the author's
estate); third, it is clear that, in the form now established, these
works are being published for the first time. For all these reasons
it was necessary to have the consent and collaboration of the Estate,
and this was readily given by the beneficiaries and the Literary
Executor for Frieda Lawrence Ravagli, Gerald Pollinger of Laurence
Pollinger Limited. Copyright will be claimed in all the texts of the
new edition in the name of the Estate; copyright of the editorial
material will be claimed in the name of the Press.

It is not intended, however, that this major editorial venture
and this first real publication of Lawrence should remain confined
to an expensive text prepared for scholars. It is essential that the
corrupt old texts should drop from sight and not have to go on being
used by readers who want the real thing. Lawrence's original publishers, Heinemann in the United Kingdom and Viking Press in the
United States, have from the first given the venture large-minded
and enthusiastic support, and the texts will be made available for
more popular editions shortly after first publication.

The Press will be publishing a scholar's or library edition, in hardback, with introduction, text, textual apparatus, and the glossarial and other notes which the student (especially the foreign student) now needs. This will also be made available in paperback. Heinemann may use the text in their Phoenix edition: a plain text in hardback for the ordinary reader. It is hoped that Viking-Penguin, the pioneers in paperbacking Lawrence, will decide to use the text in their edition for the widest public of all. In this way the fruits of scholarship will be made widely available. The greatest novelist and prose-writer of the century will at last be read in an accurate text, made available at all levels of the market.

Appendix

Conference members may be interested in some specific examples of the kinds of changes mentioned above. These are taken from two volumes which are in an advanced state of preparation.

<u>Sexual</u> <u>censorship</u>. Two examples from the short story "The Overtone," published posthumously. Even at that late date, Lawrence was being bowdlerized. The printed text currently reads:

> "I can't," she said stubbornly, with some hopelessness in her voice.
> "Yes," he said. "Yes. You trust me, don't you?"
> "I don't want it. Not here, not now," she said.

The manuscript reads:

> "I can't," she said stubbornly, with some hopelessness in her voice.
> "Yes-" he said, "Yes. You trust me, don't you?"
> "I don't want it. You wouldn't have me if I don't want to, would you?" she said.
> "Do have me," he said, "Have me then without taking your things off."
> "Not here-not now," she said.

In another place the present text reads:

> "But the fauns and satyrs are there-you only have to remove the surplices that all men wear nowadays."

The MS reads <u>look</u> <u>under</u> for <u>remove</u>: the change is an example of hypersensitivity, if ever there was one.

<u>Misprints</u> can be represented from <u>The</u> <u>Trespasser</u>, edited by Elizabeth Mansfield. There is one on the very first page: for <u>kind</u> <u>of</u> <u>a</u> <u>pathetic</u> <u>forbearance</u> read <u>kind</u> <u>of</u> <u>apathetic</u> <u>forbearance</u>. In another place <u>the</u> <u>colour</u> <u>of</u> <u>dreams</u> <u>without</u> <u>shape</u> should read <u>the</u> <u>colour</u> <u>of</u> <u>dreams</u> <u>without</u> <u>the</u> <u>shape</u>. Elsewhere, <u>amid</u> <u>the</u> <u>large</u> <u>magnificent</u> <u>sea-moon</u> should read <u>amid</u> <u>the</u> <u>large</u> <u>magnificent</u> <u>sea</u> <u>noon</u>; <u>she</u> <u>had</u> <u>no</u> <u>idea</u> <u>what</u> <u>she</u> <u>thought</u> should be <u>. . . he</u> <u>thought</u>. <u>If</u> <u>they</u> <u>rose</u> <u>up</u> <u>and</u> <u>refused</u> <u>me</u> should be <u>If</u> <u>they</u> <u>rose</u> <u>up</u> <u>and</u> <u>refuted</u> <u>me</u>.

This is just a sample. You do not have to be a scholar to reflect that a large number of errors like the above has the cumulative effect of clouding the text; a detail has been dimmed every time and is now illuminated. Each is a small point, but many small points in a single text make the difference between corruption and authenticity.

<u>House-styling</u>. This too seems like a small matter, but in fact is a large one. Printers in Lawrence's time imposed a rigid house-style

on all authors in matters of spelling, punctuation, and small conventions like hyphenization. This has a twofold effect. Like every other
human, Lawrence could make slips of the pen and fall into inconsistencies. The printers supplied a system which retrieved these small
lapses. But they also ironed out Lawrence's idiosyncrasies of style,
and, in their own way, they interpose another cloud between Lawrence
and us.

I give an instance which is in actuality a misprint rather than
a house-styling, but it shows that so-called "accidentals" are <u>not</u>
accidental, but <u>substantive</u> (another terminology we have learned to
avoid). The present text of <u>The Trespasser</u> reads, <u>The elms' great</u>
<u>grey shadows, seemed to loiter in their cloaks across the pale fields</u>;
the MS reads, <u>The elms, great grey shadows, seemed to loiter in their</u>
<u>cloaks across the pale fields</u>. Changing the apostrophe back to a comma
extends the metaphor backwards to the beginning of the sentence. It is
a change of meaning.

This happens often. For instance, <u>In the road again he lifted his</u>
<u>face to the moon</u> should read <u>In the road, again he lifted his face to</u>
<u>the moon</u>. Similarly, the present text <u>They sat opposite each other</u>
<u>with averted faces, looking out of the windows</u> should read <u>They sat</u>
<u>opposite each other, with averted faces looking out of the windows</u>.
The shift of meaning is minute, but real. Or again, <u>Faces innumerable-</u>
<u>hot, blue-eyed faces-strained to look over his shoulders</u> should read
<u>Faces, innumerable hot, blue-eyed faces strained to look over his</u>
<u>shoulders</u>. This is an even slighter shift, but still detectable.

It is rather like the many cases where the printer inserted or
deleted a question mark, as in:

> "It has been something, dear," she repeated.
> He rose and took her into his arms.
> "Everything," he said.

The first line should read:

> "It has been something, dear-?" she repeated.

Here the wistfulness of her tone is shown to be the trigger which
produces his action. As a last example, take the climactic sentences:

> So he went on amid all the vast miracle of movement in the city
> night, the swirling of water to the sea, the gradual sweep of
> the stars, the floating of many lofty, luminous cars through
> the bridged darkness, like an army of angels filing past on
> one of God's campaigns, the purring haste of the taxis, the
> slightly dancing shadows of people. Siegmund went on slowly,
> like a slow bullet winging into the heart of life.

But originally this was <u>one</u> sentence, very carefully built up:

> So he went on amid all the vast miracle of movement in the city
> night, the swirling of water to the sea, the gradual sweep of
> the stars, the floating of many lofty, luminous cars through the

bridged darkness, like an army of angels filing past, on one
of God's campaigns; the purring haste of the taxis, the |
slightly dancing shadows of people: Siegmund went on slowly,
like a slow bullet winging into the heart of life.

Lawrence was a careful punctuator, in the sense that he was a careful
sentence-constructor. His use of commas, semicolons, and colons is
clearly deliberate and skilled, and was frequently overridden; just
as his sentences were sometimes divided or joined by the printer.
He permitted this, but it was an intrusion and needs to be set aside.
Time after time, we come upon a genuinely expressive use of punctuation which has been overridden, for instance, There was a long space
between the lift of one breath and the next should read There was a
long space between the lift of one breath, and the next. The pause
in the sentence enacts the pause in the breathing.
    There are thousands of such variants in texts like The Tres-
passer, where we have a manuscript. Their removal justifies my
analogy with the removal of varnish from a great picture. We read the
text for the first time with this veil lifted.
    A final point. I said above that Lawrence, as a human being like
the rest of us, had his inadvertencies and his inconsistencies. These
were largely eliminated by the printer's house-styling. We have to
face a quite serious issue: in stripping off that house-styling, we
come back to the original text, with all its inadvertencies and inconsistencies. Do we, then, impose a new house-styling which removes
these? After a good deal of discussion we have decided that only the
absolute minimum of interference can be permitted. There are small
matters in which Lawrence can and should be allowed to be inconsistent.
It is not that these forms are in any way expressive; rather that they
are insignificant in themselves; and yet to regularize on any large
scale is to embark on a course which would eventually be inconsistent
with the main aim: to give the reader what Lawrence wrote, as little
tampered with as possible.
    In texts where we have a manuscript and this is used as base-
text, the Cambridge Edition will therefore present a number of manuscript forms. Texts where no manuscript or typescript exists will
present the original house-styling because we are unable to get
behind it. We have to accept this apparent anomaly; we should be no
more justified in stripping off the regularization where we have no
evidence to go on than we are in imposing a regularization which the
base-text does not support. In the many cases where we do get behind
the veil, the reader should feel a particular immediacy, and that
should justify us.

    The Cambridge Edition of the works of D. H. Lawrence will be
published in about thirty volumes. The Editorial Board consists of:
Professor J. T. Boulton (Birmingham) and Professor F. Warren Roberts.
The General Editors are Dr. Carl Baron (Cambridge), Professor David
Farmer (Tulsa), Mr. Andrew Robertson (Birmingham), Mr. M. H. Black
(Cambridge University Press). Each volume will be edited by an indi-
vidual scholar, and this large team will be drawn from Lawrence
scholars in Great Britain, Europe, and the United States.

Problems in Editing D. H. Lawrence

WARREN ROBERTS

Now that Michael Black has discussed the scope of the Cambridge Edition of the works of D. H. Lawrence and indicated the sad state of affairs with respect to the text of the works currently in print, perhaps it will be interesting to consider in detail the problems that the editors must face with a specific novel, Kangaroo. I shall also say something of the more extensive textual difficulties associated with Lawrence's poetry.

The first edition of Kangaroo was published in September 1923 by Martin Secker in London, and the American edition was published from new plates on 17 September of the same year in New York by Thomas Seltzer. This all seems perfectly straightforward, as indeed it probably should have been, but even a cursory comparison of the two editions reveals an extraordinary series of differences in the text, and the editors will not only have to find out how this came about and why, but also decide what the preferred reading may be in each case.

Lawrence wrote the first draft of Kangaroo in Australia during the period from 3 June 1922, when he wrote to Mabel Dodge Luhan that he had "started" a novel, to 15 July, when he wrote to Thomas Seltzer saying that he had "finished Kangaroo." The first draft manuscript was sent to the American agent, Robert Mountsier, from Australia via the S.S. Makura on 20 July. Mountsier followed Lawrence's instructions and had a duplicate set of typescripts prepared from the manuscript. By October Lawrence was busy revising the typescript; on 16 October he wrote Seltzer that he had "gone through Kangaroo, making many changes"; he also said that he had "made a new last chapter." This was not yet to be the last word, for Lawrence wrote Seltzer again 4 January enclosing the "last words of Kangaroo; the last page." In response to instructions from Lawrence, Mountsier sent the second copy of the typescript of Kangaroo to Curtis Brown, the English agent, at about the same time Lawrence received his copy in Taos. By September

Lawrence was corresponding with Martin Secker about the English edition of the novel.

A careful study of the extant manuscripts and typescripts of Kangaroo will probably reveal something about the sequence of states which the text of the novel went through between the first draft and the published versions, but it seems safe to say that the two typescripts circulating at the same time somehow resulted in significantly different texts for the English and American editions.

It also seems likely that Thomas Seltzer did lose the last of Kangaroo, as Lawrence warned him not to do in his letter of 4 January, because the English edition of the novel has several paragraphs at the end which do not appear in the Seltzer edition. This is only the beginning of the difficulty; the text for the critical "Nightmare" chapter differs radically. Someone, presumably Lawrence himself, excised whole paragraphs from the text of the English edition. As a result Lawrence's references to the war are much less severe in the English version; one might almost suppose he considered them too strong for English readers. These remarks only pose the problem, not the solution. The editor of Kangaroo will have to decide if Lawrence's letter of 16 October 1922 to Seltzer is to be taken at face value. In this letter Lawrence speaks of his revision of the Kangaroo manuscript: "--It is now as I wish it. I want to keep in the war-experience piece: and I have made a new last chapter. Now it is as I want it." If this is true, how does one explain the bowdlerized text of the Secker edition?

The key to an understanding of the situation with respect to the editing of Lawrence's poetry is to be found in his "Note" to the 1928 Collected Poems in which he says, "Some of the earliest poems, like 'The Wild Common' and 'Virgin Youth,' are a good deal rewritten." This is a classic understatement.

Lawrence has occasionally been characterized as a writer who dashed off his work spontaneously, the implication being that he did not revise in the usual sense. Nothing could be farther from the truth: more often than not he revised his work, particularly the early poems and stories, whenever an opportunity offered. Frequently, after publishing a poem or short story in a periodical either in England or in America, he published the work again in a periodical on the other side of the Atlantic. Then the work might be collected in an anthology, or he might include the piece in one of his own published collections. Often he altered the text in some way for each publication.

For example, a poem entitled "Twilight" appeared in The English Review for February 1914; a different version was published in Poetry in December 1914 as "Grief." The Poetry version was included in The New Poetry, an anthology edited by Harriet Monroe and Alice Corbin Henderson in New York in 1917. A longer version appeared in Amores with the title "Firelight and Nightfall," the same title Lawrence used for the 1928 Collected Poems. Another instance of multiple revision and change of title is the poem "A Woman and Her Dead Husband," published in Poetry in January 1914; it was included in Some Imagist Poets for 1915 with the same title; in New Poems Lawrence called the poem "Bitterness of Death," and in the 1928 Collected Poems it was titled "A Man Who Died."

An examination of the publishing history of the long six-part
poem called "The Schoolmaster," originally published in The Saturday
Westminster Gazette for May and June 1912, reveals the extent to
which Lawrence could go in revising and rearranging his work. The
original version in the Gazette contained 189 lines arranged in the
following order:

The Schoolmaster

I	Morning: Scripture Lesson
II	Afternoon: The Last Lesson
III	Evening
IV	The Punisher
V	A Snowy Day in School
VI	The Best of School

For Love Poems Lawrence used the collective title, "The Schoolmaster,"
again, but this time for a three-part poem of 116 lines arranged:

The Schoolmaster

I	A Snowy Day in School
II	The Best of School
III	Afternoon in School: The Last Lesson

"The Punisher" was included in Amores; for Collected Poems the collective title is dropped and four separate poems appear: "The Best of
School," "Last Lesson of the Afternoon," "A Snowy Day in School," and
"The Punisher." The poem, "The Best of School," which consisted of
some 65 lines in Love Poems, has only 36 lines in Collected Poems.
Some of the material eliminated from the earlier versions was incorporated in other poetry. Although Lawrence's reworking of "The Schoolmaster" may be an extreme case, the reader must always be alert not
only for a change of title, but also for possible revisions in each
publication of a given work.

The editor of Lawrence's poetry is fortunate in having the 1928
Collected Poems as a starting point for a critical edition of the
early poetry because Lawrence worked very carefully on the text, and
as a consequence the Collected Poems presents a more reliable text,
including accidentals, than the poetry published after 1928. For some
reason Lawrence did not include some of his published poetry in Collected Poems; these must be restored to the canon, and a decision
made about the retention of some of the more severely revised early
poems in an appropriate appendix.

With the publication of Pansies Lawrence experienced once again
his perennial difficulty with censorship. In December 1928 he wrote
the Huxleys that he had sent two typescripts of his book of Pansies
to his agent, Curtis Brown. These typescripts were confiscated by the
postal authorities at the request of the Home Office, probably as a
result of the furor over Lady Chatterley's Lover. Apparently Lawrence
retyped Pansies himself, and revised as he typed. Also, because of
objections on the part of the authorities or the publisher, some
fourteen poems were dropped from the Secker trade edition. As a result

of this censorship Lawrence had printed the so-called definitive edition of Pansies. One would suppose that Lawrence read proof for both the Secker edition and the privately printed Pansies, but the impression prevails that a house style was imposed on the Secker book, and the accidentals appear erratic in the privately printed edition. It seems obvious that Lawrence did not exercise the same control over the text of these books that we may assume he did for the 1928 Collected Poems.

Text for most of the poetry in Pansies and Last Poems can be found in manuscript notebooks kept by Lawrence. Many of the smaller poems were obviously written at a rapid pace; Lawrence did not punctuate consistently and he did not have an opportunity to prepare some of the poems for publication. Last Poems was edited by Richard Aldington after Lawrence's death, and the editor's responsibility in this instance must be to return to the manuscript as the source for his text.

For several reasons the Complete Poems published in 1964 is not altogether satisfactory, and in any case each generation of editors approaches the task of editing a text with its own prejudices. The project for a critical edition of Lawrence's work, which the Cambridge University Press has undertaken, cannot be an easy one; much remains to be accomplished, but scholars everywhere must remain grateful to that Press for assuming responsibility for the Lawrence project, a decision taken by the Syndics in the highest tradition of the Cambridge Press. We shall then have a reliable and authoritative text for one of the most important writers of this century, a scholarly need which has been long overdue.

Editing *Lady Chatterley's Lover*

MICHAEL SQUIRES

At first, Lawrence's famous novel appears to be an easy work to edit.
It is not. Even though Lawrence had control of all stages of the
text--correcting typescripts and proof, doing his own editing, and
publishing a private edition of 1,000 copies in Florence--corruption
still occurred, some of it extensive, some of it difficult to detect.
The variant readings sanctioned by the author are therefore, at times,
hard to identify. Complicating matters, the strategy that is used to
edit the first five chapters cannot also be used to edit the rest of
the novel. And since work on the new Cambridge Edition of the novel
is not yet complete, the editorial strategies that have been adopted
must necessarily be flexible--and necessarily tentative. But, with
most of the job finished, it is clear that not one but two editorial
approaches may be required to produce a reliable scholarly text of
the novel: first, the peculiar way in which the typing of the first
five chapters was carried out dictates that the holograph manuscript
alone should probably be followed for these chapters, with almost no
emendations from later stages of the text; and second, the unconventional way in which the novel was published dictates that some of
the accidental variants introduced into chapters 6 through 19 of the
first edition (Florence 1928) should be regarded as authorial, and
cannot as a whole be rejected. The rest of the essay will defend the
adoption of these two approaches.

     This defense will be clearest if I begin with a brief history
of the text of Lady Chatterley's Lover, from inscription to first
publication. Although Lawrence had already written two versions of
the novel, he decided in 1927 to recast the story still again. The
third version of the novel, probably begun in late November 1927,[1]
was finished on 8 January 1928--the whole manuscript written in a
month or so. About three weeks before Lawrence finished the final
version, he arranged for a friend, Nelly Morrison, who lived in
Florence, to begin making a typescript. We can be almost certain that
she made one ribbon copy (Ts-I) and only one carbon copy (Ts-II),

both in blue ink. But the novel's phallic content disturbed her, and
after typing five chapters, and feeling as self-righteous as Balaam's
ass, she quit.

Lawrence then asked Catherine Carswell to help him locate a
professional typist in London. He says in an unpublished letter of
[?] 25 January 1928: "I send you the first half--more--of the MS
today." The next sentence is crucial: "Of that which is already typed,
I only want <u>one</u> copy."[2] He needed only one more copy of chapters 1
through 5 because, while vacationing in Diablerets, Switzerland, he
had decided he needed three copies in all--one for his printer in
Florence, one for Alfred Knopf in New York, and one for Martin Secker
in London. This explanation is supported by Lawrence's instruction
on the fly-leaf of the MS book--"Continue p. 133 type"--and it seems
clear that the London typist would think she should simply follow
Nelly Morrison's typescript for chapters 1 through 5. In fact, that
is apparently what happened, as I will show. Since the London typist
made a new ribbon copy from Nelly's transcript, this new copy therefore contained two layers of corruption, as the following figure
shows:

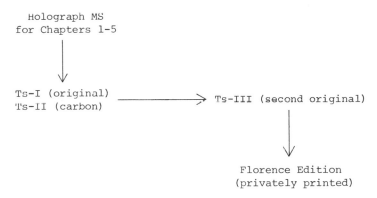

My hypothesis is that the second original of chapters 1-5 (Ts-III) is
the one Lawrence gave to the Florentine printer, and it is regrettably
the most corrupt of the three. The questions now are: Can the hypothesis be confirmed, and what are its implications for a new text of the
novel? If the following three assumptions can be supported:

1. That the London typist followed Nelly Morrison's typescript
   for chapters 1 through 5,
2. That the London typist was likely to make substantive
   alterations in Lawrence's text, and
3. That her typescript (Ts-III) served as printer's copy for
   the first five chapters,

then the way in which one edits these chapters for the Cambridge
Edition is radically different from what one might have expected
without knowing how the text of <u>Lady</u> <u>Chatterley</u> was transmitted.

First, then, did the London typist follow not Lawrence's manuscript but Nelly's typescript in making Ts-III? Obvious evidence can be cited in the corruption of Lawrence's dashes. Since Ts-I is the only typescript that has apparently survived, it is easy enough to see that Nelly Morrison corrupts most of Lawrence's dashes to ellipses: 137 are so altered in the opening five chapters. That Ts-III largely preserved these ellipses, and thus derived from Ts-I or Ts-II, can be inferred from the fact that 118 of these ellipses (86%) reappear in the Florence Edition. Had the London typist followed Lawrence's manuscript in preparing Ts-III, it is impossible to believe that the pattern of corruption would have been so nearly the same, unless the later chapters that she typed also revealed this pattern: and they do not. Moreover, the sequence of many variants, like these from chapters 1 through 5, would be virtually impossible to duplicate unless the London typist were following Nelly's typescript:

get to (MS)	get up to (Ts-I, presumably Ts-III, and Florence Edition
prowess (MS)	powers (Ts-I, presumably TS-III, and Florence Edition
sexual (MS)	sex (Ts-I, presumably Ts-III, and Florence Edition
balked (MS)	talked (Ts-I, presumably Ts-III, and Florence Edition

If therefore it is reasonably certain that Ts-III derived from Ts-I or Ts-II, then can one further argue that the London typist was likely to alter Lawrence's wording (substantives)? If so, then the many variants in working and punctuation that are revealed in a collation of Ts-I and the Florence Edition may well have been introduced not by Lawrence but by the London typist. As best I can determine, chapters 6 through 12 were typed by several typists; one, whom I call the London typist, made all three copies of chapters 6 through 8 and part of 12, and it is obvious from examining chapter 6 alone that she frequently altered Lawrence's substantives--though why she presumed to alter them is unclear. For example, she altered the MS reading "Connie pondered" to "Connie considered"; "father" to "Daddy" (twice); "smudge of blacklead" to "black smudge"; "child" to "little girl"; "slender" to "slim"; and "with curious quickness" to "quickly." These are merely a sampling. One may then infer that if the London typist altered Lawrence's substantives in chapter 6 and beyond, then it is possible--and even likely--that she altered his substantives earlier, in the first five chapters of Ts-III. And if Ts-III served as printer's copy, then all of her corruptions that Lawrence didn't detect (he noticed very few) now appear in the Florence Edition and should be removed from the new text.

But _did_ the first five chapters of Ts-III, now lost, serve as printer's copy? The evidence that they did is harder to assemble and depends on whether or not the patterns of corruption in chapters 6 through 8 and part of 12 can be shown also to occur in chapters 1 through 5 of the Florence Edition, which was apparently set from the typescript made in London. Three kinds of examples can illustrate this evidence. In chapters 6 through 8, Lawrence's paragraphing is corrupted 81 times by the London typist; in chapters 1 through 5, similarly, a collation of Ts-I and the Florence Edition reveals 25 instances of corrupted paragraphing, a figure surprisingly large when one remembers that alterations in paragraphing would often have been obvious--especially in dialogue--and that Lawrence would often have restored, in proof, the paragraphing he intended. In chapters 6 through 8, Lawrence's end-of-sentence stops are corrupted to commas 77 times by the London typist; in chapters 1 through 5 a collation of Ts-I and the Florence Edition reveals 19 instances of end-of-sentence stops corrupted to commas. In chapters 6 through 8, the London typist corrupts Lawrence's colons to semicolons and commas 60 times; in chapters 1 through 5, similarly, a collation of Ts-I and the Florence Edition reveals 77 instances of colons corrupted to semicolons and commas. What these examples all indicate is that the pattern of the London typist's later corruption matches the pattern of corruption introduced into the Florence Edition, and that Lawrence's printer followed her typescript (Ts-III) in setting up the first edition. If so--and the case seems persuasive--then the editor of a text that aims to honor Lawrence's intentions will be compelled to reject the variants introduced into chapters 1 through 5 as probable corruptions of what Lawrence intended. Only in the rare instance when variants can be confidently attributed to Lawrence should they be allowed to emend the text of the holograph manuscript, which serves as the base-text of the new edition.

To readers of <u>Lady Chatterley's Lover</u>, this editorial approach may finally introduce a number of new readings into the first five chapters. Instead of Clifford being "expensively dressed," he will in the new text be "expensively tailored in London." The Reid sisters will enjoy not "noble freedom" but "royal freedom"; and instead of Connie being "a little bit frightened of middle and lower-class humanity," she will in the new text be "a bit frightened of the vast hordes of middle and lower-class humanity." Clifford's stories will no longer take place "in a vacuum" but "on an artificial earth," while Connie will no longer wonder at his "imperious instinct," but at his "imperious necessity." And Michaelis, who once trembled "with a deep shudder," will henceforth tremble "in a sudden shudder." And so on--through dozens of examples. The point, finally, is that understanding the way in which the text of the first five chapters was transmitted can help to ensure that the Cambridge Edition will preserve the words that Lawrence intended--and not those that the London typist may well have substituted.

The second approach looks at the text of <u>Lady Chatterley</u> from the other side of the fence: whereas the approach to chapters 1 through 5 is conservative, the approach to the later chapters is necessarily more liberal. I return to a chronological account of the text only to show how the unconventional publication history partly determines the editorial strategy that an editor adopts for chapters 6 through 19 of the novel.

After Lawrence asked Catherine Carswell to arrange for the typing of chapters 1 through 5 (Ts-III only) and 6 through 12 (all three copies), he persuaded his close friend Maria Huxley to type chapters 13 through 19 in triplicate; for Maria and her husband Aldous were vacationing in Diablerets with the Lawrences. During the month of February, his typists gave him, or sent him, chapters in batches so that he could begin making corrections, preparing one typescript (Ts-III) for his printer in Florence, and then expurgating Ts-I for Knopf and Ts-II for Secker. With one small exception, there is no evidence that anyone other than Lawrence revised these three type-scripts.[3] But because the London typist was slow, Catherine may have asked others to do some of the typing--probably chapters 9, 10, and 11; hence Lawrence did not have a complete typescript until 1 March 1928.

His ribbon copy now ready for the printer, Lawrence met Pino Orioli in Florence on 9 March, and together they took the ribbon copy of Lady Chatterley's Lover to the Tipografia Giuntina, a little Italian printer's shop where the workmen still set type by hand and where--most important--"nobody knew one word of English" (A Propos, Phoenix II, p. 514). At the end of march, the proofs began to arrive, filled with mistakes--like juggling the apostrophe in contractions-- that no English-speaking compositor would have made. On 4 June 1928, after a long and irritating printer's delay, Lawrence finished cor-recting and revising the proofs; and his personal copy of the Florence Edition reached him a few weeks later, on 28 June. Once again, no ex-ternal evidence--in letters or memoirs, for instance--indicates that anyone but Lawrence corrected the proofs. Pino Orioli, who performed mechanical tasks related to the novel's publication and distribution, probably didn't know English well enough to interfere: and what com-positor, speaking no English, would have "styled" Lawrence's punctua-tion? Yet the problem remains that since both printer's copy and proofs have disappeared, an editor cannot be certain that the revi-sions incorporated in chapters 6 through 19 of the Florence Edition are authorial.

This bit of textual history leads one to pose a central editorial question: How should an editor treat the variants in chapters 6 through 19 that are revealed by a collation of Ts-I and the Florence Edition? Can he assume that Lawrence introduced them? Although respected textu-al scholars have argued various positions, most would agree that the substantive variants (new words and phrases) should be regarded as Lawrence's. But the idea of regularizing the accidentals of a text, of making its spelling and punctuation and capitalization consistent, is today unpopular. Many scholarly editors believe that a modern author should be read with his idiosyncrasies untouched. James Thorpe's view that authors often expect other hands to regularize their accidentals is not widely accepted.[4] Fredson Bowers, for in-stance, advocates relatively little regularization, believing that an editor should actively prefer the accidentals of the base-text; yet Bowers also recognizes that "an editor must resist the strong pull that the [base]-text always exerts on him to let well enough alone and to perform a minimum of critical changes, especially in respect to the accidentals."[5] Adopting a more conservative position, Hershel Parker has argued that regularization, except to correct "outright errors," should rarely be attempted, and then only to

restore "demonstrable authorial usage."[6] Michael Black, writing
about the Cambridge Edition of Lawrence's works, has said in his
essay that the original house-styling to which Lawrence's works were
usually subjected must be "set aside"--the veil of corruption lifted.
But he adds that a new house-styling, one that removes Lawrence's
original inadvertencies and inconsistencies, cannot be allowed either:
"We have decided," he writes, "that only the absolute minimum of
interference can be permitted" (see p. 57). The problem is to define
this minimum for chapters 6 through 19 of the novel. Certainly textual
chaos would come again if every volume editor corrected all inconsistencies. It is a matter, then, of fine-tuning the general editorial
principle that has been wisely established for the whole edition. In
a text like *Lady Chatterley's Lover*, which was not published in the
conventional way, a good deal of care and sensitivity will be needed
to determine how much regularization should occur.

   That some corruption of the text has occurred no one would question. The surviving typescript reveals nearly 3,000 typists' corruptions of Lawrence's substantives and accidentals. And the Italian
compositors have introduced errors of their own, such as omitting
the *i* in *yield* (chapter 1) or frequently omitting the comma before
a speaker is identified, as in "'Try an American' said Clifford"
(chapter 3). The compositors may also be responsible for the wide-
spread conversion of Lawrence's colons and dashes to commas, from
chapter 11 on. These are all varnishes that must be stripped.

   In these general circumstances, where multiple authority exists,
the normal procedure that a textual editor would follow is one established by W. W. Greg and refined by Fredson Bowers. An editor would
choose the holograph manuscript as his base (or copy) text and emend
it with those variants from later stages of the text that he judges
to represent the author's intention. Normally, in cases where both
proof and setting copy have disappeared,[7] an editor chooses the substantive variants from the text the author last revised (here, the
Florence Edition) and the accidental variants from the holograph
manuscript.

   But chapters 6 through 19 of *Lady Chatterley's Lover* do not quite
fit the norm. The novel's unconventional textual history does not permit us to infer that ordinary house-styling, where editors and compositors and publishers variously alter the text, has occurred. Apart
from the typists' corruptions, which can be identified and removed,
little interference may in fact have occurred. The textual problem,
then, concerns the extent to which the accidentals of the Florence
Edition may be assumed to represent Lawrence's intention. In principle they cannot, simply because we do not know the extent of com-
positorial sophistication. But many of the accidental variants in the
Florence Edition reflect Lawrence's normal practice. Are they to be
uniformly rejected, the waste product of a mechanical principle of
preferring the manuscript punctuation? I would suggest that such
variants are very unlikely to reflect house-styling, that Lawrence
has introduced most of them into the Florence Edition, and that an
editor must therefore be prepared to treat the accidentals of chapters 6 through 19 with more respect and more reliance on critical
judgment than would be the case if conventional house-styling had

occurred. To support this argument, I would like shortly to offer
some specific illustrations of the difficulty of choosing accidentals,
from the Florence Edition, to be emended into the base text and so to
appear in the Cambridge Edition of the novel.

Once the circumstances of the novel's publication are known,
and a mechanical method of editing chapters 6 through 19 has therefore been rejected, then a new editorial strategy must be devised.
I propose to adopt, as emendations of the base text, the accidental
variants in the Florence Edition (FE) that I can demonstrate are very
likely to be authorial, either because they are consistent with
Lawrence's manuscript usage or because they fit the pattern of TS
correction in Lawrence's hand. But in cases of doubt, a conservative
preference for manuscript readings will necessarily prevail. Here
are examples that illustrate the boundaries of the problem.

In the fairly rare case of obvious compositors' error, the FE
variants will naturally be rejected. Although the compositors'
accuracy is commendable, one does occasionally find errors like these
(in chap. 10): herselt for herself, unkowing for unknowing, word
for world; or omissions like these: his voice for came his voice,
or her contact with man for her contact with this man (chap. 9); or
natural misreadings, as in the following sequence of variants in
chapter 11: greengrocers', (MS), greengrocers! (Ts-I), greengrocers!
(FE). No one will question an editor's decision to reject such
variants from the Cambridge Edition.

But some variants in the Florence Edition are more difficult.
In one large category, Lawrence's dash in MS and Ts-I becomes a comma
in FE. For instance, in chapter 11 there - and becomes there, and; or
time - but becomes time, but; or (as a variation) after - he'd becomes
after; he'd. I am suspicious of these variants because nowhere in Ts-I,
corrected and expurgated in the author's hand, does Lawrence make such
revisions: they do not seem very likely to be authorial. Similarly,
Lawrence's use of the dash as a full stop is occasionally altered to
a period in FE, as in They might sort of graft seed - - or Mrs.
Bolton's "But it was the pit - " or "I've not much respect for people - "
in chapter 11. But again, because there is no textual evidence indicating that Lawrence was very likely to have made such a revision,
an editor ought to choose the MS reading. A much smaller category
includes various hyphenated words or phrases. In chapter 10, for
example, the Florence Edition omits the hyphens in half-an-hour's
time, yet related textual evidence proves helpful when, a few pages
later, half-a-mile appears in all three stages of the text, and when,
still later in the chapter, Lawrence himself corrects half an hour
(MS) to read half-an-hour in Ts-I. In such cases an editor, recog-
nizing that Lawrence is remarkably consistent in his accidental
preferences, would probably not fulfill Lawrence's intention by
eliminating, as FE does, the hyphens from constructions like half-
an-hour's time; he could not be expected to emend such variants into
the new text.

Some variants, however, seem very likely to be authorial, mainly
those that have a clear precedent in the TS corrections in Lawrence's
hand. What does an editor do when Lady and Ladyship are capitalized
in the Florence Edition but not in the manuscript, as in chapter 6?

Textual evidence is crucial. Since Lawrence has in the surviving
typescript frequently capitalized these words when he was expurgating (e.g., Ts-I 124, 174, 200, 216, 239, 302, 347), with the capitalization clearly in his hand, I would argue that his preference should
be adopted as a consistent emendation in the new edition. But other
variants are more troublesome and require informed judgment. To this
end, I have chosen the early pages of chapters 11, 12 and 13 (pp. 217-
29, 241-53, 263-76 of Ts-I) as a representative sample of TS correction, and will refer to this sample as a gauge of how we can expect
Lawrence to revise, of which patterns he is likely to follow. The
variants that seem authorial are all accidentals and range from
numerous commas to occasional exclamation points, colons, dashes,
and hyphens. Indeed, the Florence Edition introduces hundreds of
commas, mostly those that mark a pause in the rhythm of a sentence.
Here are some examples from chapters 8 through 11, with the commas
in question marked by a carat:

> "But he does his duty all right,̂ as far as I'm concerned."
> She was not sure whether she had been insulted and mortally
> offended,̂ or not,
> Almost it seemed to her,̂ she had married him because she dis-
> liked him.
> He began to experiment, and got a clever young fellow who had
> proved brilliant in chemistry,̂ to help him.
> Just beyond were the new school buildings, expensive pink brick,
> and gravelled play-ground inside iron railings, all very
> imposing,̂ and mixing the suggestion of a chapel and a
> prison.
> Clifford was sitting up in bed,̂ with the bed-table and type-
> writer pushed aside. . . .

Certainly these commas sound authentic. But that response is merely
subjective and therefore inadequate. Firmer evidence comes from
observing that in the 40-page TS sample Lawrence adds 21 commas,
whereas almost never in the whole of Ts-I does he delete one of his
original commas. Frequently, indeed, he restores commas that his
typists have, on their own initiative, deleted--as in Connie's statement "'Besides, we'd motor all the way'" (chap. 11), where he restores
the deleted commas in the TS. My assumption, then, is that the pattern
of correction that appears when Lawrence scrutinized the TS is very
likely to have been repeated when he corrected proof. Thus I would
argue that most of the commas introduced into the Florence Edition
should be considered authorial.

Other accidentals introduced into the Florence Edition, although
they rarely occur, can be similarly analyzed. The exclamation point
added to "'What can they do, poor chaps!'" (chap. 9) is probably
authorial, not mainly because it sounds like Lawrence but because in
the TS sample Lawrence has added five exclamation points to his text.
When the Florence Edition introduces a dash between the following
two sentences in chapter 10,

> For years he [Mellors] was gone, all the time of the war: and
> a lieutenant and all: quite the gentleman, really, quite the

> gentleman! - Then to come back to Tevershall and go as a
> gamekeeper!

the dash serves to mark the shift in Mrs. Bolton's thoughts about the
gamekeeper and, in so doing, sounds authentic; but more important, in
the TS sample Lawrence introduces dashes between his sentences three
different times. One concludes that the dash in question is likely
to be authorial, especially when one recalls that the typescript was
not subjected to a publisher's house-styling. And finally, when the
Florence Edition introduces hyphens in order to form a compound of
two words, is it reasonable to assume that Lawrence added them? Here,
for instance, are four examples of hyphens added to chapter 8 of the
Florence Edition: "under the hazel-rods," "pure reddish-white pebbles,"
"the hissing boom of the larch-wood," "under the great beech-tree."
In these cases Lawrence is almost certainly regularizing his text,
in proof, to reflect his preference for compound forms. His preference
is clearly revealed in this same chapter by "a young pine-tree," "the
old oak-wood," "some larch-twigs," and "the big holly-tree." The same
problem occurs again in chapter 10 when the Florence Edition introduces a hyphen into this abridged sentence: "He [Clifford] would
rather have been . . . listening-in to the radio." Of course it sounds
like Lawrence's punctuation, but an editor must then seek evidence,
which appears on the next page as Lawrence records Clifford's anxiety
"when he was not listening-in." Further support for assuming that all
five hyphens are authorial can be found in the 40-page TS sample,
where Lawrence has added twelve hyphens. It is very likely, then, that
Lawrence introduced most hyphens into the Florence Edition, and the
case for adopting them as emendations of the base text seems strong,
the probability of their authorial origin high. But where the evidence
is ambiguous or doubt strong, the punctuation of the manuscript must
be preferred.

I have argued that the best text of Lady Chatterley's Lover will
emerge when not one but two editorial strategies are employed--the
first using the history of the text to determine the proper editorial
stance, the second using internal textual evidence to infer an editorial stance that recovers the author's intentions as fully as the
surviving evidence permits. The mechanical principles of textual
editing must at times be tempered by judgment. As a reviewer has
recently said, "Editing is an elusive process, not often subject to
definitions, absolutes, or abstractions."[8] But it is ironic that a
work which so shocked the world for decades should continue to surprise, in a very different way: the novel that looked at the outset
easy and straightforward to edit has proved challenging indeed.

Ideas and Techniques

D. H. Lawrence's Uncommon Prayers

SANDRA M. GILBERT

> . . . we've got the world inside out. The true living world
> of fire is dark, throbbing, darker than blood. Our luminous world
> that we go by is only the reverse of this.
> > --Count Johann Dionys Psanek, in "The Ladybird"

> Who gave us flowers?
> Heaven? The white God?
>
> Nonsense!
> Up out of hell,
> From Hades;
> Infernal Dis!
> > --"Purple Anemones"

I

As the title of this essay implies, I have lately been rereading
T. S. Eliot's After Strange Gods, and as I'm sure many people will
agree, almost the only experience stranger than reading After Strange
Gods is rereading it. Indeed, most of its readers will no doubt also
agree that this frankly sermonizing work of literary criticism, which
was first incarnated in 1933 as a series of lectures at the University
of Virginia, is not just strange, it is quite distressing. Here, after
all, is the "primer of modern heresy" in which, as Nazi Germany grew
more powerful, Eliot declared that populations "should be homogeneous"
both in race and in religion, adding infamously that "reasons of race
and religion combine to make any large number of free-thinking Jews
undesirable" and that "a spirit of excessive tolerance is to be
deprecated."[1]

Almost as disturbing as statements like these, moreover, was
(and is) the tone in which modernist poetry's elder statesman made
them. Ostensibly benevolent and cautionary, it barely concealed a

sneer of social snobbery so irritating that I can still remember my
anger when I first read that "nothing could be much drearier (so far
as one can judge from his own account) than the vague hymn-singing
pietism which seems to have consoled the miseries of Lawrence's
mother, and which does not seem to have provided her with any firm
principles by which to scrutinize the conduct of her sons."[2] Because
I was naturally sympathetic to Lawrence, I felt--as I recall--like
some underservant in the Palace of Art who has suddenly gotten a
grotesquely unjust slap from a very uppity butler. My cheeks burned,
my head ached.

And yet my speculations here are going to begin with the idea
that a good deal of what Eliot said about Lawrence in After Strange
Gods was essentially accurate, accurate not in its moral evaluation
of Lawrence's work but in its perception of the radical, heretical
(and, indeed, blasphemous) mythology that is at the center of almost
everything Lawrence wrote and that specifically energizes most of his
finest poetry. I am going to argue, in other words, that Eliot was
quite right to think that what he called "the daemonic powers" had
found an instrument in Lawrence, and right to perceive that Lawrence
hated "orthodoxy" (whereas Joyce, as Eliot also saw, was a model of
"ethical orthodoxy"). In fact, from his own perspective, Eliot was
quite correct to suggest that, like Thomas Hardy, Lawrence introduces
us into "a world of pure evil."[3] For, as the Anglican/American poet
understood, the tradition in which Lawrence increasingly worked, and
worked with increasing consciousness, was that revisionary Blakeian
tradition which wants to turn the world upside down, wants, in Eliot's
words, to introduce "the diabolic into modern literature."[4]

A number of critics have, of course, noted that Lawrence was, as
Eugene Goodheart puts it, a "tablet-breaker" who assumed "at various
times the roles of nihilist, mystic, diabolist, and obscurantist"
[italics mine].[5] Since I am particularly concerned here with his
poetry, however, I want to stress my belief that, paradoxically, it
was just Lawrence's introduction of the so-called "diabolic" into
poetry that ultimately redeemed this poet-novelist's sometimes problematic work in verse. Seven or eight years ago, I wrote that I con-
curred whole-heartedly in Wright Morris's assertion that "in this
world--the one in which we must live--the strange gods of D. H.
Lawrence appear to be less strange than those of Mr. Eliot."[6] Interestingly, there were several book reviewers who took me to task even
for agreeing with Morris, suggesting that the roots of Eliotian orthodoxy clutch deep indeed, even among the "stony rubbish" of academia
in the seventies. What now interests me most about my interest in
Morris's remark, though, is how tentative it then was, how hard I
worked to prove that Lawrence's strange gods were really as comfort-
able and familiar as so many priestly grandpas, and that, indeed,
they were not very different from the gods of Eliot, or Herbert, or
Donne. I knew, I think, that Lawrence was an apparently irreligious
religious poet, but I don't think I understood just how uncommon his
book of uncommon prayers was.

What I did not know, however--or perhaps, more accurately, what
I was not yet prepared to admit to myself--is a secret truth on which
Lawrence's extraordinarily odd, elusive, glimmering, and yet powerful

reputation as a poet has been based. For years, in fact, <u>poets</u> have
read and revered Lawrence because his poems are uncommon prayers,
prayers blasphemously addressed to gods whom Eliot would define as
devils, prayers empowered by that demonic energy, that other-self-
within-the-self, which the Spanish call the <u>Duende</u>. As Karl Shapiro
wrote some twenty years ago, Lawrence is "declassed" but he "enjoys
a kind of underground popularity among writers, even though he is
outside the pale of the Tradition."[7] I would say, however, that
Lawrence's popularity among writers has grown--and indeed, lately it
has blossomed--precisely <u>because</u> he is outside what so many writers
have perceived as the impregnable tradition of Eliotian orthodoxy, a
fortress into which it has often seemed no Individual Talent could
ever penetrate. Poets love Lawrence, in other words, because he is
an underground poet--both an outsider-poet and a poet of the underground or, more exactly, the underworld. They love him because he is
a diabolical poet, a Blakeian prophet of hell.

Thus Shapiro wrote admiringly of Lawrence's "leap" into "aboriginal darkness" and of Lawrence's quest for "the aboriginal, the pure
energy of the soul,"[8] and William Carlos Williams, who so famously
thought that Eliot set poetry back half a century, obsessively eulo-
gized Lawrence (whom he considered "so English / he had thereby
raised himself / to an unenglish greatness") with a re-vision of the
Lawrentian serpent, triumphantly returning to an underwater underground world:

> Slowly the serpent leans
> to drink by the tinkling water
> the forked tongue alert.
> Then fold after fold,
> glassy strength, passing
> a given point,
> as by desire drawn
> forward bodily, he glides
> smoothly in ("An Elegy for D. H. Lawrence").[9]

Williams, of course, was a writer whose commitment to what we might
call the "hellish" or diabolic tradition in modern letters evolved
almost simultaneously with Lawrence's, for in 1920 the American
doctor published a revolutionary book of "improvisations" (or prose
poems) entitled <u>Kora in Hell</u>, one of which might serve as a motto
for the whole group of Lawrentian poets I am thinking of: "<u>Seeing a</u>
<u>light in an upper window the poet by means of the power he has enters</u>
<u>the room and of what he sees there brews himself a sleep potion.</u>"[10]

Williams's sense that the poet is <u>below</u> the phenomenal windows
of light, together with the conviction that he has magical power to
enter that room of experience and there to create a diabolical brew
of unconsciousness or darkness--together these constitute crucial
ideas that characterize the underground poetic tradition I am trying
to define here. More recent writers in this tradition would include
such diverse figures as Denise Levertov, Gary Snyder, Joyce Carol
Oates, Adrienne Rich, Ted Hughes, Robert Bly; and that is a minimal
catalogue which nevertheless includes many of the most powerful poets

writing today in English. (Moreover, if I leave out such charismatic recent artists as Sylvia Plath and Robert Lowell, that is not because I think them un-Lawrentian but because their approach to the diabolical seems to me to revise what is already revisionary even in Lawrence and his obvious disciples.)

Denise Levertov, for instance, is perhaps most frequently described as an admirer of Williams. But although her interest in organic form and specifically in the American grain of Williams's poetry would in any case bring her close to Lawrence, she has herself acknowledged a more direct connection, for she defines Lawrence as one of the major figures who was "of great importance to me as a writer, not only as a reader."[11] (And she specifically notes that Eliot did not have such importance for her.) Elsewhere, moreover, this woman whose "Song for Ishtar" is only one of a number of verses dedicated to what Eliot would have called strange gods, clarifies her sense of Lawrence's special significance. Explaining "the kind of knowledge from which [she believes] myth in poetry can grow," she quotes in full his wonderful "There are No Gods," one of a series of late "pansies" that meditate upon the demonic élan vital Lawrence thought darkly godly and Eliot considered diabolical.[12]

Like Levertov, Gary Snyder feels a special, radically theological but "post-Christian" commitment both to the poetry of the sacred and to the sacred-as-poetry. Moreover, because he is so passionate a student of comparative anthropology, both his poems and the essays he has collected in Earth House Hold are written in Lawrentian praise of "the most archaic values on earth." Particularly in his thoughtful piece on "Poetry and the Primitive" he explores the ancient connection between poetry and the demonic that is central to the underground poetic tradition of which Lawrence is an unsaintly patron. Consider, for instance, the Lawrentian implications of Snyder's remark that the "primitive ritual dramas, which acknowledged all the sides of human nature, including the destructive, demonic, and ambivalent, were liberating and harmonizing."[13]

Different as they are in other ways, such major contemporary writers as Joyce Carol Oates, Robert Bly, and Ted Hughes would clearly agree with that statement of Snyder's. Oates, who has written a perceptive study of Lawrence's poetry, notes that "the critic who expects to open Lawrence's poems and read poems by T. S. Eliot . . . is bound to be disappointed" and her realization that "Lawrence loves the true marriage of heaven and hell, illusory opposites" shows that she knows just exactly why the Eliotian reader will be disappointed in Lawrence's uncommon prayers.[14] Similarly, Robert Bly has written of the Norwegian poet Harry Martinson that "everything [in his work] feels alive, resilient, fragrant, like seaweed under water . . . a little like Lawrence in 'Bavarian Gentians,'"[15] and in a comment on Neruda's poetry he describes Neruda, perhaps his greatest master, in the same way that I would myself now describe Lawrence, as "a new kind of creature moving about under the surface of everything. Moving under the earth, he knows everything from the bottom up (which is the right way to learn the nature of a thing) and therefore is never at a loss for its name" [italics mine].[16] Such statements are mottos of underground poetry notably similar to the "improvisation" I quoted from

Kora in Hell, and they come quite inevitably from a writer whose meditation upon "A Bird's Nest Made of White Reed Fiber" ends in a vision
of an "ecstatic and black" rebirth in the other world, a vision exactly
comparable to the one Lawrence has in "Medlars and Sorb Apples."

With the problematic exception of Denise Levertov, Ted Hughes
is the only one of Lawrence's countrymen whom I feel qualified to
include in this tradition, but he is perhaps the most obvious heir
of Lawrence's diabolical vision. Bleaker than the hymn-sequences in
The Plumed Serpent, Hughes's Crow cycle nevertheless picks up where
Lawrence's Aztec imitations left off, and Gaudete, Hughes's latest
book, not only chronicles the demonic career of a "changling" clergy-
man, it is prefixed by an epigraph from Heraclitus which asserts,
diabolically enough, that "Hades and Dionysos are one."[17] Yet none
of this underground thought should come as a surprise if it is seen
in the context of other Lawrentian works by a poet whose career began
with a hellish but sacramental vision of "pike so immense and old /
That past nightfall I . . . silently cast and fished / With the hair
frozen on my head" for the "dream / Darkness beneath night's darkness
had freed, / That rose slowly towards me, watching."[18]

Interestingly, even Adrienne Rich, who is probably now best
known as a feminist poet, has acknowledged an early debt to Lawrence,
pointing out that "women can find something for themselves in the
poetry of men like Shelley and Lawrence because, while these poets
are sexist, their imaginations act from their 'feminine,' intuitive
nature."[19] In fact, despite her comment about Lawrence's "sexism,"
it seems to me that what Rich is defining here is the crucial place
the author of Birds, Beasts and Flowers occupies in a tradition of
radically revisionary underground poetry that has been of major importance not only in the lives and works of the best contemporary
poets in English but also in the lives and thoughts of most contemporary feminists. Indeed, if I had more space here, I'd probably want
to argue that the central tenets of this Lawrentian underground tradition are most likely underworld visions that have helped recent
American and British poets to appreciate those European and South
American writers, like Neruda, Rilke, Vallejo, Martinson, Tranströmer,
and Lorca, who are their most powerful non-English influences. It is
no coincidence that Lorca, for instance, shared with Lawrence a deep
admiration for the strange gods of Walt Whitman, that demonically
energetic writer whom, as Shapiro reminded us, Lawrence called the
"first white aboriginal." In fact, Lorca ended his famous "Ode to
Walt Whitman" with lines that also summarize Lawrence's underground
vision:

> I want the strong air of the most profound night
> to remove flowers and words from the arch where you sleep,
> and a black boy to announce to the gold-minded whites
> the arrival of the reign of the ear of corn.[20]

II

I think it is not only interesting but very significant that all
these passionate devotees of Lawrence's strange gods are poets (including Oates). Though I am not especially expert in contemporary

fiction, I doubt that I could make much of a case for Lawrentian diabolism among recent novelists in England and America. Lawrence's strange gods have been of greatest importance to poets, which is perhaps why they were most violently attacked by a preacher who began his theological career as a poet named T. S. Eliot. Lawrence himself, moreover, seems to me to have expressed his own devotion to these strange gods in uncommon prayers most often disguised as lyric poems. Indeed, I suspect that Lawrence's poet-disciples may have consciously or unconsciously perceived that not only such obviously prayerful works as those collected in Last Poems but even the apparently "realistic" nature poems in Birds, Beasts and Flowers originated in anti-Christian visions such as those I have been describing here. At this point, therefore, I would like to pause and consider in greater detail the possibility that Birds, Beasts and Flowers may not only be energized but organized by a subversive narrative structure.[21]

Of course, Look! We Have Come Through!, Lawrence's third book of poetry, has long been read as a narrative sequence or "verse novel." Lawrence himself provided the work with an official "Argument" and insisted that "these poems should not be considered separately. . . . They are intended as an essential story, or history, or confession, unfolding one from the other in organic development." But in any case it is easy enough to see the dramatic and narrative coherence of a group of confessional poems chronicling "the conflict of love and hate [that] goes on between [a] man and [a] woman, and between these two and the world around them, till . . . they transcend into some condition of blessedness."[22]

On first consideration, however, readers would not tend to perceive the same narrative coherence in Birds, Beasts and Flowers, the great collection whose tone and technique Look! both foreshadowed and created. With Kenneth Rexroth and Tom Marshall, most would see this volume not as a narrative sequence but as a philosophical "exploration" of the "newly valued world of birds, beasts, and flowers-- a sacramentalized, objective world" to which the poet has been mystically wedded by the ritual of holy matrimony recorded in Look![23] I myself have described the poems in Birds, Beasts and Flowers, as essays of discovery, processes of definition, with Lawrence a metaphysical or metaphorical Linnaeus cataloguing the varieties of otherness in nature.[24]

I want to argue here, however, that as a collection Birds, Beasts and Flowers is consciously or unconsciously organized and unified by a submerged narrative structure which gives it exactly the dramatic coherence Lawrence sought in Look! Further, I want to suggest that this narrative structure is not only submerged but subversive, for it seems to me to depend on a revisionary synthesis of a group of those myths of darkness to which so many poets have recently been drawn and which were to become increasingly important to Lawrence: the story of Persephone and Dis (or Pluto), the story of Orpheus and Eurydice, the stories of Osiris and Dionysus, the story of Samson, and last but not least the story of the fall of Lucifer, and the subsequent falls or failures of all humanity.

As we might expect, Lawrence does not "tell" these stories in received, official ways; at every point his perspective on them is that of the illegitimate, dangerous, Blakeian outsider he felt he had become in his postwar flight from England. Thus Persephone's marriage to Dis/Pluto is the best thing that ever happened to her (and Lawrence enacts in turn her part and the part of her dark lover); Orpheus's separation from Eurydice and journey down the "winding, leaf-clogged silent lanes of hell" (CP, p. 281) is lucky and full of wonder; Samson is not, as Milton thought, imprisoned by his blindness in the dungeon of himself but rather freed from ordinary vision to perceive that "the dome of high ideal heaven" (CP, p. 287) is his prison; and Lucifer, the Son of the morning, whom Milton called Satan and Blake called Los, is not a slimy lord of evil but a lord of life, "a king in exile . . . Now due to be crowned again" (CP, p. 351).

With Kenneth Rexroth, then, I believe that the poems of Birds, Beasts and Flowers do not have a "supernatural luster." But where Rexroth thought this luster the light "that shines through the figures of men and animals and things . . . as they are found carved around the mandala of the Blessed Virgin above some cathedral door or some rose window,"[25] I would say it is exactly the opposite. For, as my Blake reference was meant to imply, the subversive narrative of Birds, Beasts and Flowers is not a celebration of the radiant Christian sacrament of holy matrimony but a version of Blake's sardonic Marriage of Heaven and Hell, a botanist's or zoologist's Black Mass in which at one point Lawrence, speaking as St. Matthew (whom he defines as representative man) insists that since he has already "mounted up on the wings of the morning," he must now dredge "down to the zenith's reversal" (CP, p. 323). Rather than being a metaphysical Linnaeus, in other words, Lawrence is here a Satanic Darwin, journeying in thought to the black center of the earth to trace an evolutionary history we citizens of the "pussyfoot west" (CP, p. 280) have forgotten. In the radically revisionary etiology he uncovers, the sacred energy of life comes "Flying not down from heaven, but storming up . . . from the dense under-earth. . . . Setting supreme annunciation to the world" (CP, p. 304). And of course, therefore, the annunciation he imagines is an upside down (or perhaps downside up) event, not the airy visitation about which poets from Dante to Yeats have written, but a fierce kiss of darkness, even, at times, a kiss of death.

Finally, then, I want to argue that in its sophisticated and subversive engagement with Christian mythology and its consequent espousal of an alternative religion which grows from a variety of irreligious experiences, Birds, Beasts and Flowers is, as much as Aaron's Rod, The Lost Girl, and Kangaroo, a fictional link between Lawrence's great middle-period novels of society--Sons and Lovers, The Rainbow, Women in Love--and such late, openly revisionary mythologies and romances as The Plumed Serpent, "The Woman Who Rode Away," "Sun," Lady Chatterley's Lover, and The Escaped Cock. We might even speculate, indeed, that because Birds, Beasts and Flowers is a more successful and coherent work than any of the so-called "problem" novels I have mentioned, it is a far more significant bridge than they are between this author's very different middle and late periods.

Did Lawrence actually intend Birds, Beasts and Flowers to have the narrative and allusive coherence I am suggesting it has? I think that is hard to say. Because he was also a novelist, this poet did

frequently and inevitably shape literary materials into stories. As
a critic/essayist, moreover, he was highly conscious of his own
revisionary impulses. The title he gave this collection, for instance,
has been drawn from stanza two of S. Baring-Gould's "Evening Hymn":
"Now the darkness gathers, / Stars begin to peep. / Birds and beasts
and flowers, / Soon will be asleep."[26] But, given the anti-Christian
cast of Lawrence's thought in this period, it is hard to imagine that
he didn't use Baring-Gould's phrase with some conscious irony, and
hard to imagine, too, that he did not think of even the gathering
"darkness" with a very different reverence from that of the Reverend
Mr. Baring-Gould. In addition, although Lawrence did not provide
Birds, Beasts and Flowers with an "Argument"--that is, a plot sum-
mary--like the one he wrote for Look!, it is clear that he organized
the book very carefully, beginning with "Fruits" and moving through
"Trees," "Flowers," "Evangelical Beasts," "Creatures," "Reptiles,"
"Birds," and "Animals" to "Ghosts." Some explanation of why he did
this seems to me to begin to emerge when we consider that this modern
Marriage of Heaven and Hell opens with a quarrelsome poem about eating
a pomegranate, has at its center an emotionally charged but unsatisfactory confrontation with a serpent, and, after a baptismal encounter
between the poet/narrator (who renames himself "Red Wolf") and a dark
figure he dubs "Harry" or "Old Nick," ends with the speaker's acces-
sion to what we must call shamanistic powers, his summoning up of the
spirits of the dead, and his expression of interest in a kind of anti-
religious colony in the New World.

I am suggesting, in short, that the processes of discovery in
Birds, Beasts and Flowers are held together by the covert story of a
trip underground, a voyage of death and resurrection exactly like the
ones that Lawrence would describe in The Escaped Cock or "The Ship of
Death." But in the Birds, Beasts and Flowers narrative, perhaps more
than anywhere else, this Blakeian poet makes it quite clear that in
his version of the night sea-journey the protagonist does not, like
Beowulf, go down into the mere to slay the forces of darkness but
rather to be strengthened and even transformed by them; his fall is
fortunate not because it will enable him, like Milton's Adam, to rise
again by his own efforts, but because it is a fall into a hell that
he knows is really a darkly radiant heaven, and he may be lucky enough
to fall even further, deeper, into the center of all energy; finally,
when he comes back from his trip into the demonic darkness behind
appearances, he is not, like Hawthorne's Goodman Brown, horrified by
what he has learned, but ennobled, even blessed.

All this may seem quite mystical, but I think my reading (if not
my rhetoric) is fairly quickly justified by "Fruits," the opening
section of the book. This section contains (in order of their appearance) the poems called "Pomegranate," "Peach," "Medlars and Sorb
Apples," "Figs," "Grapes," "The Revolutionary," "The Evening Land,"
and "Peace." It is followed by "Trees" and "Flowers." In 1930 Lawrence
prefaced the section with an epigraph (from Burnet's Early Greek
Philosophy) declaring that "fruits are all of them female, in them
lies the seed. And so when they break and show the seed, then we
look into the womb and see its secrets. So it is that the pomegranate
is the apple of love to the Arab, and the fig has been a catch-word

for the female fissure for ages . . . the apple of Eden, even, was
Eve's fruit . . ." (CP, p. 277) and so on.

If we put all this information together, our first thought might
be that "Fruits" simply begins the collection because the book is
organized like a great chain of being, from the least animate, the
least developed life-forms (the fruit, the pit, the seed) to the most
intensely alive, the subtlest, the most complex (human beings and
their ghosts). And to some extent this is true. But we might quibble
over which came first, the fruit or the tree. And more important, we
must ask why poems which are neither about fruits nor seeds--poems
like "The Revolutionary," "The Evening Land," and "Peace"--are included in this section. (A related question would be: why have the
"Evangelical Beasts" been placed between "Flowers" and "Creatures"?)
If, as seems reasonable, we see the placement and organization of
"Fruits" as somehow paradigmatic for the volume as a whole, then we
must conclude that this section has a narrative and emotional as well
as a logical or categorizing function; it both tells a story and
begins a story. And I believe the tale it tells is an archetypal story
about eating fruit and being changed by the magical properties of
fruit.

I am sure the fruit-eater here is Lawrence himself, so I will
not refer to him as a persona but compromise and call him the poet/
narrator. This poet/narrator dramatically defines and describes himself in the very first lines of the book:

> You tell me I am wrong.
> Who are you, who is anybody, to tell me I am wrong?
> I am not wrong.

The "you" here is of course us, the audience, the bystanders, the
hypocrite lecteurs who watch but do not--cannot--participate in the
poet/narrator's ceremonial meal. Since he is writing in English, we
are also obviously English-speaking. Thus we represent or at least
we are associated with the "long ash-grey coffin"[27] of Christian/
Victorian England, the pious world in which the poet has grown up
and from which he has now been exiled because he is somehow "wrong"
(meaning evil, Satanic).

More specifically, the poet/narrator's wrongness, as the poem
makes clear, consists in what he sees: a crack in the surface of the phenomenal world," a fissure, a rupture, through which glow the begin-
nings and the ends of things. But what he sees implies also what he
does and what he will eat. The timid and genteel reader, refusing to
see the dangerous, suggestively sexual fissure, insists upon looking
only "on the plain side" of life. But from that side there is no
nourishment, and on that side there is no entrance into the mysteriously flaming realm behind the setting sun, whose fissure in the
darkness of the sky beckons like a doorway into paradoxical possibilities. When he cracks open the pomegranate, therefore, we have to assume
that this defiant speaker begins the revolutionary process of eating
and entering the fruit--that is, eating and being eaten by it. In a
sense, in this poem he is planting the seed of his whole book within
himself, and this poem/seed is the kernel of transformation.

It seems fairly clear that the poet/narrator here eats the
"glittering compact drops of dawn" that are the pomegranate's seeds
with considerable equanimity. "For my part, I prefer my heart to be
broken," he assures us. "It is so lovely, dawn-kaleidoscopic within
the crack." But as Lawrence's imagery of heartbreak suggests, the
ceremonial fruit meal is traditionally a dangerous one. In countless
folk narratives fearful metamorphoses begin with the ingestion of
some alien substance, and Judeo-Christian mythology itself, of course,
starts with such a meal of poison fruit: when Eve ate the apple she
"ate" death and, as Milton puts it, even "Earth felt the wound" and
all Nature sighed.[28] Similarly, nineteenth-century poets like Keats
(in "La Belle Dame") or Christina Rossetti (in "Goblin Market") tell
stories of transformation and self-confrontation which begin with the
eating of strange fruits or roots, and Lawrence's poem certainly
depends at least in part on our grasp of the tradition in which all
these tales of eating participate. But most particularly, Lawrence's
poem alludes to the myth of Persephone, the queen of the underworld
and the daughter of the earth goddess, who was irrevocably committed
to her half-time life in hell--that is, to her traveling back and
forth between the upper and lower worlds--when she ate a few pomegranate seeds.

That Lawrence chose to begin his account of a journey through
the alien kingdom of Birds, Beasts and Flowers not with Eve's fall
but with Persephone's seems to me significant in several ways. First,
and most obviously, it emphasizes the deliberately anti-Christian
nature of the cosmology he is outlining. Second (and perhaps more
important), it establishes the essentially amoral or at least morally
unconventional tone of this collection. For where Eve's fall (especially as Milton presents it) was a moral one, Persephone's was
mystical, or anyway mysterious. Eve wickedly ate the apple because
she was angry, but Persephone only ate the pomegranate seeds because
she was hungry. In other words, although Eve deserved punishment--
falling!--Persephone did not deserve to "fall"; she simply fell,
through the neutrality and energy of natural appetite, thereby both
entering and creating the seasonal cycle of life and death that constitutes the essence of natural process. Because Eve's fall was a
moral event, it follows, too, that the world it created is, as we
know, a sadly material and ruined landscape from which the divine
spirit has irrevocably withdrawn itself. But--and this is crucial to
Lawrence's revision of the myth of the fall--since Persephone's fall
was morally neutral, the world it brought about (especially as Lawrence
sees it) is a radiant realm the goddess herself still visits: she withdraws and returns, withdraws and returns, in a divine Heraclitean flux
that helps us understand why the poet used so many quotations from
Burnet's Early Greek Philosophy as epigraphs for this volume.

Moreover, to the extent that Lawrence wants to celebrate the
natural world he must celebrate not only Persephone, the traveler
back and forth, but also her demonic mate, the god of darkness who
first entangled her in this seasonal process. Particularly in cele-
brating this god of darkness, however, he is revising the myth of the
fall to say: no, it was not really a fall, it was a downward journey.
If it has not already been made clear, his revisionary awareness is

definitively revealed both in "Peach" and "Medlars and Sorb Apples,"
the two poems that follow "Pomegranate." Defending the fruit's
"groove," its "suggestion of incision," "Peach" continues the defiant
dialogue with a hypocrite lecteur audience that "Pomegranate" began.
At the same time, though, through a passage that wittily parodies
Blake's "Tyger," Lawrence implies that the transition from "Pomegranate" to "Peach" is a necessary fall or downward journey from
Innocence to Experience, a journey from the virginal dawn-country of
Beulah to the riper realm of Generation. "Why so velvety, why so
voluptuous heavy?" he asks. "Why hanging with such inordinate weight?
/ Why so indented?" And though (like Blake before him) he does not
answer these questions, he does playfully offer the reader a peach
stone to throw at him, showing that he at least has eaten the fruit.

In "Medlars and Sorb Apples" it becomes even plainer that in
eating the fruit the poet/narrator has not only eaten Nature but has
himself entered Nature through cracks and grooves in the "bivalve
roundness" of the seasonal world. Having "eaten death," however, he
does not despair like Eve, but instead exclaims that "Wonderful are
the hellish experiences!" and embarks upon his crucial journey down
the "winding, leaf-clogged, silent lanes of hell." And though Lawrence
describes this trip as Orphic or Dionysiac, it is also Persephone's
journey, a journey that begins with a kiss of death--"a kiss and a
spasm of farewell"--in the "flux of autumn," "a journey that is given
sacramental savour by the rambling, sky-dropped grape" and a journey
that ends with the soul entering Pluto's realm "naked-footed . . .
Ever more exquisite, distilled in separation." Along with Persephone,
Orpheus, Dionysus, and all other mortal beings, the poet/narrator
gropes downward into the "intoxication of final loneliness." As if
to show that you are what you eat, he himself has become a seed falling through the dead walls of the fruit into the labyrinthine ways
of an underworld where he must re-create his own energies.

Approached by winding lanes and "orgasm[s] of rupture," this dark
central hell is not, of course, so much a tomb as it is a womb; as
Lawrence's epigraph noted, "fruits are all of them female" so that
entering the labyrinth of nature "we look into the womb and see its
secrets." "Figs," therefore, quite appropriately follows the journey-
imagery of "Medlars and Sorb Apples" with a meditation upon the place
that is the journey's goal, or one of its goals. For years, I must
confess, I have been troubled by what has seemed to be the anti-
feminism of this poem, and I am still disturbed by Lawrence's comparison of a "bursten fig" to a "prostitute . . . making a show of her
secret," and by his editorial insistence that "women the world over"
who burst "into self-assertion" are like "bursten figs [which] won't
keep." Nevertheless, it is easier to understand and at least partly
justify "Figs" when we consider its position in the submerged narrative that structures Birds, Beasts and Flowers. Having begun his
journey into the center of nature, the poet/narrator becomes ever
more certain that the natural world is divinely emblematic. "The fig,
the horseshoe, the squash-blossom. / Symbols," he says, as if murmur-
ing this hard-won information to himself. And the fig, as he sees it,
symbolizes not only female creative energy but the mystical darkness
or secrecy in which female energy generates and regenerates life.

In a real sense, then, the magical interior of the fig, "where everything happens invisible, flowering, fertilisation, and fruiting / In the inwardness of your you," is analogous to the secret central chamber of hell where Persephone lies with Dis in what Lawrence was later to call "the marriage of the living dark" (CP, p. 960), that continually restores life. But to shed any light in this room other than the paradoxical light of "torches of darkness" (CP, p. 697) would be (as in the tale of Cupid and Psyche) like bringing to consciousness what must be done intuitively. In folk tale after folk tale we learn, after all, that to tell the secret is to lose the power, and indeed, in Birds, Beasts and Flowers this notion links "Figs" to the forth-coming story of Samson, who lost his (male) power by kissing and tell-ing. It explains, too, why the stone in "Peach" is "wrinkled with secrets and hard with the intention to keep them," and why the poet/ narrator only half-ironically invites his hostile reader to throw a peach stone at him, the speaker. Self-enclosed, dense with the power of secrecy, the peach pit is yet another talisman of transformation by which one may pass from here to there, from this foolishly asser-tive upper world to the magic shadows below.

Lawrence elaborates even further in "Grapes" on the virtues of secrecy and the disadvantages of what he calls "the universe of the unfolded rose, / The explicit / the candid revelation." His attack upon the "rose of all roses, rose of all the world" which has begun to "simper supreme" in western culture is an attack upon both Yeats and Plato (or neo-Plato), for the heavenly beauty that Yeats defined in his rose poems[29] as not only eternal but emblematic of eternity was clearly a Platonic ideal: abstract, brilliant, disembodied, exist-ing to be seen and not touched, a symbol of the mind willfully yearn-ing to separate itself from nature rather than the body reincarnating itself in nature. Lawrence's journey, however, continues to be a trip into an antediluvian and anti-Platonic Hades--a fleshly cave--that he defines as the true Eden, the primordial place of origin we must re-remember. In this "dusky, flowerless, tendrilled world" the vine bears an invisible rose whose blue-black sacred grapes hang "globed in Egyptian darkness." And modern westerners, the prissy readers who were the "you" of "Pomegranate" and "Peach," fear re-remembrance of such a dangerously invisible kingdom, fear substituting Pluto for Plato. Indeed, the poet/narrator sometimes seems himself to feel such fear, for despite his obvious scorn of his contemporaries, he speaks throughout this poem as "we" (rather than "I" versus "you"). "We must cross the frontiers, though we will not," he notes, adding with grim determination that we must "take the fern-seed in our lips, / Close the eyes, and go / Down the tendrilled avenues of wine and the other-world." Here, blind, fallen from our daylight lives, intoxicated with loneliness, shrouded in secrecy, we must seek our own lost powers.

Since both the horror and the necessity of blindness are almost insurmountable obstacles to the fall or downward journey that is the subject of the Birds, Beasts and Flowers narrative, it seems inevit-able that the poet/narrator should pause here to consider the implica-tions of blindness for one famously sightless hero, Samson. Not surprisingly, however, Lawrence drastically revises the story that is told in the Bible and in Milton's Samson Agonistes, and there are

enough allusions to the latter source for us to be certain that just
as he was attacking Yeats in "Grapes," he is here severely criticizing
Milton. To begin with, as I noted earlier, Lawrence's Samson does not
mourn his blindness, the way Milton's does. Rather, he vaunts it, as
if having rashly told one secret he has luckily learned another.
Captive and defeated, Milton's agonized hero complains that he has
been "exiled from light" to "a living death . . . Myself my sepulcher,
a moving grave."[30] But Lawrence's Samson makes plot necessities into
mystical virtues.

Because he is an exile, this revisionary hero is a revolutionary,
setting himself sardonically against the "pale-face authority" of
those pillars of society who hold up "the high and super-gothic
heavens." Because he is blind, he need not "yearn" or "aspire," for
"what is daylight to me that I should look skyward?" Because he is
imprisoned in the "living grave" of his own body, he experiences
things as Pluto and Persephone must in their hot black chamber--
intuitively, receptively: "To me, the earth rolls ponderously, superbly
. . . To me, men's footfalls fall with a dull, soft rumble . . . To me,
men are palpable, invisible nearnesses in the dark." Most important,
perhaps, where Milton's warrior defines the labor to which he had been
condemned as the ultimate sign of degradation--for is he not "eyeless
in Gaza, at the Mill with slaves?"[31]--Lawrence's revolutionary seems
actually to take pride in his work: "Am I not blind at the round-
turning mill? / Then why should I fear their pale faces? / Or love
the effulgence of their holy light?" We might almost speculate, in
fact, that for Lawrence the "round-turning mill" is a kind of genera-
tor, an energy source that gives his hero the power to make the skies
of piety come tumbling down. And unlike the Bible's and Milton's Samson, Lawrence's will certainly survive: "My head," he says, "is thick
enough to stand it, the smash."

Indeed, not only will Lawrence's revolutionary survive, he will
be "Lord of the dark and moving hosts / Before I die." As such a lord,
however, this blind and blinding hero begins to seem like someone
other or larger than simply the Samson of Biblical or Miltonic legend.
Lawrence has in any case been careful only to refer to him as "the
revolutionary," never specifically naming him Samson. Now we begin to
see why, for this speaker does seem to have a multiple identity.
Blind and vengeful, he is Samson. But potent with dark energy, mysteriously regal, he is also Lucifer (who was exiled in darkness but lived
to create an alternative kingdom), Osiris (who was torn apart in defeat
but reconstituted as the ruler of the underworld), and Dis/Pluto (who
has been defined as the Lord of the Dead but whose marriage with
Persephone sustains the "moving hosts" of the living).

Lawrence has been suggesting, then, that at the center of things,
when one has embarked upon the journey into darkness, tombs become
wombs, hell becomes an experience more ecstatic than heaven, and night
implies fiercer energies than day. His exploration of such mystical
paradoxes neatly links "The Revolutionary" with its successor, "The
Evening Land," for although the latter work seems at first like just
another one of this poet's characteristically apocalyptic polemics
on the subject of America, much of its imagery extends and elaborates
upon the story of the Black Mass voyage that Birds, Beasts and Flowers

is covertly narrating. As most Lawrence critics have noted, at this
point in his career--before he had literally left the old world for
the new--Lawrence's America was as mythic a realm as Shakespeare's
or Blake's. The poet/narrator of Birds, Beasts and Flowers is quite
willing to confess this. "Oh, America / The sun sets in you. / Are
you the grave of our day?" he asks, then devotes the rest of the poem
to an analysis of his own anxiety about the "death" America promises.
Is it what Lawrence's own revolutionary lord would define as a real
death, the death that permeates the long ash-gray coffin of England,
the "winding sheet of . . . boundless love / Like a poison gas?" Or
is it a death that implies Osiris-like rebirth? America has an
"elvishness," he declares, that "carries me beyond . . . what we call
human, / Carries me where I want to be carried." Perhaps then, he
implies, America as the "evening land" is a way station on the downward, night sea-journey that began when the Persephone-like speaker
of "Pomegranate" ate a few "glittering compact drops of dawn." If so,
the real goal is still ahead; it is the raging central core the poet/
speaker sees in a kind of dream-vision that ends this section.

     Perversely entitled "Peace," this concluding poem is about the
volcanic apocalypse that would occur if the Satanic/Plutonic energy
Lawrence seeks should suddenly surface, unbidden, as "Brilliant,
intolerable lava," engulfing "forests, cities, bridges," all the
historical monuments of "pale-face authority." Would it be "Peace"?
Would the traveler's urge to journey toward a blinding center finally
be satisfied? Or would the "dark and nude vast heaven" of that pre-
history we pious readers have labeled Satanic be fearsome and intolerable? Looking forward to the dramatic climaxes of this collection's
underground narrative--the unsuccessful meeting with the snake in
Sicily and the successful encounter with "Old Nick" in America--
Lawrence's wonderful image of lava "walking like a royal snake down
the mountain towards the sea" gives us an obvious clue to the hellish
consummation he undevoutly wishes. But although the poet/narrator has
here a definitive vision of the energy roaring behind the fissure in
the pomegranate, we are still left wondering, as the section concludes,
whether he himself will have the energy to take us further into the
heart of darkness.

                              III

     Those who have read all the way to the end of Birds, Beasts and
Flowers will know, of course, that Lawrence as poet/narrator does
seem, symbolically speaking, to reach his journey's goal, the promised
end of a penetration into the invisible fire behind the visible world.
Or rather, more accurately, his journey ends in a series of increasingly intense meetings with hell on earth, for more often than not
in these poems the underworld sends emissaries out or up to the poet
and his world. Thus almost all the poems in "Trees" are wondering
re-examinations of demonic plants that grow like trunks of darkness
out of what might be called the buried life. Just as the cracking
open of a pomegranate appropriately began the "Fruits" section, a
meditation upon cypresses--in fact, an attempt at dialogue with them--
significantly begins this section. Associated with Tuscany and the

lost, supposedly "evil" Etruscans (whose reputations Lawrence wishes to rescue), the cypress is also traditionally the death tree, dark, immortal, hovering like a black flame over the tombs of "the silenced races and all their abominations" as if it rose straight from the breast of hell. In this poem, therefore, Lawrence for the first time becomes openly shamanistic, summoning ghosts while repudiating the rational, pale-face optimism of Darwin: "They say the fit survive, / But I invoke the spirits of the lost." By the end of this section, moreover, his invocations no longer need the solidity of trees to focus them; they are addressed directly to larger forces—to the "Sun of black void heat" (_CP_, p. 301) and the "red thing . . . blood-dark" for which we have no word but "moon" (_CP_, p. 302).

Similarly, in "Flowers" more messengers from the underground kingdom appear in the country of daylight to declare esoteric meanings to the poet/narrator. Almond blossom storms up from the center of things to set "supreme annunciation to the world." Purple anemones rise like hell on earth, "little hells of colour, caves of darkness" in pursuit of a lost Persephone. Sicilian cyclamens whisper "witch-craft / Like women at a well, the dawn-fountain." Royal hibiscus, worn by a pagan Eve "Before she humbled herself, and knocked her knees with dirt," offers an "exquisite assertion . . . Risen from the roots," and furious salvia flower, red as an "extinct race" of "red angry men," flickers like "living wrath / Upon the smouldering air" with a "throat of brimstone-molten angry gold." It is no wonder that, having con-fronted and contemplated so many emissaries of hell, Lawrence feels he must pause in the next section to attempt an even more direct re-examination of the Christian Bible, and specifically of the New Testament's Evangelistic Beasts.

As I commented earlier, his Matthew is a traveler back and forth exactly like his Persephone. Since Lawrence is subversively revising Christian mythology, however, he inevitably emphasizes the necessity of the downward plunge rather than the joys of the upward flight. Thus many of Matthew's self-defining statements could act as Blakeian epigraphs for the book as a whole: "Put me down again on the earth, Jesus, on the brown soil / Where flowers sprout in the acrid humus, and fade into humus again," or "At evening I must leave off my wings of the spirit . . . And I must resume my nakedness like a fish, sink-ing down the dark reversion of night / Like a fish seeking the bottom, Jesus," or "Remember, Saviour / That my heart . . . Throws still the dark blood back and forth / In the avenues where the bat hangs sleep-ing, upside-down / And to me undeniable."

Upside-down: as so often, Lawrence is his own best exegete, for the remaining three Evangelical Beasts present images of Mark, Luke, and John that are as upside-down as any bat. The poet-narrator's bat-vision of a "reversed zenith," creates, for instance, a Blakeian parable of the fall of the lion of the spirit from a savage king of the beasts to an ignominious servant of the redcross Lamb, a Urizenic sheepdog with a bourgeois Victorian family. Similarly, Lawrence's upside-down consciousness leads him to argue that "Luke, the Bull, the father of substance," has been sadly bewitched by the Lamb, while in the most inevitable yet sardonic joke of all the phoenixlike Eagle of St. John, once the symbol of pure intellect, has become merely "the

badge of an insurance company," the emblem of profit-and-loss
capitalism. Serving as a kind of bridge between Lawrence's con-
frontations with the apparently inanimate vegetable kingdom and the
journey his poet/narrator must now take through the animal world,
these subversive redefinitions of Biblical symbols prepare us,
finally, for even more outrageous reappraisals to come: the snake who
is poisonous but lordly, the ass who was foolish because he carried
Jesus into Jerusalem, the demonic turkeycock who should replace
the ethereal peacock, the mountain lion who is more valuable than a
million people, the bulldog who ought to "learn" pagan loyalty rather
than Christian loving, and the tortoise whose inchoate orgasmic scream
is a kind of anti-Platonic paradigm for human speech.

As the creatures the poet/narrator encounters grow more complex,
more neural, more autonomous, it becomes increasingly clear that now,
besides being talismans of Hades, they are totemic familiars, spiritual guides and judges; besides representing the underworld, they
incarnate its grave ruler. Paradoxically, in other words, the "higher"
Lawrence's quest takes him on the evolutionary scale, the closer he
comes to a significant dialogue with the "lower" kingdom. But the
obstacles to true communion are of course very great. Like the space
traveler that in a sense he is, this poet/narrator must catch at
obscure hints and decipher mysterious signs as if he were a linguist
decoding an extragalactic language on the basis of only a few fragmentary clues. The Christian humanist assumptions that he cannot
escape, moreover, cause attempts at dialogue to break down on several
occasions--in "The Mosquito," in "Man and Bat," and in "Fish," for
example, and most famously in "Snake." By the end of "Reptiles,"
however, in "Tortoise Shout," the poet/narrator has heard what we
might define as the primal scream of hell, the "strange faint coition
yell / Of the male tortoise at extremity / Torn from under the very
edge of the farthest far-off horizon of life," and he has grasped the
deep metaphysical connection between this cry, "the first elements of
foreign speech / On wild dark lips," and the "Osiris-cry of abandonment" uttered in extremis by Christ, whose crucifixion plunged him
from the upper air into the shadowy underworld of the Egyptian god.

It is significant, I think, that after "Tortoise Shout" Lawrence
as poet/narrator begins to engage in far more vigorous dialogue with
the beings he encounters, translating the ass's speech, for instance,
and himself admonishing the he-goat ("Fight, old Satan, with a selfish
will") and the elephants ("Serve, vast mountainous blood"). Finally,
at the edge of a canyon--a fissure in the earth not unlike the crack
in the pomegranate--in "the heart of the west," in the symbolic shadow
of a subversively "black crucifix like a dead tree spreading wings,"
this phenomenal traveler has his visionary encounter with the shrouded,
demonic Indian who calls himself "Old Harry" or "Old Nick." "Across
the pueblo river"--a stream as mystically significant, in this context, as Styx or Lethe--"That dark old demon and I / . . . say a few
words to each other," Lawrence tells us. But the few words they say
are important indeed: "Where's your God, you white one? / Where's
your white God?" the Indian/demon asks, and the poet/narrator confesses that "He fell to dust as the twilight fell, / Was fume as I
trod / The last step out of the east." At this, albeit reluctantly,

the dark interlocutor renames him "Red Wolf," and metaphorically
speaking Lawrence does become a red wolf, symbolically entering the
realm of Birds, Beasts and Flowers that has grown increasingly less
alien throughout his narrative. For when the "dark old father" pro-
tests fastidiously that "We take no hungry stray from the pale-face,"
the poet declares "Father, you are not asked. / I am come. I am here.
/ The red-dawn-wolf / Sniffs round your place."

As I began by arguing, this transformation is the principal
denouement of Lawrence's narrative. Like the protagonist of Look!,
the poet/narrator has here entered into some "condition of blessedness," although its characteristics are subversive indeed. Nor do
they always seem like blessings, even after Lawrence's Blakeian redefinitions. We are told in "Men in New Mexico," for example, that
in this new world there is "a dark membrane over the will, holding a
man down / Even when the mind has flickered awake." This black membrane is perhaps the weight of blind Samson's "dark and nude vast
heavens," finally experienced firsthand; this is perhaps what it
means, not just to imagine Osiris but to become Osiris, if only for
a moment.

Still, despite its dangers, a demonic blessedness does now
permeate everything, and Lawrence says he wants it to. Not only has
the poet/narrator himself become a beast, a red wolf, in "Autumn at
Taos" the whole landscape becomes animal and magical: the pines are
bear fur, the desert a wolf pelt, the aspens, significantly, the
"glistening-feathered legs of the hawk of Horus," legs of the divine
son of Osiris who was conceived through a downside-up annunciation
from the kingdom of the dead. In "Spirits Summoned West," moreover,
Lawrence's poet/narrator asks others from that kingdom to forget
their old rational/social functions as "wives and mothers" and join
him in this new world as newly powerful virgins, Persephones to his
Dis. Then, as if wondering how long a new world can stay new, in
"The American Eagle," he adds a last ironic question about his own
vision of a new hell and a new earth: can the eagle of the Rockies,
the demonic "bird of men that are masters," sustain its attack upon
the redcross Lamb, or will the emblematic American bird itself be
tamed by the "dove of Liberty," and become a mere goose laying an
"addled golden egg"?

                              IV

As this last poem suggests, and as most students of Lawrence
will suspect anyway, America both as myth and as reality is crucial
to the metamorphic journey Birds, Beasts and Flowers describes.
Indeed, some readers may object that the narrative I have defined
so far is simply an account of this writer's famous emigration from
the old world to the new one, a trip which accompanied and inspired
his composition of this cycle of poems. For my purpose here, however,
what is most significant about this journey--at least as the poet/
narrator of Birds, Beasts and Flowers presents it--is the paradoxical direction in which it was taken. "I'm a pale face like a homeless
dog / That has followed the sun from the dawn through the east,"
Lawrence writes in "Red Wolf," "Trotting east and east and east till

the sun himself went home, / And left me homeless here in the dark
at your door." And of course that is simply true. Lawrence and Frieda
went east from England to Italy, then east from Italy to Ceylon,
Australia, San Francisco, and Taos. Both in reality and in these poems,
in other words, Lawrence went west paradoxically, by going east. He
did not take the conventional "westward ho" journey that rational
"empire" supposedly ought to take in western culture, nor did he
ride consciously, wearily westward like Donne riding toward death.[32]
Thus he seems really to have confirmed his own subversive desire for
a downside-up annunciation by going east to get west, entering the
dawn fissure of the pomegranate to reach the evening land of America.

Prepared as he was for transformation, every place Lawrence
touched upon in the course of his actual journey was, as we know,
radiant with a "symbolic meaning." England, pious and rational, was
the Urizenic heaven from which he had fallen--or exiled himself--like
a new Lucifer. In the garden of his childhood, he obviously felt,
Blakeian priests in black gowns were walking their rounds and binding
with briars his joys and desires. Italy, closer to the pagan world
yet ruined by history, must have seemed to be a kind of purgatorial
paysage moralisé, offering him the talismanic pomegranate through
whose crack he could enter like Persephone into the roaring energy
behind appearances. Even the southward journey within Italy may have
seemed symbolic, for in a sense the Lawrences traveled backwards in
time, from Renaissance Tuscany to pagan Sicily, and, going south, they
journeyed from the calm vineyards around Florence to the quaking
slopes of Aetna, from common ground to royal lava. Finally, like his
own Persephone, Lawrence went west by going east; he reached the
country he defined as the evening land of death--and rebirth--by entering the morning and groping his way to the darkness behind the light,
the numinous behind the luminous. As he traveled, moreover, he passed
(both literally and figuratively) through a cycle of seasons--fall,
winter, spring/summer, fall--and these help structure his narrative
almost as much as its paradoxical geography.

Did Lawrence do any of this consciously, intentionally--that is,
did he travel east-west for mystical as well as practical reasons? Or
was the conjunction of real voyaging and fantasy voyage merely a coincidence? Given Lawrence's Romantic tendency to mythologize himself,
his habit of divining meanings by reading the entrails of his own
experience, I think we have to assume that he did perceive a message
both in his poems and in his east-west passage, and that perhaps
intuitively, perhaps intellectually, he arranged his poems so as to
present this message as dramatically as possible. He may have understood, too, that the journey his poems described was a voyage of
literary as well as spiritual metamorphosis, a journey from one genre
into another. For, depending as they do on folk tales, myths, and
revisionary encounters with the invisible powers that manifest themselves in the visible, Lawrence's poetic notes from underground not
only linked two stages in his career, they actually played a crucial
part in his transformation from the romantic yet realistic novelist
of Women in Love and Aaron's Rod to the mythic romancer of The Plumed
Serpent, The Escaped Cock, "The Woman Who Rode Away," and Last Poems.

As he traveled away from England, I believe, Lawrence traveled
continually away from the traditional novel and increasingly toward

the fabulist mode in which he was to be one of our century's major
pioneers. And though this will sound like yet another paradox, I
would speculate that it was important to this poet-novelist's novelistic evolution that the narrative of Birds, Beasts and Flowers
was submerged in poetry. Liberating him temporarily from the exigen-
cies of all plot except those mythic paradigms which seemed to him
to be implicit in his own voyage, the composition of this poem
sequence prepared him not only for such a generic experiment as The
Plumed Serpent but also for the revisionary mythmaking of The Escaped
Cock and other late tales. Ultimately, by going east toward the primitive dawn-sources of all culture, toward the poetry at the heart of
prose, Lawrence had gone further west, deeper into what we call
modernism. In a sense, then, the poems of Birds, Beasts and Flowers
not only tell the story of his transformation, they are the story.

V

Of course, as most of the contemporary Lawrentian poets mentioned
earlier would understand, this story is one that continues throughout
the rest of Lawrence's life-and-poetry, for, like a subversive form of
the plot that organizes all Christian liturgy, it is a tale of the
cyclical mysteries of transformation that must be re-enacted time and
time again. Certainly, although most of the meditative verses in Last
Poems are more overtly religious than the Birds, Beasts and Flowers
works, they are just as diabolically unorthodox. Indeed, like the
Birds, Beasts and Flowers poems, they frequently present downside-up
versions of Christian myths. Thus, where the central Christian transformation is from flesh to spirit, the crucial Lawrentian transformation, throughout both Last Poems and the late stories, is from spirit
to flesh, as if Lawrence were now actually writing the uncommon prayers
he wants spoken as part of the Black Mass he imagined in Birds, Beasts
and Flowers. Even the newly fleshly Jesus of The Escaped Cock seems
rather Satanic, with his black pointed beard and "dusky skin" that has
a "silvery glisten,"[33] so that it is quite appropriate for the priestess of Isis to identify him with Osiris, another demonic power of the
lower depths. (In Apocalypse, moreover, Lawrence actually does conflate
Christ with the "Lord of the Underworld [and with] Hermes, the guide
of souls through the death-world, over the hellish stream. . . ."[34]
    It is not surprising, then, that More Pansies includes a cheeky
little anti-sermon called "The Church," in which Lawrence sketches a
few theological pointers for his heretical new Church of spirit-
turned-flesh:

      If I was a member of the Church of Rome
      I should advocate reform:
      the marriage of priests
      the priests to wear rose-colour or magenta in the streets
      to teach the Resurrection in the flesh
      to start the year on Easter Sunday
      to add the mystery of Joy-in-Resurrection to the Mass
      to inculcate the new conception of the Risen Man (CP, p. 609).

Yet another late Pansy, simply entitled "Lucifer," is even more
specific about the poet's allegiance to the Blakeian angel whose fall,
according to Lawrence, paradoxically intensified his brightness:

> Angels are bright still, though the brightest fell.
> But tell me, tell me, how do you know
> that he lost any of his brightness in falling?
> He only fell out of your ken, you orthodox angels,
> you dull angels, tarnished with centuries of conventionality
>
> (CP, p. 614).

Finally, in a revision of this poem that was included in the Last
Poems notebooks, Lawrence revealed himself, in a kind of Satanic
epiphany, as the diabolist that I believe he always was:

> Angels are bright still, though the brightest fell.
> But tell me, tell me, how do you know
> he lost any of his brightness in the falling?
> In the dark-blue depths, under layers and layers of darkness,
> I see him more like a ruby, a gleam from within
> of his own magnificence
> coming like the ruby in the invisible dark, glowing
> with his own annunciation, towards us (CP, p. 697).

"Glowing with his own annunciation": proud as any devil, this Lucifer
is clearly a demonically self-made god, and thus it is the "magnificence" of his fallen flesh that magically hushes and darkens even the
brightest noon in which Lawrence finds himself. Similarly, his emissaries, the pomegranate flowers of Andraitx that Lawrence describes
in yet another late poem, mysteriously make "noon . . . suddenly dark
. . . lustrous . . . silent and dark." At the same time, testifying
to the sacred erotic power of the god, the poet notices that in this
anti-Miltonic darkness at noon "from out the foliage of the secret
loins / red flamelets here and there reveal / a man, a woman there"
(CP, pp. 605-6).

Significantly, the holy Lucifer to whom Lawrence alludes in all
these poems is the same subversive god that Denise Levertov describes
in a 1966 poem called "Eros,"[35] for as she says,

> simply he is
> the temple of himself,
>
> hair and hide
> a sacrifice of blood and flowers
> on his altar
>
> if any worshipper
> kneel or not.

In the end, Levertov's revision of Lawrence's re-vision of Lucifer
suggests that, though Lawrence himself may once have fallen out of
the ken of orthodox literary critics, though he would never be praised

at Mr. Eliot's Sunday Morning Service, he still hangs gleaming, like the demonic Morning Star he loved, on the horizon of contemporary verse. Insisting that "the only Riches" are the self-created "Great Souls,"[36] he hymns a world without Established Churches, a world with only the flickering of sacred pomegranate seeds in the shadows behind the crack of dawn.

D. H. Lawrence and the Resurrection of the Body

JAMES C. COWAN

"I believe in the resurrection of the body," Lady Constance Chatterley says (LCL, p. 98),[1] and she means it rather literally in the here and now. D. H. Lawrence uses the Christian mystery of resurrection as a profound symbol for the emergence into living sensuality which he wanted to see humanity make in his time from the torpor, indeed the death and putrefaction, of an overintellectualized established religion that supported the economic and social status quo of an industrial society that turned people of flesh and blood into machines.

T. S. Eliot's Prufrock, though so far as I know in normal health physically, had experienced this death-in-life state as the walking zombie of the room where "the women come and go/Talking of Michael-angelo," whose magnificent masculine figures stand in sharp contrast to Prufrock's physique, with its thinning hair and thinner arms and legs. In the opening lines of "The Love Song of J. Alfred Prufrock," as Stephen Spender suggests, Prufrock projects his condition outward upon the landscape in the simile of the "patient etherised upon a table," an image unsuitable to describe an evening but singularly accurate in characterizing Prufrock and his anaesthetized society.[2] As Spender points out, Lawrence, rather than projecting modern man's torpor upon the natural environment, internalizes nature itself as a resurrective principle:[3]

A sun will rise in me,
I shall slowly resurrect,
already the whiteness of false dawn is on my inner ocean (CP, p. 513).

In his review of Tolstoi's Resurrection, Lawrence declares: "We have all this time been worshipping a dead Christ: or a dying." Christians should know better: "The Cross was only the first step into achievement.

94

The second step was the tomb. And the third step, whither?" In Tolstoi, he felt, "the stone was rolled upon him" (P, p. 737), leaving Christ a God of death and spirit, not of life and flesh. In "The Risen Lord," Lawrence claims that "the Churches insist on Christ Crucified, and rob us of the fruit of the year," for in the liturgical calendar, all the months from Easter to Advent belong to "the risen Lord" (P, p. 571). For Lawrence, "resurrection of the body" meant, in part, "resurrection of the flesh":

> If Jesus rose from the dead in triumph, a man on earth triumphant in renewed flesh, triumphant over the mechanical anti-life convention of Jewish priests, Roman despotism, and universal money-lust; triumphant above all over His own self-absorption, self-consciousness, self-importance; triumphant and free as a man in full flesh and full, final experience, even the accomplished acceptance of His own death; a man at last full and free in flesh and soul, a man at one with death: then He rose to become at one with life, to live the great life of the flesh and the soul together, as peonies or foxes do, in their lesser way. If Jesus rose as a full man, in full flesh and soul, then He rose to take a woman to Himself, to live with her, and to know the tenderness and blossoming of the twoness with her; He who had been hitherto so limited to His oneness, or His universality, which is the same thing (P II, p. 575).

Lawrence's theology perhaps owes something to the medieval Adamites, who sought to return man to the state of innocence before the Fall; or at least to Joachim of Flora, the thirteenth-century abbot, whose division of history into the epoch of the Father before Christ, the epoch of the Son from the Advent of Christ to the present, and the epoch of the Holy Ghost yet to come Lawrence had cited favorably in Movements in European History (MEH, pp. 193–94).

Without elaborating further on Lawrence's theological position, I want to suggest that "the risen Lord" throughout his canon, particularly in his later work, is a paradigm for a resurgence of the flesh and the deep, intuitive knowledge available to man through sensual awareness as equal in value to the mind and the mental-spiritual knowledge elevated by the Protestant-capitalist-materialist ethos of modern industrial society. If the emphasis in Western culture upon rational, objective knowledge validated in the laboratory may be seen as the masculine thrust of spirit, the externalization of Idea in the technological penetration, control, and exploitation of nature, from the smallest organism to the moon and stars, in the quest for immutable scientific law, then Lawrence's reaffirmation of intuitive, subjective knowledge validated experientially in the body is an attempt to redeem the feminine, the inward, the mutable as a significant mode of knowing lost to whole generations immured in the scientific method.

Lawrence's treatment of physicians is not kind--when they lend their skills in the once priestly art of medicine to the warfare state in conducting pre-induction physical examinations. In Kangaroo the first examining physicians encountered by Lawrence's persona, Somers, address him as one gentleman to another and reject the thin, apparently consumptive man for military service (K, p. 233). At a later stage in the war, when almost no one is being rejected, the doctors at the induction center treat him in far less gentlemanly fashion. They are contemptuous of his body, Somers feels, and sneeringly skeptical when he tells them he has had pneumonia three times and is threatened with consumption. He submits in silent rage as they examine his genitals and rectum. "Never again," he vows to himself, "never would he be touched again. And because they had handled his private parts, and looked into them, their eyes should burst and their hands should wither and their hearts should rot. So he cursed them in his blood . . ." (K, p. 261). And why? Why should Lawrence recoil from the same kind of physical examination which millions of men have undergone for military service? Lawrence's own neurotic motives aside, he recoils not from another's touching his body but from the body's being objectified, reduced to a static part in an inexorable mechanism for killing in a world without grace, rather than being treated reverently as subject and human, functional in an organic and holy world. Somers is not the German spy his Cornish neighbors accuse him of being; his subversion goes much deeper than that: "This trench and machine warfare is a blasphemy against life itself, a blasphemy which we are all committing" (K, p. 225).

In such a world, touch is violation. As Lawrence puts it in "Touch," a poem from Pansies:

> Since we are so cerebral
> we are humanly out of touch.
> And so we must remain.
> For if, cerebrally, we force ourselves into touch,
>   into contact
> physical and fleshly,
> we violate ourselves,
> we become vicious (CP, p. 468).

A basic tenet of Lawrence's thinking is that sensory or sensual experience should not be dominated by ideas or ideals mentally derived. Hence his pronouncements against "sex in the head" and his cry in another poem from Pansies:

Noli me tangere, touch me not.
O you creatures of mind, don't touch me!
O you mental fingers, O never put your hand on me!
O you with mental bodies, stay a little distance from me! (CP, p. 468).

And hence, in a third poem in the sequence, his call for "Chastity, beloved chastity" in "this mind-mischievous age":

> O leave me clean from mental fingering
> from the cold copulation of the will,
> from all the white self-conscious lechery
> the modern mind calls love! (CP, p. 469).

The alternative, in our age, as he suggests in a fourth poem in the sequence, is a resurrection of touch in the very blood:

Touch comes when the white mind sleeps
and only then.
Touch comes slowly, if ever; it seeps
slowly up in the blood of men
and women.

Soft slow sympathy
of the blood in me, of the blood in thee
rises and flashes insidiously
over the conscious personality
of each of us . . . .

Personalities exist apart;
and personal intimacy has no heart.
Touch is of the blood
uncontaminated, the unmental flood (CP, pp. 47-48).

There was an age, Lawrence postulates in Etruscan Places, when
touch had the nonmental yet sacramental quality he wants. In describing the wall paintings in the Tomba dei Vasi Dipinti (Tomb of the
Painted Vases), Lawrence remarks on the banquet scene with "the
bearded man softly touching the woman with him under the chin":

Rather gentle and lovely is the way he touches the woman under
the chin, with a delicate caress. That again is one of the
charms of the Etruscan paintings: they really have the sense
of touch; the people and the creatures are all really in touch.
It is one of the rarest qualities, in life as well as in art.
There is plenty of pawing and laying hold, but no real touch.
In pictures especially, the people may be in contact, embracing
or laying hands on one another. But there is no soft flow of
touch. The touch does not come from the middle of the human
being. It is merely a contact of surfaces, and a juxtaposition
of objects. . . . Here, in this faded Etruscan painting, there
is a quiet flow of touch that unites the man and the woman on
the couch, the timid boy behind, the dog that lifts his nose,
even the very garlands that hang from the wall (EP, pp. 77-78).

So it seems to Lawrence because he envisions ancient Etruria as a
civilization whose knowledge emerged from integrated physical, intellectual, and emotional being instead of compartmentalizing both knowledge and being into so many intersecting surfaces and manipulatable
fragments:

It must have been a wonderful world, that old world where
everything appeared alive and shining in the dusk of contact
with all things, not merely as an isolated individual thing
played upon by daylight; where each thing had a clear outline,
visually, but in its very clarity was related emotionally or
vitally to strange other things, one thing springing from
another, things mentally contradictory fusing together
emotionally (EP, pp. 112-13).

     This vitalistic philosophy was rooted in a nonanthropomorphic
religion whose gods "were not beings, but symbols of elemental powers":
"The undivided Godhead, if we can call it such, was symbolised by the
mundum, the plasm-cell with its nucleus: that which is the very beginning, instead of, as with us, by a personal god, a person being the
very end of all creation or evolution" (EP, pp. 87).
     The mundum as plasm-cell is the central metaphor for man in the
psychological theory which Lawrence elaborates in Psychoanalysis and
the Unconscious and Fantasia of the Unconscious. In Lawrence's mythic
metaphor, "The original nucleus, formed from the two parent nuclei at
our conception, remains always primal and central, and is always the
original fount and knowledge that I am I" (FU, p. 75). As the first
of four dynamic psychic centers in what Lawrence calls "the first
field of consciousness," this center remains "within the solar plexus"
as the medium of a sympathetic, positive mode of knowing by incorporating the outer world into the self. Through this medium, in vital
polarity with the mother's solar plexus, the infant maintains a pure,
effluent, preverbal communication with her. Individuation occurs as
the original nucleus divides (though paradoxically Lawrence suggests,
in contradiction of the principle of cell division, that it remains
in the solar plexus): "This second nucleus, the nucleus born of recoil,
is the nuclear origin of all the great nuclei of the voluntary system,
which are the nuclei of assertive individualism" (FU, p. 76). In the
adult, this second center remains in what Lawrence calls "the lumbar
ganglion" as a subjective medium of differentiation and negativity:
"I am myself, and these others are not as I am" (FU, p. 79). The
third and fourth centers emerge as the first two divide horizontally.
Whereas the centers of the lower dynamic plane are subjective in
nature, those of the upper dynamic plane are objective, and upper and
lower are supposed to complement each other (PU, p. 34). The cardiac
plexus has the same relation to the thoracic ganglion that the solar
plexus has to the lumbar ganglion. Like the solar plexus, the cardiac
plexus is positive and sympathetic, but rather than incorporating the
other into the self, it sees in the other an object of worship in
which to lose the self: "The wonder is without me. . . The other being
is now the great positive reality, I myself am as nothing" (FU, p. 78).
The thoracic ganglion, like the lumbar ganglion, is negative in polarity, but whereas the lumbar ganglion functions instinctually, for
example in expressing rage, the thoracic ganglion is the seat of the
spiritual will whereby one manipulates others. In harmonious balance
with the lower centers, the upper centers serve useful functions. The
thoracic ganglion becomes the source of "eager curiosity, of the delightful desire to pick things to pieces, and the desire to put them
together again, the desire to 'find out,' and the desire to invent
. . ." (FU, p. 80). In the integrated individual, Lawrence suggests,
not only do the four dynamic psychic centers function harmoniously
together but also they function in balanced polarity with the psychic
centers of the other in a human relationship.
     In May 1918, Lawrence wrote to Edith Eder, the wife of Dr. David
Eder and the sister of Barbara Low, both of them London psychoanalysts,
asking her to find him a book on the human nervous system with maps.
Had she referred him to a standard medical text such as Gray's Anatomy

of the Human Body, then available in the twentieth edition revised, edited by Warren H. Lewis (Philadelphia: Lea and Febiger, 1918), pp. 701-21, he would have found a scientific exposition of the two broad divisions of the human nervous system into the central nervous system, the brain and spinal cord, and the peripheral nervous system, composed of the voluntary nervous system, which mediates voluntary movements, and the autonomic, or as Lewis's edition of Gray calls it, the sympathetic nervous system, which mediates involuntary physical functions of the glands, blood vessels, and the like.

But Lawrence, while sometimes claiming scientific validity and sometimes admitting to scientific inexactitude, "particularly in ter- minology" (FU, p. 36), makes no claim to objective scientific knowl- edge based on the doctrines of logical positivism, which limits science to what can be deduced by rigorous logic from the observation and classification of factual data and sensory phenomena. Rather he posited a "subjective science," as he called it, derived from the ancients, from the vitalists and the animists, from the Etruscans and the Egyptians; a science of intuition and imagination rather than of cause and effect; a science in which poet and healer are not separate, as in the modern world, but the same, as in the poet-priest-king- medicine man tradition.

Lawrence's "science" is that of a poet. He wrote: "This pseudo- philosophy of mine--'pollyanalytics,' as one of my respected critics might say--is deduced from the novels and poems, not the reverse" (FU, p. 57). Even so, he does not proceed deductively but declares: "I proceed by intuition" (FU, p. 54). And the system he proposes is not based on objective fact but on metaphor. His four dynamic psychic centers are all parts of the autonomic nervous system, transmitting impulses and mediating involuntary functions, not, as he seems to sug- gest, the great integrative centers, which modern neuroanatomy locates in the central nervous system, of such complex functions as integra- tion, origin of impulses, and consciousness. So what is the value of a metaphor rooted in inaccuracy or of a nonscientific science? For Lawrence the value lies in formulating a personal myth to affirm what the body knows as opposed to what the mind knows. Implicit in his theory is the criticism that in the modern world the upper centers of mind and spirit have gained the upper hand while the lower centers of body and blood have declined. The will dominates; instinct atrophies.

To resurrect the science of the ancients, then, is to resurrect the body. That is what Lawrence undertakes imaginatively in Lady Chatterley's Lover. From the beginning of her marriage, Lady Constance Chatterley had wanted children, but at that time she had thought that "sex was merely an accident, or an adjunct, one of the curious, obso- lete, organic processes which persisted in its own clumsiness, but was not really necessary" (LCL, p. 11). Now as Sir Clifford, who has returned from the war paralyzed from the waist down, sits with his friends in long, intellectual conversation, she muses on their curious one-sidedness: "How many evenings had Connie sat and listened to the manifestations of these four men: . . . It was fun. Instead of kiss- ing you, and touching you, they revealed their minds to you. It was great fun! But what cold minds" (LCL, p. 39). Formulating a vague plan to have a child, she recalls the Biblical text, "Go ye into the streets

and byways of Jerusalem and see if you can find <u>a man</u>" (<u>LCL</u>, p. 73).
The relationship might even be impersonal if forces greater than their
social selves were present. Shortly after this Connie comes upon
Mellors, the gamekeeper, bathing in the back yard of his cottage:

> He was naked to the hips, his velveteen breeches slipping down
> over his slender loins. And his white slim back was curved over
> a big bowl of soapy water, in which he ducked his head, shaking
> his head with a queer, quick little motion, lifting his slender
> white arms, and pressing the soapy water from his ears, quick,
> subtle as a weasel playing with water, and utterly alone (<u>LCL</u>,
> p. 75).

This scene, which resembles closely the bathing girl scene at the end
of Chapter 4 of James Joyce's <u>A Portrait of the Artist as a Young Man</u>,
recounts an experience as remarkable as Stephen's epiphany of dove-
like female beauty, yet this is an ephiphany, as it were, of the solar
plexus, not of the mind:

> In spite of herself, she had had a shock. After all, merely
> a man washing himself; commonplace enough, Heaven knows!
> Yet in some curious way it was a visionary experience: it
> had hit her in the middle of her body. She saw the clumsy
> breeches slipping down over the pure, delicate, white loins,
> the bones showing a little, and the sense of aloneness, of a
> creature purely alone, overwhelmed her. Perfect, white, soli-
> tary nudity of a creature that lives alone, and inwardly alone.
> And beyond that, a certain beauty of a pure creature. Not the
> stuff of beauty, not even the body of beauty, but a lambency,
> the warm, white flame of a single life, revealing itself in
> contours that one might touch: a body!
> Connie had received the shock of vision in her womb,
> and she knew it; it lay inside her (<u>LCL</u>, p. 76).

That evening, looking at her own body in the mirror, Connie thinks,
"What a frail, easily hurt, rather pathetic thing a human body is,
naked; somehow a little unfinished, incomplete!" (<u>LCL</u>, p. 79). She
sees that, "instead of ripening its firm, down-running curves, her
body was flattening and going a little harsh. It was as if it had not
had enough sun and warmth; it was a little grayish and sapless" (<u>LCL</u>,
p. 80). Deprived of its very existence, "her body was going meaningless, going full and opaque, so much insignificant substance" (<u>LCL</u>,
p. 80). Tommy Dukes, who seems at times to deliver Lawrence's own
criticism of his society and his age, confirms Connie's judgment of
their bodiless and meaningless existence, but looks to the future:
"There might even be real men, in the next phase. . . . <u>We're</u> not
men, and the women aren't women. We're only cerebrating makeshifts,
mechanical and intellectual experiments" (<u>LCL</u>, p. 86).
     What is it that stands between Connie Chatterley and the life
of her own body? Lawrence suggests that it is mental life, the habit
of living from the mind alone instead of the vital centers of the
body, or, worse, the motivating of these centers of spontaneous

instinct by ideas: "How she hated words, always coming between her and life: they did the ravishing, if anything did: ready made words and phrases" (LCL, p. 108).

Yet opposed to the world of words, Sir Clifford Chatterley's trivial if fashionably witty writing and conversation, the intellectual counterpart of his mining industry, is the world of organic nature, the forest preserve of the old England on which the mines encroach further and further. Connie's second epiphany of the body comes at the gamekeeper's hut as she watches a pheasant chick, which has just emerged from the mundum of the egg, bravely asserting its identity to the universe:

> . . . it was the most alive little spark of a creature in seven kingdoms at that moment. Connie crouched to watch in a sort of ecstasy. Life, life! Pure, sparky, fearless new life! New life! So tiny and so utterly without fear! (LCL, p. 133).

Mellors gives her a chick to hold:

> She took the little drab thing between her hands, and there it stood, on its impossible little stalks of legs, its atom of balancing life trembling through its almost weightless feet into Connie's hands. But it lifted its handsome, clean-shaped little head boldly, and looked sharply round, and gave a little "peep."
> "So adorable! So cheeky!" she said softly.
> The keeper, squatting beside her, was also watching with an amused face the bold little bird in her hands. Suddenly he saw a tear fall on to her wrist (LCL, p. 135).

The resurrection of the flesh begins almost immediately as Mellors, who in his taciturn disappointment in marriage had thought the sexual life was finished for him, feels "the old flame shooting and leaping up in his loins, that he had hoped was quiescent for ever" (LCL, p. 135). The two make love in the hut on an army blanket on the floor. Connie lies as if in a dream:

> The activity, the orgasm was his, all his; she could strive for herself no more. Even the tightness of his arm round her, even the intense movement of his body, and the springing seed in her, was a kind of sleep, from which she did not begin to rouse till he had finished and lay softly panting against her breast (LCL, p. 137).

Feminist critics like Kate Millett have deplored Connie's passivity[4] and missed the genuine tenderness of Mellors's regard for her. I do not think that Lawrence sees himself as writing a poetic marriage manual any more than I think that his direct description of sexual acts in the novel tends to deprave and corrupt. Lawrence is neither prescribing passivity for women nor titillating bourgeois men. I take Connie's sleep-like state as a symbolic death of her mental life presaging a resurrection of the body.

This rebirth is an evolution into life, developed gradually in the novel in the sexual experiences which Connie and Mellors share. For valid medical description of sexual data, phenomena observed and catalogued with scientific conclusions drawn from it, Masters's and Johnson's Human Sexual Response is, perhaps, more reliable than Lady Chatterley's Lover. But having said so, I am reminded that in Human Sexual Inadequacy, Masters and Johnson as sex therapists characteristically turn to the touch and tenderness that informed Lawrence's last major novel. Sir Clifford Chatterley, his lower centers literally paralyzed, rolls over the flowers of the wood in his motorized wheel chair, a symbol for his whole mechanical being. Connie and Mellors, vulnerable but reborn, reject the single-minded life of surface mentality and the machine civilization that it serves. Hermits of love, as impractical as the love saints of John Donne's "The Canonization," they burn like tapers and rise in the flame like the phoenix, Lawrence's image of resurrection par excellence. "We fucked a flame into being," Mellors writes to Connie:

> You can't insure against the future, except by really believing in the best bit of you, and in the power behind it. So I believe in the little flame between us. . . . It's my Pentecost, the forked flame between me and you. . . . That's what I abide by, and will abide by, Cliffords and Berthas, colliery companies and governments and the money-mass of people all notwithstanding (LCL, p. 364).

Although the civilization as a whole seems doomed, the "forked flame" of sexual tenderness and the baby Connie carries in her womb are symbols of the hope for individual love with which the novel ends.

The "resurrection of the body" becomes, finally, the central theme in the last novella Lawrence published in his lifetime, appearing in London under the title The Man Who Died but published first in Paris as The Escaped Cock (1929), titles which reflect opposing cultural emphases on death and rebirth. Although Lawrence clearly bases his story on Biblical accounts of Christ's appearances after death, he does not identify the protagonist as Christ, because he has rejected His messianic mission, or Jesus, because that would restrict him to the historical Jesus, but simply as "the man," for the purpose of wholly humanizing and secularizing the figure by embodying in him the principle of life renewed in the flesh rather than in the spirit. The essay "The Risen Lord," written in the same year, is an excellent gloss on the novella.

In another paper, I have demonstrated Lawrence's technique of making Biblical allusions in a context which consistently alters the original heavenly or spiritual meaning to an earthly, physical one. For example, John's account of Christ's words to Mary Magdalene, "Touch me not; for I am not yet ascended to my Father: but go to my brethren, and say unto them, I ascend to my Father, and your Father; and to my God, and your God" (John 20:17), is revised in Lawrence's version to read, "Don't touch me, Madeleine. . . . Not yet! I am not yet healed and in touch with men" (MWD, p. 24), for the purpose of suggesting a shift in allegiance from the spiritual forces implied in

ascending "to my Father" to the physical awareness of being "in touch
with men." Lawrence had been hostile to John's doctrine of creation
by the Logos (John 1:1) at least as far back as the unpublished Foreword to Sons and Lovers, which attempts to restore the primacy of
flesh over word. Now the risen man concludes:

> The Word is but the midge that bites at evening. Man is tor-
> mented with words like midges, and they follow him right into
> the tomb. But beyond the tomb they cannot go. Now I have passed
> the place where words can bite no more and the air is clear,
> and there is nothing to say, and I am alone within my own skin,
> which is the walls of all my domain (MWD, p. 38).

The Apostle Paul's definition of the meaning of the Resurrection is
that "our Saviour Jesus Christ . . . hath abolished death, and hath
brought life and immortality to light through the gospel" (II Timothy
1:10), but Lawrence's risen man wants only to heal his wounds and
enjoy "the immortality of being alive without fret. For in the tomb
he had left his striving self . . . ." (MWD, p. 39).

The escaped cock of Lawrence's title, an allusion to the cock
that crowed after Peter's third denial of Christ on the night of his
trial, refers literally to a gamecock which breaks his fetters at
the same moment that the man awakens "from a long sleep in which he
[has been] tied up" in the tomb, and figuratively, of course, to the
phallus and the new vital life of the blood. Part II of the novella
introduces the Isis-Osiris myth in the risen man's journey to the
temple of Isis in Search, where he stays in a cave of goats, an obvious
reference to Pan. Both his sepulchre, "a carved hole in the rock"
(MWD, p. 7) and the cave, a dark place in which there is "a little
basin of rock where the maidenhair fern [fringes] a dripping mouthful
of water" (MWD, p. 62) are womb symbols. His emergence from the tomb
marks his rebirth into physical life, but his emergence from the cave
signals a rebirth of long repressed sexuality. When he goes to the
priestess, who identifies him with the lost Osiris, he admits to
himself, "I am almost more afraid of this touch than I was of death.
For I am more nakedly exposed to it" (MWD, p. 84). "It has hurt so
much!" he says to her. "You must forgive me if I am held back." But
the woman answers softly, "Let me anoint you! . . . Let me anoint
the scars!" (MWD, pp. 87-88). Through this touch, he realizes why
he had been put to death: "I had asked them to serve me with the
corpse of their love. And in the end I offered them only the corpse
of my love." But his followers could not love "with dead bodies,"
and he reflects, "If I had kissed Judas with a live love, perhaps he
would never have kissed me with death" (MWD, pp. 89-90).

This new self-knowledge signals a growth in being that is inwardly organic: as in the poem "Sun in Me," "a new sun was coming up
in him" (MWD, p. 93). Whereas Christ had built his church upon the
rock of St. Peter (Matthew 16:18), the risen man, touching the woman,
thinks, "On this rock I built my life" (MWD, p. 94). Having rejected
the spiritual communion of the broken body that he had instituted
earlier, he wants now only the sacrament of the communion of flesh
with flesh. In a multileveled pun that is, at once, an allusion to

Scriptural Resurrection (Luke 24:6) and a literalization in sexual
terms of the Laurentian "resurrection of the body," the man says, at
the very moment of phallic erection, "I am risen!" (MWD, p. 94). After
their sexual consummation, he says, "This is the great atonement, the
being in touch," for in the new life "atonement" means human related-
ness that does not depend on the sacrifice of the divine pharmakos.
     Nevertheless, Lawrence's risen man, though de-Christianized,
is subtly mythicized through blending with the figure of Osiris. Both
Osiris and Christ are associated with the miracle of wine, both were
betrayed by "brothers," slain, and deified. But Christ's Resurrection
was followed by his Ascension, whereas Osiris, in the version of the
myth that concerns Lawrence, did not, properly speaking, rise. Instead
the goddess Isis went in search for the pieces of his body, which his
evil brother Set had dismembered and scattered along the Nile, and
she found all but the phallus. Lawrence so carefully fuses the two
figures that his risen man, though based on the celibate Jesus, is
made to supply what is missing in the Osiris myth. "Rare women," the
philosopher has told the priestess of Isis in Search, "wait for the
re-born man" (MWD, p. 58), and she is one of those rare women. Identified on the one hand with the Magna Mater archetype and on the other
with the tradition of the sacred prostitute, she is presented primarily
in terms of her priestly function of healing. Even her pregnancy is
not treated realistically but, in keeping with the tone of solemnity
appropriate to the quest romance, is linked with the fruition of the
natural cycle of the seasons. The man, too, rather than ascending in
a vertical, linear thrust of spirit like his Biblical counterpart,
identifies himself, like Osiris, with the seasonal cycle as he departs:
"Be at peace. And when the nightingale calls again from your valley-
bed, I shall come again, sure as Spring" (MWD, p. 100).

Lawrence versus Peeperkorn on Abdication; or, *What Happens to a Pagan Vitalist When the Juice Runs Out?*

MARK SPILKA

My text for this belated speculation on Lawrence's impotence is drawn from Thomas Mann's The Magic Mountain, which first appeared in Germany in 1924. Given Lawrence's classification of Mann as early as 1913 as "the last sick sufferer from the complaint of Flaubert," who "stood away from life as from a leprosy,"[1] this novel about isolated invalidism may seem more like a proof of Lawrence's charge than a likely source of illumination. But let us apply to it for the moment the generous maxim of another sick sufferer, John Stuart Mill, who believed that we need our enemies if we are to avoid our own weaknesses and complacencies.[2] Certainly we also need our friends, whatever their complacencies, especially those who have long known or suspected that Lawrence was impotent over the last five years of his life, but who still count themselves--as I complacently do--among his admirers. So let us be generous too with ourselves as we look at Mann's version of the same deficiencies--impotence, life abdication, self-destruction-- of which Lawrence had first accused him.

My text, then, is that late section of The Magic Mountain in which Mann introduces a richly attractive and grandly comic character, Mynheer Pieter Peeperkorn, into the hermetically feverish atmosphere of the tuberculosis sanatorium in which his young protagonist, Hans Castorp, has been entrapped for almost seven timeless years. Mynheer Peeperkorn is an elderly colonial Dutchman, a coffee planter from Java, a retired plutocrat whom Castorp himself describes as tall and lean, sparse-whiskered and bewrinkled, with small pale eyes and a high red forehead, yet unmistakably robust in his majestic stance. This newcomer at the international House Berghof is in his sixties; he suffers from a "catarrhal condition due to alcoholism" and from an intermittent malignant tropical fever. He arrives, however, with Madame Clavdia Chauchat, the "little puss" whose favors Hans had earlier enjoyed, and so brings "some dismay and perplexity" upon the hero of

Mann's tale.[3] But as usual Hans is able to extract some wisdom from
his dismayed perplexity, as with luck we may from ours.

In his essay of 1953 on "The Making of The Magic Mountain" Mann
describes how in 1912 he visited his ailing wife for three weeks at
a Swiss sanatorium high in the alps, how a doctor there discovered a
moist spot in his lungs and advised him to join his wife for the six
months' cure, and how--instead of taking his advice--he began writing
The Magic Mountain:

> In it I made use of the impressions gathered during my three
> weeks' stay. They were enough to convince me of the dangers of
> such a milieu for young people--and tuberculosis is a disease
> of the young. You will have got from my book an idea of the
> narrowness of this charmed circle of isolation and invalidism.
> It is a sort of substitute existence, and it can, in a rela-
> tively short time, wholly wean a young person from actual and
> active life. Everything there, including the conception of time,
> is thought of on a luxurious scale. The cure is always a matter
> of several months, [more] often of several years. But after the
> first six months the young person has not a single idea left
> save flirtation and the thermometer under his tongue. After the
> second six months in many cases he has even lost his capacity
> for any other ideas. He will become completely incapable of life
> in the flatland (MM, p. 719; italics mine).

Hans Castorp is not, finally, one of these cases. Within the
narrow pound here described he comes to entertain many ideas designed
to equip him for reentry into the life below. But Mann's awareness of
the incapacitating nature of sanatorium life gives us our first clue
to Lawrence's resistance to the idea of tuberculosis and the going
treatment for it.

As Mann also knew, the luxury of such prewar institutions was
economic as well as temporal: "They were only possible in a capital-
istic economy that was still functioning well and normally. Only under
such a system was it possible for patients to remain there year after
year at the family's expense" (MM, p. 719). His novel became "the
swan song" of that expensive way of life, which the retired coffee-
king Peeperkorn might well afford for his several ailments, but which
D. H. Lawrence could not afford until his waning years, long after
the decay within him had taken hold--and this too may explain his
long refusal to seek such treatment. Meanwhile, with uncanny prescience, Mann had placed his more opulent advocate of "actual and
active life" in the very setting Lawrence struggled to avoid, as if
to discover by alpine experiment how a captive pagan king reacts to
the loss of ithyphallic powers.

Aside from his robust leanness, and perhaps his fleshy nose,
Mann's majestic pagan bears little physical resemblance to Lawrence.
He differs also in his bibulous or bacchic disposition, for Lawrence's
capacity for the wines of life was limited and his more Puritan pagan-
ism made for modest rather than grand displays of the carnival spirit
which Hans once enjoyed with Clavdia, and which Mynheer Peeperkorn
seems to incarnate. But the force of Peeperkorn's vital personality

and the fresh life he brings to demoralized spirits at the sanatorium
are not altogether un-Lawrentian.

Mann did not, of course, have Lawrence in mind in creating
Peeperkorn. Though he wrote to a fellow mythologist (Karl Kerenyi)
in 1934 that he knew Lawrence's work "quite well" and found him "a
significant phenomenon and characteristic of our times," he said also
that he preferred Aldous Huxley--"one of the finest flowerings of
West European intellectualism"--to Lawrence, whose "fevered sensuality"
had "little appeal" for him.[4] Such "fevered sensuality" might give
us pause, especially in the tubercular and mythic context of The
Magic Mountain; but there were plenty of German models for Mann's
mythic sensualist, and German sources for his ideas: that "late-born
son of romanticism," "the thoroughly voluptuous Richard Wagner," for
example, whom Mann admired as "a great and greatly fortunate self-
glorifier and self-consummator" (L, pp. 136, 145); or the social
theoriest Hans Blüher, whose Role of the Erotic in Male Society seems
to have influenced Mann's views on male sexuality and on the ironic
and erotic relation between life and mind (L, pp. 103-6); or the
philosopher Friedrich Nietzsche, whose Dionysian and Apollonian
phases in The Birth of Tragedy speak to the same erotic ironies of
life and mind (L, pp. 108, 152); or, finally, the dramatist Gerhart
Hauptmann, whose kingly ways provided Mann with the external features
and mannerisms and with the "powerful and touching personality" of
the mighty Peeperkorn (L, pp. 131-33, 140-41). Mann's loving attitude
toward his comic creation, in a book whose design--he says--"repeatedly refers back to the mysticism of the body, the organic mystery"
(L, p. 139), is as evident in his letters as his text; but it is the
ironic play of mind upon that beloved embodiment of life's mystery
that concerns us here.

The organic properties of the robust Peeperkorn may be quickly
delineated. Though he speaks in broken sentences and unfinished
thoughts, his articulate hands complete his meanings, orchestrate
his implicit views, command the felt comprehension of his entranced
admirers. His gestures and his olympian presence suggest those histrionic gifts which Mann elsewhere attributes to artistic faking, but
here reclassifies as gifts of nature (MM, p. 584). Peeperkorn is a
magnificent mime whom even the deaf might comprehend. He moves from
gothic anguish to pagan jollity to jovian rage with measured ease.
He displays also an enormous capacity for oral enjoyment, imbibing
an endless flow of wines, coffees, liqueurs, ordering copious viands
for himself and his enravened guests, treating them to picnic lunches,
excellent dinners, midnight snacks. Further, he makes indiscriminate
love to all women present, rousing pride and gratitude, but "without
detriment to the delicate homage" he meanwhile pays to the devoted
Madame Chauchat (MM, p. 572). A swanlike lover, then, for whom all
women are inviting and admiring Ledas. Finally, his infectious "receptivity for life" (MM, p. 572) commands Hans Castorp's reverence.
Hans' previous mentors, Naphta and Settembrini, are dwarfed beside
this giant presence, who dispels their antinomies with summoned
eagles, emasculates their finest arguments with wordless gestures,
reduces them to intellectual babblings.

Mann attributes such powers to "the mystery of personality";
but since he views personality in organic terms, perhaps "mystery of

being" would serve as well. His homage to that "intelligent heart" and that knowledgeable belly and penis which Lawrence also celebrates seems obvious. He even offers a version of blood-brotherhood when Hans and Pieter drink to each other in the name of their common feeling for Clavdia. And the theology of feeling for which Pieter speaks--often with Hans' assistance--seems in many ways Lawrentian. It is Hans, for instance, who develops the distinction between his own refined self-indulgences and Pieter's devotion to "the simple, the great, the primeval gifts of God," and who ascribes the word "impotence" to his own indulged refinements (MM, pp. 564-65). In doing so, he more or less acknowledges the validity of Lawrence's charges of 1923 against the modern school of hyperconscious fiddling with one's buttons and one's twinging toes. The childish self-absorption of Joyce, Proust, and Richardson may be permissible, says Lawrence, at 17, or even 27; but at 37 it becomes "a sign of arrested development" and at 47, of "senile precocity."[5] The latter phrase recalls Lawrence's dismissal of Mann in 1913 as old and outdated in his Flaubertian artistry, his refined retreat from leprous life. Though Mann was then 38, only ten years older than himself, Lawrence had mistaken von Aschenbach's age in Death in Venice--53--for Mann's, reducing him thereby to the same debility he would later ascribe to all self-conscious moderns.

Through Hans Castorp, then, Mann graciously admits to his own senile precocity. But in Peeperkorn's theology of feeling he also finds its vitalist equivalent. The word "impotence" frightens Peeperkorn: it is the final inadmissible horror, the "unpardonable sin" against "the holy, the feminine claims life makes upon manly honour and strength" (MM, p. 565). For "Life," as Pieter explains to Hans, "is a female":

> A sprawling female, with swelling breasts close to each other, great soft belly between her haunches, slender arms, bulging thighs, half-closed eyes. She mocks us. She challenges us to expend our manhood to its uttermost span, to stand or fall before her. To stand or fall. To fall, young man--do you know what that means? The defeat of the feelings, their overthrow when confronted by life--that is impotence. For it there is no mercy, it is pitilessly, mockingly condemned. . . . Shame and ignominy are soft words for the ruin and bankruptcy, the horrible disgrace. It is the end of everything, the hellish despair, the Judgment Day (MM, p. 566).

Later the frightened Peeperkorn will justify--or perhaps merely add to--these apocalyptic pronouncements while explaining to Hans "our sacred duty to feel":

> Feeling, you understand, is the masculine force that rouses life. Life slumbers. It needs to be roused, to be awakened to a drunken marriage with divine feeling. For feeling, young man, is godlike. Man is godlike, in that he feels. He is the feeling of God. God created him in order to feel through him. Man is nothing but the organ through which God consummates his marriage with roused and intoxicated life. If man fails in feeling, it is blasphemy; it

is the surrender of [God's] masculinity, a cosmic catastrophe, an irreconcilable horror (MM, p. 603).

Hans speaks now with respectful deference to the alarming side of Peeperkorn's "austere" theology, which ascribes to man, he says, a "highly honourable" but perhaps "one-sided religious function"; and certainly the religious weight so placed upon the human organ is sufficient cause for anyone's alarm. Most of us, like Hans, are "built on modest lines" and would prefer that God attend to His own masculinity, or, at the least, that life would behave less like a sexually demanding odalisk. But putting these anthropomorphic metaphors and their somewhat drunken accents aside, Lawrence often talked like this about life's--if not Frieda's--demands.

"We are transmitters of life," he tells us in a famous poem, "And when we fail to transmit life, life fails to flow through us."[6] Or again, in "Cabbage Roses," if we fail to "smell the breath of the gods in the common roses, and feel the splendour of the gods go through" us, then we "are suffering from an amnesia of the senses," we "are like to die of malnutrition of the senses," and our "sensual atrophy" will at last send us "insane" (CP III, p. 91). Elsewhere in Lawrence's work the declaratives are less strident, the admonitions less abstract; but loud or subtly rendered, there is always the demand that we put the life-quality where it was not--into "the whiteness of a washed pocket-handkerchief" for one modest instance (CP II, p. 179), but beyond that, into nothing less than the totality of our lives and loves, indeed, our very deaths. We may willingly begin, of course, with enlivened handkerchiefs and enlivening roses; but whether we can go the whole way with Lawrence, and "ripple with life" through all our days (CP II, p. 178), seems questionable. He tells us frankly enough that giving and receiving life "is not so easy" (CP II, p. 179), and that "only the few, the very few," can do it well enough to "matter in the sight of God" (CP III, p. 72); and yet he asks us all to join that holy company. An austere religion, then, with severe demands and punishments, and with few genuine initiates--perhaps because, like the band of ascetic monks to whom one critic compares them, they ask more of themselves "than ordinary human nature can be expected to give."[7]

So too does Mann's Mynheer Peeperkorn. When his ailments finally begin to affect his potency, he invites his friends to a picnic beside a thundering mountain waterfall; and there, with every word drowned out by the deafening priapic flow, he delivers what turns out to be his farewell mime-address. Then late that night, by applying the principle which he once coherently articulated to Hans--that every food that nurtures may also poison--he distills an organic poison into a cobra-mechanism of his own devising and injects it into his veins. Faced with that sorry outcome, Hans pronounces Pieter's view of himself as "the [failed] instrument of God's marriage . . . a piece of majestic tomfoolery"; but Clavdia more eloquently explains his principled action as "une abdication" (MM, p. 624).

The obvious moral of this somewhat lugubrious tale is that Lawrence, under similarly distressful circumstances, refused to abdicate. Though his long avoidance of medical treatment for tuberculosis may be seen as a gradual form of suicide, in all likelihood the

treatment itself would have dispatched him even sooner. He seems to
have known instinctively that confinement in some alpine sanatorium
might rapidly destroy his will to live, or, as with Peeperkorn, drive
him to destroy himself, and he wisely chose to live as long as possible.[8] Even before Mann he had depicted alpine retreats in his fictions
as centers of European decadence, playgrounds of the idle rich, where
romantic self-destruction flourishes, where the love-modes are death-
modes, forms of spiritual disintegration in the northern ice-destructive
manner; and, through Tyrolean climbers like Captain Hepburn, he too
decried the deadly spiritual uplift, he too exclaimed: "Yes . . . it
is wonderful. But very detestable. I want to live near the sea-level.
I am no mountain-topper."[9] He knew something about the hazards, then,
of substitute existences on magic mountains and preferred the green
and sunny life below.

Hence his fear of tuberculosis, which meant the end of life itself as he wished to live it: in discriminating and active touch with
friends, loved ones, uncaged places. As we shall see, he showed no
apparent fear of impotence, which he could and did accommodate; indeed, he seems to have taken it as the "creative pause" before Resurrection, the blankness which he shared with a dying civilization.
"Desire is dead," he says with perfect frankness in a dozen poems of
this period,[10] meanwhile expanding his theology of phallic consciousness to include "the greater life of the body" in its conceptual range.
Whereas Peeperkorn's wider-ranging theology of feeling would contract,
at the end, to the narrow sphere of phallic uplift.

For Lawrence, apparently, God's marriage with the living universe
could proceed with or without the telltale phallus; and yet his insistence during these years upon the phallic consciousness, and the phallic powers of heroes like himself, would seem to belie that generous
notion. Either he no longer practiced what he preached, or preached
more variously than he practiced, or preached with an enormous faith
in future resurrection. Whatever the case, we need to look more
closely at his closing years--the years of Lady Chatterley's Lover,
"Sun," Pansies, The Man Who Died, the London exhibition of his paint-
ings--if we are to understand how he came to terms with sexual impotence, and so come to terms with our own complacencies on that score.

According to that critical godfather of all true Lawrentians,
Harry Moore, Lawrence's impotence "dates from that terrible illness
in Mexico in 1925, from which Lawrence never recovered."[11] It was
induced, then, by the inroads of tuberculosis on his body, and not
by any psychic wound like the Oedipus complex nor any inherent sexual
deficiency, as his many adverse critics assume. There seems to me no
question that Lawrence did experience genuine sexual fulfillment in
his previous relations with Frieda, such critics to the contrary
notwithstanding. His poems and novels tell us that much, whatever
their conflictual nature, and Frieda supports their eloquent testimony. The quarrels between the Lawrences were founded, I think, in
quite other considerations--in aristocratic versus working-class
willfulness, for instance, rather than sexual incompatibility. But
beginning in 1925 their sexual relations were of necessity infrequent,
and by the end of 1926, as Frieda later told her friends, they ceased

altogether. These several friends related what Frieda had told them
to one of Lawrence's many biographers, Richard Aldington, who in turn
told it to Harry Moore in the late 1950s. Moore aired the information
for the first time in his 1960 revision of The Intelligent Heart, then
five years later revealed its source in a memorial tribute to Aldington.[12] There the information rested until 1972, when Frieda's biographer,F. L. Lucas, made the first of many current appropriations of
"the fact, later revealed by Frieda, that towards the end of 1926
[Lawrence] had become sexually impotent" (italics mine).[13] Of course,
"facts" come in different sizes. As Moore privately observes, all we
have to go on here are the second-hand reports of unnamed friends.[14]

In 1974, however, just before her death, Lawrence's once-faithful
disciple Dorothy Brett published a revised version of her 1933 memoirs
which offers firsthand evidence of his impotence. Early in 1926, when
Lawrence was apparently trying to break away from Frieda, he joined
Brett and the Brewsters on Capri and, when the Brewsters left, traveled with Brett to Ravello, Italy, where they occupied separate rooms
in the same hotel. In her original account of the episode Brett implies that they slept in their separate rooms at all times; but in
her revision she reveals what she apparently could not disclose in
1933, that Lawrence came to her hotel room on two successive evenings
and was impotent on both occasions. As Emily Hahn reports the episode
in her Lorenzo (1975), the astonished Brett, her dreams come true,
was trying hard "to be warm and loving and female" on these occasions
while Lawrence--who believed that their relationship had to be physical to succeed--was "struggling to be successfully male." But the
flustered Brett did not know how to rouse him, nor was Lawrence able
to rouse himself. "Your boobs are all wrong," he told her when stalk-
ing off on the second evening, leaving her "ashamed, bewildered,
miserable." Next day she found him packing "in a towering rage," on
his way back to Frieda, consigning the faithful Brett--who would
never see him again--to look after his ranch in Taos, New Mexico.[15]

Whatever we may wish to say in Lawrence's defense--that his
fidelity to Frieda was so strong he could not overcome it, that he
did not find his adoring deaf disciple sexually attractive, that her
tin ear-trumpet (which would have delighted Peeperkorn) was too much
for him--the fact remains that he blames her for his own boobish
failure. As we shall see, this was one of his most successful ways
of coping with impotence in the years ahead; but it seems at this
point a peevish, spiteful way, lending substance to what his detrac-
tors say about these final years, and we shall be hard put to condone,
much less explain it. Meanwhile, let us at least acknowledge that
Brett's testimony tends to confirm what Frieda is said to have told
her several friends: that by the end of 1926, when he began writing
Lady Chatterley's Lover, Lawrence was wholly impotent.

It seems to me, if not a critical embarrassment, at least a
critical perplex, or better still, a critically embarrassing perplex,
that Lady Chatterley's Lover was written by an impotent man. His
enemies have often said so. His friends and admirers, myself among
them, have long refused to say in public what they have either privately known or long suspected, perhaps out of admiration for the
defiant courage, and for the courageous vision, of a slowly dying
man. In a sense we have all trusted Lawrence as much as, if not more

than, his prophetic tale--trusted his integrity, his honesty as a prophetic artist, whatever his phallic condition. But now that others have spoken for us, now that the bald truth is public knowledge, our grounds for trusting him must be reassessed. After all, despite Lawrence's famous maxim, no tale is more trustworthy than the sensibility which created it; and when that sensibility suffers blankness, nullity, in the phallic region, then its renderings and appraisals of sexual experience may well seem questionable to many readers. This is what the novel's many adverse critics have always argued. If we are to stave them off once more, this is the embarrassment we must unperplex.

"One sheds one's sicknesses in books--repeats and presents again one's emotions, to be master of them." So runs another famous Lawrence maxim. The sickness which he tried to shed in Lady Chatterley's Lover-- and in that sense, the novel's oddly "generative" source--must have been impotence. Just as Hemingway moved from a piece of shrapnel in his scrotum to Jake Barnes' missing penis, and Joyce from the practice of coitus interruptus to Leopold Bloom's long abstinence, and Eliot from sexual revulsion to the fisher king's sterility, so Lawrence moved from his own tubercular debility to Clifford Chatterley's paralysis from the hips down. Chatterley's war wound, externally imposed, irreversible, was like the inroads of the disease whose name Lawrence would not speak and whose irrevocable spread he could not acknowledge. It was always his "broncs," his bronchial tubes, and never his lungs, which troubled him. But through Clifford he admitted to the condition he so much dreaded; and onto Clifford he projected a version of his own infirmity, a form of irreversible impotence. But he did not otherwise identify himself with Clifford, as Hemingway, Joyce, and Eliot--though still potent themselves--may be said to identify with their variously unmanned protagonists. Instead he created someone whose reaction to impotence would contrast with his own, someone he could blame for failing to reach his own accommodations.

In Women in Love he had used the same contrasting method with Hermione and Birkin, both of whose heads need bashing if they are ever to become "spontaneously passionate" and truly sensual; and with Birkin and Gerald, both of whom must pledge themselves with a man before they can join with a woman "in absolute mystic marriage": but it is only Birkin who is released to real sensuality through head-bashing, and to mystic marriage through blood-brotherhood. In Lady Chatterley there is no contrasting cripple whose reaction helps us to judge poor Clifford: only the gamekeeper, Oliver Mellors, who has withdrawn from the sexual and industrial wars to school himself in sylvan solitude and nurse his emotional wounds. In some ways the situation comes closer to that in Sons and Lovers (Chap. 4) when the boy Paul jumps from the sofa and accidentally smashes the face of his sister's beloved doll, Arabella. Though bereaved sister Annie eventually forgives him, Paul decides to sacrifice Arabella on a funeral pyre, so rejoicing while she burns that Annie is inwardly dismayed: for she sees that he hates the doll intensely "because he had broken it." In Lady Chatterley Clifford may be Lawrence's Arabella, his sacrificial wounded doll, upon whom most of the ills of modern civilization and not a few of his own fears and failings are heaped (e.g., his increased fear of emotional dependency, his

breast-fetishism, his occasionally spiteful stories), at some cost,
some critics say, to credibility.

One thing seems certain: the question as to why Lawrence made
him crippled need no longer puzzle us. Though understandably evasive,
his own answer to that question, in "A Propos of Lady Chatterley's
Lover," speaks honestly enough to the crucial issues:

> I have been asked many times if I intentionally made
> Clifford paralysed, if it is symbolic. And literary friends
> say, it would have been better to have left him whole and
> potent, and to have made the woman leave him nevertheless.
>
> As to whether the "symbolism" is intentional--I don't
> know. Certainly not in the beginning, when Clifford was created.
> When I created Clifford and Connie, I had no idea what they were
> or why they were. They just came, pretty much as they are. But
> the novel was written, from start to finish, three times. And
> when I read the first version, I recognised that the lameness
> of Clifford was symbolic of the paralysis, the deeper emotional
> or passional paralysis, of most men of his sort and class to-
> day. I realised that it was perhaps taking an unfair advantage
> of Connie, to paralyse him technically. It made it so much more
> vulgar of her to leave him. Yet the story came as it did, by
> itself, so I left it alone. Whether we call it symbolism, or not,
> it is, in the sense of its happening, inevitable[16] (italics mine).

The story and its characters came "inevitably," then, out of the
creative unconscious, whose dispensation Lawrence honors. We can see
in retrospect how they must have emerged, within that dispensation,
from an unconscious blending of his early elopement with Frieda and
his present impotence, as projected back upon her displaced husband.
A "pure personality" himself--cold, disconnected, bodiless--Professor
Weekley is the initial prototype, at the least, for all those eminently
dispensable husbands one meets in Lawrence's fiction, from the Reverend
Mr. Massy onwards. Lawrence now burdens such a man, at any rate, with
his own disability, his own accidental impotence, as if to test against
that shared condition the strength of his own shaky marriage. Sir
Clifford is "purely a personality," he tells us in the passage preceding his remarks on symbolism; he is disconnected from humanity
because "he does not know what warm sympathy means." On the other hand,
Mellors, who "still has the warmth of a man . . . is being hunted down,
destroyed. Even it is a question if the woman who turns to him will
really stand by him and his vital meaning" (AP, pp. 119-20; italics
mine).

Will Frieda stand by Lawrence and his "vital meaning," now that
he is technically as disconnected from her as the otherwise potent
Weekley? Well, suppose the odds were evened: then the differences
between the disabled Lawrence and such disabled displaced husbands
would at least be clear, and the "vulgar" grounds for leaving a sexually crippled man might be compared. By fictional skewing, then,
Lawrence evens the odds: makes himself whole and potent again, as he
was when he and Frieda awakened each other; disables Weekley, or a

type more fully representative of modern coldness, so as to clarify
for himself as well as Frieda what there is to stand by under those
conditions; and, with past awakening made present, with present disability set off to advantage by invidious contrast, speaks out for
his own continuing warmth and courage.

I think Lawrence must have been wrestling, perhaps half-con-
sciously, with some such total complex of personal problems when he
created his story and his characters. If his own fidelity had its
foolish limits, he was never very sure of Frieda's. As he seems to
have told David Garnett, she had once defiantly stressed her independence, after a row during their elopement, by swimming across the
Isar to make love to a woodcutter on the opposite bank.[17] According
to Aldous Huxley, such "erotic excursions" occurred "now and then"
throughout their marriage; but the only other recorded instances
were an approchement with John Middleton Murry in 1923, while Lawrence
was in America, which became an affair only after his death, and a
more Chatterley-like sortie with her future third husband, Angelo
Ravagli, in 1928.[18] Huxley says that Lawrence took such excursions
more or less in stride, being too dependent on Frieda to break away.
After the Ravagli affair, for instance, he is said to have told her:
"Every heart has a right to its own secrets."[19] But as we know, he
did try to break away with Brett in 1926; and he was deeply troubled
by the half-baked affair with Murry, whom he lampoons in several
stories of this period--most notably in "The Border Line" (1924),
where his prototype returns after death, finishes off an expiring
Murry (whom Frieda has meanwhile married), and makes love to Frieda
with the dead Murry in an adjoining bed. As this macabre tale suggests,
Lawrence's sex-ghost stories are like metaphors for transcended impotence: his phallic powers endure in ghostly form long after their
technical relapse.

Certainly his fear of Frieda's infidelity, or more accurately,
of her imminent departure, endured. In Lady Chatterley's Lover,
accordingly, Connie is unable to leave Clifford until she can blame
him for denying simple human warmth and for displacing his own life-
responsibility onto supporting props like Mrs. Bolton's boobs, his
spiteful literary soirées, and his chugging motor chair. As I argued
with some prescience in 1955, the assault on good will which the novel
makes through Connie's departure involves a clash of moral systems,
with Connie sinning against bourgeois sentiments which turn counterfeit before our eyes, and with Clifford sinning against organic life.[20]
Let me again point out, in the light of Lawrence's impotence, that
Clifford's sin is sensual and emotional rather than sexual, that his
paralysis helps to isolate and heighten that distinction, and that
Lawrence's novel--and his case for his own worth with Frieda--rests
upon it. Thus, when Connie compliments Mellors for having the courage
of his own tenderness, a form of courage "that will make the future,"
Mellors too defuses sex--or better still--diffuses sex by placing it
on a wide sensual spectrum:

> Ay! it's tenderness really; it's cunt-awareness. Sex is really
> only touch, the closest of all touch. And it's touch we're
> afraid of. We're only half-conscious, and half-alive. We've got

to come alive and aware. Especially the English have got to get in touch with one another, a bit delicate and a bit tender. It's our crying need.[21]

It is not sexual potency, then, which makes Mellors superior to Clifford, but his insistence on a range of sensual consciousness wide enough to "make the future." Like Lawrence, he understands the sensual basis of human sympathy, its physical or creaturely foundation; and if, like Lawrence, he forgets here the maternal orgins of human warmth, he at least breaks through--in his surly and often willful way--to a viable form of male as well as female nurture.

Thus tenderness, not willfulness, is the novel's theme, and its emergence at this late stage in Lawrence's career may have something to do with the humbling onset of impotence. If the "militant ideal" was now a "cold egg," as he wrote to Witter Bynner in 1928, so too was passionate desire. But out of that warm egg, tenderness, he might still be able to hatch another phoenix. And so he tells us, in "A Propos of Lady Chatterley's Lover," that "all the emotions belong to the body," that "the higher emotions" especially--meaning "love in all its manifestations, from genuine desire to tender love, love of our fellow men, and love of God"--are centered in the body (p. 96); that the "instinct of fidelity" is the deepest sexual instinct (p. 104); and that it thrives best when set in relation "to the rhythmic cosmos" (p. 114). And these larger conceptions of what he means by the "phallic consciousness" arise phoenix-like from dying sexual embers. He has no need to commit suicide, then, like Peeperkorn, with the lapse of desire; he can still invoke this "greater consciousness," this broader sense of the body's ongoing vitality.

Indeed, in the same pamphlet, impotence itself is accommodated by life's larger rhythms. While writing about the sexual swindle of counterfeit emotions, Lawrence speaks of "the time of great sexual change" when men and women "are nearing fifty": if the love between them has been false in the intervening years, sex lashes out through cataclysmic hatred and the marriage smashes. But when marriage is sacramental, with sex as the act of communion, then it provides "for the complex development of the man's soul and the woman's soul in unison, throughout a lifetime" (p. 107); and included in this provision is "the period of waning passion but mellowing delight of affection" (pp. 109-10). That passion wanes for men as well as women at this difficult time seems evident from the context; but as Harry Moore reports, Lawrence also made the point clear in a conversation with Earl Brewster in 1927:

> He pointed out that he and Brewster were now "at the âge dangereux for men: when the whole rhythm of the psyche changes. . . . It is well to know the thing is physiological: though that doesn't nullify the psychological reality." Too many people resented the sex swindle of modern life, which was not completely the fault of the individual but was to a great extent a product of the age. One had to go through the process of change, without too much exasperation.

"I try," Lawrence told his Buddhistic friend, "to keep
the <u>middle</u> of me harmonious to the <u>Middle</u> of the universe.
Outwardly I know I'm in a bad temper, and let it go at that."[22]

Lawrence was then 42, not 50; but he was plainly describing that
mythic state, the male menopause, when passion wanes and desire lapses
and men lash out in irritability and hatred against the modern sexual
swindle. The acrimonious tone of <u>Pansies</u>, the harsher passages in
<u>Chatterley</u>, may proceed as much from that "dangerous" condition as
from tubercular irascibility. But what matters most is that Lawrence
saw his situation as transitional rather than cataclysmic, a period
of psychological and biological change; and that he steadied himself
emotionally through that broader sense of the body's ongoing life.
The appeal to cosmic attunement suggests also why he could identify
with that cosmic lover, the sun, in tales of this period, and from
that vantage point speak contemptuously, as he does at the end of
the unexpurgated edition of "Sun" in 1928, of a husband's "futile
little penis" stirring inside a wife who prefers the sun's penetra-
tions. Such cosmic conceit, given the greater futility of his own
little penis at this time, seems hard to justify unless we grant him
his sunlike perspective of the body's changing phases.
We must make a similar concession, I think, for <u>Lady</u> <u>Chatterley's</u>
<u>Lover</u>, a novel which proceeds through a series of explicit sexual
encounters so as to demonstrate a change of being in one protagonist
and, in the other, a renewed commitment to life. This experience of
sexual rebirth and renewal became the novel's dramatic center only in
the third and final version, when Lawrence decided to make the act of
love itself the dramatic medium for Connie's rite of passage and
Mellors' change of heart. It was Connie's experience, however, which
chiefly engaged his creative interest: for in order to convey it he
would have to perform a sustained act of sexual sympathy, the success
or failure of which would depend upon the courage of his own considerable tenderness. This imaginative rendering of a woman's sexual experience seems to me the novel's unassailable triumph; and when we reflect that it was performed by an impotent man we have to grant its
exemplary value, its demonstration that Lawrence himself--whatever
his limitations--could still appreciate the sensual otherness of a
woman much like Frieda. In Chapter 9, moreover, just before the
first sexual encounter with Mellors, he made it abundantly clear that
he hoped to inculcate the same sensual sympathy in his readers, explaining there how the novel itself, as a generic medium, "can inform
and lead into new places the flow of our sympathetic consciousness,
and . . . can lead our sympathy away in recoil from things gone dead."
Connie's experience of revulsion and renewal fits this generic prescription: her experience is ours, and Mellors' <u>subordinate</u> role is
to assist her and us in achieving it.
Still, however subordinate, Mellors' role is problematic in that
it lends itself to authorial wish-fulfillment. He is not reborn as a
man as Connie is reborn as a woman; he is already manly, and while
his creaturely sureness may be necessary to Connie's transformation,
it is almost a given condition. True enough, he undergoes his own
struggle, his own painful reawakening, and wins through, as I have

said, to a valid version of male nurture. But his grizzled wisdom
and experience come ready-made to his and Connie's rescue. Was
Lawrence projecting his own need for fleshly resurrection onto this
phallic hero? Or was he relying on earned past experience so as to
focus more sharply on Connie's transformation? I think the answer to
both questions is "yes."

Given his sense of the body's changing phases, Lawrence could
legitimately look back to his own embattled years of potency, fulfillment, reciprocity, and could imagine for this novel a man who
has already acquired his own hard-won apartness, his own hard-lost
capacity for tender reconnection. Unlike Stephen Crane, he had at
least been to the civil wars he wanted to re-create, and we have no
reason to doubt his retrospective wisdom. It seems to me instructive,
even so, that his bets on Mellors' potency were carefully hedged.
Our first glimpse of Mellors' nakedness, for instance, is from the
hips up, so that Connie's shock of recognition when she comes by
chance upon him, her vision of warm single sensual life in Chapter 6,
is an exact reversal of Clifford's hips-up blankness, coldness, and
dependency. In the same vein our last glimpse of Mellors is through
a Jane-Austenish epistle written in his fortieth winter--the last
year of Lawrence's potency; its subject is chastity, "the peace that
comes of fucking," the "pause of peace" that flows between these
separated lovers like a cool refreshing river--an extension then of
sexual fulfillment, its lingering aftermath, as we see when Mellors
compares it to the weary impotence of philanderers like Don Juan,
who "are unable to be chaste in the cool between-whiles." Interestingly, both letter and novel end with John Thomas saying goodbye to
Lady Jane "a little droopingly, but with a hopeful heart." So that
Mellors' intensely phallic activity in the novel is framed, as it
were, between these cautionary images of hips-up vitality and a
droopingly satisfied penis.

His hopeful heart speaks, I fear, to my first embarrassing
question. Whatever his steadying sense of the body's changing phases,
Lawrence did understandably hope that his impotent condition was only
temporary; he did try to inspire his drooping penis by creating a
phallic hero after his own lost desire. The frequent easy replenish-
ment of Mellors' sexual powers, his wide and varied sexual history,
his advantage in age as well as experience over Connie, the special
pleading on his behalf (as in the famous night of searing anal passion
when Lawrence condones or forgets his hero's obvious hostility)--
surely these are signs of the author's self-aggrandizement and wishful
blindness. And Mellors' cocksure manner as Connie's mentor seems, at
times, like the author's sexual swagger. Lawrence would finesse such
aberrations with far greater skill in The Man Who Died, where his
impotence gave him imaginative entry into Christ's nullity in the
tomb; and where his own desire for fleshly resurrection could be
imagined as the awakening and healing of a numbed and badly wounded
man. Here too the puncturing of self-importance, of cosmic vanity,
which is one of the tale's most effective and most obviously self-
critical themes, keeps the imagined resurrection within plausible
human bounds. Again, unlike Peeperkorn, Lawrence knew when to retire
as God's world-saving instrument and seek his own salvation in the

body's "greater life." In this humbler mood, within this mythic context, and on these more personal grounds, his "escaped cock"--as the novella was originally called--could be wishfully restored.

Or perhaps--as seems possible--the novella celebrates a brief return to actual potency, the uncertainty of which would also account for the new cosmic humility. We know that Lawrence composed the first half of the tale, in which the healing "man who died" abandons his prophetic role without achieving potency, in April 1927, and then published it as a separate story; and that he did not write the second half, in which the ex-prophet is restored to potency by the priestess of Isis, until August 1928. Perhaps a brief flareup of sexual powers occurred between these dates and inspired the second section. If so, it was not sufficient to prevent Frieda's affair with Angelo Ravagli in October 1928; but, along with the second section of The Man Who Died, it may explain the hopeful patience of the poems of this period, where--as Lawrence seeks his own fleshly renewal in some future cultural rebirth--"the new word is Resurrection" (CP II, pp. 246-47).

Yet suppose he understood such wishful thinking even as he indulged it; suppose he meant something else by personal resurrection, something more durable and more within his reach. In "A Propos of Lady Chatterley's Lover," for instance, he seems to want to think his way back--not to potency--but to chastity, "the peace that comes of fucking," the lingering aftermath of sexual fulfillment which he defines so lovingly as the novel ends:

> And this [he stresses] is the real point of this book. I
> want men and women to be able to think sex, fully, completely,
> honestly and cleanly.
> Even if we can't act sexually to our complete satisfaction,
> let us at least think sexually, complete and clear. . . . Years
> of honest thoughts of sex, and years of struggling action in
> sex will bring us at last where we want to get, to our real and
> accomplished chastity, our completeness, when our sexual act and
> our sexual thought are in harmony, and the one does not inter-
> fere with the other. . . . A great many men and women to-day
> are happiest [he continues] when they abstain and stay sexually
> apart, quite clean: and at the same time, when they understand
> and realize sex more fully. Ours is the day of realization
> rather than action. . . . To-day the full conscious realization
> of sex is even more important than the act itself (pp. 92-93;
> italics mine).

Some critics find this passage inconsistent with Lawrence's previous railings against the "lordly mind," cerebral, analytic, which can never understand the body's mysteries (CP II, p. 205). But Lawrence was always partial to the mind's intuitive and instinctive reaches, its imaginative apprehensions, and this is what he means now by "conscious realization" and "thinking fully." It is in this sense, too, that his new prescription for the age applies to his own condition. He had written Lady Chatterley to balance his own realization of the act with the act itself, to bring his own intuitive ideas into balance with his past experience. No longer potent, he could at least

restore and extend his accomplished chastity, his past completeness
in "the cool between-whiles," the peaceful pauses; and his new sequential harmony would cover phases of his life rather than sequential
deeds and pauses. This must have been how he justified to himself
those final years when--like Renoir--he wrote and painted pictures
with his otherwise drooping penis, when he could only realize sex
in his mind through the flow of pen and brush, and could not act.
As he puts it in "A Propos," "thought and action, word and deed, are
two separate forms of consciousness, two separate lives that we lead"
(italics mine); for "while we think, we do not act, and while we act
we do not think" (p. 92).

Confined now to the separate life of thought, Lawrence continued
to think and write about sex as one who abstains from it as if by
choice. But this is how all who write about sex must proceed, whatever their potency. The old adage that Harry Moore cites to me in a
recent letter--"Sex books are written only by the impotent"--is true;
you cannot write about sex while experiencing it--except of course
as an aid to masturbation or wet daydreams, as in Joyce's letters
of 1909 to Nora.[23] But as I have already indicated, there is a difference between imagining sex fully, as Lawrence asks, and the various forms of mental excitation he called sex-in-the-head, of which
masturbation--literary or otherwise--was for him a major instance.
In Lady Chatterley Connie's private oracle, Tommy Dukes, is Lawrence's
example of one modern sexual abstainer who tries and fails to realize
sex in his mind, but who meanwhile distinguishes for us between "the
mental life," with its many forms of sexual exploitation, and the
intelligence which comes from "the whole corpus of the consciousness,"
and is therefore fully alive. Thus, in the Wragby parlor in Chapter 4,
when asked what he believes by his shy friend Berry, Dukes replies
that "intellectually" he believes "in having a good heart, a chirpy
penis, a lively intelligence, and the courage to say 'shit' in front
of a lady"; and when Berry says he has them all, Dukes laughs in
denial:

> No [he says]; my heart's as numb as a potato, my penis droops
> and never lifts its head up, I dare rather cut him clean off
> than say 'shit!' in front of my mother or my aunt . . . they
> are real ladies, mind you; and I'm not really intelligent, I'm
> only a 'mental-lifer.' It would be wonderful to be intelligent:
> then one would be alive in all the parts mentioned and unmen-
> tionable. The penis rouses his head and says: How do you do?
> to any really intelligent person. Renoir said he painted his
> pictures with his penis . . . he did too, lovely pictures! I
> wish I did something with mine (italics mine).

This passage seems a little quaint, in these advanced days of
the sexual revolution, when it takes more courage to say "lady" in
front of a shit than to follow Dukes' advice. But it speaks freshly
nonetheless to Lawrence's personal predicament and his solution for
it. In the novel, where commentary, description, dialogue, inner
speech, and narrated action make their imaginative appeal to "the
whole corpus of the consciousness," it is possible to convey the

range and quality of sexual experience, its self-absorptions and predations, its nurturing fulfillments, and so bring imaginative life--
as opposed to titillation--to private parts. Connie's relations with
Michaelis and with Mellors, her experience of the mental life at
Wragby and the sensual life at Mellors' cottage, where her talks and
quarrels with Mellors advance the deeds which foster satisfying chastity, suggest the qualitative contrasts Lawrence realized in this book.
In the novel, then, as in his paintings, his creative intelligence
could enliven "all the parts mentioned and unmentionable"; he could
still be whole and vital through that greater phallic consciousness,
and could lead his readers to the same imaginative satisfactions.

Compare, in this light, the erotic ironies between life and mind
in The Magic Mountain, where Hans and Clavdia are given the last
ironic words--"a piece of majestic tomfoolery" and "une abdication"
on Peeperkorn's dying fall. Whatever his own loving reverence, the
triumph of the moral intelligence over pagan vitalism is Mann's
ironic answer to his own implicit--and distinctly irreverent--ques-
tion: what happens to a pagan vitalist when the juice runs out?
Lawrence's very different answer was to enlist the moral intelligence
in service of the body's greater life. If, as Taylor Stoehr asserts,
he had little use for self-absorbing dream and fantasy, and if he
failed to conceive of the novel as an imaginative self-enclosed medium
where the intense play of consciousness is always self-absorbing, he
used that medium nonetheless to awaken and enliven sensual sympathy
and to dispel predations and obsessions.[24] And if, as the Sartrean
critic T. H. Adamowski argues, the narrative voice in Lawrence's
novels is "the light of consciousness which gives the lie to the dream
of darkness," the mindless union of perfected lovers--if the conscious
mind can only reflect such mindless joys--Lawrence made of narration
nonetheless a potent apprehension of equilibrated selves and others,
an instance of sequential harmony by which we glimpse unconscious
possibilities.[25] In his final years he converted impotence itself
into a creative medium, and so consciously recovered the artistic
ground on which he always stood; and that conscious conversion, more
than anything else, helped him to prepare his ship of death, his
bravest demonstration of faith in the body's changing phases, by
which--and not incidentally--his wife's precarious fidelity, her
commitment to see him through to the last resurrection, was finally
assured.

Immediacy and Recollection:
The Rhythm of the Visual in
D. H. Lawrence

L. D. CLARK (with photographs by LAVERNE HARRELL CLARK)

Lawrence once said that he created by "continual, slightly modified repetition."[1] He was referring to his written style, but the same phrase may be applied to his visual sense. So many key images appear from work to work, though always in newly elaborated combinations and expansions, that we might almost consider this his fundamental creative process. The discussion that follows is based on selected passages of prose in which Lawrence repeatedly seeks out nuances in concrete perceptions of place that will carry him on to larger meanings. For the sake of reference and for further investigation by any reader so inclined, the complete passages, along with photographs of some of the scenes, will be found at the end of the general discussion.

The highly visual quality of Lawrence's writing came to public attention early in his career, as when a reviewer of The White Peacock found certain of the scenes "cinematographic."[2] Of the various later treatments, the most extensive I know is Keith Aldritt's book, The Visual Imagination of D. H. Lawrence. Aldritt stresses the kinship between Lawrence the painter and Lawrence the writer, and takes up at length his evocation of landscape. I wish to refer also to Lawrence on landscape and painting, but only as a point of departure. What I intend to explore is a certain mobility of vision by which Lawrence captures immediate impressions of place and then draws on them for a long time to come in rhythmical patterns of recollection.

While such a faculty may in part rely on a painter-like use of composition, color, and perspective, its chief expression comes in forms unique to language. Whatever mental visions a painting may suggest to a beholder, they arise from an illusory arrangement of paint and canvas, from a fixed material image, thus demanding an initial

121

leap from the world of matter to the world of spirit. But the word is
of itself a spiritual agent, and the images born of it enjoy a complete
freedom of movement. At least this is what Lawrence the writer appears
to have in mind when he turns to painting in search of meaning. He
struggles to counteract the original fixity of images in that art by
attributing to it a sort of flexibility more natural to the art of
language. To show what I mean, let me begin with Paul's rejection of
"form" in Sons and Lovers. "The shape is a dead crust," he explains
to Miriam. He wishes to capture instead the innate motion of things,
to render leaves as shimmering protoplasm and the trunks of pines as
"standing-up pieces of fire" in darkness. Certain he has created such
pines in the canvas he is working on, he cries out, "There's God's
burning bush for you, that burned not away."[3]
     Of course, Paul's low opinion of "shape" may be open to question.
A burning bush, yes. But how would we know it's a bush--or the trunk
of a pine--without the form within the fire, and why not be struck by
the unconsumed form as well as by the quiver and dazzle of the blaze?
Without the impossible conjunction of the two, who could recognize
the miracle?
     But it was not really to form itself that Lawrence objected. He
puts the matter more clearly in the late essay "Introduction to These
Paintings." What he condemns here is the form dictated by the habitual
mental concepts of the artist, the cliché, while he applauds the form
congenital to the object itself, to which the artist can only respond
by circumventing habit and trusting to the quickness within himself.
The only artist of his time that Lawrence credited with such sensitivity was Cézanne, and when he defines the creation of living form
by this painter we note that his convictions have not changed since
the early novel. Fluidity is still for him the supreme quality of
being. Cézanne's apples and human figures are certainly forms, but
vital forms, "mobile but come to rest" with all the mobility still
in them. Cézanne also achieves this feat in some of his later land-
scapes. In these, according to Lawrence, "We are fascinated by the
mysterious shiftiness of the scene under our eyes; it shifts about
as we watch it. And we realize, with a sort of transport, how intuitively true this is of landscape. It is not still. It has its own
weird anima, and to our wide-eyed perception it changes like a living
animal under our gaze."[4]
     A landscape astir with an animal life of its own--as I say,
Lawrence really seems to have in view what writing accomplishes more
easily than painting, having at its command the almost infinite mobility of image in the word and never having to translate image from
mental to physical form. At least, Lawrence might here be alluding
to his own writing rather than Cézanne's painting, for in a landscape
that he describes the "weird anima" of place seldom fails to emerge,
in a "curious rolling flood of vision"[5]--again to borrow Lawrence's
words. Let us take, for example, the famous opening pages of The
Rainbow. There is plenty of vividness akin to painting here, but what
truly presents the landscape of Marsh Farm as "mobile but come to
rest" is a vast interaction of human and natural elements where the
visual images revolve in an obscure and ever-changing rhythm of time
and space. Images of the seasons rise and fall as "the wave which
cannot halt."[6] We sense the dual vision, what the men see looking

inward and the women outward. Bodies of imagery suggest in this
countryside a balance-imbalance of vertical and horizontal that keeps
the Brangwen family always in expectation of something imminent but
unknown and lends them the air of inheritors of the earth. These effects of environment are concentrated in the immediate present and
yet imbued with the flux between past, present, and future. It would
be impossible to paint all this, but the language can unite with
space the time flow essential to bringing the landscape to life.

   We find these characteristics of landscape all through Lawrence's
fiction. But I would like to begin closer to the source, to take up
some of Lawrence's observations from their earliest recording and move
forward through various written forms to trace the workings of immediacy and recollection.

   First, the crucifixes that symbolized for Lawrence the Alpine
region of Germany, Austria, and Italy. He wrote a sketch of these in
three versions, one not long after first seeing them in the fall of
1912, another a short while later, and a third in the fall of 1915
for the volume Twilight in Italy. The seriousness of his intention
here is evident in his assertion that this was to be "a book of
sketches, about the nations, Italian, German and English, full of
philosophising and struggling to show things real."7 In the earliest
form of the piece, published in Love Among the Haystacks and Other
Pieces after his death, we find discussion of many differences in the
crucifixes according to whether they were carved by highland or low-
land inhabitants, or by Germans, Austrians, or Italians. But any correlation between Lawrence's re-creations of the landscape containing
the crucifixes and what he observes of religious feelings in the popu-
lace remains diffuse. In the Westminster Gazette version, as if remembering evidence overlooked in a descriptive detail that recollection
had not supplied the first time, he replaces some general observations
on Austrians with these sentences: "As one goes higher the crucifixes
get smaller and smaller. The wind blows the snow under the tiny shed
of a tiny Christ."8

   This leap from general to particular without transition is not
merely a stylistic quirk, for when we come to Twilight in Italy we
discover that Lawrence was advancing toward a fully developed insight,
which he inserts in about eight lines of text between restatements of
the details just cited. The remembered smallness of the crucifixes
high in the mountains has now led him to the conclusion that only
these embody any longer "the old beauty and religion."9 Curiously,
there occurs here also what we would normally expect to find in an
earlier rather than a later version: an exact description of the
crucifixes. And it is through this concreteness that the narrator
experiences the awe which the crucifixes create in relation to their
own snowbound landscape, especially the highest "crucifix, half
buried, small and tufted with snow."10

   But this is not yet the end of the meanings suggested by the
little crucifixes of the Alps. At least four years after the event,
Lawrence called it to mind once more and utilized such a little
crucifix to objectify the uncontrollable urge to self-destruction
that Gerald Crich suffers in Women in Love. The "little Christ under
a little sloping hood" arouses a "dread of being murdered. But it was
a dread which stood outside him like his own ghost."11

The range of imagination opened up by the sight of a few arti-
facts in a foreign land is clearly immense. What began as a small
travel article recurs as concrete evidence in a searching analysis of
the character of nations and at last furnishes a drastic turn of action in one of the author's greatest pieces of fiction. No example
could serve better to demonstrate what a creative potential lay in
"the mysterious shiftiness of the scene" that Lawrence was capable
of absorbing from landscape.

The example of the crucifixes indicates deepening vision in a
single scene over several years of repeated remembrance. Another
direction such a vision may take is toward a comparison or contrast
of places, anything from a simple connection between a present and
an absent place to far more complex parallels. We still meet with
strong emotional, moral, or philosophical significance in the visual
details of the writer's surroundings. I have selected an example
from the letters, the most extensive source in Lawrence of a juxtaposition of places, the source in which an experience is set down as it
happens or just after, and carries with it an urgent sense of personal problems, though these may be cast in national or geographic
terms.

The letter I quote dates from early in Lawrence and Frieda's
stay at Lake Garda, where they settled for a while after their walk
across the Alps. We should keep in mind that Lawrence was at this
time preoccupied with his first great novel, Sons and Lovers. England
thus stood off in distant and powerful contrast to Italy: the freedom
of the Mediterranean south against the restriction of the Atlantic
north. For Lawrence the contrast could not have been more personal.
England signified the illness of the past he was attempting to write
out of his system in the novel. Italy with Frieda promised health and
wonder and unbounded love in a glorious future. Brilliant word pictures of the lake, the villages, the lemon gardens, the olive orchards
and the vineyards abound in the letters. One day Lawrence received a
package of English books, among them Arnold Bennett's Anna of the
Five Towns, which he read and attacked in a letter on the same day
the package arrived. This was during Lawrence's first trip abroad.
He had not read a book in English, he reported, since leaving home
five months ago. Bennett's novel had lifted him out of his foreign
country where the people speak a strange language and spirited him
back to the Midlands to hear almost his own dialect.

England--or his own past, if you will--appears "grubby" and hopeless, and Bennett seems resigned to that hopelessness.[12] This is enough
to provoke in Lawrence a hatred of England and, further, a denunciation of all literature since Flaubert as "acceptance" of the horror of
modern life. In a rush to conclusion so typical of Lawrence, he snatches
at a definition of tragedy: a concept he has been trying off and on to
define for himself since the death of his mother in 1910. "Tragedy
ought to be a great kick at misery," he exclaims.[13] But the personal
involvement does not stop here. The physical presence of the lake
region, almost without transition from the concrete to the abstract,
becomes a set of terms to express the writer's repugnance for England
and his overwhelming exultance in his Italian surroundings. For instance, two such sentences as the following stand in emotional if

illogical support of one another: "The vines are yellow and red, and
fig trees are in flame on the mountains. I can't bear to be in England
when I am in Italy."[14] He has already worded his repudiation of England as "washing it off." Now a scene breaks into the page that is
probably the source of the metaphor. The day before, he and Frieda
had gone out to swim in the lake under a stormy sky. After an excited
recounting of that event he climaxes the paragraph with another jump
from description to conviction: "Then great lightnings split out.--No,
I don't believe England need be so grubby."[15]

It is revealing, after this letter, to turn at once to a sketch
that Lake Garda stirred Lawrence to write: "The Lemon Gardens." It
exists in two forms, one appearing in the English Review in 1913, a
later one in Twilight in Italy, whose avowed purpose, we recall, was
to analyze nations. This sketch, like that of the crucifixes, pursues
a deepening significance through successive interpretations of remembered exotic sights, but a contrast of places is now uppermost and
themes develop with particular reference to elements of time and space.
Let us consider one small scene in which the narrator and his landlord, owner of the lemon gardens, come out on the roof of a lemon-
house and stop here high above the lake to gaze and talk. In the first
version of the scene, which is only about half as long as the later
one, the object is to clarify two contrasts: one between the little
signore and his lovely environment, another between two nations. The
"shabby, shaky little figure" of the Italian is "lifted up like an
image of decay"[16] against the undying radiance of snow on the mountains opposite and the vivid colors on the hills and the lake. When
the signore begins to complain of the deterioration of his lemon business, the narrator, about to introduce the simplistic argument that
natural surroundings make up for economic disadvantage, exclaims on
the beauty of the scene and begins the contrast with England. But the
signore interrupts with his opinion: England is where the wealth is.
Italians have only the sun, which is no adequate compensation. But
the narrator goes on simplifying, with an image of the sun as a lemon
in the signore's garden, a heavenly lemon that in his avarice the
Italian would seize and sell if he could. And the narrator concludes,
almost priggishly, that unlike his landlord, he wouldn't sell a
particle of the sun.

The "Lemon Gardens" of Twilight in Italy seeks out a more profound
meaning in the same situation. Lawrence is now back in England, with
the recollection of Italy vivid in the past, but it is a cross-pene-
tration of memory, since he deals with what it was like back then to
be in Italy remembering England. This hovering of memory sets up a
whole new range of thematic concerns dependent on new spatial and
temporal perspectives. The two men are not now simply above the ground
looking across the lake at lovely mountains. Their position is on a
certain upper "level" of a world. Another "level," that of the lake
surface, runs below them. Villages like "groups of specks" have been
added to the far shore, augmenting the feel of distance. The signore
is speaking, as he did not in the first version, with "distant, perfect melancholy," and the narrator adds a similar distance to his own
vision of the ruined lemon-houses and the villages, which seem to be
"lingering in bygone centuries."[17] He then makes his protest, as
before, on the beauty of this land compared with England, and is

interrupted in like manner. Only now the Italian is not avaricious but envious of English industrial achievement and aching to undergo that experience himself. It is now the moment for the narrator to draw his final lesson from the scene, which turns out to be far different from that of the first version, and is truly unexpected. He mentions for the third time on this page that he is sitting on his "level" in the upper world, a simple emphasis giving an exactness of outlook in space to assist a casting back and forth in time. Now he sees himself in Italy feeling what he probably did not feel at all when he was actually there, for the war has changed much of his outlook. He sees himself recovering in Italy "the peace of the ancient world" along "the old, olive-fuming shores," and then looks still further from that point into the past, "backwards, only backwards," as though losing himself in antiquity. But then he goes on to report a memory doubly removed as his conclusion. He thought of England then-- where of course he is now--he thought of it as "horrible . . . black, and fuming." But surprisingly enough he decides that England is after all better than Italy. Because the problem is one of life-direction, after all. And then comes the moral of the whole sketch: "It is better to go forward into error than to stay fixed inextricably in the past."[18]

In the previous example of a visual detail appearing repeatedly in lesser prose and culminating in the fiction, the image was single and definite. In my next example the recurrent element is a scene, and the process of creation is more like that of the passage cited from The Rainbow. Once more we begin with a letter. The place is Fiascherino, Italy, and the time is about one year after the Lake Garda period. This was where Lawrence came to the realizations that largely made The Rainbow and Women in Love what they are. His receptivity to the impressions of place and his facility for turning them to account were never greater. The language of the letters vibrates with the results. We find, as always, the intensely visual descriptions. We find more than ever the imagination poised in awareness of its spatial and temporal relation to the physical world. The cottage where they live, Lawrence writes, is on "a little tiny bay half shut in by rocks." But the olive woods that "smother" the bay "slope down swiftly"[19]: as if the spot were both cosily enclosed and at the same time precipitated into motion. The implications of movement are far greater at another moment when Lawrence is out on a ship near this delightful spot and gazing out in the midst of writing a letter. Here is "a massive dark sea" against a sky "pearl white" and far off yet "level with one's eyes." In the rhythm of the vessel he cannot be sure whether he will thrill next to "a sensation of gradual, infinite upslope, or of slow, sure stooping into the spaces."[20] There could be no better illustration of absolute immersion in surroundings to the limit of one's being.

Still in the letters, a little further on, we discover a connection between a sense of place and a sense of the past like that alluded to in Twilight in Italy. But here the association is mythical rather than historical. Lawrence writes of how he walks along on the heights above the sea, with the olive trees all around. It is so Biblical, so reminiscent of the Sea of Galilee apparently, that he expects at any turn "to meet Jesus gossiping with his disciples as he goes along above the sea, under the grey, light trees."[21]

Now this might be taken as a fancy soon to pass, if we did not know Lawrence well, know of the recall and transformation of bygone moments and places in later work. We come to fiction again, and to a far later time in this case, all the way to The Escaped Cock, written some sixteen years afterwards. The setting of the temple of Isis in this story owes some of its most significant details, it seems to me, to a recollection of Fiascherino. The Christ association is obvious, but we find also the same sense of steepness, the same tints the olive trees lend to the atmosphere, and the pine trees mentioned often in other letters. To help us fix the identity, the temple stands, "on a little, tree-covered tongue of land between two bays"[22] that closely resembles the situation of Fiascherino.

Concerning the Fiascherino setting, some of the photographs will demonstrate my point. The next place, however, is so fantasized to start with that photographs can portray only a single aspect of the whole, the aspect of loftiness. For the rest, I think you will be content with Lawrence's own word pictures. The landscape I speak of now fulfills more than any yet mentioned, perhaps, Lawrence's insistence on living motion in a natural scene.

In Sea and Sardinia, nearing Cagliari, the port where he landed on the island, Lawrence sees the city in a plainly emblematic light. As visible from the ship Cagliari is "a naked town rising steep, steep, golden-looking. . . . The city piles up lofty and almost miniature, and makes me think of Jerusalem." The sense of illusion grows: "It is like some vision, some memory, something that has passed away. Impossible that one can actually walk in that city."[23]

It is the habit of mythical vision for strange locations again, but with some nuances not encountered in our examples so far. This passage, written soon after Lawrence's quick trip through Sardinia, suggests a more deliberate distortion of reality into illusion as a way of absorbing new places. But half of the parallel has no origin in reality at all, for Lawrence had never been to Jerusalem. He meant the Jerusalem of a Biblically oriented mind, of course, and fortunately we can verify much about this tendency of his by referring to such other writing as the essay "Hymns in a Man's Life." He recalls here the effects on him in childhood of places from the Nonconformist hymns, of "Galilee and Canaan, Moab and Kedron."[24] These were magic worlds that came to "exist in the golden haze of a child's half-formed imagination."[25] And the impressions have lasted untouched into manhood, their wonder never dimmed: a principal source in the development of imagination. As for Galilee, we are reminded naturally of Fiascherino. Jerusalem itself is not mentioned in the "Hymns" essay, though obviously the Holy City belongs to the same category as the other localities. We might think here too of the statements in the early pages of Apocalypse, also written late in life, concerning the growth of childhood vision through exposure to the Book of Revelations with, among other things, its New Jerusalem.

But it is not till we turn to one of Lawrence's outright fantasies that the Jerusalem image falls into place in relation to the curious description in Sea and Sardinia. I refer to the utopian fantasy that Keith Sagar has entitled "A Dream of Life,"[26] written in the same general period as Apocalypse and "Hymns in a Man's Life," with its

picture of Lawrence's native Midlands a thousand years hence and its
narrator awakened from his millennial sleep to witness mankind reborn.
"The ugly colliery townlet of dirty red brick" where he was born has
become a golden city set on a hill, and to describe it he calls up
from memory how that town looked to him as a child when he would
approach it from a distance in afternoon light. It was like the "walls
of Jerusalem . . . a golden city, as in the hymns we sang in the Congregational Chapel."[27] An image of childhood contributes now to a
perfected future. For all his travels over much of the earth between
his early life and the date of this fragment, Lawrence goes back for
a vision of the future to what lay about him in his infancy. The discovery in adult years of a mysterious symbolism in a Sardinian city
proves to be, then, but a piece in a life-long design. This sort of
quest for perfection is not far from that of the New Testament myth-
maker who wrote, "For here have we no continuing city, but we seek
one to come."[28]

There is yet a further dimension to this whole pattern of inner
and outer, past and present vision--and I should say "future vision"
as well. It has to do with Lawrence's vision of America. In this case
the portrayal in the mind comes before any actual contact with the
place--a "prophetic" vision, if you will. Certainly Lawrence held it
to be such. He fashioned it out of an interpretation of early American
literature--following that power of the written word discussed at the
start of this paper. It was not only that he pictured in a sort of
dreamland, like most sensitive readers, the scenes in the fiction he
read. Out of Cooper and Melville and others he invented a whole continent of America and treated it in essays on these writers just as
he had treated Italy by recollection in Twilight in Italy: as a route
to philosophic truth by symbolic creation of a place on a mythical
plane. The imaginative span of the various symbological essays written
during the Great War is in fact a leap from Italy as past place to
England as present place to America as future place. The most effective presentation of this clairvoyance is in the essay on Cooper's
Leatherstocking novels. And if we take account of the whole personal
context of Lawrence's fascination with these books, we will understand
better why at the time he thought Cooper to be the greatest novelist
in the world. He sorely needed what Cooper had to offer: escape into
the promising unknown.

Lawrence becomes ecstatic over Cooper's description of a pioneer
village in the forests of upstate New York, and of the limitless
prairies to the west. A mystic "consummation"[29] with these scenes
which he ascribes to Cooper he plainly shares and brings home to himself in Europe. He calls the New York State village an extension of
England, but of England "in the toils of the great dark spirit of the
continent"[30] of America. All this is past, perhaps, but no, not as
Lawrence conceives it--though of course the fact that it is a vision
out of history supplies the potential for further vision. But what
truly captures Lawrence's attention, strangely enough, is what the
scene holds for him of the future, what he refers to as the "pristine
magic of futurity, like the Odyssey."[31] Both Cooper and Homer are, in
other words, prophets of the coming time for their respective peoples.

Now we may soon realize that this dream-like future of America is
mainly a projection of Lawrence himself out of a dark and dying Europe

at war into a land of rebirth, but the point here is that the concept of being which the writer feels essential to his emotional being emanates from a place and a time that can represent the past, much more so the future, and yet possess all the immediacy of present reality.

When Lawrence's enthrallment with remote America came to actuality several years later, Cooper's world still assisted his views. The first Indians he saw that he could take to be "wild" were the Jicarilla Apaches of New Mexico, and he responded, he reports, in a heart "kindled with Fenimore Cooper," seeing the Apaches as "nomad nations gathering still in the continent of hemlock trees and prairies,"[32]— again the magnificence of the virgin conifer forest and the vast expanse of the prairie. From this time on Lawrence spoke much of the primeval spirit of America in terms of a geographical balance between the pine forests of the New Mexico mountains and the great open spaces around them, a balance focused eventually on the setting of Kiowa Ranch, with its many pine trees and broad view to the west. In this landscape Lawrence felt in touch with the cosmic energy once available to animistic man, that god-stuff as "shaggy as the pine-trees, and horrible as the lightning."[33] On first going up to Kiowa Ranch--called that name by Lawrence because the Kiowa Indians used to camp there--he had the aid of some Taos Indians in making the cabins liveable. After they left he and Frieda went out to sleep one time where they had camped. He elaborates the marvel of this place in a letter, how "something wild and untamed, cruel and proud" comes to him "out of the air," here with the "trees and mountains" and "only the great desert below," and a squirrel that "runs up the balsam pine."[34]

Frequently this spirit of the American landscape was manifested for Lawrence in a single tree, a big pine in front of his cabin. When the Taos Indians were at their camp, their drumming and dancing at night furnished much of the substance of the essay "Pan in America," which Lawrence worked on sometimes as he listened to them. The big pine appears, "like a guardian spirit in front of the cabin where we live," that tree which "is still within the allness of Pan"[35] and thus carries much of the essay's theme. A little later that year Lawrence wrote St. Mawr, the short novel in which Lou Witt makes the crucial decision of her life at a ranch based on Kiowa, as does another woman who precedes her, the New England wife of a previous owner. The first woman eventually succumbs to "the animosity of the spirit of place"[36] here and much of this spirit attacks her through the pine-trees. One aspect of their malevolence is visually reminiscent of those trees that Paul Morel painted in Sons and Lovers--"at evening, the trunks would flare up orange-red."[37] To this Lawrence adds a new image, a typical glimpse of animation in the landscape: the branches of the pines rise in "dark, alert tufts like a wolf's tail touching the air."[38] This awful beauty that finally defeats her is centered from time to time in the single tree, "the great pine-tree that threw up its trunk sheer in front of the house, in the yard. That pine-tree was the guardian of the place. But a bristling, almost demonish guardian, from the far-off crude ages of the world. Its great pillar of pale, flaky-ribbed copper rose there in strange callous indifference, and the grim permanence, which is in pine-trees."[39]

Lou Witt, unlike the other woman, finds her highest inspiration and the perfect retreat from modern decadence in the ranch, in the "great desert-and-mountain landscape."[40] Here she expects to escape involvement with the "phallic male,"[41] unless it be with "the mystic new man"[42] she despairs of ever meeting. Here she will surrender herself to the "wild spirit more than men"[43] which is the spirit of the place itself. The pine-tree embodies just that, for it has already been described as "a passionless, non-phallic column, rising in the shadows of the pre-sexual world, before the hot-blooded ithyphallic column ever erected itself."[44]

Lawrence comes back to this pine-tree in one of his fullest parallel evocations of two places at once, the little sketch with which he ended Mornings in Mexico, written two months after he left America for good and was living at Spotorno on the Italian Riviera. The moon on the Mediterranean calls up an analogous scene at Kiowa Ranch, and in a free play of imagination the writer turns back and forth between his actual surroundings and the former surroundings made highly desirable by memory. He is not in the "Old World" at all, for the Mediterranean is "eternally young," and America represents a "wonderful, hoary age." As he sees it, "the time is different there," moonlight and all. The ranch in his mind is empty of human presence, but for all that not deserted, for there is "the big pine tree in front of the house, standing still and unconcerned, alive." He purposely distorts his sense of time and place: "I wonder if I am here, or if I am just going to bed at the ranch,"[45] among all the ghosts that never leave the pine woods around. They reproach him for going away. All the same they gather round him like his own family, and stay close by while he sleeps. And when he wakes he will "see the trunk of the great pine tree, like a person on guard,"[46] like one of the ghosts incarnate.

Immediacy and recollection--a long chain of impulses born of immersion in place: born, facing, and returning in a rhythm that underlies a great part of Lawrence's whole creative genius.

Passages

I

A. "As one goes higher the crucifixes get smaller and smaller. The wind blows the snow under the tiny shed of a tiny Christ" (Phoenix, p. 85).

B. "Only high up, where the crucifix becomes smaller and smaller, is there left any of the old beauty and religion. Higher and higher, the monument becomes smaller and smaller, till in the snows it stands out like a post, or a thick arrow stuck barb upwards. The crucifix itself is a small thing under the pointed hood, the barb of the arrow. The snow blows under the tiny shed, upon the little, exposed Christ. All round is the solid whiteness of snow, the awful curves and concaves of pure whiteness of the mountain top, the hollow whiteness between the peaks, where the path crosses the high, extreme ridge of the pass. And here stands the last crucifix, half buried, small and tufted with snow" (Twilight in Italy, pp. 13-14).

C. "Having gained one ridge, he saw the vague shadow of something higher in front. Always higher, always higher. . . . He had lost all his sense of place. . . . How frail the thread of his being was stretched! He would perhaps climb the ridge. The snow was firm and simple. He went along. There was something standing out of the snow. He approached with dimmest curiosity.

It was a half-buried crucifix, a little Christ under a little sloping hood at the top of a pole. He sheered away. Somebody was going to murder him. He had a great dread of being murdered. But it was a dread which stood outside him like his own ghost" (Women in Love, p. 465).

Passages

II

A. "I have read Anna of the Five Towns today, because it is stormy weather. For five months I have scarcely seen a word of English print, and to read it makes me feel fearfully queer. I don't know where I am. I am so used to the people going by outside, talking or singing some foreign language, always Italian now: but to-day, to be in Hanley, and to read almost my own dialect, makes me feel quite ill. I hate England and its hopelessness. I hate Bennett's resignation. Tragedy ought really to be a great kick at misery. But Anna of the Five Towns seems like an acceptance--so does all the modern stuff since Flaubert. I hate it. I want to wash again quickly, wash off England, the oldness and grubbiness and despair.

Today it is so stormy. The lake is dark, and with white lambs all over it. The steamer rocks as she goes by. There are no sails stealing past. The vines are yellow and red, and fig trees are in flame on the mountains. I can't bear to be in England when I am in Italy. It makes me feel so soiled. Yesterday F. and I went down along the lake towards Maderno. We climbed down from a little olive wood, and swam. It was evening, so weird, and a great black cloud trailing over the lake. And tiny little lights of village came out, so low down, right across the water. Then great lightnings split out.--No, I don't believe England need be so grubby" (Collected Letters, pp. 150-51).

B. "We went out of the shadow of the lemon-house on to the roof of the one below us. When we came to the brink of the roof, I sat down. The Signore stood behind me, a shabby, shaky little figure on his roof against the sky, lifted up like an image of decay. Yet the mountain snow was radiant opposite, and a film of pure blue was on the hills. The water breathed an iridescent dust on the far shore. An orange-sailed boat leaned slim on the dark-blue water, where crisp flecks of foam were fluttering. A woman went downhill with two goats and two sheep. Among the olives someone was whistling.

'Yes,' said the little Signore, musing, looking down from his height. 'That was once lemon-garden down there--you see the stumps of the pillars, between the vines. Twice as much, twice as much lemons, I had. . . .'

I sit and look at the lake. And now the lemon-gardens in ruin among the hills stand out to me. . . .

'But it is beautiful!' I protest. 'In England--'
'Ah,' cries the Signore, 'in England you have the wealth--
les richesses--but here we have the sun'; he waved his hand heaven-
wards towards the wonderful source of the blue day. But he sounded
sadly, as if he were making the best of it. If the sun had been a big
lemon hanging in his garden, I am afraid he would have sold it by
weight" (English Review, September 1913, pp. 219-20).
    C. "We went out of the shadow of the lemon-house on to the roof
of the section below us. When we came to the brink of the roof I sat
down. The padrone stood behind me, a shabby, shaky little figure on
his roof in the sky, a little figure of dilapidation, dilapidated as
the lemon-houses themselves.
    We were always level with the mountain-snow opposite. A film
of pure blue was on the hills to the right and the left. There had
been a wind, but it was still now. The water breathed an iridescent
dust on the far shore, where the villages were groups of specks.
    On the low level of the world, on the lake, an orange-sailed
boat leaned slim to the dark-blue water, which had flecks of foam. A
woman went down-hill quickly, with two goats and a sheep. Among the
olives a man was whistling.
    'Voyez,' said the padrone, with distant, perfect melancholy.
'There was once a lemon garden also there--you see the short pillars.
. . . Once there were twice as many lemons as now. . . .'
    Suddenly his face broke into a smile of profound melancholy,
almost a grin, like a gargoyle. It was the real Italian melancholy,
very deep, static. . . .
    I sat and looked at the lake. It was beautiful as paradise,
as the first creation. On the shores were the ruined lemon-pillars
standing out in melancholy, the clumsy, enclosed lemon-houses seemed
ramshackle, bulging among vine stocks and olive trees. The villages,
too, clustered upon their churches, seemed to belong to the past.
They seemed to be lingering in bygone centuries.
    'But it is very beautiful,' I protested. 'In England--'
    'Ah, in England,' exclaimed the padrone, the same ageless,
monkey-like grin of fatality, tempered by cunning, coming on his face,
'in England you have the wealth--les richesses--you have the mineral
coal and the machines, vous savez. Here, we have the sun----'
    He lifted his withered hand to the sky, to the wonderful
source of that blue day, and he smiled, in histrionic triumph. But his
triumph was only histrionic. The machines were more to his soul than
the sun. . . . As for the sun, that is common property, and no man is
distinguished by it. He wanted machines, machine-production, money,
and human power. . . . He wanted to go where the English have gone.
. . .
    I sat on the roof of the lemon-house, with the lake below
and the snowy mountain opposite, and looked at the ruins on the old,
olive-fuming shores, at all the peace of the ancient world still
covered in sunshine, and the past seemed to me so lovely that one
must look towards it, backwards, only backwards, where there is peace
and beauty and no more dissonance.
    I thought of England, the great mass of London, and the black,
fuming, laborious Midlands and north-country. It seemed horrible. And
yet, it was better than the padrone, this old, monkey-like cunning of

fatality. It is better to go forward into error than to stay fixed inextricably in the past" (<u>Twilight in Italy</u>, pp. 51-53).

Passages

III

A. "I am so happy with the place we have at last discovered, I must write smack off to tell you. It is perfect. There is a little tiny bay half shut in by rocks, and smothered by olive woods that slope down swiftly. Then there is one pink, flat, fisherman's house. Then there is the <u>villino</u> of Ettore Gambrosier, a four-roomed pink cottage among vine gardens, just over the water and under the olive woods" (<u>Collected Letters</u>, p. 227).

B. "It is very lovely here. I sit on the rocks against the sea all day and write. I tell you it is a dream" (<u>Collected Letters</u>, p. 230).

C. "I am writing on the steamer, going to Spezia. It is a wonderful morning, with a great, level, massive blue sea, and strange sails far out, deep in a pearl glow, and San Terenzo all glittering pink on the shore. It is so beautiful, it almost hurts: so big, with such a massive dark sea and such endless, pearl white sky far away and level with ones eyes. On this sea, looking at the horizon, I never know whether I shall feel a sensation of gradual, infinite up-slope, or of slow, sure stooping into the spaces" (<u>Collected Letters</u>, p. 241).

D. "You have no idea how beautiful olives are, so grey, so delicately sad, reminding one constantly of the New Testament. I am always expecting when I go to Tellaro for the letters, to meet Jesus gossiping with his disciples as he goes along above the sea, under the grey, light trees" (<u>Collected Letters</u>, p. 255).

E. "The temple, facing south and west, towards Egypt, faced the splendid sun of winter as he curved down towards the sea, and warmth and radiance flooded in between the pillars of painted wood. But the sea was invisible, because of the trees, though its dashing sounded among the hum of pines. The air was turning golden to afternoon. The woman who served Isis stood in her yellow robe, and looked up at the steep slopes coming down to the sea, where the olive-trees silvered under the wind like water splashing. She was alone, save for the goddess. And in the winter afternoon the light stood erect and magnificent off the invisible sea, filling the hills of the coast. She went towards the sun, through the grove of Mediterranean pine-trees and evergreen oaks, in the midst of which the temple stood, on a little, tree-covered tongue of land between two bays" (<u>The Escaped Cock</u>, p. 35).

Passages

IV

A. "And suddenly there is Cagliari: a naked town rising steep, steep, golden-looking, piled naked to the sky from the plain at the head of the formless hollow bay. It is strange and rather wonderful, not a bit like Italy. The city piles up lofty and almost miniature,

and makes me think of Jerusalem: without trees, without cover, rising
rather bare and proud, remote as if back in history, like a town in a
monkish, illuminated missal. One wonders how it ever got there. . . .
It has that curious look, as if it could be seen but not entered. It
is like some vision, some memory, something that has passed away.
Impossible that one can actually walk in that city" (Sea and Sardinia,
p. 52).
    B. "At the top of the hill was a town, all yellow in the late
afternoon light, with yellow, curved walls rising massive from the
yellow-leaved orchards, and above, buildings swerving in a long, oval
curve, and round, faintly conical towers rearing up. It had something
at once soft and majestical about it, with its soft yet powerful
curves, and no sharp angles or edges, the whole substance seeming
soft and golden like the golden flesh of a city.
    And I knew, even while I looked at it, that it was the place
where I was born, the ugly colliery townlet of dirty red brick. Even
as a child, coming home from Moorgreen, I had looked up and seen the
squares of miners' dwellings, built by the Company, rising from the
hill-top in the afternoon light like the walls of Jerusalem, and I
had wished it were a golden city, as in the hymns we sang in the
Congregational Chapel" (Phoenix, p. 829).

                              Passages

                                 V

    A. "Five minutes' walk from here are the tents and beds of the
Indians, still standing. Frieda and I slept there once, under the big
stars that hang low on the mountains here. Morning comes and a beautiful grey squirrel runs up the balsam pine and scolds us. No one else
in the world, only the great desert below, to the west. . . . Here,
where one is alone with trees and mountains and chipmunks and desert,
one gets something out of the air, something wild and untamed, cruel
and proud, beautiful and sometimes evil--that is really America"
(Collected Letters, pp. 794-95).
    B. "A big pine tree rises like a guardian spirit in front of the
cabin where we live. Long, long ago the Indians blazed it. And the
lightning, or the storm, has cut off its crest. Yet its column is
always there, alive and changeless, alive and changing. The tree has
its own aura of life. And in winter the snow slips off it, and in
June it sprinkles down its little catkin-like pollen-tips, and it
hisses in the wind, and it makes a silence within a silence. It.is a
great tree, under which the house is built. And the tree is still
within the allness of Pan" (Phoenix, p. 24).
    C. "Her cabin faced the slow down-slope of the clearing, the
alfalfa field: her long, low cabin, crouching under the great pine-
tree that threw up its trunk sheer in front of the house, in the yard.
That pine-tree was the guardian of the place. But a bristling, almost
demonish guardian, from the far-off crude ages of the world. Its great
pillar of pale, flaky-ribbed copper rose there in strange callous indifference, and the grim permanence, which is in pine-trees. A passionless, non-phallic column, rising in the shadows of the pre-sexual world,
before the hot-blooded ithyphallic column ever erected itself. . . .

Past the column of that pine-tree, . . . from which silent,
living barrier isolated pines rose to ragged heights at intervals, in
blind assertiveness. . . . At evening, the trunks would flare up
orange-red, and the tufts would be dark, alert tufts like a wolf's
tail touching the air" (St. Mawr, pp. 145-46).

D. "There is a bright moon, so that even the vines make a shadow,
and the Mediterranean has a broad white shimmer between its dimness.
By the shore, the lights of the old houses twinkle quietly. . . .
[But] what about the ranch, the little ranch in New Mexico? The time
is different there. . . . The moon shines on the alfalfa slope, between the pines, and the cabins are blind. There is nobody there.
. . . Only the big pine tree in front of the house, standing still and
unconcerned, alive. . . . Here, the castle of Noli is on the western
skyline. . . . There it has snowed, and the nearly full moon blazes
wolf-like, as here it never blazes; risen like a were-wolf over the
mountains. . . . The Mediterranean whispers in the distance, a sound
like in a shell. . . . I wonder if I am here, or if I am just going
to bed at the ranch. . . . The pine trees make little noises, sudden
and stealthy, as if they were walking about. And the place heaves
with ghosts . . . that never go beyond the timber. . . . At the ranch,
to-night, . . . I should . . . dart to bed, with all the ghosts of
the ranch cosily round me. . . . Waking, I shall look at once through
the glass panels of the bedroom door, and see the trunk of the great
pine tree, like a person on guard" (Mornings in Mexico, pp. 80-82).

"Only high up, where the crucifix becomes smaller and smaller, is there left any of the old beauty and religion"--Twilight in Italy, p. 13.

"The crucifix itself is a small thing under the pointed hood, the
barb of the arrow"--Twilight in Italy, p. 14.

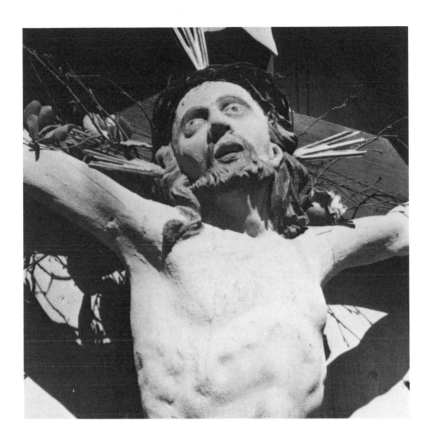

"A little Christ under a little sloping hood at the top of a pole.
He sheered away. Somebody was going to murder him. He had a great
dread of being murdered. But it was a dread which stood outside
him like his own ghost"--Women in Love, p. 465.

"Today it is so stormy. The lake is dark, and with white lambs all over it"--<u>Collected</u> <u>Letters</u>, p. 150.

"That was once lemon-garden down there--you see the stumps of the
pillars, between the vines"--English Review, p. 220.

"The villages, too, clustered upon their churches, seemed to belong
to the past. They seemed to be lingering in bygone centuries"--
Twilight in Italy, p. 52.

"The black, fuming, laborious Midlands and north-country"--
<u>Twilight</u> <u>in</u> <u>Italy</u>, p. 53.

"A little tiny bay half shut in by rocks, and smothered by olive woods that slope down swiftly"--Collected Letters, p. 227.

"A four-roomed pink cottage among vine gardens, just over the
water and under the olive woods"--Collected Letters, p. 227.

"You have no idea how beautiful olives are, so grey, so delicately sad, reminding one constantly of the New Testament"--<u>Collected Letters</u>, p. 255.

"The grove of Mediterranean pine-trees and evergreen oaks, in the
midst of which the temple stood, on a little, tree-covered tongue
of land between two bays"--The Escaped Cock, p. 35.

"And suddenly there is Cagliari: a naked town rising steep, steep, golden-looking, piled naked to the sky. . . . The city piles up lofty and almost miniature, and makes me think of Jerusalem"--
Sea and Sardinia, p. 52.

"The circling guard of pine-trees, from which silent, living
barrier isolated pines rose to ragged heights at intervals.
. . . At evening, . . . the tufts would be dark, alert tufts
like a wolf's tail touching the air"--St. Mawr, p. 146.

"The cabins are blind. There is nobody there. . . . Only the big
pine tree in front of the house, standing still and unconcerned,
alive"--Mornings in Mexico, p. 80.

"The Mediterranean whispers in the distance, a sound like in a
shell. . . . I wonder if I am here, or if I am just going to bed
at the ranch"--Mornings in Mexico, p. 81.

"The great pine-tree that threw up its trunk sheer in front of the house, in the yard. That pine-tree was the guardian of the place. But a bristling, almost demonish guardian, from the far-off crude ages of the world"--St. Mawr, p. 145.

Lawrence's Major Works

Lawrence's Major Work

EMILE DELAVENAY

The theme of this Conference is "D. H. Lawrence Today" and the title originally suggested for this session "Lawrence's Major Novels," subsequently changed to "Lawrence's Major Works," but I do not think this need trouble us much, since I doubt anyone would challenge the position of the novels as the major works. Therefore my remarks will relate to some limited aspects of Lawrence today and to what I consider his major novel.

Let me begin with a few words on the state of Lawrence criticism today. This Conference has given ample evidence that the Lawrence industry is flourishing. In fact, publishers will accept, it seems, almost anything, good or indifferent, which contains his name in the title, and the substantial number of books sent out for review each year confirms the prosperity of the business, if not always the value of the criticism. Here, we have some first-rate scholarly criticism and also some highly elegant variations on familiar themes. And yet, especially when so much emphasis is placed on Lawrence's "rehabilitation" of the phallus, as if Lady Chatterley's Lover were his major work, can we altogether dismiss the thought that critics are now scraping the bottom of the barrel?

A ray of hope is, however, brought into this Conference by the timely initiative of the Cambridge University Press and the teams they have put to work on the textual editions of the letters and of the complete works. I have no doubt, as one who has suffered, despite the noble efforts of Aldous Huxley and Harry T. Moore, from the chaotic state of the so-far-published letters, that, when they are at last available in their chronological sequence and without excisions and expurgations, and when all the variants of the different works are printed in a format allowing easy comparison, future students will be able to concentrate more effectively than was possible to us of the older generation on the significance of the man and his works.

Let us hope, indeed, that the availability of these definitive texts will soon make it possible to review constructively the aims and means of future Lawrence criticism. As Lawrence becomes part of the history of bygone days rather than the prophet, interpreter, and stimulator of the dissatisfactions of his contemporaries and immediate successors, the need to see him in the perspective of his own time and place will grow. There will then be room, as well as means, for new and fertile critical studies, and for assessments free from the critics' personal reactions to social and psychological conditions closely resembling those from which Lawrence himself suffered. Those of us who were at the Taos conference in 1970 will be struck, as I am, by the change in the critical atmosphere since that conference. The element of the cult is less evident, and there are healthy signs of an approach closer to that of the laboratory than of worship at a shrine. For this our thanks are due, at least in part, to the directors of this Conference.

On the theme of "the major works" I may perhaps be allowed to make a personal contribution both as one who first approached Lawrence from a foreign culture, and as a teacher of French students who are fascinated by him but nonetheless experience various difficulties in fully understanding both his writing and the characters in his novels. While many of you may feel that the world we live in, which is increasingly "one world," owes some of its characteristics to Lawrence's message, I for one am prepared to put greater emphasis on his Englishness, on an Englishness which indeed now belongs to the historical past, even though many of his themes anticipate some present preoccupations.

Lawrence has of course been translated into French, but often so incredibly badly that one wonders what the reader can make of him. And there is a Lawrence legend, built upon hearsay and approximations. If you were to ask the French equivalent of "the man in the street," "Who was Lawrence?" you would probably obtain an answer roughly of this order: "That chap from the Intelligence Service who wrote dirty novels? Wasn't there one called The Seven Pillars of Lady Chatterley's Lover?" This is not in the least improbable, even in a place like Vence, where the boosters of the local tourist industry calmly write newspaper articles about the people who allegedly "knew him well" and "had many conversations with him" in the days when he "lived at Vence." Even literary gentlemen who should know better are all too prone to seize on colorful bits of the legend when writing about him.

At a more responsible level, that is to say among academic critics and advanced and middle-grade students, we find a continuing, serious, and often passionate interest in Lawrence, not unconnected sometimes with a young student's personal problems of family relationships and revolt against a home environment felt to be constraining. After all, French society, especially in the Latin South, is not as permissive as our newspapers and magazines and film festivals might suggest.

This is where Sons and Lovers comes into its own as what I unhesitatingly call, from the special angle from which I have chosen to speak, THE major novel. By this I mean the one from which the French student will draw maximum profit in terms of knowledge of Lawrence the man, Lawrence the artist, and of understanding the late-Victorian and post-Victorian England.

I am not concerned here with "pure" literary values, if there are such things, but with the capacity of a novel both to shock the reader into recognition of greatness and to communicate a wide range of human experience, personal, social, psychological, economic, geographical, and historical--in other words, to enlarge the field of consciousness of the careful reader not only in relation to a chosen course of studies (in this case, English civilization and literature) but also to his understanding of human nature. In this context, I certainly rate Sons and Lovers above The Rainbow and Women in Love. In those two later works, the information is transmuted and polarized, in the way dextrose polarizes a ray of light. The artistic distortion of the raw experience raises literary problems of a different order, which can only be treated in class after certain basic facts about English life and about Lawrence have been fully assimilated. And I rate it high above Lady Chatterley's Lover, even after taking into account the scenes describing life in the mining town of Tevershall, as compared with the colliery and the collier's home scenes in Sons and Lovers.

Having taught French students Chaucer and Shakespeare, Milton, Pope, and Byron, to name but a few, I wish to stress that teaching Sons and Lovers today in France offers an equally rich and rewarding experience and requires the use of similar techniques: those are writers who call on the whole range of scholarly treatment, from philology through the history of ideas and literary history to personal psychology and stylistic analysis.

First of all, there is the problem of language: even the advanced student of English who has acquired fluency during a year or more spent in Boston or Austin, or in London, Edinburgh, or Bristol, has to master the Eastwood dialect, at least enough to understand the dialogue if not to reproduce the accent orally. This is for him an exercise not unlike that which was common in the days when we still taught the Canterbury Tales or The Tale of the Coffers in the original Middle English and not in modern English or even a French translation.

In addition to this philological effort the student has to strive to acquire historical and cultural notions often unfamiliar to him. He must learn something of the English working-class culture and politics of the nineties and the early twentieth-century, to penetrate in depth the religious background of the Morel and Leivers households. Because the novel was first conceived as a realist piece of literature, because every scene had been lived by the author, Sons and Lovers can be exploited in class as an invaluable document illuminating working men's ways and philosophy in England in the Age of Improvement. Mrs. Morel appears as the true inheritor of the workers' educational tradition in the nineteenth century, of which the choice agents were the cooperatives, the women's guilds, the Mechanics' Institute and its library, the Congregational chapel and its ministers. The Coop office is the means for Mrs. Morel to elevate her son William into the middle class. In describing life in Eastwood in the eighties and nineties, Lawrence has given us a coherent and almost complete picture of the England of Samuel Smiles, striving like Mrs. Morel and her sons, in its own blind way, for social mobility through thrift and self-improvement.

I need not enlarge on the colliery scenes and the descriptions of Walter Morel's side of Eastwood life: everything essential has been said about that. Nor need I emphasize the unique introduction Lawrence provides for foreign students to English farm life and the beauties of the natural environment in Derbyshire and Nottinghamshire. The powerfully written early part of the novel, conceived as a paean of praise for Gertrude Morel, is a fine educational tool, almost exempt from the distortions and exaggerations which lessen the usefulness of scenes in some of the later novels, from those Van Gogh-like effects one comes across, in Women in Love for example. And yet, as Lawrence himself said, Sons and Lovers is art, great art, and as such provides the student with a powerful incentive to assimilate its rich and varied content.

Equally illuminating in the classroom is an analysis of Lawrence's gradual self-discovery as the novel progresses, the realization, partly due to the advice given him by Jessie Chambers and partly to the incipient influence of psychoanalysis, of his mother's role in destroying his early love. In other novels, the more brutal, more sarcastic treatment of the mother-son relationship is less effective in helping students analyze their own problems. Better than The Rainbow or Women in Love, Sons and Lovers helps them shed their own sickness.

And yet the germs of Lawrence's future development are there, for instance in the discussion between Paul and Gertrude of his attachment to "his common people." Paul, the young twentieth-century artist, has begun to see through the fallacies and inadequacies of Samuel Smiles. "Improvement," in the old-fashioned sense, has now but little attraction for him. He is not yet ready to "drop out of the rat race," but his attitudes are a prefiguration of Ursula's in The Rainbow and Birkin's in Women in Love. Here again, the very gradualness of the process has untold pedagogical value and leads to heated discussions, especially as Paul's attitude to class and to social mobility remains equally ambiguous, as do his judgments of Gertrude Morel. But is it really more ambiguous than Ursula's or Birkin's? Does Lawrence really set up his own standards of a popular culture? or is he merely aware of an impasse in which the rising working-class boy finds himself? All the conflicts and ambiguities of the later novels, including Lady Chatterley's Lover, are already in Sons and Lovers, in a form which makes them palpable and acceptable to the student, perhaps more so than in the later works.

To sum up, Sons and Lovers seems to me today to be still the best introduction to Lawrence the man and Lawrence the writer. Some of the reasons I have just given are, admittedly, pragmatic. But are there any absolutes in literary criticism? Since one of the main objectives of criticism is, after all, to help others enjoy works of literature, may I simply conclude that, without close familiarity with the world of Paul Morel, there would be much of value in the other major novels which would remain obscure or even unintelligible to the foreign reader.

The Loving of Lady Chatterley: D. H. Lawrence and the Phallic Imagination

> "A man's most dangerous moment," he said, when his head emerged, "is when he's getting into his shirt. Then he puts his head in a bag."[1]

I

The title of Lawrence's novel, Lady Chatterley's Lover, with its indicated emphasis on the male (as her lover), suggests the phallic preoccupation of the work. Lady Chatterley herself does occupy dramatic center-stage, related as she is by plot and theme both to the impotence of Clifford, and to her rebirth through Mellors. But Lawrence's recognizable intention in this novel is to illustrate those modes of belief and manners of sex which men display in their various ways of "loving" Lady Chatterley. Such a commitment, in a single work of fiction, is part of Lawrence's focus throughout his writing career on the revivification of healthy sexual passion between men and women, which Lawrence believes starts with the male expression of what I have called elsewhere "the phallic imagination": the fundamental source of masculine energy and force that begins with existential uncertainty, in a willing and courageous surrender of ego and consciousness in the sex act, and concludes with the pure "singling out," the "star-equilibrium" described by Lawrence in his "pollyanalytical" essays and in Women in Love.[2]

It must be stressed, in this decade of rabid sexual politics, that Connie's renewal is just as important--to her, to Lawrence, and to us--as Mellors'. Yet in the insistent dialectic of this novel, and in the symbolic manifestations of its vision, it is true that Lawrence places first blame and first responsibility on the male; as Mellors is the primary organ for one of Lawrence's last novelistic attempts to formulate his priapic concerns, so does Mellors' organ-- that very root of his being--loom unashamed and active in page after page in this fiction. As Lawrence writes away his dying days, his message must be clear: this novel might be disliked or bowdlerized, but it would not be misunderstood. Indeed, the phallus itself is both instrument of recovery and injured patient in Lady Chatterley's Lover, as its rise, fall, and dismissal becomes a literal and metaphoric index to the health or disease of a fragmented culture.[3]

The men at Wragby who (like Clifford) sit and complain, or who (like Tommy Dukes) pontificate about a "chirpy penis" even while they exempt themselves from passion, or who (like Michaelis) continue to play out their adolescence, all reflect, in different ways, the crippling of their phallic imagination. These men limit, or pervert, or deny the sexual love of women, and this failure merges with and exascerbates their inability to respond confidently, with a proud and existential urging of the whole self, to the postwar issues of the growing power of the machine, the entrenchment of industry, and the social and psychic devastation occasioned by the slaughter of a generation of English men. The instinctive execution of such assertion by a male, as Lawrence first suggested when he derived himself as man and artist in Sons and Lovers, is symbolized by an erect phallus, even in those "wounded" days after 1918 in Lady Chatterley's Lover, and even when that sexual thrusting out involves the disapprobation of society, the vagaries of the law, or the open-ended terrors of uncertainty.[4] Clifford's war injury does not exempt him from Lawrence's scorn for his dead sensual self. We need only recall our essentially sympathetic reaction to Hemingway's Jake Barnes, another representative of the wounded, to realize how the erect moral backbone can begin to compensate for a lack of performing sexual life which is beyond a character's control.

The Lawrence-Hemingway connection is useful, and not only because Hemingway writes about Jake Barnes in the same months that Lawrence begins his first tentative versions of Clifford Chatterley. Lawrence had reviewed Hemingway's first full-length work, In Our Time (1925), and as Lawrence describes the prominent tone of Hemingway's portrait of Nick Adams and what the war has done to that character, he unknowingly anticipates the unmistakable quality of his own characterization of Clifford, and the honest lack of resolution in the last lines of Lady Chatterley's Lover. Here is a passage from Lawrence's criticism of Hemingway: "It is really honest. And it explains a great deal of sentimentality. When a thing has gone to hell inside you, your sentimentalism tries to pretend it hasn't. But Mr. Hemingway is through with sentimentalism."[5] It is not surprising that the author of Lady Chatterley's Lover, who himself both endured and portrayed the damaging effects of cultural barbarism on the organic self, should express an appreciation of the quality of emotional honesty in Hemingway's work. Lady Chatterley's Lover is so free from sentimental bias that it confidently requires its readers not only to understand the needs of Lady Chatterley's loving, but also to condone a woman's abandonment of a crippled husband for the love of her spouse's gamekeeper. It is that same unsentimental quality echoed in the symbolic final lines of the novel. Lady Chatterley's Lover ends without any claims for Connie and Mellors' chances together in the real world, and with a recognition of the exhaustion of the most basic evidence of Mellors' phallic imagination: "But a great deal of us is together, and we can but abide by it, and steer our courses to meet soon. John Thomas says goodnight to Lady Jane, a little droopingly, but with a hopeful heart" (LCL, p. 375).

II

In Lady Chatterley's Lover, more than in his other major fiction, the full force of Lawrence's integrated art and prophesy is devoted to his expression of the phallic imagination. In the novel's view of social culture in England after World War I, in its biting criticism of subordinate characters, in its animus to the machine, in the repetitious, overlapping tone and symbols of its design, and in its unself-conscious use of sharp puns and irony, Lady Chatterley's Lover becomes both a visionary hymn to the phallus and a stylistic homage to the rhythm of sexual intercourse. Whether the phallus is addressed as "John Thomas," or anthropomorphically celebrated as merely "it," or hypocritically theorized upon by the talkers at Wragby, or dismissed as irrelevant by Clifford, Lawrence employs all the staples of novelistic art (including its drama, use of repetition, and its ability to "convey a metaphysic") to write a work of fiction prophetically devoted to the need for phallic renewal and geared for the dramatic representation of such achieved renewal.

In his last full-length novel, Lawrence did not write his greatest work, but he may have created his most integrated piece of literature. Lady Chatterley's Lover uses the whole form of this novel the way Lawrence speaks of his need to catch the "whole hog" of "man alive";[6] he writes the work as simultaneously a method, justification, and metaphor for the intimate process of sexual discovery which Lawrence charts through Connie and Mellors. As if to complete the daring implications of such unity in one novel, Lawrence states his case for the pursuit of this aesthetic integration in a few seminal lines in the work itself. It is rare for such a literary explanation of form to link so organically to theme, as Lawrence explains both his topic and its treatment:

It is the way our sympathy flows and recoils that really determines our lives. And here lies the vast importance of the novel, properly handled. It can inform and lead into new places the flow of our sympathetic consciousness, and it can lead our sympathy away in recoil from things gone dead. Therefore, the novel, properly handled, can reveal the most secret places of life: for it is in the passional secret places of life, above all, that the tide of sensitive awareness needs to ebb and flow, cleansing and freshening (LCL, p. 146).

This is the announcement of the phallic theme of the novel, related intrinsically to the language of literary analysis, to the developing affair of Connie and Mellors, and to our experience of reading the work. For Lady Chatterley's Lover will "inform" us about the loving of Lady Chatterley; it will "lead" us, as it also teaches Connie, to recoil "from a thing gone dead" called Clifford, and from the deathly life he represents. The "passional secret places" in this novel have a complex literal and figurative significance which Lawrence must

intend. Whether the "places" connote the largely unexplored areas of
sexual life which Lawrence will battle to portray against the restric-
tions of censorship, or whether the "places" are the actual openings
to Connie's body which Mellors will discover, Lawrence announces in
those lines of Chapter Nine a large ambition: he makes the declared
doctrinal responsibilities of his art into metaphoric extensions of
its plot, preoccupations, and stylistic rhythms.

As this novel probes the "passional secret places" which Lawrence,
as a writer, penetrates in his work, we are urged to follow the phallic formulation of Lawrence's artistic credo, to the correlative lines
of Mellors' probing phallic imagination; in the following passage we
move through the graduated prose and through Mellors' reactions,
around the curves and folds of Connie's body, as we participate,
with Mellors, in the varieties and repetitions, the highs and the
lows, the ups and the downs, the "flows and recoils" of his discovery:

> She dropped her blanket and kneeled on the clay hearth, holding
> her head to the fire, and shaking her hair to dry it. He watched
> the beautiful curving drop of her haunches. That fascinated him
> today. How it sloped with a rich downslope to the heavy round-
> ness of her buttocks! And in between, folded in the secret warmth,
> the secret entrances! . . . All the while he spoke he exquisitely
> stroked the rounded tail, till it seemed as if a slippery sort
> of fire came from it into his hands. And his fingertips touched
> the two secret openings to her body, time after time, with a
> soft little brush of fire (LCL, p. 284).

For Mellors as for us, it is an appropriate prospecting metaphor of
a digger after gold, and Mellors--who already is familiar with his
find--has that healthy existential urge to find the crucial difference
in the essential patterns of repeating experience. The passage conveys
the notion of a Mellors who can find again, as if he opens a new vein
of ore within the old one. "That fascinated him today"--Mellors is
open to the spontaneity of his day's admiration, as on another day
he is captivated by the pendulum motion of her breasts.

This depiction of the variety of Mellors' interest in her body
is neither a radical view to Lawrence nor a stunning development in
his ideas about sex or about the responsibilities of fiction. To the
Lawrence of Chapter Nine in Lady Chatterley's Lover it is reflective
of a man caught up in the moving "tide of sensitive awareness," which
makes Mellors' eminently phallic imagination "ebb and flow" with the
new rhythms of each sexual encounter. Note, of course, that this
rhythm of "ebb and flow," if it is reduced to its clinical significance, is the natural psycho-sexual rhythm of the sex act itself,
which similarly builds and retreats on the way to climax. Lawrence
includes this pattern of repetition in his earlier fiction, and he
even has created a dialectic response to adverse criticism about the
frequency of tumescent and detumescent rhythm in his prose. In his
"Foreword" to Women in Love, Lawrence writes a few lines that can be
read as a complement to the explanation of Chapter Nine in Lady
Chatterley's Lover, as they involve a similar appeal about his organic
approach to his art; he argues that the repetitive rhythms of style
necessary to embody his phallic imagination in fiction are part of

his vision of the workings of that imagination itself. Repetition
becomes not only necessary to his meaning, it is the form that his
meaning must take to be true to the repetitive rhythms of the phallic
imagination:

> In point of style, fault is often found with the continual,
> slightly modified repetition. The only answer is that it is
> natural to the author; and that every natural crisis in emo-
> tion or passion or understanding comes from this pulsing,
> frictional to-and-fro which works up to culmination.[7]

The "natural crisis" which Lawrence mentions here so defensively
creates the repetition in Lady Chatterley's Lover that is at the
heart of the phallic vision and rhythmic structure of that novel.
The pulsing toward culmination, and the repetition of such incre-
mental rhythms, are most evident in the many explicit scenes of intercourse in the novel, where the stylistic significance is integratively
tied to the physiology it describes.[8] The sexual awakening of Connie
and Mellors does not guarantee their organically complete life, but
it does increase the probability of a happy conclusion to the "passionate struggle into conscious being"--a phrase also from the foreword to Women in Love.
    Note that such a foreword introduces a novel which does not have
the explicit sexuality of Lady Chatterley's Lover. The point is that
the relevant lines from a foreword in 1920 and from Chapter Nine in
Lady Chatterley's Lover in 1928 reflect not only the connections between his use of style and his representation of sexual rebirth, but
also the relation of Lawrence's pulsingly rhythmic prose to his belief
that all of life's personal struggles--of which the sexual is often
the most prominent--reflect the advances and disruptions of this slow
"movement to culmination." Although the "passionate struggle" continues throughout one's life, Mellors' sanguine, phallic-centered
view is supported by Lawrence in the twilight of his own career: "I
believe if men could fuck with warm hearts, and the women take it
warm-heartedly everything would come all right. It's all this cold-
hearted fucking that is death and idiocy" (LCL, p. 266). In Lady
Chatterley's Lover, an impotent and dying author has no time for anything less than naked truth, and he makes his two lovers speak directly to the phallus. It is as if the dark god of D. H. Lawrence's
obsession for twenty-five years is now let loose as a living presence,
to be decked with flowers and worshipped for its idiosyncracy as well
as its power. Lawrence's phallic imagination had always infiltrated
his great major fiction, but usually in a slightly transposed, or
politicized, or mystified form; the phallic imagination had been con-
founded by the inevitable self-consciousness of his self-derivation
in Sons and Lovers, by his understandable need to absorb that theme
into the sweep of female generations in The Rainbow, by the double
burden of a truncated love theme and undigested theory in Women in
Love, and by his unfortunate linkage of the phallic to the province
of political power in Aaron's Rod, The Plumed Serpent, and Kangaroo.
But in the loving of that woman called Lady Chatterley, the phallic
imagination roams free and unadorned, and it is to that loving and
that imagination that I wish to turn.

III

Oliver Mellors is not always as untroubled or ecstatic about Connie's sexual offerings of herself. Mellors must struggle against the memories of his former marriage, just as he must surmount his fear of re-engagement in the world of passion; both battles are caught in that characteristic "flow and recoil" of his sympathies toward Connie. But there is no doubt, from the moment we meet him, of his awareness of the "vast importance" and responsibility inherent in sex. Lawrence has--to continue my transposition of words from Chapter Nine--"properly handled" the form of a novel about the "vast impor-tance" of the phallic imagination, just as Mellors will emerge as the only man who, as he lingers over the "passional places" on Connie's body, will be the first man to "properly handle" the form of Lady Chatterley.

For the other men can only handle petty ideas, and when they touch Connie it is only with the kiss of ego. Michaelis, for instance, is an acquiescent, cynical, and submissive lover, whose physical love for Connie is so masturbatory that he is described as "working his hands furiously in his trouser pockets" (LCL, p. 93) just before his loving of Lady Chatterley; he remains so passive and self-involved that he becomes furious when Connie, who knows she is making manipu-lative love with him, requires him to hold on longer so she can reach her orgasm. The only difference between the immature lovers here is that Connie recognizes the onanistic nature of their affair, so she is shocked for Mick to pretend that deep needs were being served. Lawrence is quite explicit in his essays, fiction, and letters on how strongly he holds account of the inadequacy of a male who does not come to the female for full, complete sexual satisfaction. In one letter he writes: "It is the hardest thing in life to get one's soul and body satisfied from a woman so that one is free from oneself."[9] Michaelis never makes the attempt, and as he desperately clutches his trousers and ego, his loving of Lady Chatterley illustrates one failure of phallic responsibility.

As Lawrence demonstrates in "Pornography and Obscenity," and as W. D. Snodgrass implies in his important essay on "The Rocking-Horse Winner," masturbation and worship of the machine are related perver-sions of passion: erotic desires brought back to oneself or devoted to the inanimate are similar evasions of Lawrence's dictum that sexual energy must seek for the transcendent.[10] Lawrence dramatizes this unholy relationship in the marvelous stalled chair scene. The episode is significant because it combines the poignancy of romantic drama with the bitterness conveyed by double-entendre and blunt symbology. Mark Spilka provocatively explained a quarter of a century ago that by the time of this scene we have learned to hate Clifford, that "thing gone dead," as much as Connie does.[11] By now the affair of Connie and Mellors is well-advanced. Lawrence's confidence in our own awareness of the proper place for "sympathy" is so great that even a radical reordering of the most basic gestures of social con-vention seems easily justified; that is, we clearly side with the adulterous wife of the crippled husband as she touches the hand of her lover, while that lover pushes the woman's ignorant and cuckolded husband up a hill. Clifford's motorized wheelchair, into which (as

Spilka indicates) Clifford has sunk the roots of his _moral_ being, is
his only means of feeling erect and potent. The chair has stalled
going up a hill, and Clifford refuses to call for help. He is wedded
to his machine for support, and he treats it with all the cruel ex-
cesses of displaced libido; he hysterically insists that his machine
can make it. After repeated efforts to start an obviously _improperly
handled_ engine himself, Clifford must call on Mellors. Thus the functioning lover is asked by the broken husband to fix the unfixable
motor; Clifford wants the impossible--he wants Mellors to miraculously
make potent the impotent props of industrial support. But Mellors
knows more about ignored women than he does of modern machines, and
he cannot fix the motor of Lady Chatterley's husband. After an exas-
perated Clifford guns the engine several times, he climaxes his frustrations and his masturbatory evasions by "putting her in gear with
a jerk, having jerked off his brake" (_LCL_, p. 246). Now that Clifford
has so brutally forced a conclusion, the lover of his real woman peers
under Clifford's mechanical lady for a little peek, as "the keeper lay
on his stomach again." Connie watches with concern the exertions of
her lover, who is as confused and ineffective with her husband's
machine as he is confident and nurturant with her. The multiple ironies
and puns about the perverse distortion of the phallic imagination in
this scene all depend on the realization that Lawrence does not make
sport of Clifford or of his paralysis; rather, he criticizes the extent to which Clifford permits his own incapacity to blind him to
what is sustaining, unmechanized, and external. When the chair breaks,
he screams for his toy to be fixed. Clifford is spoiled, not used to
waiting. His childish fondling of Mrs. Bolton's breasts epitomizes
his sexual capacity, as does Lawrence's comment that it is through
Mrs. Bolton that Clifford "got his pecker up" (_LCL_, p. 153).

What matters to Clifford is his reliance on the machine and his
related belief in a consistent arrangement of social conventions. He
does not want to be surprised or disappointed by people, or betrayed
by the motors which run his life; people and machines are useful only
if they can be employed to keep the unexpected and organic claims of
life away from him. When Clifford makes the perverse proposition to
Connie that she have a child for _them_ by a lover of her own choosing,
his justification is his advocacy of a philosophical corruption of
what he calls "the integrated life." As he spells out the practice
of this life to Connie, he reveals the extent to which he can ignore
organic claims in favor of self-indulgence and petty practicality:

> Don't you think one can just subordinate the sex thing to the
> necessities of a long life lived together. . . . Isn't the whole
> problem of life the slow building up of an integral personality,
> through the years. . . . But only do those things so that you
> have an integrated life, that makes a long harmonious thing.
> And you and I can do that together . . . if we adapt ourselves
> to the necessities, and at the same time weave the adaptation
> together into a piece with our steadily lived life (_LCL_, p. 83).

Here Clifford's jargon, with its rampant behavioristic ring, employs
a closed-ended tapestry metaphor to stress qualities of adaptation,

harmony, necessity, and steadiness. But it is precisely Lawrence's
point, dramatized most notably in the contrasting male figure of
Mellors, and in the open-ended conclusion to the novel, that it is
the fundamental and unending momentum toward vital, organic complication which makes life worth living; such momentum comprises that
"ebb and flow" rhythm which moves through the rites of passage from
youth, to maturity, to marriage, and to progeny. Early in their affair
Mellors summarizes to Connie the healthy inevitabilities of their
love-making, when he says: "There's always complications. . . . It's
life. . . . There's no keeping clear. And if you do keep clear you
might almost as well die" (LCL, p. 165).

Thus the phallus in Lady Chatterley's Lover becomes the appropriate index of this commitment to disruptive life over stagnant
death; it is the most direct gauge of the devotion of the phallic
imagination to the necessary uncertainties of the "passionate struggle
into conscious being." In his brilliant defense of D. H. Lawrence in
The Prisoner of Sex, Norman Mailer writes: ". . . The phallus was the
perfect symbol of man, since no matter how powerful a habit was its
full presence, it was the one habit which was always ready to desert
a man."[12] Late in the novel, as Connie and Mellors must decide whether
to inherit the burdens of an unpredictable future together, they discuss their prospects without a hint of the adaptive totalitarianism
of Clifford's prescriptions. They speak only with a sane tentativeness
about their future, which is buttressed by Lady Chatterley's epigram-
matic formulations of the sustaining value of Mellors' brand of loving.
She begins with existential catechism, then slowly strengthens Mellors'
confidence, and finally helps him articulate the power of what he
provides:

> "What else are you?"
> "You may well ask. It no doubt is invisible. Yet I'm some-
> thing to myself at least. I can see the point of my own exis-
> tence, though I can quite understand nobody else's seeing it."
> "And will your existence have less point, if you live
> with me?"
> He paused a long time before replying:
> "It might."
> She, too, stayed to think about it.
> "And what is the point of your existence?"
> "I tell you, it's invisible. I don't believe in the world,
> not in money, nor in advancement, nor in the future of our
> civilization. If there's got to be a future for humanity,
> there'll have to be a very big change from what now is."
> "And what will the real future have to be like?"
> "God knows! I can feel something inside me, all mixed up
> with a lot of rage. But what it really amounts to, I don't know."
> "Shall I tell you?" she said, looking into his face.
> "Shall I tell you what you have that other men don't have, and
> that will make the future? Shall I tell you?"
> "Tell me, then," he replied.
> "It's the courage of your own tenderness, that's what it is,
> like when you put your hand on my tail and say I've got a pretty
> tail."

The grin came flickering on his face.
"That!" he said.
Then he sat thinking.
"Ay!" he said. "You're right. It's that really. It's that all the way through" (LCL, pp. 345-46).

So Lady Chatterley, who gets her real loving from Mellors, helps him to identify the special quality and energy of that loving; she helps him see that his affectionate, naked, and direct admiration of her sexual self is the verbal expression of his revivifying phallic imagination. Connie has heard the pompous twitterings of the emasculated wags at Wragby; she now tells Mellors that she knows the sounds of men from the noise of defaulting aesthetes or passion brokers. From Mellors himself there is the appropriate litany of phrases about the inexplicable and the uncertain: "Invisible . . . invisible . . . something . . . I don't know." Mellors' doubt about how to describe, through language, the root of what D. H. Lawrence calls the "otherness" of sexual being, contrasts with Clifford's willingness to provide prefabricated rationalizations about "the integrated life." It is not an easy integration which this couple faces, but a dislocation which is the mandate and effect of their love. They are willing to bet their "future for humanity" on the polarized connection between John Thomas and Lady Jane.

Such a gamble is complicated by the disruptions of their personal histories and by the confining prejudices of their social environment. Note what the "courage of their own tenderness" must encounter. Gamekeeper Mellors dares the vicious class antagonisms to claim his "Lady" and his unborn child, while he simultaneously tries to recover from his own recent marital experience and attempts to dissolve the authority of another man's marriage. Lady Chatterley must survive the legal and social censures of middle-class and titled morality, as she leaves her title and her crippled husband for a commoner; she is without any assurance that she can live with Mellors and become his wife. Oliver Mellors and Constance Chatterley defy the conventions of a mechanical and sexually fragmented world, and all because of their instinctive belief that the one pure thing in a world of coal, gossip, and "integrated" lives is what Mellors calls "the little flame between us" (LCL, p. 373). Such a fire guarantees nothing, but without it, according to Lawrence, there is nothing; recall how the phallic imagination was derived and affirmed by Paul Morel in his speech to Miriam in Sons and Lovers fifteen years earlier:

> "That's what one must have, I think," he continued--"the real, real flame of feeling through another person--once, only once, if it only lasts three months. See, my mother looks as if she'd had everything that was necessary for her living and developing. There's not a tiny bit of feeling of sterility about her."
> "No," said Miriam.
> "And with my father, at first, I'm sure she had the real thing. She knows; she has been there. You can feel it about her, and about him, and about hundreds of people you meet every day;

and, once it has happened to you, you can go on with anything
and ripen."[13]

IV

In a crucial passage from Armies of the Night, Norman Mailer
writes:

> For guilt was the existential edge of sex. Without guilt,
> sex was meaningless. One advanced into sex against one's sense
> of guilt, and each time guilt was successfully defied, one had
> learned a little more about the contractual nature of one's own
> existence to the unheard thunders of the deep--each time guilt
> herded one back with its authority, some primitive awe--hence
> some creative clue to the rages of the deep--was left to brood
> about.[14]

It is the clarion call of Mailer's sexual aesthetics--sex as the one
pure act of existential definition. Three years later, in his discussion of D. H. Lawrence in The Prisoner of Sex, Mailer broadens
the issues of "sex with guilt" to an understanding that summarizes
the crux of Lawrence's message about the phallic imagination:

> Lawrence's point, which he refines over and over, is that the
> deepest messages of sex cannot be heard by taking a stance on
> the side of the bank, announcing one is in love, and then pro-
> ceeding to fish in the waters of love with a bread basket full
> of ego. No, he is saying again and again, people can win at
> love only when they are ready to lose everything they bring to
> it of ego, position, or identity--love is more stern than war--
> and men and women can survive only if they reach the depths of
> their own sex down within themselves. They have to deliver
> themselves "over to the unknown." No more existential statement
> of love exists, for it is a way of saying we do not know how
> the love will turn out.[15]

When sex is not shorn of this self-defining guilt, when it is con-
fronted with all the fears, doubts, and anxieties that comprise the
necessary baggage of one's personal history, when sex is faced dir-
rectly, without affectation or bromide, then it becomes (in Mailer's
analysis and in Lawrence's fiction) the polarized equilibrium of
isolate sexual selves. Both Lawrence and Mailer dislike the modern
tendency to promote the many tonics that are geared to delimit the
jarring but pure delivery "over to the unknown"; precoital confes-
sions with a lover, postcoital analysis with a group, the self-
indulgent use of contraception--all are the resources which represent
a mechanical, hypochondriacal civilization's willingness to enclose
the existential arena of sex in favor of sex which has known and safe
boundaries--indeed, sex which has been organized to be satisfying,
certain, and unimplicating.

The loving of Lady Chatterley, before she meets Clifford, provides an obvious example of Mailer's detested "sex without guilt."
As a young and intelligent woman, with all the fashionable notions

about liberation and the rights of the female, she accepts her Fabian indoctrination that the mind is more important than any sexual self-knowledge. So her first affairs become virtually asexual offerings of herself to emasculated "humble and craving young men," who conveniently never demand "otherness" from her, and only provide the protectiveness of political discussion:

> It was the talk that mattered supremely. Love was only a minor accompaniment. . . . So they had given the gift of themselves . . . each to the youth with whom she had the most subtle and intimate arguments. The arguments, the discussions were the great thing: the love-making and connection were only a sort of primitive reversion and a bit of an anti-climax. One was less in love with the boy afterwards, and a little inclined to hate him, as if he had trespassed on one's privacy and inner freedom (LCL, p. 39).

Those "unheard thunders of the deep" are not felt because they are not generated; the existential element is ripped out by a need to articulate some spurious concept of independence amid the sweat of passion. Lawrence mocks the Fabians here, as his portrait of Connie's early sex life recognizes that little frightens a socialist more than ineradicable differences between people. So Connie Reid dispenses with her soul-sucking brand of sex to marry Clifford, who returns home in no condition to initiate her to the deeper secrets of the flesh.

Connie's adjustment to Clifford's absolute incapacity is at first helped by her history of programmatic, dispassionate sex as a young woman on the Continent. Connie tolerates her paralyzed husband at Wragby, where she wilts away listening to tired, bruised, and pretentious men denigrate sex with their self-serving discussions. A passive Connie takes her cue from the blasted sexuality around her, as she moves easily from the androgynous visions of utopian politics in France to the cynical complaints of a disillusioned elite in England after the war: "As for sex, the last of the great words, it was just a cocktail term for an excitement that bucked you up for a while, then left you more raggy than ever" (LCL, p. 102). Into this empty life comes Mellors. Her attraction to him, which is developed over a few short meetings before their first sexual encounter, is primarily a product of the appealing privacy of his endurance, of her recognition of his obviously silent and primitive control of his life next to the communal spirits at her husband's country estate. He may be poor, coarse, and insolent, but he is also refreshingly unapologetic and self-sufficient. Mellors' first "loving" of Lady Chatterley, which—given its compulsions—is understandably manipulative and abrupt, is hampered by her old need to have the sex without guilt. She still plays doctrinaire liberationist, as she is more involved in formulating epistemological questions for herself than in feeling her connection with a man. Listen to her use feminist manifestoes to shield herself from the "unknown": "Was it real. Her tormented modern-woman's brain still had no rest. Was it real. And she knew, if she gave herself to the man it was real. But if she kept

herself for herself, it was nothing" (LCL, p. 164). Recall Mailer's
reference to the "primitive awe" with which "one was left to brood
about" after sex. For Connie reaches her room to think more about
Mellors, and in a blunt and beautiful paragraph, clearly written
from her perspective, she manages to make all the right observations
about her experience with Mellors. But she provocatively stops just
short of the conclusion she will reach about her loving by Mellors
later in the novel:

> It really wasn't personal. She was only really a female to him.
> But perhaps that was better. And after all, he was kind to the
> female in her, which no man had ever been. Men were very kind
> to the person she was, but rather cruel to the female, despising
> her or ignoring her altogether. Men were awfully kind to Constance
> Reid or to Lady Chatterley; but not to her womb they weren't kind.
> And he took no notice of Constance or of Lady Chatterley; he just
> softly stroked her loins or her breasts (LCL, p. 169).

Connie's linguistic peroccupations sound familiar--shades of "Ms."
and "Chairperson" in the ideological wars of the 1970s. It is not
difficult to sense how Lawrence would feel about those silly games of
title and politics. For Lady Chatterley almost concludes what Mellors
already knows: she nearly understands that the names and titles are
unimportant social indices, and they properly have no relation to
Mellors' understanding of her real being--that is, her sexual identity.
Connie is almost ready to assert what oddly sounds reactionary fifty
years after Lawrence's death: that her "female" is the most important
part of her, and that she knows men and women before she knows persons.
Easy for the ineffectual men at Wragby to be "kind to Constance Reid
or to Lady Chatterley," so kind that they treat her as one of the guys.
Such is the sexual distortion implicit in their intellectual egali-
tarianism, which Lawrence knows is the socially acceptable form of
their indolent androgyny. The conclusion which Connie feels but does
not as yet comprehend is that Mellors' eminently "male" appreciation
of her womb, or her own acceptance of such fundamental homage, is not
common, not to be taken for granted, and not to be dismissed as mere
chauvinism. Mellors' kindness to Connie's womb is both his ultimate
tribute to her as a woman, and--the essential paradox which today's
ideologues refuse to accept--the place from which any honest communication between the sexes always begins.
      It is a measure of the prescience of Lawrence's fears about the
future of sexuality in an increasingly technologized society, that
today it might be regarded as inappropriate for a woman to acknowledge that she feels the "male" in a man with whom she speaks; the
compulsion of the apologist would be to explain "how minor are the
differences between . . .," or "how stereotyped to consider . . ."--
we know the story well, and Lawrence demurs. Any basis for any relationship between the sexes, Lawrence insists, which attempts to substitute for the fundamental awareness of gender difference is merely
pomposity, priggishness, or sexual evasion. The "men" Connie thinks
about remain kind to "Lady Chatterley" so they need not face the
requirement of the complementary assertion of male "otherness" from

themselves; a title demands easy amenity, while a female demands the
respect of a male. Oliver Mellors supplies this respect, as he warms
to the loving of Lady Chatterley despite the disturbing memories of
his recent relation to women. That healthy fire in him, which Paul
Morel had described to Miriam, cannot be extinguished. So when Connie
bends before the chicken coop and cries in front of Mellors, "in all
the anguish of her generation's forlornness" (LCL, p. 163) a scarred
Mellors struggles to stay uninvolved, struggles to deny the sexual
urges which have been unleashed by his awareness of Connie's sexual
otherness. Mellors' phallic strength makes demands, he is as if summoned by a God of fire, against his will, and that is Lawrence's point.
Will does not stand a chance:

> And he stood up, and stood away, moving to the other coop. For
> suddenly he was aware of the old flame shooting and leaping up
> in his loins, that he had hoped was quiescent for ever. He fought
> against it, turning his back to her. But it leapt, and leapt
> downward, circling in his knees (LCL, p. 162).

The full fascination of this scene, and of the love-making which immediately follows, is often misunderstood by critics as either an example of Mellors' pity for Connie or of his manipulative use of her
vulnerability.[16] As for the former criticism, only the most weather-
beaten and insensitive stud (which Mellors clearly is not!) can make
love for charity and stay reasonably sane. The charge of sexism in
this scene is patently foolish because Connie takes all but the very
final initiative with him; in addition, Mellors before, during, and
after the sex is racked with concern not about his performance, or
Connie's perception of him, but about the "complications" that such
an act must bring upon them. He knows that he cannot merely clean up
and say goodbye, and he significantly refers to love-making as "life."
In short, Mellors in no way treats the sex as if it were the hot passion of an afternoon's seduction, although that option, given Connie's
desperate situation, certainly was open to him.

Sex remains the sacramental act for Lawrence, and so Oliver
Mellors, from the beginning of his affair with Connie, has a resolute
inability to envisage the act of love divorced from the potential of
a longer and more complicated connection with her. During their second
sexual encounter Mellors begins to accept the likelihood of their
deepening involvement; as if to attest to the broadening nature of
his affection, he becomes more tender and worshipful during the physical act, as his phallic imagination moves from the phallus to a gentle
caressing by voice and hand. But Connie persists in having "sex without guilt" in a manner somewhat reminiscent of Miriam Leivers; she
watches Mellors and observes her own reactions as he enters her, so
she misses her orgasm, as "she knew, partly it was her own fault. She
willed herself into this separateness" (LCL, p. 174). The next day,
harboring that mixture of desire and antagonism for Mellors, which
is a concomitant of the abrupt nature of their affair, Connie and
Clifford visit an elderly and aristocratic bachelor. The man is aware
of Connie's sexual charm, and his glib, class-conscious "kindness" to
a Lady confounds Connie's sense of what she has learned from Mellors

about real sexual appreciation. Here Lady Chatterley forgets that Mellors' kindness to the womb comes first, as she regresses, once again, to the platitudes of her Fabian womanhood: "After all, Mr. Winter, who was really a gentleman and a man of the world, treated her as a person and a discriminating individual; he did not lump her together with all the rest of his female womanhood into his 'thee' and 'tha'" (LCL, p. 178).

Fortunately, Connie's trite rationalizations do not last. As part of that characteristic "ebb and flow" rhythm which Lawrence, in Chapter Nine, related both to the form of the novel and to its erotic preoccupations, Lady Chatterley's appreciation of the phallic loving she gets from Mellors is revived when she sees Mrs. Flint and her baby. Later she thinks fondly of her visit to Mrs. Flint, and her illuminating thoughts occur just before another visit to Mellors: "Yes, Mrs. Flint had flaunted her motherhood. And Connie had been just a bit, just a little bit jealous. She couldn't help it" (LCL, p. 181). Connie has been roused by Mellors' loving to a yearning for that further step in female sexual emergence, symbolized to Lawrence by the prospect of motherhood. Her sex with Mellors right after her acknowledgement of a healthy and primitive envy of motherhood provides the first experience for Connie of orgasmic sex with Mellors, as she suspends her will during the rhythms of intercourse. The orgasm is hers because the jealousy was her "guilt," and she appropriates the bile of her envy into the magic of sexual self-definition. Connie did not talk out the jealousy with the men at Wragby or dismiss it with the apologetics of her political indoctrination; she takes the jealousy to bed with Mellors, where she uses it, in Mailer's terms, as the "existential edge" of her sex--sharp enough this one time to produce the sexual gratification. In the midst of her orgasm note the prose: "Her womb was open and soft . . . and softly clamoring for him to come in again and make a fulfillment for her" (LCL, p. 183). The "clamor" here is not only for orgasm, not right after her trip to Mrs. Flint, and not with a womb that from the beginning, at the chicken coop, has seemed to beg for the planting of a seed in her. Sex is regarded as mere sensation by the talkers on the Chatterley estate, but, for the loving of Lady Chatterley to have transcendent value, it must promise to move beyond sensual stimulation to the apocalyptic possibility of conception.

V

Connie does experience periods of uncertainty about her sexual experience with Mellors after this crucial meeting with him. She is particularly prone (a bit like Ursula in Women in Love) to the need for verbal assurance from him about why they make love, and how well they perform, as if she cannot quite abandon her college training to seek to know the just cause of everything. Oliver Mellors, from his defiant private life to his unwillingness to formulate dialectic, remains the existential sexual hero; his loving of Lady Chatterley requires him to respond to her anxious questions, and he characteristically answers with the uncertainty of "I don't know," or with the existential fiat, "Tha knows what tha knows. What dost ax for" (LCL, p. 272). He is a special breed of man--his phallic imagination

so enduring, his respect for unadorned honesty so uncompromising.
Lawrence cautions us against the facile belief that, if it were not
Oliver Mellors loving Lady Chatterley so wisely and so well, it would
have been any mature and sexually energetic man. For Connie herself
shows evidence of the discriminating education she receives about men
from her loving by Mellors. She makes a perfectly balanced judgment
of the men in the pits, as she shows an awareness of their primitive
strength, and also an unsentimental recognition of their lack of
phallic imagination:

> The common people were so many, and really, so terrible. So she
> thought as she was going home, and saw the colliers trailing
> from the pits, grey-black, distorted, one shoulder higher than
> the other, slurring their heavy, iron-shod boots. Underground
> grey faces, whites of eyes rolling, necks cringing from the pit
> roof, shoulders out of shape. Men! Men! Alas, in some way patient
> and good men. In other ways, non-existent. Something that men
> should have was bred and killed out of them. Yet they were men.
> They begot children. One might bear a child to them. Terrible,
> terrible thought! (LCL, pp. 212-13).

Connie easily puts to rest the romantic stereotype of the begrimed
and sensual man in the pits. What sounds like class snobbery in Lady
Chatterley is really a blunt and accurate appraisal by a woman who
has begun to understand the full measure of a male's sexual responsibility. What has been killed off in these men, as Connie captures so
well, is any sense of phallic imagination, any sense that they could,
like Mellors, find the source of their primitive strength, and enter
the life and body of a Ladyship. But unlike Mellors they are described
as passive creatures of the underworld, who can only ride down poisonous, mechanical shafts into mother earth. They are dying under the
ground and have even lost the blood knowledge that knows better. They
are without the ambitious fire of Mellors' loins.

Later in the novel, fully aware of the value of Mellors' brand
of loving, Lady Constance Chatterley engages in a naked dance of communion in the rain before Mellors. The dance has all the rhythms, and
almost the identical images, of Anna Brangwen's dance before her emasculated husband in The Rainbow. Recall that Anna's dance was to annul
Will for his defaulting; the dance did not mediate through her husband
to the transcendent unknown, but rather Anna danced

> in exultation beyond him. Because he was in the house, she had
> to dance before her Creator in exemption from the man. On a
> Saturday afternoon, when she had a fire in the bed room, she
> took off her things and danced, lifting her knees and her hands
> in a slow, rhythmic exulting . . . she would dance his nullifi-
> cation. . . . And with slow, heavy movements she swayed back-
> wards and forwards, like a full ear of corn.[17]

Now Lady Chatterley appropriates the same rhythms, but she uses her
ritualistic choreography as a homage to Mellors' phallic power:

> It was a strange pallid figure, lifting and falling, bending so
> the rain beat and glistened on the full haunches, swaying up
> again and coming freely forward through the rain, and then swoop-
> ing again so that only the full loins and buttocks were offered
> in a kind of homage towards him (LCL, p. 282).

Thus the loving of Lady Chatterley has charted the development of
Connie from adolescent feminist to frustrated wife, to masturbatory
lover, to the vital and warm exponent of sex with guilt. The final
stage of her sexual emergence, related to the theme of the phallic
imagination, is most evident when she can enjoy the cathartic function of sex as, in Lawrence's terms, a "phallic hunting-out." It is
not normative sex in the fiction of Lawrence, but a form of sexual
purging, which roots out shame and fear by using that shame and fear
as the cutting edge of a lusty, exploratory sex. Such loving of Lady
Chatterley provides Lawrence with a final opportunity to reiterate,
in explicit terms, the primacy of the phallic imagination over the
modern world's penchant for evasion, reductive mechanization, and
aesthetic pretense:

> Shame, which is fear: the deep organic shame, the old, old
> physical fear which crouches in the bodily roots of us, and
> can only be chased away by the sensual fire, at last it was
> roused up and routed by the phallic hunt of the man, and she
> came to the very heart of the jungle of herself. . . . The
> phallus alone could explore it. . . . She had needed this
> phallic hunting-out. What liars poets and everybody were. They
> made one think one wanted sentiment. When what one supremely
> wanted was this piercing, consuming, rather awful sensuality.
> To find a man who dared do it, without shame or sin or final
> misgiving (LCL, pp. 312-13).

The achieved integration in Lady Chatterley's Lover of form and doctrine is stressed in a passage which--like the words of Chapter Nine--
must refer to the daring of a novelist and the special power of his
hero. Amid the confrontational sounds of "they" and "to find a man"
Lawrence's personal pride is unmistakeable: the only act comparable
to the courage of Mellors' tenderness is a dying man's shameless
depiction of it.

D. H. Lawrence and the Resacralization of Nature

SCOTT SANDERS

If authors were islands, Lawrence would be one of the most carefully scrutinized pieces of real estate on earth. Most of what can usefully be said about him has already been said many times over. Why is that? Why have so many readers, critical and casual alike, been attracted to his work in recent years? This is a question partly about the work, partly about the cultural frame within which we read it. The answer I am proposing concerns Lawrence's view of nature, and of our place in nature. I will lead you back across only as much of the familiar Lawrentian terrain as I need to in order to suggest why it has become so familiar.

What does Lawrence offer his readers? When you read one of his novels or tales, what sort of tracks does it leave in your mind? You are rarely left with memorable characters or the afterglow of verbal ingenuity or the satisfactions of plot. You are left instead with the vivid impression of living in the flesh. You are made to feel like a creature within creation, like a participant in the sacred, unified surge of life. Abstractly phrased in this manner, belief in nature's unity and sacredness is just an article of faith. But for Lawrence, despite his excursions into philosophy, this was always an article of experience. And he made it so for his readers. He taught us to dwell in our flesh, to commune with nature, in a way that, for all the precedents in the literature of mysticism and Romanticism, had never been so powerfully expressed before in English.

All of Lawrence's writing, in every genre and period, is saturated with awareness of an underlying ground, a god-process. His characters intuit that divine process through sex, through childbirth and death, through birds and beasts and flowers, through the wails of babies and the motions of rivers and the shining of stars. Readers come away from Lawrence, not with a theory about the meaning of the mystical experience, but with glimmerings of the experience itself.

Wherever you open Lawrence you will find this intuition of the unity of mind and flesh and nature. Here is a familiar example from Sons and Lovers. Paul and Clara have just made love:

> They had met, and included in their meeting the thrust of the manifold grass stems, the cry of the peewit, the wheel of the stars. . . . To know their own nothingness, to know the tremendous living flood which carried them always, gave them rest within themselves. If so great a magnificent power could overwhelm them, identify them altogether with itself, so that they knew they were only grains in the tremendous heave that lifted every grass blade its little height, and every tree, and living thing, then why fret about themselves? They could let themselves be carried by life, and they felt a sort of peace each in the other.[1]

This sense of being carried along by a transcendent power, overwhelmed and yet at peace, is the authentic moment in Lawrence's world. It is the touchstone against which all lesser experiences are measured. Whatever his evolving opinions about politics or race or education or sex, he always returned to that primal awareness of nature's enveloping power, like a bather to a spring.

To put it simply, he valued those influences which fostered this awareness, and condemned those which hindered it. Insofar as science pretended to capture nature in its formulas, insofar as any church pretended to house the divine presence, it was in Lawrence's eyes a delusion, a tyranny. "Outside the cathedral were many flying spirits that could never be sifted through the jewelled gloom," Anna remarks in The Rainbow. Self-consciousness is another obstacle to communion, for it locks one inside the ego, and the ego is another imprisoning fiction, like the cathedral, like scientific formulas. "Self was a oneness with the infinite," Ursula concludes later in The Rainbow. "To be oneself was a supreme, gleaming triumph of infinity." One sustains the fiction of the all-powerful and self-sufficient ego, according to Lawrence, by continually exerting the will. The compulsion to dominate other people, to assert control over nature--as Gerald Crich forces his mare to front the clattering railroad cars--cuts one off from awareness of the sacred and injures the delicate fabric of nature itself. And that Lawrence regarded as the cardinal sin of industrialism.

He did not advocate any simple-minded "return to nature," any retreat to the caves or gnawing of raw meat. The use of the African carving in Women in Love or the treatment of Indians in the New Mexican writings should be reminders enough of that. For him it was not a matter of giving up consciousness, or renouncing "civilization," but of progressing into higher levels of consciousness, advancing to the point where the limitations of reason and technology and social forms might be acknowledged and direct apprehension of nature's sacred way becomes possible.

Lawrence's suspicion of reason, ideas, even language itself--so paradoxical in a writer and so troubling to many readers--was another expression of his belief in the primacy of direct communion with the god-process. Thus we find in John Thomas and Lady Jane:

If man could once be reasonable enough to know that he is <u>not</u> a
creature of reason, but only a reasoning creature, he might avoid
making himself more prisons. Man is a creature, like all other
creatures. And all creatures alike are born of complex and intricate passion, which will for ever be antecedent to reason.[2]

The chief impediments to religious experience, he maintained, are
fixed ideas. "Man creates a God in his own image," Kate reflects in
The Plumed Serpent, "and the gods grow old along with the men that
made them. But storms sway in heaven, and the god-stuff sways high
and angry over our heads. Gods die with the men who have conceived
them. But the god-stuff roars eternally, like the sea, with too vast
a sound to be heard."[3]

As in all the world's mystical traditions, so in Lawrence, the
direct apprehension of the god-stuff is far more important than philosophies of the sacred. This conviction was one source of his quarrel
with science, since the mechanistic version of science that he knew
from school pretended to have substituted rational laws for a brutal
and slovenly nature. To borrow a saying that has gained currency in
linguistics and the philosophy of science, Lawrence maintained that
"the map is not the territory," whether the map is religious doctrine
or scientific formulas or language itself. We must never confuse our
symbols with the reality to which they refer. Like the Taoist, Hindu,
and Buddhist writers whom he resembles in so many other respects,
Lawrence regarded mental constructs as veils that must be swept away
to allow for mystical communion. Language carves up the world into
bundles, and we must go about mending the cuts. This suspicion of
language is a special burden for the writer, who mistrusts words and
yet is saddled with using them.[4]

Mention of parallels with Eastern traditions is a reminder that
virtually all aspects of Lawrence's religious vision had been antici-
pated in the literature of mysticism. Indeed a summary of the meta-
physics and psychology implicit in his writing would closely resemble
what Aldous Huxley, studying the world's mystical lore, called "the
perennial philosophy." His dualism, for example, his stress on the
dynamic balance between complementary life-principles, has been fully
worked out in the yin/yang philosophy of Taoism. The sacred underlying
unity to which he so frequently appeals has been called Brahman by
Hindus, Dharmakaya by Buddhists, and Tao by Taoists. What is remarkable
in Lawrence is not the terms of his religious vision, but the power
with which he displayed it, and the fact that he pursued it without
the aid of any well-established literary or philosophical tradition.
Had he been born in China or India or Japan he would have found many
models near at hand. In England he found helpful insights in Hardy,
of course, and in Blake and the Romantics generally. In America he
discovered mystical elements in Melville and Whitman. But none of
these English-language predecessors offered more than partial literary
models.

If he was far from original in his mysticism, he was highly original in the literary forms he evolved to give it expression. He invented
a physics of character, a language of energy and matter, designed to
exhibit the impersonal, transcendent layers of the self. Here, for
example, is an interlude between Will and Anna in The Rainbow:

He called, not to her, but to something in her, which responded
subtly, out of her unconscious darkness. So they were together
in a darkness, passionate, electric, for ever haunting the back
of the common day, never in the light.[5]

Or consider this exchange from Women in Love:

Minette sat near to Gerald, and she seemed to become soft, subtly
to infuse herself into his bones, as if she were passing into him
in a black, electric flow. Her being suffused into his veins like
a magnetic darkness, and concentrated at the base of his spine
like a fearful source of power.[6]

Describing emotion in terms of natural imagery--electricity, magnetism,
seeds, birth, rivers, wind--Lawrence goes beyond romantic analogy to
assert a profound connection: emotion does not simply mimic natural
processes; it is a force of nature. This groping for a rhetoric of
impersonal energies, to replace the familiar rhetoric of private feeling, is responsible for what is most remarkable and most wearying in
Lawrence's style.

   In his treatment of character, Lawrence broke with the two dominant trends in the English novel, the social and the psychological.
Instead of presenting character as the product of "personality" and
social determinants--class, job, family, and the like--he treated it
as the temporary coalescence of natural forces. One constantly feels,
reading him, that the ultimate reality is the field of energy, out of
which individuals flicker and into which they fade again. He thus cuts
against the whole drift of the bourgeois novel, from Defoe onward,
where character was interesting in its own right, either as the representative of a social group or as an idiosyncratic individual.

   By contrast to the "psychological" fiction for which he had so
little use--Proust, Joyce, Woolf, James--his work is very little concerned with thought-processes or memory, very much with immediate
sensation. Ursula's impatience with memory is typical:

She wanted to have no past. She wanted to have come down from
the slopes of heaven to this place, with Birkin, not to have
toiled out of the murk of her childhood and her upbringing,
slowly, all soiled. She felt that memory was a dirty trick played
upon her. What was this decree, that she should "remember"! Why
not a bath of pure oblivion, a new birth, without any recollections or blemish of a past life.[7]

As in mystical training, so in Lawrence's fiction one seeks to escape
the entanglements of memory, to silence the inner babblings of thought,
so that voices from beyond the self can be heard.

   He developed rhythms of prose and narrative structures which communicated the biological patterns, the god-processes underlying all
the surface action in his fiction. Here is a characteristic passage
drawn from John Thomas and Lady Jane:

Constance sat down with her back to a young pine-tree, that swayed
against her like an animate creature, so subtly rubbing itself
against her, the great, alive thing with its top in the wind! And

she watched the daffodils sparkle in a burst of sun, that was warm on her face; and she caught the faint tarry scent of the flowers; and gradually everything went still in her, so still, so still and disentangled.[8]

That is sexual, of course. But sexuality, here and elsewhere in Lawrence, is a pathway toward stillness, clarity, and illumination, toward apprehension of the god-stuff. To take another example, consider this moment during the honeymoon of Will and Anna in The Rainbow:

As they lay close together, complete and beyond the touch of time or change, it was as if they were at the very centre of all the slow wheeling of space and the rapid agitation of life, deep, deep inside them all, at the centre where there is utter radiance, and eternal being, and the silence absorbed in praise; the steady core of all movement, the unawakened sleep of all wakefulness.[9]

Lovemaking is a journey inward. Sensuality is a more appealing mystical path than meditation, yogic exercise, fasting or drugs; and it is also the easiest path to abuse. One abuse is to regard sensuality as an end in itself, as those critics do who turn Lawrence into a prophet of simple-minded eroticism. Sex pervades his writing like an aroma, but only because it is the most immediate, powerful evidence of the self's participation in nature.

By consistently describing emotion in terms of natural imagery, Lawrence dramatized the connection between the dynamics of the self and the dynamics of the rest of the created world. "The quick of the universe is in our own bodies, deep in us," he wrote in the second version of Lady Chatterley's Lover. Although he was a rhapsodist of the body, and highly original in the language he evolved for speaking of bodily states, he subordinated even the flesh to the transcendent process of which it is a manifestation. The effect is reminiscent of a maxim from Heralictus: "It ever was, and is, and shall be, everliving Fire, in measures being kindled and in measures going out." The actual imagery of fire was one of his favorites. Here is another glimpse of the relation between Will and Anna:

But to him, she was a flame that consumed him. The flame flowed up his limbs, flowed through him, till he was consumed, till he existed only as an unconscious, dark transit of flame, deriving from her.[10]

One comes away from Lawrence affected less by the characters or events or settings than by the fire burning in them all.

Unlike Blake, Lawrence did not concoct an idiosyncratic pantheon of gods to dramatize his mystical insights. Unlike Eliot, he did not try to resuscitate an institutional religion. Unlike Yeats, he did not seriously try to resurrect dead gods or devise a private mythology. His one extended attempt at such a revival, The Plumed Serpent, failed to convince him any more than it has convinced most of its readers. And his sundry "pollyanalytics"--those prolonged ventures into philosophy--are usually turgid commentaries on his fiction and poetry and travel essays. Lawrence is at his strongest when he deals with the experience of the sacred directly, without the mediation of cult or theology or institution.

So much for the familiar terrain. Why has it attracted so many explorers? The answer, I believe, is that these elements of Lawrence's vision are at the center of a major shift in our thinking about mind and nature. Here I must be even more sketchy, and more open to challenge, since I am attempting to compress a vast amount of cultural history into a few paragraphs.

We are in the midst of a revolution in thought, as significant as--and in some respects contrary to--the revolution that accompanied the rise of modern science and industrialism. This revolution could be described briefly as a recovery of a sense of the sacredness and unity of all creation, an assertion of the creatureliness of humankind, and an associated recovery of respect for those modes of knowledge which allow for the apprehension of that unity and sacredness. The seeds of this shift in outlook were already present in eighteenth-century deism, in the Romantic cult of wilderness, in Darwin's evolutionary theory, and in many other places. But in the past two decades so many intellectual influences have come together, all pointing toward a resacralization of nature, that only now can we begin to speak of what Thomas Kuhn--writing of the tidier world of scientific thought-- has called a shift in paradigm, or what Raymond Williams--writing of cultural history--has called a shift in the structure of feeling.

Of course I cannot prove that such a shift is taking place, any more than a contemporary of Descartes and Newton could have proved that a radical turn from the medieval outlook was taking place in the seventeenth century. I can only point to a few of the intellectual trends which, taken together, seem to form a critical mass: the congruence between the philosophies of modern physics, biology, and mysticism; the growth in ecological thinking, in fields ranging from information theory to theology; the interest in Oriental philosophies; the interest in American Indian and other so-called "primitive" cultures; the stress within psychology on intuition, imagination, and what could be called the left-handed qualities of mind; the stress within anthropology on the animal origins of humanity; the growth in respect for wilderness, for endangered animals, and for the integrity of the environment; the interest in altered states of consciousness, in dream, trance, and vision.

The earlier paradigm, on which the scientific and industrial revolutions were based, might be summarized as follows: nature can be wholly known by reason; it is a medium alien to us, perhaps hostile, certainly amoral, on which we must impose our will and our values; if there is a divine presence at all, it is wholly cut off from the material world. On such a view, the mind's relation to nature is instrumental: whatever cannot be measured or shaped cannot be reliably known. Nature is only real insofar as it can be manipulated. The consensus emerging in our own time might be summarized as follows: we belong to nature, root and branch; our task is to discover and cooperate with the rhythms of nature itself; reason can only guide us part way to that discovery, and must be supplemented by intuition and vision. We are gradually coming to recognize that the world, ourselves included, is a unified system. We can no longer sustain the illusion of the isolated, objective, observing reason, set off against nature, nor the view of nature as raw "stuff" upon which we work our designs. We are coming to regard mind's relation to nature as participatory rather than instrumental: we gain ultimate knowledge of the world, not by manipulating it, but by listening, by patiently attending. I call this an "emerging" consensus, because large-scale shifts in world-view are always fuzzy, intangible, long drawn-out affairs. They can never be confidently described until long after they have been completed, as we can now describe the shifts in world view associated with the breakup of the medieval religious consensus or the rise of industrial and urban society.

Lawrence caricatured the old paradigm in his portrait of Gerald Crich, the industrial magnate:

> He had a fight to fight with Matter, with the earth and the coal it enclosed. This was the sole idea, to turn upon the inanimate matter of the underground, and reduce it to his will. . . . And the whole productive will of man was the Godhead. . . .[F]or was not mankind mystically contradistinguished against inanimate Matter, was not the history of mankind just the history of the conquest of the one by the other?[11]

The radical opposition between humanity and·nature, the deification of technology, the military contempt for the earth: all these attitudes were necessary for the triumph of industrialism, all were repugnant to Lawrence, and all have come to be regarded by many people in our own time as suicidal. Lawrence was able to see the dangers of the ethic of exploitation earlier than most people, because he grew up amidst the spoils of Britain's industrial revolution. Like Blake, he observed humankind at war with landscape and with its own flesh.

He was fond of reminding us that old ways of seeing are constantly being outmoded. In his "Study of Thomas Hardy," for example, he wrote:

> The little fold of law and order, the little walled city within which man has to defend himself from the waste enormity of nature, becomes always too small, and the pioneers venturing out with the code of the walled city upon them, die in the bonds of that code, free and yet unfree, preaching the walled city and looking to the waste.[12]

The point is not just that any code becomes a fetter, but that the fundamental opposition between city and nature, the erecting of the wall, is wrong. Unlike Hardy, say, or George Eliot or Cobbett, Lawrence no longer wrote of the countryside from within an assumed agrarian order. He was already divorced from the country by education and by knowledge of mines, mills, cities. His going back to nature was a conscious movement, taken with an awareness that modern society had largely left nature out of account: hence his appeal to jaded urban readers in the 1960s and 1970s. There is another familiar example of his invocation of nature's wider life in The Rainbow, where Ursula reflects upon her college life:

This inner circle of light in which she lived and moved, wherein the trains rushed and the factories ground out their machine-produce and the plants and the animals worked by the light of science and knowledge, suddenly it seemed like the area under an arc-lamp, wherein the moths and children played in the security of blinding light, not even knowing there was any darkness, because they stayed in the light. But she could see the glimmer of dark movement just out of range, she saw the eyes of the wild beast gleaming from the darkness, watching the vanity of the camp fire and the sleepers; she felt the strange, foolish vanity of the camp, which said, "Beyond our light and order there is nothing."[13]

Provoked in part by the global environmental crisis, in part by discoveries of alternative states of consciousness, in part by an awareness of the self-destructive tendencies within technological society, many have now come to admit, with Lawrence, the foolish vanity of the camp.

If we persist in that vanity, mistaking our lighted circle of consciousness for the whole of reality, building our wasteful cities without regard to the larger environment in which we must survive, then our tenure on earth will be far shorter than the dinosaur's. Lawrence clearly recognized that Homo sapiens might easily pass away, and in that regard he was even more profoundly respectful of the unsearchable godhead than the anthropocentric religions have been:

Whatever the mystery which has brought forth man and the universe, it is a non-human mystery, it has its own great ends, man is not the criterion. . . . The eternal creative mystery could dispose of man, and replace him with a finer created being. . . . It could bring forth miracles, create utter new races and new species in its own hour, new forms of consciousness, new forms of body, new units of being. To be man was as nothing compared to the possibilities of the creative mystery. To have one's pulse beating direct from the mystery, this was perfection, unutterable satisfaction.[14]

Such an outlook is humbling. It runs counter to the main current of Western thought since the Renaissance.

If it was necessary for nature to be desacralized before the scientific and industrial revolutions could flourish, so nature must be resacralized in order for us to survive the after-effects of those revolutions. This shift in the structure of feeling toward nature has been underway at least since the time of the Romantics. But only in this century, and especially in the past two decades, have large numbers of people, across the whole spectrum of arts and disciplines and social classes, come to recognize that a radical rethinking of our relation to nature is urgently needed. The Romantics were already critical of the overweening claims of reason and of the early results of industrialization. But their response seemed a luxury at that time, an elitist nostalgia for some green and pleasant past. Now, faced with an environmental and spiritual crisis, we can no longer discount this

shift in feeling toward nature as nostalgic. We live in a time when
the inherited notion of conquering nature, the arrogance of reason,
the anthropocentrism of thought, threaten our existence.

So we read Lawrence until the corners wear off his books, until
the edges wear off his imagery, because he articulated powerfully and
memorably this shift in our view of mind, nature, and ourselves. He
felt that the experience of nature's divine process was endangered by
industrialism, democracy, the labor movement, by churches and schools.
Thus he was unable to offer any political vision. In the end he was
unable to connect the mystical experience with any form of society: it
remained private, isolated, beleaguered by the world. We are left with
the task of imagining what social forms this new outlook might take.
What forms of work, of community, of housing, of technology, what forms
of loving and learning are compatible with a view of nature as sacred?
Many in this generation are groping for answers.

It could be argued that the resacralization of nature is only
possible now that nature has apparently been subdued by technology.
And it might be argued further that the change of outlook I have
described is only temporary. Both may be true. Certainly there are
still powerful influences at work in our society, bent on conquering
nature and denaturing humankind. But in my opinion, if the resacralization of the created world is a short-lived phenomenon, then our
species will also be short-lived.

Homoerotic Feeling in *Women in Love*: Lawrence's "struggle for verbal consciousness" in the Manuscripts

CHARLES L. ROSS

> "Man struggles with his unborn needs and fulfilment. New
> unfoldings struggle up in torment in him, as buds struggle
> forth from the midst of a plant. . . . This struggle for
> verbal consciousness should not be left out in art."
> --D. H. Lawrence, Foreword to Women in Love.

The homoerotic aspect of Women in Love has stirred controversy
ever since Lawrence's publisher Martin Secker silently excised several paragraphs so that the book might pass the "censor morons" (as
Lawrence called them) who had succeeded in banning and burning The
Rainbow. In recent years critical debate has shifted from questions
of seemliness to allegations of authorial duplicity in the treatment
of homoerotic feeling. Speculation has been roused by the printing of
a rejected opening chapter, "Prologue," in which Rupert Birkin is
attracted to the athletic and sensual bodies of men like Gerald Crich
while carrying on a half-hearted affair with the "spiritual" Hermione
Roddice.[1] Most critics have found the published novel more reticent
on the subject of homosexuality than the "Prologue" seems to imply
the earlier version would have been. Hence the almost universal query:
Why was Lawrence reticent by his own, implied standards?

The most common explanation for Lawrence's rejection of such an
opening is that, after the banning of The Rainbow, he felt constrained
by the prospect of adverse public opinion to alter what would have
been a more explicit treatment of homosexuality.[2] Evidence supporting
the hypothesis of duplicity, however, is quite tenuous. After publication of the first edition Lawrence did make a few cosmetic changes to
avoid a libel suit. But he had written and revised several drafts of

the novel years earlier, when he had little or no hope of finding a
publisher.[3] A more ambitious, Freudian explanation finds the answer
in Lawrence's ambivalence towards homosexuality and his consequent
unconscious psychological defense: "Lawrence transferred to [Gudrun]
the feelings that would have been Birkin's if his homosexuality had
become explicitly the central issue in the fiction. . . . Her responses give evidence of Lawrence's shame and anxiety over such
desires."[4] Such an explanation assumes generally that revision is an
attempt to hide the author's real psychology, and specifically that
Lawrence unconsciously distorted his inspiration. The argument inevitably follows that the story of Birkin and Gerald reveals Lawrence's
need "to escape to a man from the misery of his own failure with a
woman," but that "his deep residue of puritanical repression and certain intellectual scruples prevent the successful culmination of this
friendship."[5] The critic who argues this last case believes that
Lawrence wanted to write in praise of homosexuality, which he saw as
a "higher" form than heterosexual love, but lacked the courage to
treat "this intensely personal theme." The result was that Lawrence's
real interest in homosexuality underwent a sea change into an otherwise inexplicable dwelling on the shameful experiences of the heterosexual couples: "The anal intercourse in 'Excurse' . . . sublimates
Birkin's homosexual desires by satisfying them in an alternative and
perhaps even more perverse way."[6]

The voluminous manuscripts of the novel may help us escape from
this biographical cul-de-sac. For in their entirety they yield a very
different picture of Lawrence's developing artistic intentions--one
that shows him creating rather than disguising meaning. They form a
bridge from the author's intentions, as divined in letters and other
extra-textual sources, to the enacted intentions of the finished,
published novel.[7] To begin with, it is wrong to assume, as most
critics do, either that the Prologue is the only or principal prepublication version, or that Lawrence "cancelled" or "suppressed" an
integral chapter from the finished novel. On the contrary, the Prologue is one of two chapters that survive from an early draft: part
of a fragmentary beginning, soon abandoned, and succeeded by three
full-length drafts.[8] Thus there are three prepublication versions of
the novel, one fragmentary and two complete, which are essential to
an understanding of Lawrence's intentions in the treatment of homoerotic feeling. I shall call them, respectively, the Prologue, the
penultimate draft (I) and the final draft (II).[9] They reveal that,
while reconsidering the friendship of Gerald and Birkin, Lawrence
grasped the ideal of male comradeship as a possible though difficult
alternative to the deathliness of modern sex relations, an "additional"
and complementary (not higher) relationship to the new type of "mystic"
marriage that Birkin and Ursula strive to realize.

Early Versions: The Love That Dare Not Speak Its Name

In the Prologue, Birkin, whose affair with Hermione has become
merely destructive, is acutely conscious of his desire for the bodies
of men:

All the time, he recognized that, although he was always drawn
to women, feeling more at home with a woman than with a man,
yet it was for men that he felt the hot, flushing, roused
attraction which a man is supposed to feel for the other sex.
Although nearly all his living interchange went on with one
woman or another, although he was always terribly intimate
with at least one woman, and practically never intimate with
a man, yet the male physique had a fascination for him, and
for the female physique he felt only a fondness, a sort of
sacred love, as for a sister.[10]

But he will not admit the beauté mâle, despising his innate feelings
yet "inevitably" drawn to "exchange intimacy" with men. Nor can he
love the whole person of the men to whom he is attracted. Just as he
is split in his relations with women between spiritual affection and
lust, so he looks upon the men of his secret desire as physical speci-
mens but not intellectual companions. In fact, his feelings are shaped
by a class consciousness similar to that in the homosexual literature
of the late Victorian and Edwardian years, as described by Timothy
d'Arch Smith in Love in Earnest.[11] To Hermione, Gerald is "common"
and coarsely stupid; even to Birkin, he is "limited." yet this obtuse-
ness attracts Birkin, who enjoys having a "hard-limbed traveller and
sportsman" in his power: "Birkin felt a passion of desire for Gerald
Crich, for the clumsier, cruder intelligence and the limited soul,
and for the striving, unlightened body of his friend."[12] Gerald recip-
rocates with a "reverence" for the higher understanding of his physically frail friend whom he can protect with his "superior physical
strength." Throughout the chapter Birkin is drawn to "ruddy, well-
nourished fellows, good-natured and easy," that is, men who are
intellectually if not socially inferior but physically desirable.
Even the details of male physique are imbued with class values, as
when Birkin admires a soldier with "large, dumb, coarsely-beautiful
hands . . . [and] strong knees." But these homosexual desires are
rigorously repressed or "cast out" so that there is never any "demonstration" of affection in a series of friendships which are once
likened to the passionate attachment of David and Jonathan. Moreover,
Birkin's inability either to love women or to admit his love for men
seems an inevitable symptom of the degeneracy of the times, and is
the occasion for despair and fatalism:

And Birkin was just coming to a knowledge of the essential
futility of all attempts at social unanimity in constructive-
ness. In the winter, there can only be unanimity of disintegration. . . . He ran about from death to death. Work was
terrible, horrible because he did not believe in it. . . .
In his private life the same horror of futility and wrongness dogged him.[13]

The finished novel, on the other hand, holds out hope for the
regeneration of mankind in two, complementary relationships: the
tentatively affirmed "mystic marriage" between Birkin and Ursula, and
the Blutbrüderschaft of Birkin and Gerald. Yet the transition from

the Prologue's mood of despair to the muted hope of the novel was a gradual process of discovering possibilities of life amid death. In the novel Lawrence expressed the latent content or hidden subject of the early versions, diagnosing Birkin's (and perhaps his own) fear of homosexual desire.

The penultimate draft, then, retains many of the features of the Prologue. Birkin's desire for a male friend is wholly conscious and coupled with his failure to form a stable, loving relationship with a woman, either Hermione or Ursula. In the original ending to chapter 2, for example, Birkin and Gerald are aware of their proclivities and consciously reject the "unmanly" examples of classic male friendships. The passages in square brackets below (and hereafter) indicate expressions in the original version which were revised in the final version to the expressions in angle brackets.

> It was always the same between them; always their talk brought them into a [fearful] ⟨deadly⟩ nearness of contact, a strange, perilous intimacy which [neither of them would avow] ⟨was either hate or love, or both⟩. And the tacit disavowal made almost a hatred between them. . . . they were not going to be so unmanly and unnatural as to allow any heart-burning of love between them. They had not the faintest belief in [love] ⟨deep relationships⟩ between man and man, [and even the classic friendship, such as that between David and Jonathan, they looked upon with suspicion and contempt, as being in some way unmanly or unclean. To them the relationship of Achilles and Patroclus was moving, but womanly and suspect.] ⟨and their disbelief prevented any development of their powerful but suppressed friendliness⟩ (II, p. 45).

Some critics have been quick to interpret the deletion of the allusions to classic homosexual friendships as evidence of Lawrence's covert desire which he feared. But the deletions are also part of a new direction in characterization. The final version makes their attraction "powerful but suppressed," a pressing but not fully conscious need that the two friends will discover in the course of the novel. The changes from "love" to "deep relationships" and "Achilles and Patroclus" to "suppressed friendliness" move in the direction of vagueness—but for a purpose. Together with the elimination of "avow," they suggest that the men are largely unconscious of their deep affection for each other. In other words, the revised language is evasive because they are unconsciously evading the truth of their feelings. Lawrence decided to make their unconscious desire—its initial suppression and eventual revelation—an explicit theme. This altered intention is the crucial reason why he deleted the allusions, and not a fear of censorship or an unconscious wish to disguise the issue. At least such an interpretation of artistic intention should cast doubt on charges that the passage is "more covert and defensive" than the Prologue, and that the tone betrays Lawrence's "uneasiness with this intensely personal theme." It seems more probable that the disavowal of "unmanly and unnatural" emotion is an ironic comment on the characters' defensiveness than a jibe of Lawrence's.[14]

Another reason for Lawrence's decision to delete the allusions to the loves of Achilles and Patroclus or David and Jonathan may have been

that they were part of the repertoire of homoerotic poets who wanted
to express their passion without rousing the ire of a prudish public.
These classical and Biblical themes gave an air of historical or literary legitimacy to wayward emotions. They had become coterie clichés.
Thus the touchstone quotation from 2 Samuel--"Thy love to me was wonderful, passing the love of women"--became "well-nigh a fiat for
paederasty," and poems like "The Meeting of David and Jonathan" by
J. A. Symonds were designed to be read one way by the initiated and
quite another by the reading public.[15] It seems probable that Lawrence
would not have wanted to evoke literary homoeroticism, which would
have suggested that Birkin and Gerald are deliberately concealing
what they regard as aberrant feelings. Moreover, by omitting the
allusions Lawrence dignifies the relationship above the gay clichés
and facile gossip of the times.

He may also have wanted to dissociate his novel from the patrio-
tism commonly associated with the Homeric ideal of comradeship in war.
While at work on the novel, he was summoned to an army physical examination and spent the night in barracks with other "incipient soldiers."
Sympathy for his fellow recruits soon turned to revulsion at the fore-
taste of military life. He saw acutely that the men were being lured
to their deaths in the trenches by the reflected glamour of a literary
stereotype. As he explained to Amy Lowell in America:

> The whole thing is abhorrent to me--even the camaraderie, that
> is so glamorous--the Achilles and Patroclus business. . . .
> How [Richard] Aldington will stand it I don't know. But I can
> tell that the glamour is getting hold of him: the "now we're
> all men together" business, the kind of love that was between
> Achilles and Patroclus. And if once that lays hold of a man,
> then farewell to that man forever, as an independent and con-
> structive soul.[16]

It is significant that the letter was written at the same time as the
penultimate draft, in which Lawrence failed to separate himself from
Birkin, for whom homosexuality is a forbidden subject. Hence the letter
contains both good sense and, in the last sentence, defensive prejudice. Like Birkin in the penultimate version, as we shall see, Lawrence
could not yet imagine or admit that manly love could become a primary,
liberating relationship. Having decided in the final version to exalt
male comradeship to equality with heterosexual love, Lawrence dropped
all allusions to the Greek heroes.

Prelude to Intimacy: "In the Train," "Breadalby" and "Water-Party"

Unlike the Prologue or penultimate version, the novel we now read
develops the mutual need and affection of the two men indirectly,
through casual conversations. Chapter 5, "In the Train," begins the
process. In the penultimate version, Gerald listens in silence to an
overbearing lecture on the "new life" that a creative love between man
and woman will bring. Birkin is adamant that heterosexual love, a bonding with one woman, will bring personal and social regeneration--or
nothing will. But his stridency appears defensive, an unconscious

strategy to evade the knowledge of his need for male love. He sup-
presses any such knowledge together with any sign of affection for
Gerald; so, having raised the need for manly love, he hastily retracts.
As a result, Gerald listens in silent hostility to the narrowly exclusive alternatives offered by Birkin, either heterosexual marriage
or despair and death.

> "It isn't children I want to bring forth with a woman,
> but hope and truth and a new understanding," said Birkin.
> "And it needs you and a woman?" asked Gerald.
> "It can only be born of the love between a man and a woman--
> the living spirit, the new understanding. . . . There is only
> physical procreation in the world now--no spiritual begetting
> and bringing forth. Children are a stumbling block, parenthood
> is a pis-aller. It is the men, now, who should bring forth
> truth and understanding. But we are all barren, as men. We can
> only beget children, and suffer death." . . .
> "I can't help thinking that is rather narrow, limited, what
> you say," said Gerald.
> ". . . it is in my own, particularised self, united in love
> with a particular woman, that the hope lies, the germ of creation
> --nowhere else. . . ."
> "But you haven't found the woman yet," said Gerald, almost
> sarcastically (I, pp. 63-64).

In the final version, Birkin still believes in heterosexual love
as the primary relationship, but he is not adamant. His mood now passes
from anger at Gerald's unbelief, through self-doubt, to "rich affec-
tionateness and laughter." Although neither man voices his need for
the other, their conversation implies that male friendship might prove
the missing term between Birkin's insistence on heterosexual marriage
and Gerald's skepticism about any lasting relationship. So their new
dialogue, which replaces Birkin's monologue, reveals both Gerald's
bafflement at his failure to find an individual purpose beyond the
perfecting of a social mechanism and Birkin's response to his indirect
plea for advice and companionship.[17] This revision has the great advantage of holding Gerald's underlying insecurity in balance with his
"manly" exterior:

> "And you mean if there isn't the woman, there's nothing?"
> said Gerald.
> "Pretty well that--seeing there's no God."
> "Then we're hard put to it," said Gerald. . . .
> Birkin could not help seeing how beautiful and soldierly
> his face was, with a certain courage to be indifferent (II,
> p. 82).

The limitation to this brand of courage becomes plain later when Gerald
has the courage to face and experience the deathliness of modern love
but not the courage to envisage an alternative in the love of man for
man. Yet the revision also controls our criticism of Birkin who sounds
to Gerald "insistent rather than confident." Finally, Birkin confesses
his own perplexity together with his affection for Gerald as a person,

no matter how unwilling a convert. He has become a troubled searcher
for the truth rather than an inflexible prophet. His humanity as well
as Gerald's has been deepened.

Henceforward in the final version, Lawrence accentuated the ambivalence of their friendship. In the early version of Chapter 8
("Breadalby"), for instance, Gerald is merely suffering from a bad
conscience because he did not pay Minette after their brief affair.
This trivial decision whether to give Minette her due becomes in revision a symptom of Gerald's perplexity about what to do with his
life and of his ultimate cynicism about saving himself through friendships with either sex. Notice how his good-humored banter modulates
to an intense question that tacitly admits an inadequacy.

Penultimate version:

>"I can't see why I should be any better if I didn't want to
give Pussum some money."
>
>"You feel there's a spot on your soul, so you'll put a penny
over it, and it won't be there--. . . . And it will help your
digestion, if you give her a ten-pound note?"
>
>"Yes, it will. I feel the affair's over, then."
>
>"That's where you are a fool. The ten pounds makes not the
slightest difference to your own inside. Ask yourself what you
wanted of her, what you got, and what you didn't, and see why
you are at outs over it. Don't wrap the whole question in a ten-
pound note, and throw it out the window. You'll find it on the
lawn, later on."

>"I can't see what you will leave me at all, to be interested
in. . . . Neither the Minettes, nor the mines, nor anything else.
. . ."
>
>"You see," said Birkin, "part of you wants Minette, and
nothing but Minette, part of you wants the mines, the business,
and nothing but the business--and there you are--all in bits--"
>
>"And part of me wants something else," said Gerald, in a
queer, quiet, real voice.
>
>"What?" said Birkin, rather surprised.
>
>"That's what I hoped you would tell me," said Gerald. . . .
>
>"I can't tell you--I can't find my own way, let alone yours.
You might marry," Birkin replied. . . .
>
>"That is your panacea," said Gerald. "But you haven't even
tried it on yourself yet, and you are sick enough."
>
>"I am," said Birkin. "Still, I shall come right."
>
>"Through marriage?"
>
>"Yes," Birkin answered obstinately.
>
>"And no," added Gerald, "No, no, no, my boy."
>
>There was a silence between them, and a strange tension of
hostility. They always kept a gap, a distance between them,
they wanted always to be free each of the other. . . . (II,
pp. 147-48).

The revision enforces links between Gerald's public and private lives, which he would deny. He accedes to Birkin's analysis that he is "all in bits," oscillating between random affairs and the unfulfilling business of the mines, with no "centre" or "single pure activity." But he will not look too long beneath the surface of his activities. Having forced Birkin to suggest "something else," he derides marriage with an Edwardian, man-of-the-world complacency. The movement is typical of the altered intention of the final version to show the conflict within Gerald between naiveté and cynicism, vulnerability and strength. On the other side, the obstinacy of Birkin on the subject of marriage seems an evasion of self-knowledge. Lawrence has captured the unstable blend of love and hate that characterizes their friendship.

Declaration of Friendship: "Man to Man"

The chapter "Man to Man" represents the first climax of the theme of male friendship, as the strong but hitherto repressed affection is openly acknowledged. Now the conflict within the men between outward reserve and the growing pressure of desire has become an explicit theme rather than a hidden subject. Lawrence was distancing himself from the emotional blindness of Birkin in earlier versions by probing the reasons for Birkin's as well as Gerald's unwillingness to countenance the forbidden subject. In the penultimate version male friendship appears hopeless and "perhaps death" because it is merely the complement to "the hatred of woman." In sickbed Birkin thinks that his affair with Ursula has reached an impasse. Humiliated by the thought of being loved in equality by woman, he demands of Ursula an absolute surrender like that of Mohammed's wives "who believed utterly" (I, p. 244). For her part, Ursula is hostile and equally absolute in her assertions of female superiority. If Birkin appears a male chauvinist, Ursula has a good deal of the overweening female or Magna Mater about her.

> Was she not enthroned, the female, as the first and the highest? Was not woman the creator of man, did she not bring him forth? . . . Was she not the guardian and sustainer of all life, the greatest principle within humanity? (I, p. 245).

Recoiling from this impasse, Birkin turns to his love for Gerald as a despairing consolation. He has no hope in the revivifying possibilities of male friendship; without woman there can be no life. He has placed himself in a false position, split between dogmatic and unreciprocated claims on Ursula and a love for Gerald that is "impossible" because largely a reaction from the failure with Ursula.

> For the present, there was only Gerald who had any connection. Gerald and he had a curious love for each other. It was a love that was perhaps death, a love which was complemented by the hatred for woman. It was a love that tore apart the two halves, and brought universal death. It tore man from woman, and woman from man. The two halves divided and separated, each drawing away to itself. And the great chasm that came between the two sundered halves was death, universal death.

But if this was so it was so. There was the love between
him and Gerald and the other was denied. . . . Then there must
be death. . . . So be it. No man can create life by himself. It
needs a man and a woman. And if the woman refuse, then the life
is uncreated and death triumphs. Il Trionfo Della Morte.

That allusion to the title of D'Annunzio's novel betrays the false
note in Birkin's reveries: he is indulging in self-pity. Indeed the
fatalism and melodramatics recall the situation of the Prologue where
Birkin's unadmitted love for men was a symptom of a general failure
in human relations. Consequently Birkin's preaching about the inevitability of death for the present era, with which the reverie in the
penultimate version ends, seems a rationalization of his personal case:

For us, the imminent experience is the experience of death. . . .
It is our desire, it is our necessity, it is our fate. There is
a life which is over-dry and which must pass away. This is our
universal life. We must die, we must all die, because the term
of our living is over (I, p. 246).

Since Birkin has decided that neither female nor male friendship offers
an alternative to the imminent experience of death, he responds to
Gerald's passionate approach with only "cold weariness":

"Yes," Birkin admitted, "I like you better than anybody
else--any other man." He put out his hand from the bed, and took
Gerald's brown, sinewy hand in both his, and sat with lips parted,
breathing short and fast, his eyes set. Birkin looked at him,
with unchanging eyes. He felt a hot pang of love for him, and a
deep pity, a deep sorrow. Then finally a cold weariness.
"We'll stand by each other, Gerald," he said slowly.
Gerald's face changed swiftly, he looked aside. He wanted
the other man to put his arms round him, and hold him. He could
not look at Birkin's dark, steadfast eyes any more, he turned
aside, panting slightly, because he so much wanted the other man
to take him in his arms and hold him close in peace and love. Yet
it was so impossible.
"A Blutbrüderschaft," said Birkin, sadly, reassuring, as
if to comfort the other (I, pp. 330-31).

That is the sole use of the Germanic term in the penultimate draft.
But Birkin's offer carries no conviction because neither man has the
courage to challenge stereotyped sex roles. Their friendship, like that
of Birkin and Ursula, seems to have ended in frustration and unfulfill-
ment.

While rewriting the final version, Lawrence grasped the vital
potential in what had appeared the impossible love of man for man.
He amplified the solitary and tentative suggestion of Blutbrüderschaft
into the main theme of the friends' conversation.[18] Now Birkin sees,
with sudden clarity, the need for an equally creative love between men.
However, his manner of advancing the idea is not dogmatic but dramatic.
He looks at Gerald "with clear, happy eyes of discovery," but he must

search for the right words to express the love he has been denying
all along:

> "We will swear to each other, one day, shall we?" pleaded
> Birkin. "We will swear to stand by each other--be true to
> each other--ultimately--infallibly--given to each other,
> organically--without possibility of taking back" (II, p. 330a).

The revision focuses on the urgency and sincerity of his words rather
than their programmatic content. Birkin, we feel, has seized on the
Germanic conception of Blutbrüderschaft so as to appeal to his "sol-
dierly" friend who considers him too "uncertain" in the man's world.
Nor was Lawrence interested in elaborating the archaic form of pledging friendship. He seems to have chosen the foreign term because he
found the English connotations of "homosexual" both too narrow and
socially inadmissible. Casual homosexual relations were as repugnant
to him as heterosexual promiscuity. This attitude can be seen in his
extreme reactions to the "corruption"[19] of Bloomsbury homosexuals and
the "thin rationalism, libertinism and irreverence" of John Maynard
Keynes and his set at Cambridge.[20] By contrast to that image of homosexuality, Lawrence wanted to suggest the sort of relationship which
might find an acceptable social expression for the love that dare not
speak its name. In fictional terms a secret liaison with Birkin would
have been quite out of character for Gerald. As an artist Lawrence
was interested in the differing reactions of the friends to the notion
of Blutbrüderschaft. Birkin lectures eagerly while Gerald, though
deeply attracted, holds himself in reserve:

> Gerald looked down at him, attracted, so deeply bondaged in
> fascinated attraction, that he was mistrustful, resenting the
> bondage, hating the attraction. . . . Gerald hardly listened.
> His face shone with a certain luminous pleasure. He was pleased.
> But he kept his reserve. He held himself back (II, p. 330a).

The ambivalence of Gerald's response to Birkin's offer, his desire and
reserve, will come to seem a sign of his fatality.

Thus the rewriting of "Man to Man" marks a great advance in
Lawrence's exploration of the text. Whether or not male comradeship is
a necessary or possible complement to heterosexual marriage will concern not only Birkin and Gerald but Birkin and Ursula. Whereas the
early versions present a conscious but hopeless desire for men which
is merely the obverse of a failure with and hatred for women, the novel
persuades us that male friendship can complement a revitalized relationship with women. Lawrence transformed a repressed desire, breeding
misanthrophy and despair, into an admitted and conceivably sustaining
Blutbrüderschaft.

Achievement or Failure?: "Gladiatorial" and "Marriage or Not"

Inspired by the discovery of male comradeship, Lawrence used it as
the growing point for the remainder of the Birkin/Gerald story. Moreover, the manuscript reveals his wish to stress the physical and frankly
sexual aspect of Blutbrüderschaft. His motives will never be fully

known, but it seems likely that he became aware of an inconsistency in his treatment of sexuality. We may imagine this more or less conscious recognition in the form of a question: if he wanted Brüder-schaft to be considered (in Birkin's words) "equally creative" with heterosexual love, why didn't he describe a homosexual experience comparable in intensity and completeness to the experiences of the heterosexual couples? The wrestling in "Gladiatorial," for all the virtuosity of its description, remains incomplete--a sublimated form of homosexuality. Nor does Birkin there confront the necessity of a homosexual embrace, preferring to deal in generalities: "We are mentally, spiritually intimate, therefore, we should be more or less physically intimate too--it is more whole" (W, p. 310).

When rewriting, Lawrence tried to resolve this inconsistency. First he heightened the sexual import of the wrestling:

> Birkin's intelligence [flickered over] <interpenetrated into> Gerald's body . . . like some [spell] <potency> . . . . So they wrestled swiftly, [astonishingly] <rapturously>. . . (II, p. 427).

In the final version Gerald then asks explicitly "Is this the Brüder-schaft you wanted?" but only after he has betrayed an instinctual reticence, in a passage inserted to recall and foreshadow other fleeting moments of love. The revision suggests not only the greater intensity of Birkin's love but Gerald's repression of affection:

> And Gerald's hand closed warm and sudden over Birkin's, they remained exhausted and breathless. . . . <the one hand clasped over the other. It was Birkin whose hand, in swift response, had closed in a strong, warm clasp over the hand of the other. Gerald's clasp had been sudden and momentaneous.> . . . Gerald's hand slowly [relaxed its hold] <withdrew>. . . (II, p. 430).

And finally Lawrence inserted a sentence prophesying their tragic failure: "The wrestling had some deep meaning to them--an unfinished meaning" (II, p. 430).

That unfinished meaning is confronted for the last time in "Marriage or Not." It is a brief chapter over which Lawrence took great pains, but which is usually ignored by critics who argue that Lawrence "exorcises the demons of his homosexual desire" by "ratifying the love for Ursula and condemning the love for Gerald."[21] Their final conversation about comradeship is crucial, coming directly after the climaxes of heterosexual love in "Excurse" and "Death and Love" and before Gerald is swept away from Birkin into the mere destructiveness of the closing Tyrolese chapters. Lawrence not only revised thoroughly in 1917, but returned in 1919 to reconsider a passage in which Birkin all but admits the "physical basis" whereby manly love might become an additional form of sexual marriage. Far from disguising or displacing homoerotic implications, Lawrence was clarifying and extending them in revision.

In the penultimate version, the opening witticisms about Gerald's possible marriage to Gudrun serve as prologue to a strident "dissertation" by Birkin. Male comradeship is never mentioned, in keeping with

the reticence of early versions. Instead, Birkin lectures Gerald on
how the knowledge of death gives one confidence to ignore the falsity
of life and start to build a new world around the nucleus of a "living"
marriage. It is a stump speech that antagonizes Gerald, who feels "as
if he were being forced in some direction," and that is dramatically
unconvincing on several counts. Birkin does not achieve such a marriage with Ursula in the penultimate version of "Excurse," and he
considers his love for Gerald to be impossible. Consequently the vivid
presentation of the deathliness of modern society far outweighs his
insistence that "we know . . . our lives contain the inception of a
new earth" (_I_, p. 564).

Lawrence reconsidered this exchange in the light of Birkin's
avowal of love for Gerald in "Man to Man." What had been merely jocu-
lar repartee now gives way, under Birkin's questioning, to a tormented
though unspoken plea for love by Gerald:

> "Yes," he said, "one must consider marriage coldly. It is
> something critical. One comes to the point where one must take
> a step in one direction or another. And marriage is one direc-
> tion--"
> "And what is the other?" asked Birkin quickly.
> Gerald looked up at him with hot, strangely-conscious eyes,
> that the other man could not understand.
> "I can't say," he replied. "If I knew _that_" . . .
> "You mean if you knew the alternative?" asked Birkin.
> "And since you don't know it, marriage is a _pis aller_."
> Gerald looked up at Birkin with the same hot, constrained
> eyes.
> "One does have the feeling that marriage is a _pis aller_,"
> he admitted (_II_, p. 563).

In the 1917 version, however, there follows a quite different
middle to the chapter. It is more physically immediate than the final
version of 1919, as Birkin clasps Gerald's hand in "a sudden spasm of
love" and once again pleads for an avowal of love: "that we will stick
to each other, and love each other, to the end of all things, no matter
what happens . . . swear it with me" (_II_, p. 564). Yet is is also less
hopeful because the affection is so one-sided in Birkin, and because
their feelings for one another remain largely unspoken. It resembles,
in fact, a reprise of the early version of "Man to Man" quoted above.

> Birkin was strangely sensible and matter-of-fact about this
> very important measure. But Gerald wanted to cry, to cry and wail
> aloud, like an infant that is hopelessly sick. He averted his
> face slightly, leaving his hand in the hand of his friend. He
> just had not the strength to swear.--Birkin felt a terrible con-
> traction at his heart. He watched the other man strangely, all
> the while. And he saw the curious dumb, unborn helplessness of
> Gerald's face.
> "Never mind," said Birkin, "we have sworn in silence."
> His fingers gently contracted over the hand of Gerald, then he
> released his grasp. He had a strange dazed pain at his heart
> (_II_, p. 564; i.e.,--first layer of interlinear revisions,
> crossed out).

Then the chapter ends as in the published novel with Gerald choosing marriage as a "doom," remaining split between his public persona and his "underworld" desires, never to be fulfilled in a love that would express his whole self.

The manuscript indicates that Lawrence wholly replaced the middle section (W, pp. 402.17-403.21) in 1919, when the novel had lain dormant for two years. Again the motive may have been an awareness in retrospect of the inequality between the heterosexual and homosexual experiences. So, in the 1919 version, Birkin speaks frankly of the "additional" homosexual marriage that would be "equally important, equally creative." No longer relying on the analogy of the Germanic pledging ceremony, he articulates at last the hitherto unadmitted content of a Blutbrüderschaft:

> "Surely there can never be anything as strong between man and man as sex love is between man and woman. Nature doesn't provide the basis," said Gerald.
> "Well, of course, I think she does. And I don't think we shall ever be happy till we establish ourselves on this basis. You've got to get rid of the exclusiveness of married love. And you've got to admit the unadmitted love of man for man. It makes for a greater freedom for everybody, a greater power of individuality both in men and women."
> "I know," said Gerald, "you believe something like that. Only I can't feel it, you see" (II, pp. 564-65).

To one acquainted with the early drafts, it may seem that Lawrence is arguing through Birkin with his past self and his insistence on heterosexuality to the exclusion of manly love.

Nevertheless, even on second and third thoughts Lawrence did not create a sexual scene for Birkin and Gerald that is fully comparable to those between the heterosexual couples. Why didn't he? The late additions show that he was aware of an inconsistency, and that he strove to give comradeship a theoretical parity. Was he prevented then by fear of public reaction or his own ambivalence? I think not. The logic of characterization, not the perplexity of life, lies behind the revision. It would have been improbable for Gerald to relinquish his Wille zur Macht in favor of an "eternal" commitment to another person of either sex. As though to buttress this interpretation, Lawrence rewrote their last words to stress Gerald's cynical indifference to Birkin's offer of love. Gerald chooses to repress manly love and thereby commits himself to the dissolution of all attachments:

> And the two walked on. [But Birkin wanted to hear the sledge bells. He felt under an unbearable oppression, walking with Gerald, as if he were in a vice.]
> <"I've loved you, as well as Gudrun, don't forget," said Birkin bitterly. Gerald looked at him strangely, abstractedly.
> "Have you?" he said, with icy scepticism. "Or do you think you have?" He was hardly responsible for what he said> (II, p. 711).

Their failure to consummate is an inevitability of Gerald's character, not a sign of any "deep residue of puritanical repression" in Lawrence.

Moreover, Lawrence's reticence about the exact nature of the physical contact in a _Blutbrüderschaft_ need not imply defensiveness. As the long and fruitless controversy about exactly what kind of sex Lawrence is depicting in certain scenes in _Lady Chatterley's Lover_ should have made clear, Lawrence is seldom explicit on this subject. He is always less concerned with which parts of the body are in contact than with the range of sensual and emotional response in any relationship: "And what is sex, after all, but the symbol of the relation of man to woman, woman to man? And the relation of man to woman is wide as all life. It consists in infinite different flows between the two beings, different, even apparently contrary. Chastity is part of the flow between man and woman, as is physical passion. And beyond these an infinite range of subtle communication we know nothing about."[22] Similarly, when describing the friendship of Birkin and Gerald, Lawrence is more concerned with the psychological "basis" for love between men than with physiological specification.

Finally, as a record of the writer's own desires, _Women in Love_ shows Lawrence to have been not only passionately committed to manly love and "mystic" heterosexuality but skeptically aware that the achievement of either would be difficult if not impossible. Hence the novel ends questioning the feasibility, if not sincerity, of Birkin's fixed idea about _Blutbrüderschaft_. Originally the last scene was a longer, pathetic version of Birkin weeping over Gerald's corpse in unassuaged grief. In the final version Lawrence added a short dialogue between Birkin and Ursula, in which Birkin reiterates his desire for "eternal union with a man too" but Ursula heatedly replies that it is "an obstinacy, a theory, a perversity." Whether or not our judgment is as harsh, we are left to contemplate an unresolved problem.

Thus the record of Lawrence's intense struggle for verbal consciousness, preserved in the manuscripts, suggests that charges of covert and defensive writing are ill-founded. Accusations that he evaded or displaced the central issue of manly love could be levelled with more justice at the early versions of the novel. There the distance between Lawrence and Birkin was negligible, with the result that Birkin's blindness to his need for such love might be interpreted as Lawrence's. Whether or not Lawrence was translating his unreciprocated, repressed affection for men into the liberating medium of fiction, he did not create a compensatory fantasy. The published novel leaves open the question whether one can achieve "equally creative" bisexual friendships.

Whatever Lawrence's unconscious motives may have been, his artistic intentions are reasonably clear. The manuscripts provide an aesthetic rationale for omitting the Prologue and deleting allusions to the classic friendships of David and Jonathan or Achilles and Patroclus. Lawrence decided that knowledge of the need for a _Blutbrüderschaft_ should remain submerged or unconscious until it surfaced with sudden clarity midway through the novel in a chapter aptly titled "Man to Man."[23] What had been a despairing consolation for the general disruption of sexual life in the original versions became in theory a necessary, sustaining complement to heterosexual marriage. One measure of

this altered intention is the prominence of the term <u>Blutbrüderschaft</u>
in the latter half of the novel, and the frank conversations of Gerald
and Birkin. Homoerotic feelings, which had been feared and repressed,
are now openly discussed and potentially part of a new society. The
novel we read, unlike its early versions, is balanced and mutedly
hopeful without being complacent or dishonest.

Lawrence and Women

The Boy in the Bush in the Lawrence Canon

CHARLES ROSSMAN

I

Ever since the generally favorable reviews that greeted the 1924 publication of The Boy in the Bush, critics have largely ignored D. H. Lawrence's other Australian novel. When Southern Illinois University Press reprinted the novel in 1971, for example, Harry T. Moore's preface nearly equalled in length all previous critical commentary. Like Shakespeare's Two Noble Kinsmen, The Boy in the Bush has been neglected owing to the "taint" of collaboration--owing, that is, to the critically unpalatable fact that, in Moore's phrase, "Lawrence shares the title page" with the little-known M. L. Skinner.

Such critical neglect is, although mistaken, understandable. If we are to assess The Boy in the Bush as specifically a Lawrence novel or to assimilate it in our assessments of the whole Lawrence canon, we must know how much of the book Lawrence actually wrote. Yet critics have ignored the book undeservedly. Even though Mollie Skinner's original manuscript (from which Lawrence fashioned the published novel) has apparently disappeared, enough evidence survives for us to make an informed estimate of Lawrence's particular contributions to the collaboration. There is, for instance, the recently discovered holograph manuscript, and two copies of the typescript are extant, both corrected in Lawrence's hand, one at the University of Texas and the other at Columbia. But most important is the copy of the novel that Mollie Skinner marked for Edward Garnett, soon after publication, to indicate Lawrence's share of the book. Such valuable documents are illuminated by the surviving correspondence between Lawrence and Skinner, as well as by Skinner's own memoirs.

Surprisingly, the only scholarly appraisal of these materials published so far is that made by Harry Moore in his preface to the 1971 reprint of the novel.[1] In the remarks that follow, I briefly reexamine the details surrounding Lawrence's collaboration with Mollie Skinner. My aim is not, to be sure, to "correct" Moore's account. Rather, I hope to give other scholars an even fuller picture of the chronology, details, and substance of the collaboration, in order to lay the basis for the sort of informed assimilation of The Boy in the Bush into the Lawrence canon that has been long overdue. For the present, my own effort at such an assimilation will be confined to a tentative assessment of Lawrence's particular attitudes toward male-female relationships in the novel, as embodied in its fiercely solitary hero, Jack Grant.

II

Frieda and Lawrence met Mollie Skinner in May 1922, when they lodged for a few days at the guest house she operated in Western Australia. While there, Lawrence read a sample of Skinner's novel-in-progress that she later published as Black Swans. Lawrence was impressed, but critical. He urged her to begin a new novel about subjects closer to her experience, specifically, about her "strange country" and its early settlers.[2] Apparently inspired by his encouragement, Mollie Skinner finished a new novel within ten months. During the spring of 1923 she posted the manuscript of "The House of Ellis" to Lawrence, probably in care of his publisher in New York. Lawrence himself was by then in Chapala, Mexico, writing the first version of The Plumed Serpent.

Surviving letters show that as late as 26 July Lawrence, by then in New York, had not yet received Skinner's manuscript. Within six weeks, however, he had arrived in Los Angeles and had the manuscript with him. He wrote her from Santa Monica 2 September with the news that he had read "The House of Ellis." As before, he praised her work with reservations: "Such good stuff in it: but without unity or harmony. I'm afraid as it stands you'd never find a publisher" (CL, p. 751). In the same letter, Lawrence made his startling offer of collaboration: "If you like I will take it and re-cast it, and make a book of it." She cabled her approval.

Skinner next heard from Lawrence in a letter written 1 November 1923 from Guadalajara, in which he informed her that he had been revising her novel while he traveled in Mexico: "I have been busy over your novel, as I travelled. The only thing was to write it all out again, following your MS, almost exactly, but giving a unity, a rhythm, and a little more psychic development than you had done. I have come now to Book IV. The end will have to be different, a good deal different" (CL II, p. 760). Mollie Skinner wrote, nearly thirty years later, that Lawrence could not have had her cable of approval for very long when he sent her this letter. To her, anxious to establish herself as principal author of The Boy in the Bush, Lawrence's following letter of 15 November, in which he announces that "I finished the novel yesterday" (AH, p. 585), indicates that he spent only a couple of weeks on her manuscript. Skinner's clear implication is that Lawrence worked at the novel all too briefly to accomplish much more than minor revisions of what remains essentially her work.

Precisely what did Lawrence contribute to the published version of Millie Skinner's original manuscript? In his letter to her of 2 September, proposing the collaboration, Lawrence had asked for "a free hand" to "make a complete book out of" her manuscript. Two months later, in a letter of 1 November describing his revisions through chapter 3, he remarked that "the only thing was to write it all out again." Similarly, Lawrence wrote to his London agent, Curtis Brown, the day after he finished his work on the book, declaring that "I tackled the thing, and wrote it all over afresh" (AH, p. 586). Years later, in his preface to Skinner's novel Black Swans, Lawrence reiterated that "I am not good at suggesting and criticizing. I did the only thing I knew well how to do: that is, I wrote the whole book over again, from start to finish, putting in and leaving out, yet keeping the main substance of Miss Skinner's work" (P, II, pp. 294-95).

Despite qualifying phrases like "yet keeping the main substance of Miss Skinner's work," Lawrence's words have been interpreted as leading to claims of an inflated share in the collaboration. Katherine Susannah Prichard, for example, an Australian novelist who befriended Mollie Skinner, has bluntly declared that any statement "that 'Lawrence re-wrote the whole of Mollie Skinner's Australian novel The Boy in the Bush' cannot be accepted" (Nehls, II, p. 274). Mollie Skinner has written approvingly of Prichard's words and has asserted that she wrote "about three-fourths of the book" (Nehls, II, pp. 139, 273). And despite the eagerness with which Skinner accepted Lawrence's offer to "recast" her book in 1923, she wrote in 1950 that "what amused me later was that he used my construction until the end, when he worked on the last two chapters" (Nehls, II, p. 271).

Despite Mollie Skinner's assertions, the evidence supports Lawrence's account of his contribution to the book. In the first place, although his own letters (quoted above) make it clear that he devoted only the two weeks from 1 November to 14 November to the actual writing of chapter 4 through the end of the novel, Skinner is certainly wrong in inferring that he had not even begun his revisions until 1 November. He had left Los Angeles on 25 September and had arrived in Guadalajara 16 or 17 October, carrying "The House of Ellis" with him. He may have received her cable of approval before he left Los Angeles; but, if not, he must have found it awaiting him in Guadalajara, where he had his mail forwarded. Lawrence therefore must have received her cable between two and five weeks before he wrote her on 1 November that "I have been busy over your novel, as I travelled." That gave him ample time to study the manuscript, to ponder the changes in characterization and development that he would make, to think through the new ending that he would add, and to do the actual rewriting as far as the beginning of chapter 4.

Mollie Skinner herself, in the copy of the novel that she marked for Edward Garnett, indicates that, regardless of when Lawrence revised chapters 1 through 3, he changed them extensively. Of the forty-seven pages comprising the first three chapters, she claims as her own unaltered writing only twenty-two pages, while indicating that Lawrence composed all or most of six pages, that he made revisions of a full paragraph or more on five additional pages, and that he made frequent minor changes on the remaining fourteen pages.

Examination of the rest of Skinner's marked copy indicates that Lawrence's writing is frequent and extensive throughout. For example, Skinner left only 137 pages out of the novel's total of 369 completely unmarked, by which she presumably meant to claim only those as pages to which Lawrence contributed little or nothing. On the other hand, she credits Lawrence with writing (or with heavily rewriting) almost as many pages: between 100 and 130 complete pages of the book, depending upon how one interprets her marginal comments. She has marked five additional pages as nearly all Lawrence's, and 65 more as containing at least one full paragraph of his work. Despite the remark that "he used my construction until the end, when he worked on the last two chapters," Skinner's marginal designations reveal that Lawrence's writing was by no means confined to the end of the novel, but rather is frequent from the first page to the last.

The typescript corrected in Lawrence's own hand reveals that he made changes from beginning to end in it, too. He made more than two hundred alterations involving 119 of the typescript's 543 pages. Once again, however, as with the marked copy of the novel, these changes become more frequent and more extensive near the end. For instance, Lawrence marked only eighteen of the first two hundred pages of the typescript, for the most part making additions or deletions of single words, with only four instances of revisions involving an entire sentence. In contrast, forty-five out of the last ninety-three pages (i.e., pp. 450-543) contain Lawrence's written afterthoughts, sometimes involving an entire page or more. Interestingly, several revisions, which were carried over into the published book, were not marked by Mollie Skinner to indicate them as Lawrence's work. Such oversights suggest that, in marking the book for Garnett, she may also have omitted many other passages written by Lawrence.

And, indeed, close reading of the novel reveals dozens of passages unmarked by Skinner that Lawrence almost certainly wrote. Such passages frequently echo earlier sections ascribed by her to Lawrence and deal with, for example, Jack's speculations about his dark "Lord of Death," with Jack's consuming anger, with his urge to kill Easu, or with his speculations about the nature of women and his desire to have more than one woman. Other unmarked passages contain recognizably Lawrentian diction or themes, sometimes with overt parallels to Kangaroo or foreshadowings of The Plumed Serpent. A good case could be made that Skinner, in marking the book, noted the passages that she wanted to disown, as well as many that she easily recognized as Lawrence's, but that she overlooked a good deal of his writing.

While Lawrence did not conceive The Boy in the Bush, then, he reworked the first version in the same free manner with which he revised early drafts of his own novels. He no doubt "wrote the whole book over" in the literal sense that he physically copied an existing text, assimilating it in the process by freely making numerous, often extensive, deletions, changes, and additions. More than that, much of The Boy in the Bush did in fact originate with Lawrence. Nearly ninety of the last hundred pages are all, or nearly all, Lawrence's writing. Of the final sixty pages, Skinner claims only one, page 329, as containing her unrevised words. Lawrence therefore appears to be responsible for the creation of Hilda Bessington, for the death of Easu at Jack's hands, and for the final stages of Jack's development, which reveal him as a "Lord of Death" living in a state of extreme psychological isolation, suspicious of everyone but nevertheless desiring two or more women simultaneously as his mates. Mollie Skinner felt such a jolt at Lawrence's new ending that, as she confessed, "I wept."

Mollie Skinner's feeling of shocked alienation from the final version of "her" novel is a measure of just how completely Lawrence made it _his_ novel. Moreover, since Lawrence completed it during a hiatus in the composition of The Plumed Serpent, the critical measure of his crucial "leadership period" cannot be taken without considering it.

III

In rewriting Mollie Skinner's manuscript, Lawrence converted what was apparently a vividly concrete adventure story, with abundant sentimental love interest, into a bildungsroman wherein Jack Grant is educated to some rather startling principles which he boldly implements in action.

The novel opens with Grant, not yet eighteen years old, stepping ashore in a West Australian port in 1882. He has arrived from his native England, an innocent who looks "just a little too lamb-like to be convincing" (p. 1). Jack has been sent out to the colony, following some small problems in secondary school, where his father expects him to sow his wild oats, to learn something of Australia, and ultimately to find some land and a wife and to settle down to a life of convention and farming.

That much of the story Lawrence took from Skinner. But whereas her version apparently depicted Jack as a "good bad boy," something like an Australian Tom Sawyer, Lawrence re-created Grant as genuinely "bad," that is, as an aggressive, revolutionary sensibility who departs radically from both accepted social norms and "normal" personality. Nearly every significant formal element in the novel's opening eight pages delineating Jack's character and circumstances and anticipating his future development occurs in passages that Mollie Skinner has marked as revised by Lawrence. For example, Skinner wrote the word "changed" in the margin next to the second new paragraph of page 4, and then ran a red, nearly continuous marginal line to the center of page 7. These pages treat of Jack's relationship with his parents, their relationship with each other, Jack's repudiation of conventional notions of "sin," his sympathy with convicts, his fascination with the "non-moral bush" with "a devil in it," and, most importantly, the first hint of his "dark god" in the speculation that "it didn't matter what you did, as long as you were good inside yourself."

From this carefully reshaped opening, Lawrence developed his Jack Grant. This Grant can stand neither fences nor any enclosed spaces, rejecting them as the impositions of a false and pious civilization. Similarly, he despises landowning and farming, feels a deep spiritual kinship with convicts and other renegades who are antagonistic to establishment values, hates both the "stolid new Victorian church" in the port-city (the "one thing he knew he disliked in the view," Lawrence adds) and the Christian religion to which it ministers. As the story unfolds, Jack kills a rival in love, asserts an ethic of masculine supremacy (rooted in a private, mystical religion of power and death), and attempts at book's end to establish a harem, seemingly with good prospects for success. By this time, Jack regards himself, without a hint of self-doubt, as superior to everyone else in the book and immune from their judgments. He feels himself a "Lord of Death" whose behavior expresses the will of an uncompromising "dark god" who speaks to Jack alone.

Although Skinner wept at Jack's development, Lawrence portrays him without irony and with so little esthetic distance that Jack's consciousness and the narrator's are frequently indistinguishable. Lawrence, that is, endorses Jack's conviction that his deeds are divinely sanctioned. Thus, when Jack kills his rival Easu with impunity, when he dominates the once bold and independent Monica, when he turns with sudden hatred against Tom and Lennie, who have been worshipfully loyal, and when he abruptly despises Mary for having refused his unreasonable demand that she sleep with him in the stable, Lawrence-as-narrator not only _presents_ these developments, he affirms them.

One sequence in which Lawrence's revisions demonstrate his attitude is that of Jack's evolving relationship with Easu. During the first third of the novel, the antagonism between them develops much like a conventional rivalry between aggressively masculine adolescents vying for the same girl, in this case Monica. But when Jack and Easu at last come to blows, the description takes on radically different tones in different passages. For instance, Jack dwells on his hatred of Easu and his desire to hurt him with these words:

> He had never before had this strange lust dancing in his blood,
> the lust of rage dancing for its consummation in blows. He had
> known it before, as a sort of game. But now the lust bit into
> his very soul, and he was quivering with accumulated desire,
> the desire to hit Easu hard, hit him till he knocked him out.
> He wanted to hit him till he knocked him out (p. 166).

Skinner marked this passage "very little changed." Whatever Lawrence's changes might be, they no doubt include the remarks about lust, blood, and rage--sentiments and language recognizably Lawrence's. On the other hand, the comparatively wholesome masculine desire, twice expressed, to "knock out" a rival sounds incongruously meek in the overall atmosphere of bloodlust and brutality. This desire to "knock out" Easu very much reflects the tone of the earlier development of their relationship, and must certainly be a vestige of Skinner's original version.

Just a page earlier, in a passage marked by Skinner to indicate Lawrence's writing, Jack considers the prospect of a fight with Easu in considerably more violent and far less preppie terms: "How he hated Easu's ugly, jeering, evil eyes, how he would love to smash them out of his head" (p. 165). Jack's reveries after the fight are even more violent. "Lord, I'll kill him if you want me to," he prays (p. 174), a sentiment echoed over the following pages. It is important to see, too, that the desire to kill Easu and to possess Monica are linked: "Lord, _if_ _you_ _don't_ _want_ _me_ _to_ _have_ _Monica_ _and_ _kill_ _Easu_, _I_ _won't_. _But_ _if_ _you_ _want_ _me_ _to_, _I_ _will_ (p. 180, passage marked as Lawrence's, with italics in the original). Within a few more pages, all Jack's doubt about his "Lord's" will is dissolved, and he dwells on "that dark vibration which made him want to kill Easu" (p. 184, marked by Skinner as "ALL DHL").

In such passages, we can see the precise overlayering of Lawrence's material on the matrix of Skinner's original. Skinner had set up a contest for Monica which probably ended in a fistfight in which Jack emerges victorious after "knocking out" Easu. Lawrence adds to this the young man's passionate hatred and his "Lord of Death" who sanctifies him and justifies whatever extremes of behavior Jack's impulses lead him to.

These impulses lead, of course, to Easu's death nine chapters later, in "The Last of Easu." As might be expected, Skinner has marked this chapter as containing a large proportion of Lawrence's original writing, running a continuous marginal line down twelve of the sixteen pages (pp. 283-88 and 288-97), while leaving only a single page (p. 286) totally unmarked. Lawrence provides Jack the ostensible justification for the killing of self-defense, since Easu is killed during an attack on Jack with an ax. Yet, even though the plea of self-defense satisfies the jury, as it had witnesses to Easu's attack, it accounts only superficially for either Jack's behavior or, more importantly, his motivation.

Just before the killing, Jack has privately concluded that Easu is the father of Monica's illegitimate child. Jack feels a certain rage over the "wrong" done Monica. But his deepest anger, as we learn after the killing, has sprung from sexual jealousy, from the personal insult that Easu has had the nerve "to spoil Monica," his possession. Jack feels such disgust at the thought of Monica "all messed up by that nasty dog" that he "felt that she was a little repulsive, too" (p. 298). His sense of betrayal and dirtiness is so intense that, for the moment, he "felt he could never follow where Easu had been messing." We can assume that these were Jack's unspoken feelings the morning when, for no apparent reason, he rides by Easu's place with a gun in his belt, en route to visit Monica. Jack confronts Easu with patronizing haughtiness. He provokes Easu with remarks calculated to humiliate him and arouse his anger. Then, when Easu makes his predictable attack, Jack coolly aims his cocked gun and contemplates the spot on Easu's forehead, "that mystic place," where the bullet would enter.

As with the death of Banford in "The Fox," Easu's death is a carefully orchestrated "accident." Jack has created a situation which allows him to kill Easu in "self-defense," to remove a personal rival with trumped-up moral justification. There is a moment some fifteen pages after the killing when Jack allows himself to wonder "why had he taken the trail past where he and Easu had fought" (p. 313, marked as Lawrence's writing). But Jack quickly dismisses such speculations: "But for what unconscious purposes who shall say?" Jack now acts with divine sanction, and questions of conscience have been laid to rest forever.

With Easu out of the way, Jack is free at last to claim Monica as his own. He locates her and her two illegitimate children, and, without discussion or courtship, takes possession of her. (The word "possession" recurs frequently in the text.) Monica willingly assents to his precondition to the relationship: "And you won't oppose me when there's anything I want to do, will you?" (p. 317). Similarly, she understands that she must worship him, "the eternal stranger," from afar, that she will "never finally know him, and never entirely possess him" (p. 318). But she concludes, "So be it. At least it relieved her of the burden of responsibility for life. . . . After all, this man was magical." At times she questions her fate, wonders about Jack's "power over her," and asks herself why she couldn't "be a free woman . . . and a complete thing in herself" (p. 320). But when she is near Jack she dismisses her opposition as mere "perverseness." Her will "evaporates," and all she desires is to be subsumed into the world of Jack's will: "Her own freedom was worth less than nothing." (All passages quoted in this paragraph have been marked by Skinner to indicate Lawrence's writing.)

Thus Jack achieves the relationship with Monica that he had yearned for 150 pages earlier: "But she must give up to him. She must give herself up. He demanded this submission, as if it were a submission to his mysterious Lord" (p. 175, marked as "all" Lawrence's). With Monica, then, as in the killing of Easu, Jack equates his desires with those of his Lord. His "dark god" and "Lord of Death" are all an ecstacy of self-justification, of elevating his personal desires to the level of divine principle. As the book draws to a conclusion, Jack's desires become increasingly bolder, his fears and isolation increasingly paranoid, as we see in particular with his attempt to bring Mary under his sway in addition to Monica.

Jack's attempt occurs in Chapter XXIX, "The Offer to Mary," which Skinner has attributed almost wholly to Lawrence.[3] Jack, Mary, and Old George are inspecting some property that Jack has inherited but which he wants to settle on Mary. Disgusted by the day's social intercourse with human beings, Jack prefers, Gulliver-like, to sleep in the stable with his horse. Quite suddenly he says, "Come and sleep in the stable with me" to Mary (p. 351). They quarrel. Mary insists that, since he is married to Monica, he belongs to her. Jack replies that he does not belong to Monica, although he concedes that he will "love Monica again, another time." But, he tells Mary, "I love you, too." Mary cries out, "Oh, you are cruel to me! You are wicked!" She abruptly returns to the house, leaving Jack to meditate the simplicity and honesty of horses.

At first Jack's response is comparatively subdued. He thinks that Mary, and that all women by themselves, "were only parts of some whole, . . . fragments" (p. 353). He reaffirms that he was right in wanting Mary in addition to Monica, that he needs "wives, not wife," and he concludes that he will return to his camp, and to Lennie, Tom, and Monica. But on the way back to Perth, Jack's thoughts take a startling and unprepared-for turn. He now regards Mary's refusal as a betrayal. Moreover, he believes, oddly, that "Mary would want me killed." As his thoughts tumble forward, he begins to loathe himself for even having offered himself to her, who ought to have gone "down on her knees before the honour, if I want to take her" (p. 356). He begins to regard Mary as a "brown snake," and next to regard everyone, "man or woman, wife or friend," as "silent, damp, creeping snakes" anxious to bite him. Earlier in the five-page chapter, he had expressed good will toward Monica, Lennie, and Tom, but now he repudiates them all as vipers and declares that, in self-defense, he "will crush their heads" (p. 357). Previously, Jack had hoped to found a Rananim-like

colony with a "few aristocrats-to-the-bone" (p. 325). Now he scorns
the idea: "As if I could make it with the people that are on earth
to-day! No, no, I can do nothing but stand alone" (p. 358).

Jack's conclusions and the depth of his passion both strike the
reader as grossly exaggerated. His proposition to Mary had been, after
all, a daring one that would have been very difficult for her to accept. Moreover, Jack never makes any further effort to reason with
her or to draw her slowly to him. He makes his proposal to her abruptly
and demands that she comply immediately or be despised as denying his
"dark god." Similarly, his fears of Monica, Lennie, and Tom have no
basis in the facts of the story. Rather, they have all agreed to
Monica's precondition of not opposing him, in fact of standing beside
him, in anything that he attempts. Jack's raging passion is paranoid
megalomania, pure and simple.

Where does Lawrence stand in relation to Jack's final stage of
development? Of course, Lawrence is no more Jack than he is Birkin or
Somers--nor any less. If it is true that no author ever simply is one
of his characters, even one intended as autobiographical, it is also
true that Lawrence had special affinities for several of his characters, like Birkin, Somers, and, I would add, Jack Grant. As I have
said, Jack acquired his basic personality from Lawrence, who narrates
that development without irony or esthetic distance. To these facts
must be added that of the disproportionate and exaggerated response
that Jack makes to Mary's refusal to sleep with him. If we fail to
find Jack coherent here, we may be tempted to look, as Eliot did with
Hamlet, behind the character for his source in his creator--to inquire,
that is, whether the extremes of feeling and the incoherence of the
fictional character may not reflect those of the author.

As it happens, Lawrence rewrote The Boy in the Bush at a time
when he had recently relived the horror of World War I during the
composition of "The Nightmare" chapter of Kangaroo. It was also a
time of painful estrangement from Frieda, who had returned to Europe
without him. Moreover, as the letters of the period reveal, Lawrence
was especially capable at this time of intense hatred for people in
general. We may safely conclude, at the least, that Lawrence worked
on Skinner's manuscript during one of his most extreme and painful
periods of psychological isolation and distaste for the world. It is
worth noting that within a three-year-period embracing the composition
of The Boy in the Bush, Lawrence also completed "The Ladybird," "The
Fox," "The Captain's Doll," "The Princess," and "The Woman Who Rode
Away," all depicting efforts by men to bring a woman into submission,
even if it means raping or killing. This is the period, too, of the
final version of Studies in Classic American Literature, Kangaroo, and
The Plumed Serpent, with their obsessive concern for leadership (over
the masses in general but women in particular), submission of women
and lesser men to a single strong man, and the mystical relationship
of the strong man to his "dark god."

Seen in this context, The Boy in the Bush appears to bring these
concerns to their most intense development in Lawrence's canon, with
the possible exception of The Plumed Serpent, written concurrently.
As a whole, these concerns illustrate a movement in Lawrence's work
of the 1920s, completed by Jack Grant and The Boy in the Bush, away

from "love" as the basis of human relationships, and toward "power" as that basis. This shift of emphasis may have earlier glimmerings, but it is overtly articulated as a necessity in the conversations between Aaron and Lilly near the conclusion of Aaron's Rod (completed only slightly more than two years before The Boy in the Bush). In numerous ways, Jack embodies the yearned-for figure of masculine "power": in his psychological isolation and his indifference to the judgment of others, in his magical ability to compel people to accept his will as their own, in his intense and exclusive allegiance to his "dark god," and, perhaps most significantly, in the relationship that he demands with women--their submission to his lordship.

As Middleton Murry has suggested, Jack accomplishes what Somers in his frustration and many of Lawrence's other male characters can only wish for. The evidence leaves little doubt that Jack fulfills Lawrence's wishes and eases his frustrations as well. Whatever Lawrence had been before taking up Mollie Skinner's manuscript, and whatever he became later, during the composition of The Boy in the Bush he was often, not in simple but in complex ways, Jack Grant. For those of us who believe that the genesis of a work of art has something essential to do with its meaning, that is important to know. If, on the other hand, we disregard the sources of art in the author, and wish only to place The Boy in the Bush within Lawrence's canon, or if we wish to locate Lawrence on the spiritual and ideological landscape of the early twentieth century, Lawrence's contributions to the creation of Jack Grant, and Lawrence's complex endorsement of Jack, are matters worth dwelling upon.

D. H. Lawrence in Ascona?

ARMIN ARNOLD

In July and August 1978 an exhibition entitled "Monte Verità" was
shown in Ascona and on the nearby islands of Brissago in the Lago
Maggiore. It was organized by Harald Szeemann. The catalogue, entitled Monte Verità, published by Electra Editrice in Milano, is
written in German; it contains hundreds of photographs and about
three hundred thousand words of text. In the autumn of 1978 the exhibition was shown in Zurich, and in spring 1979 it arrived in
Berlin.[1] The purpose of the exhibition was to give a history of
Locarno, Ascona, and the Monte Verità (part of Ascona), with the emphasis placed on the artists, anarchists, nudists, communists, the-
osophists, and other eccentrics who had assembled there since about
1870.
　　Locarno and Ascona have been the center of several revolutionary
movements. Bakunin had been one of the first to settle, for a time,
in Locarno. After 1900 Ascona had become a refuge of German anarchists
(Erich Mühsam), of liberated women (Franziska zu Reventlow), of pro-
gressive psychologists (Otto Gross), and of their sex-centered
patients and friends. The link between Munich and Locarno became so
close that the railway provided direct daily service from Munich to
Bellinzona (still in effect in 1979). More and more Germans settled
in Ascona. The former fishing village, where only Italian had been
spoken, grew into a German colony of about five thousand people. A
considerable number of more or less well-known German authors and
artists settled permanently in the region of Locarno. The former
bohemian hovels on and around the Monte Verità were torn down and
replaced by a hotel and by rather expensive bungalows. As time went
along, the reputation for gross immorality shifted from the mountain
to the vast camping ground on the Maggia River which divides Ascona
from Locarno.
　　We know from Robert Lucas and Martin Green[2] that Otto Gross had,
specifically in 1910-1913, divided his time about equally between
Munich and Ascona. We know that Gross' wife, Friedel[3] Gross-Schloffer,

195

had lived in Ascona from 1910 until well into the twenties. In fact, her husband had turned her over, in 1911, to his friend, the painter and anarchist Ernst Frick (1881-1956). In 1920 Frick fell in love with the photographer Margaretta de Fellerer with whom he lived after he had left Friedel sometime after 1922. We also know that Frieda Weekley, later the wife of D. H. Lawrence, visited her friend Friedel in Ascona in 1911, that Frieda invited Frick to England and met him there later in 1911, and that Frieda wrote to Friedel that she intended to visit her and Frick in Ascona later in 1912--accompanied by D. H. Lawrence. We read in the exhibition catalogue (p. 113) that Ernest Frick had stated that Lawrence and Frieda had, in fact, visited him and Friedel in Ascona in 1912. If the Lawrences really did so, it must have been on a trip from Lake Garda, where they lived from September 1912 to April 1913. A trip from Gargnano would have been a matter of three days at least, but there is no mention of such a trip in Lawrence's or Frieda's letters or other writings.

From René Schickele's book _Liebe_ _and_ _Aergernis_ _des_ _D._ _H._ _Lawrence_ (1934), the editors of the catalogue learned that Lawrence describes in _Twilight_ _in_ _Italy_ a commune of anarchists whom he had met on his walk through Switzerland in 1913. They think that he might have referred to the anarchists in Ascona (p. 113). In fact, he did not. The anarchists Lawrence met were Italians working in a factory at Adliswil near Zurich. Nevertheless, it is quite possible that Lawrence did visit Ascona, but in 1913.

Lawrence and Frieda had, in September 1913, planned to walk from Basel over the Gotthard to Milano and had probably intended to visit, on the way, Friedel and Ernst Frick in Ascona. Frieda then decided to let Lawrence walk by himself; she would meanwhile visit her mother and later join Lawrence in Milano. Did Frick remember Frieda's visit in 1911 and Lawrence's in 1913? Or did he remember that they intended to visit Ascona in 1912 and/or 1913? Let us look at the evidence in _Twilight_ _in_ _Italy_, at the last two chapters which are a record of Lawrence's walk from Schaffhausen to Como.[4]

It was the first time that Lawrence and Frieda separated since they had decided to stay together in May 1912, sixteen months previously. During his trip Lawrence often thought of Frieda and of Ernest Weekley, but also of Otto Gross. In Frieda's life Lawrence was not so much the successor of Weekley as of Otto Gross, and Lawrence was aware of the fact. As to Frieda, he loved and missed her; as to Weekley, Lawrence had a bad conscience.

In a postcard to Enid Hilton, written in Konstanz 18 September 1913, Lawrence had said that he intended to walk from Schaffhausen to Zurich, then to Lucerne, and then over the Gotthard. This he did, but in a strange and devious way. He had walked two-thirds of the way from Zurich to Lucerne when, in Zug, he suddenly decided to make for Arth-Goldau instead of Lucerne. It would have been fifteen miles from Zug to Lucerne, but Lawrence made up his mind to go directly to the Gotthard. In Arth-Goldau he decided to climb the Rigi; once on top, he felt that he wished to go to Lucerne after all. He walked down to Küssnacht and from there back to Lucerne. Instead of the fifteen miles from Zug, he had walked at least twice that distance. Why did Lawrence not go to Lucerne from Zug, then from Lucerne to the

Rigi, then from the Rigi to the Gotthard, as he had intended and as
anyone in his right mind would have done? I think there is evidence
in the text which explains the matter.

When Lawrence set out from Adliswil on the morning of Sunday,
21 September 1913, he said, "I went quickly over the stream, heading
for Lucerne."[5] Evidently his intention was to reach Lucerne the same
day, an easy walk. As pointed out, he changed his mind in Zug and
headed for the Gotthard. The following day he did go to Lucerne, but
he stayed there less than an hour, just long enough to write a few
words on a postcard. And what does he say about Lucerne? "Lucerne
and its lake were as irritating as ever--like the wrapper round milk
chocolate. I could not sleep even one night there: I took the steamer
down the lake, to the very last station. There I found a good German
inn, and was happy"[6] (T.i.I., p. 148). Not one other word about
Lucerne. How can Lawrence say, "Lucerne and its lake were as irritating as ever"?--he had never been there before. Does he mean that a
picture of Lucerne appears on the wrappers of some milk chocolate
and that it is irritating to have to take those wrappers off? Maybe.
But I am convinced that Lawrence was rather irritated about the fact
that several years before, on 29 August 1899, in the Hotel Schweitzerhof in Lucerne, Ernest Weekley and Frieda had spent their unhappy
wedding night, so vividly described by Frieda in her memoirs.[7] Lucerne
had irritated Frieda, and now it irritated Lawrence. This would explain the "as ever." In September 1913 Weekley was a bitter reality
in Lawrence's life: Lawrence was conscious that he had harmed a former friend. Weekley still refused to agree to a divorce; he refused
to allow Frieda to meet her children; as a consequence Frieda was
often depressed and made life miserable for Lawrence. Lucerne reminded
Lawrence too much of Weekley, and that is probably the reason why at
first he balked at going there; later he felt attracted nevertheless,
but he fled immediately he set eyes on the Hotel Schweitzerhof.

After Lawrence had left the road to Lucerne in Zug and gone on
towards the Gotthard, he came to Walchwil and went into a tea-room
run by two old ladies. They asked him, "You are Austrian?" "I said
I was from Graz; that my father was a doctor in Graz, and that I was
walking for my pleasure through the countries of Europe. I said this
because I knew a doctor from Graz who was always wandering about"
(T.i.I., p. 147).

The only doctor from Graz whom Lawrence could have heard about
was Otto Gross, Frieda's lover of a few years previously. Apparently
Lawrence never met him, but he knew all about him: Otto Gross was
the father of Else Jaffe's son Peter and the husband of Frieda's
friend Friedel Schloffer. Through Else, Lawrence must have been aware
of all the scandals about Otto Gross. When Lawrence says that this
doctor was always wandering about, he meant that Gross was continually moving about between Munich and Ascona. Martin Green suggests
that Lawrence was at that moment thinking of Otto Gross because Gross
had been associated with anarchists, and Lawrence had met a group of
Italian anarchists the night before in Adliswil.[8] Maybe. But it is
just as probable that Lawrence, having left the road to Lucerne and
proceeded directly to the Gotthard, had been thinking about Ascona
which he could now reach tomorrow or the day after. There he could

look up Friedel, and perhaps Gross or Ernst Frick would be in Ascona as well.[9] Lawrence, of course, might also have been jealous. After all, Frieda might at this very moment be meeting Gross who was "always wandering about." When Lawrence wrote, or re-wrote, those two chapters of Twilight in Italy in 1915, he could afford being ironical about Gross. It is, of course, ironical when he throws himself into the role of the son of Otto Gross.

Having been reminded of Gross in Walchwil and of Ernest Weekley in Lucerne, Lawrence arrived in Hospenthal the evening of 23 September, went to bed, and meditated, "Why am I here, on this ridge of the Alps, in the lamp-lit, wooden, close-shut room, alone? Why am I here?" (T.i.I., p. 157). One cannot help feeling that Frieda's absence is one reason why Lawrence hated Switzerland so much. Why, for instance, does he mention "the detestable Rigi, with its vile hotel" (T.i.I., p. 148)? Because Frieda and Weekley had stayed there of course.

On Wednesday evening, 24 September, Lawrence came to Bellinzona. If he visited Ascona, then he must have done so on the following day. He says, "I was no longer happy in Switzerland, not even when I was eating great blackberries and looking down at the Lago Maggiore, at Locarno, lying by the lake" (T.i.I., p. 165). He was probably on the Monte Ceneri looking across the Magadino Plain towards Locarno, but there is the distinct possibility that he was on the Monte Verità looking down at Locarno. We just do not know. It is interesting, however, that here, near Ascona, for the first time on his trip, Lawrence feels sexually attracted by a girl; he is "fascinated by her handsome naked flesh that shone like brass" (T.i.I., p. 166). She calls to him, but Lawrence is "afraid" and hurries on. He is still thinking about her later in Lugano. Could this have been an incarnation of the pretty Friedel Schloffer in Ascona? Was Lawrence "afraid" that Friedel might want to have an affair with him? After all, Frieda had had an affair with Friedel's husband, Otto Gross. Friedel might consider it nothing but natural justice to have, in turn, an affair with her best friend's lover! Lawrence was, of course, aware of the situation. If he did in fact meet Friedel in Ascona, he might, with regard to Frieda's reaction, not have mentioned it in Twilight in Italy or anywhere else.

The following day Lawrence witnessed the scene when a group of men tried to get control of "an immense pale bullock" (T.i.I., p. 167), a scene which in this book fulfills the same function as (in Lawrence's interpretation) the final hunt in Moby Dick. The bullock is the symbol of the old, natural, sensual, healthy world which modern man, an admirer of things mechanical, is doing his best to destroy. This is the main topic of Twilight in Italy.

Two days later, on Saturday, Lawrence was in Milano. On Sunday, 28 September, Frieda arrived punctually.

The "Real Quartet" of *Women in Love*: Lawrence on Brothers and Sisters

LYDIA BLANCHARD

Brotherhood, whether in literature or in life, is traditionally a positive bond, the fellowship of men with other men offering a relationship both sought after and power-filled. But the two great myths of sisterhood, the stories of the Amazons and the Graiae, suggest that communities of women provoke a quite different response; women together are both unnatural and powerless.[1] The enduring force of that mythology helps to explain, at least in part, the unusual general agreement among critics that D. H. Lawrence also exalts the strength of brotherhood--and ignores, distrusts, or fears communities of women: such an assumption falls within an old tradition. But it is also an assumption that Lawrence--both in his life and in his work--did much to encourage.

Emphases in interpretation of Lawrence's attitudes toward brotherhood and sisterhood do, of course, vary. With certain notable exceptions, critics writing before 1970, particularly those who drew heavily on an understanding of Lawrence's life, assumed that Lawrence was simply more interested in male friendships than in female; most critics did not talk--or did not talk much--about women-together in Lawrence.[2] In 1963, for example, George Ford called Lawrence's preoccupation with male friendship "a well-known and well-documented aspect of Lawrence as man and writer,"[3] but like most other critics Ford did not consider Lawrence's attitudes about female friendships. Subsequent studies as different as Emile Delavenay's D. H. Lawrence and Edward Carpenter and Paul Delany's D. H. Lawrence's Nightmare continued to build on the same assumption.[4] Like nearly every other major critic of Lawrence, whatever the primary thesis, Delavenay and Delany consider Lawrence's ideas about blood-brotherhood and his concern with homosexuality, but include no similar discussion of sisterhood.

Within the last decade, however, this general silence about
Lawrence's understanding of women-together has been increasingly chal-
lenged--with strong and often bitter indictments of his attitudes.
Although psychological critics had earlier considered Lawrence's understanding of lesbianism, and found that understanding in at least some
respects faulty,[5] it is the feminist literary critics who have argued
most powerfully for the fear, the dread, that Lawrence often has of
woman-woman relationships, the extent to which Lawrence sees such
relationships as unnatural and therefore condemns them. In 1969, in
Sexual Politics, Kate Millett maintained that Lawrence "has a bitter
dread of female alliances of any kind,"[6] and her judgment has been
subsequently and frequently echoed. Florence Howe writes that "nothing
disgusts the Puritan in Lawrence more than female homosexuals"; Deborah
Core argues that when Lawrence shows a woman "in close relation to
another woman, she is near spiritual death"; even Janice Harris, who
presents a spirited defense of Lawrence against a number of feminist
indictments, agrees: Lawrence "strongly distrusts . . . any and all
friendships between women, although he celebrates friendships between
men."[7]

In a writer so complex--indeed, so contradictory--there is, of
course, ample evidence to support either of these two major critical
assumptions about attitudes toward women-together; Lawrence feeds both
camps. Certainly in some of his least interesting fiction--in Aaron's
Rod, for example--as well as in his essays and letters, there is a
concentration on male-male friendship; throughout his work, as in his
life, Lawrence explored the possibilities of brotherhood. And while
the evidence that Lawrence distrusts or fears female friendship is
more mixed than Lawrence's harshest critics usually acknowledge (Lady
Chatterley, for example, does want to avoid other women, but Mellors
has also withdrawn from contact with other men), there still remain
times when Lawrence's treatment of women-together is harshly negative.
"The Fox" is an often cited example.

However, to impose on all of Lawrence's fiction either of these
assumptions is to reduce Lawrence significantly, to distort what are,
in a number of instances, quite different ideas that Lawrence chooses
to consider. The rich texture of Lawrence's work, the sensitivity of
his understanding of the way in which people interact, his willingness
to explore every possible human relationship, these demand that each
of Lawrence's texts be approached anew, without bias, if the reader
is to hear, as the title of a recent essay on The Plumed Serpent urges,
what the male chauvinist is really saying.[8]

With a novel like Women in Love, for example, either of these
critical assumptions--that Lawrence is not interested in or has great
fear or distrust of women-together--distorts the actual importance of
the relationship between Ursula and Gudrun, the sisters of Lawrence's
original title and the women for whom the novel is, of course, named.
George Ford, to cite one instance, has argued that Women in Love is
"a real quartet, not two duets, and . . . the testing of some phases
of the relationship between men is as dominant in its subtle counterpointing as the testing of the relationships between men and women."[9]
Thus Ford simply ignores--as have most other critics--a significant
part of the counterpointing, the relationship between women. It is a
relationship obviously necessary for a "real quartet," a connection

that Lawrence explores at almost the same length as he explores the
connections between Birkin and Gerald and one that Lawrence sustains
long after the possibility of blood-brotherhood has been exhausted.

In March 1916 Lawrence wrote to Middleton Murry and Katherine
Mansfield: "All is well between us all. No more quarrels and quibbles.
Let it be agreed for ever. I am Blutbruder: a Blutbrüderschaft between
us all."[10] To be sure, such a use of "blood-brotherhood" to include
relationships with women is not common in Lawrence, but his concern
with "us all" does indicate the importance that he placed, in life,
on the two couples becoming a unit, a "real quartet." It is such a
real quartet that also exists in some of his fiction, particularly
in Women in Love, a novel that counterpoints men and women not only
with male-male relationships, as Ford suggests, but with connections
between women as well. For although Lawrence recognized the extraordinary difficulties of forming satisfactory friendships, he also
recognized, in both literature and life, the possibility of such
friendships for both men and women. The tension between Katherine
Mansfield and Frieda could hardly have encouraged him, but in November 1918 Lawrence nevertheless wrote to Mansfield: "I do believe in
friendship. I believe tremendously in friendship between man and man,
a pledging of men to each other inviolably. But I have not ever met
or formed such friendship. Also I believe the same way in friendship
between men and women, and between women and women, sworn, pledged,
eternal, as eternal as the marriage bond, and as deep. But I have not
met or formed such friendship"[11] (emphasis added). Lawrence's interest
in relationships that would supplement marriage was clearly not restricted, either in his life or in his work, to friendship between men.

To argue, as Kate Millett has argued, that Women in Love is "the
story of Birkin's unrequited love for Gerald, the real erotic center
of the novel" or that Lawrence uses the novel to explore the "natural
repugnance of women toward each other,"[12] is to ignore one entire and
important movement, a movement established in the first chapter--called,
of course, "Sisters." Nearly every stage of the development of the
relationship between Gerald and Birkin is balanced by a similar movement in the relationship between Gudrun and Ursula, such development
forming an intricate pattern that works to help clarify the numerous
other threads of the novel, the development of Birkin paralleling the
development of Ursula, the destruction of Gerald working against the
increased decadence of Gudrun, all building, of course, to the failure
of Gerald and Gudrun juxtaposed against the new marriage of Ursula
and Birkin.

To call the structure of this extraordinary counterpointing "excessively arbitrary"[13] is thus to ignore the effect of that careful
balance, a balance that reinforces Lawrence's affirmation of the importance of heterosexual union. For while Lawrence, as he indicated
to Katherine Mansfield, believed in single-sex friendship, he never
found it--either between man and man or between woman and woman.[14]
Finally Lawrence places his trust in the marriage of man and woman.
To see Women in Love as an exploration of brotherhood, without also
considering it as an exploration of sisterhood, distorts that final
statement, giving too much weight to the power of the male bond.

Much has been written about what Paul Delany has recently called
Lawrence's "nightmare years," the years between Lawrence's completion

of The Rainbow and the publication of Women in Love, and the way in
which the original conception was changed by the extraordinary difficulties, for Lawrence, of that period: the personal battle with Frieda,
Lawrence's disappointment over the reception of The Rainbow and search
for a publisher for Women in Love, his anger and frustration about the
Great War. But if the change in tone and style is great, Lawrence continued to see Women in Love, at least in terms of its focus, as an
extension of The Rainbow, the story of a "woman becoming individual,
self-responsible, taking her own initiative."[15]

Whatever growing interest in brotherhood Lawrence personally
felt, as late as 1919 he still considered using "The Sisters" as a title
for the second work, and in 1920, writing to Martin Secker, he defended
the final choice--Women in Love is "an excellent title"--arguing that
The Rainbow and Women in Love are "an organic artistic whole." Although
another proposal to Secker, to reissue The Rainbow under a new title
(Women in Love, Vol. I),[16] was surely motivated in part by an attempt
to avoid the censors, all of these decisions reinforce Lawrence's
interest in the women of the second volume. Whatever the bitterness
of Birkin and the decadence of Gudrun and Gerald, Ursula is a healthy
figure, the imagery of potential growth which is associated with her
at the end of The Rainbow continued in the first chapter of Women in
Love and on through the second novel. Further, in both The Rainbow
and Women in Love, Ursula moves toward that individuality, the self-
responsibility Lawrence described to Edward Garnett, not only through
her relationships with men--the rejection of Anton Skrebensky and the
more important decisive union with Birkin--but also through her asso-
ciations with other women: her mother, her grandmother, Winifred Inger,
Maggie Schofield, Hermione Roddice, her sister Gudrun.

Ursula's relationship with Gudrun in Women in Love is set in The
Rainbow, Lawrence establishing in the first reference to the sisters
together the framework which will both sustain and then separate them.
"Ursula was three years old when another baby girl was born. Then the
two small sisters were much together, Gudrun and Ursula. Gudrun was
a quiet child who played for hours alone, absorbed in her fancies.
She was brown-haired, fair-skinned, strangely placid, almost passive.
Yet her will was indomitable, once set. From the first she followed
Ursula's lead. Yet she was a thing to herself, so that to watch the
two together was strange."[17] Even in The Rainbow Lawrence stresses
Gudrun's unhealthy wish to live through Ursula--Gudrun's self-absorption, her indomitable will, those diseases of the modern ego that will
destroy not only her relationship with Gerald but Gerald himself,
qualities that also appear in Gerald and that destroy the possibility
of his brotherhood with Birkin. But Gudrun also provides support for
Ursula, as Birkin hopes for support in a brotherhood, and these early
relationships establish the dual pattern that the sisters follow in
the second novel. The relationship between the two sisters is as complex in its way as the relationship between Gerald and Birkin, containing the potential for growth, realizing some of that potential,
but ultimately failing.

However, the woman other than her mother who figures most significantly in Ursula's early maturing is not Gudrun but Winifred Inger,
and it is their relationship, the only one involving Ursula's physical
love for another woman, that is frequently singled out by critics who

object to Lawrence's treatment of women-together. For while Ursula is in love with her class-mistress, and the early stages of their relationship are filled with bliss, teaching Ursula both physically, about intimacy and passion, and intellectually, about a new world of ideas, Ursula soon breaks decisively with her class-mistress, perceiving Winifred, described at first as rather beautiful, becoming ugly and clayey, Ursula's earlier admiration giving way to feelings of shame. The reasons for this rejection of Winifred are more complex than shame about single-sex relationships, however. Although the episode does show Lawrence's hostility toward lesbians, that hostility is not, in fact, significantly different from Lawrence's attitude toward homosexuals. The relationship fails because Winifred is corrupt; she wishes both to serve Ursula and also to impose her will on the younger girl. Such a power relationship, in which one or the other is stronger, is always destructive in Lawrence, whether it involves a man and a woman, or two men, or two women.

Whatever attraction Lawrence felt for other men--and critics like Emile Delavenay have argued persuasively for Lawrence's interest in a homosexual relationship during the period when he was working on "The Sisters"--Lawrence consistently shows a revulsion against physical consummation of a blood-brotherhood. The strong beetle imagery that pervades the letters in which he describes his reactions to the homosexual liaisons that he observed at Cambridge are at least as strong as anything he wrote about Ursula's eventual disgust with Winifred Inger. Lawrence does not approve of lesbian relationships, but he also does not approve, whatever he writes about brotherhoods, of homosexual relations: "These horrible little frowsty people, men lovers of men, they give me such a sense of corruption, almost putrescence, that I dream of beetles. It is abominable."[18] More importantly, the language with which Lawrence condemns the love of Winifred and Ursula is as strong as the language with which he later has Birkin and Gerald condemn Loerke and Leitner([Loerke] "lives like a rat in the river of corruption, . . . he's the wizard rat"[19]), as strong as the language with which he condemns the potentially homosexual relationship between Gerald and Birkin.

When Lawrence eliminated from Women in Love the prologue that makes more explicit the physical attraction between Birkin and Gerald, he also excised several other passages, including a passage from the "Man to Man" chapter in which the love between the men is described as "ultimately death . . . death, universal death."[20] As George Ford has suggested, more than fear of censorship probably accounts for Lawrence's decision to cut these passages.[21] The effect of the decision is to minimize Gerald's importance as a physical alternative to Ursula, as corrupting as Winifred Inger; thus the negative quality of the Winifred-Ursula experience is balanced not against the positive hopes of brotherhood for Gerald and Birkin, but against the deadly experience of Loerke and Leitner.

In "The Sisters," then, Lawrence has hope for both "brothers" and sisters: Birkin argues in Women in Love for a blood-brotherhood which will complement his relationship with Ursula, as Ursula had dreamed of a "rich, proud, simple girl-friend" in The Rainbow (p. 420)--only one of a number of times in which Ursula moves, in her development, ahead of Birkin. It is true, of course, that Ursula does not argue

for a female alliance in the way in which Birkin argues for a male
alliance. The rhetoric is clearly not there. Such a disparity is consistent, however, with the literary tradition that Nina Auerbach has
recently described, a tradition in which codes for male communities
are "explicit, formulated, and inspirational," and those for women
are "a buried language [rather] than a rallying cry."[22] Moreover,
Women in Love is a work that explicitly expresses distrust with language. Birkin's retort to Hermione early in the novel--that she is
"merely making words" (WIL, p. 35)--emphasizes that Hermione represents precisely those qualities of self-consciousness against which
she argues, but such a disparity between language and action is true
of all the other major characters in the novel as well, with the possible exception of Ursula. For both reasons then--because codes for
sisterhoods are traditionally not articulated, and because what people
say in Women in Love is unreliable and contradictory (particularly, of
course, with Birkin)--it is important to look at a number of other
indicators for Lawrence's attitudes. If Ursula does not argue for a
sisterhood, the work nevertheless makes clear that she achieves one
that is, in its strengths and weaknesses, very similar to what Birkin
envisions for and finds in his brotherhood.

Gudrun and Ursula sustain each other. Their discussion in
"Sisters," the opening chapter of Women in Love, in which they agree
that marriage is likely to be the end of experience, foreshadows a
series of incidents in which Ursula and Gudrun come together as a
unit, self-sufficient of men. Often this self-sufficiency is frightening to the men in the novel, for example, during the dance at Breadalby
in which they are joined by Hermione, and often it overcomes men, as
their father becomes inarticulate and helpless against them. They are
like a knife and a whetstone, "the one sharpened against the other"
(WIL, p. 44); their bonding may even take them "over the border of
evil" (WIL, p. 255). Lawrence has shown as well as anyone the strength
of female community--and the subsequent male fear of that strength.

Nevertheless, for most of the novel the bond is, for the sisters,
a positive one; they have already achieved, at the beginning of the
work, that complement to a heterosexual relationship that Birkin desires with a man. At the water-party at Shortlands, for example,
Gudrun and Ursula swim together naked, and then dance and sing, in a
foreshadowing, although a more peaceful one, of the physical intimacy
of the wrestling match between Birkin and Gerald. Lawrence writes,
"When they were together, doing the things they enjoyed, the two
sisters were quite complete in a perfect world of their own. And this
was one of the perfect moments of freedom and delight, such as children alone know, when all seems a perfect and blissful adventure"
(WIL, p. 156).

The general rhythm of the book is to bring the sisters together,
alternating with encounters between Gerald and Birkin, or Gudrun and
Gerald, or Ursula and Birkin. Through this rhythm as much as anything
else Lawrence shows how Ursula and Gudrun sustain each other in the
complexity of their relationships with men--particularly with their
father and with Birkin and Gerald. He writes: "[Ursula] was perfectly
stable in resistance. . . . Only Gudrun was in accord with her. It
was at these times that the intimacy between the two sisters was most

complete, as if their intelligence were one. They felt a strong, bright
bond of understanding between them, surpassing everything else. . . .
It was curious how their knowledge was complementary, that of each to
that of the other" (WIL, p. 255). This strong bond continues through
most of the novel. Of their reunion in Innsbruck, for example: "It
was curious, the delight of the sisters in each other, at this meeting.
It was as if they met in exile and united their solitary forces against
all the world" (WIL, p. 383). The very structure of the novel itself
supports the contention that the relationship between the sisters is
as strong and as important as that between the men; the space that
Lawrence gives in Women in Love to Gerald and Birkin together, without any other person involved, is slightly more than the space he
gives to similar descriptions of Gudrun and Ursula, but contacts between the men fall off more dramatically, and earlier in the novel,
than they do for the sisters.

More importantly, however, the structure of the novel supports
Lawrence's emphasis on heterosexual relationships; men can support
each other, and women can support each other, but in Lawrence's fiction, ultimately, primary relationships must become heterosexual.
Early in the novel, Ursula and Gudrun as a pair, and Birkin and Gerald
as a pair, appear with frequency. But after the first hundred pages,
these encounters become relatively less and take up a proportionately
smaller percentage of the work. The last chapter devoted exclusively
to Gerald and Birkin, Chapter XXV ("Marriage Or Not"), is the shortest
chapter in the novel, two-and-a-half pages, a dramatic structural
indication of the failure of that brotherhood; the rhythm which has
been established of Ursula-Gudrun and Gerald-Birkin gradually switches
over to Ursula-Birkin and then, significantly later, Gudrun-Gerald.
In the final two hundred pages of the novel, after the gladiatorial
encounter between Gerald and Birkin, Gudrun and Ursula are together
more than twice as much as the men, but in both cases these single
sex meetings are substantially reduced from the opening sections;
there is a careful formal correlation between the space given to the
single-sex relationships and the novel's increased disenchantment
with their possibility. For by the end of the novel, both the sisters
and the blood-brothers have failed, have come apart, whatever strength
Ursula and Gudrun had earlier shown, whatever Birkin's continued
rhetoric about their desirability. Just as Ursula sees herself as a
separate unit from Gudrun (WIL, p. 400), so Birkin and Gerald revoke
one another (WIL, p. 427).

It is Ursula's wisdom that the structure of Women in Love finally
reinforces--a man and a woman should be enough for each other; "you
can't have two kinds of love" (WIL, p. 473). Florence Howe, then, is
correct but only in a most limited way when she writes that Women in
Love "begins with a close relationship between two sisters, [and]
effects their alienation from each other. A married woman, Lawrence
insists in this novel and in others, does not need even a blood sister;
she ought to be content with her husband's friendship and love,
period."[23] The structure of the novel, the conclusion of the work,
makes precisely the same point about brotherhoods. Although Birkin
tells Gerald, in their final meeting, "I've loved you, as well as
Gudrun, don't forget," and although the parting, we are told, freezes
Birkin's heart, it is Ursula'a desire to go south that commands him
(WIL, p. 431).

For if this book is about brotherhoods and sisterhoods, and it is certainly about both, it is about them primarily to clarify Lawrence's more important, more immediately challenging concern with addressing the disease of the modern spirit--its release into sensation and decadence, its immersion into will and power. Whether the result of the self-absorption of Gerald and Gudrun, or of some larger failing in brotherhoods and sisters that Lawrence knew from personal experience and carried over into the fiction, it is not possible to sustain these relationships in Women in Love. As acted out by Ursula and Gudrun, or as contemplated by Birkin with Gerald, single-sex relationships ultimately do not work. At the end of the chapter "Gladiatorial," when Birkin has argued that his mental and spiritual intimacy with Gerald should be combined with a "more or less" physical intimacy, Lawrence nevertheless writes, "really it was Ursula, it was the woman who was gaining ascendance over Birkin's being at this moment" (WIL, p. 266).

In Women in Love, the only hope that Lawrence holds out against what he and Bertrand Russell called the "subjectivism" of the twentieth century is the creative conflict of Ursula and Birkin, the balance that is so tenuously held by them and that sets them apart from the other characters of the work, the star equilibrium that neither Gerald nor Gudrun can sustain. Both Gudrun and Gerald are absorbed in their own egos; the thin line that divides individual self-responsibility from the will-full ego is delineated nowhere so well as in Lawrence's contrast between Ursula and Birkin on the one hand, and Gudrun and Gerald on the other. For whatever strengths that Ursula and Gudrun or Birkin and Gerald can give to one another, ultimately Ursula and Birkin move out of their single-sex relationships.

Women in Love thus argues for the central importance of male-female relationships in sustaining individual self-responsibility, clarifying that importance through a simultaneous examination of Lawrence's hope for and recognition of the failure of single-sex friendships. Lawrence would go on in subsequent fiction, of course, to consider at greater length the strengths and weaknesses of both brotherhoods and communities of women, and he would come, in some of his work, to different conclusions. But to impose on Women in Love the critical judgment that Lawrence therefore is either not interested in women-together, or that the strengths and weaknesses of female bonds are significantly different from those of blood-brotherhood, is to distort seriously what is probably Lawrence's greatest novel. Traditionally brotherhoods are destroyed when women intrude on them (as, for example, in The Man Who Would Be King[24]). In Women in Love Lawrence operates within that tradition, but he also shows that such destruction can be redemptive for both men and women. This redemption Lawrence clarifies through an examination of his hope for friendship between man and man and between woman and woman--his hope and the simultaneous realization, as he wrote to Mansfield, that he had not ever met or formed such friendship. For finally Women in Love shows, as Lawrence wrote to Bertrand Russell in 1915, his belief that "the great living experience for every man is his adventure into the woman."[25]

Women in Love and The Myth of Eros and Psyche

EVELYN J. HINZ and JOHN J. TEUNISSEN

In an essay entitled "Do Women Change?" D. H. Lawrence brings into sharp focus the issue which seems to constitute the major challenge to anyone ascribing to a mythic world view today. "They say the modern woman represents a new type," he observes, "but does she?"[1] If the true answer is a feminist "Yes," then the basic premise of archetypalist philosophy--that there is nothing new under the sun--is dealt a fatal blow.

Lawrence's answer is a firm "No": modern woman does not differ in essentials from women of the past. His method of argumentation, however, is the reductive kind which could rightly infuriate academic females to classify much archetypalist criticism as the literary equivalent of cultural attempts to impose masculine ideology upon feminine expression. Instead of illustrating concretely wherein the experience of modern woman has precedents, Lawrence simply invokes the theory that history repeats itself and asserts that modern woman has her counterpart in women of the past.

Nor, at first glance, does it appear that he is any more convincing in his fiction. Indeed, that to espouse a mythic world view is incompatible with a just and positive appreciation of the character of the modern woman would, perhaps, seem at first glance to be the moral of the difference between the two "Ursula" novels. In The Rainbow, which is generally regarded as Lawrence's most mythic work, the realism of his characterization of modern woman is highly questionable. Not only does he present Ursula as yearning for a man who will relieve her of the burden of self-responsibility, but the emotions and experiences with which he endows her seem to be too closely Lawrence's own to be recognizably feminine.

In Women in Love, in contrast, Lawrence does give the modern woman her say and does respect the positive aspects of her liberationist tendencies. But the price of this fidelity seems to entail the

collapse of a controlling mythic perspective. There are, of course,
numerous direct allusions to myth in Women in Love, but instead of
creating the sense of a prevailing mythic cohesion, the impression
they generate is similar to that of The Waste Land. Furthermore, the
apparent irreconcilability of a mythic perspective and the spirit of
modern woman seems to be the point of many of the conversations in
the novel. For example, outraged by Birkin's assertion that it is in
woman's best interests to accept the dominance of the male, Ursula
cries out:

> "Ah----! Sophistries! It's the old Adam."
> "Oh yes. Adam kept Eve in the indestructible paradise when
> he kept her single with himself, like a star in its orbit."
> "Yes----yes----" cried Ursula, pointing her finger at him.
> "There you are--a star in its orbit."[2]

And a little later she pointedly criticizes the tendency to invoke
precedents as symptomatic of a weak and defensive argument: "'I don't
trust you when you drag in the stars' she said. 'If you were quite
true, it wouldn't be necessary to be so far-fetched. . . . You wouldn't
talk so much about it'" (p. 144).

If we recall, however, that central to the myth of Eros and Psyche
is precisely Psyche's refusal to be content with the terms which Eros
has established for their love, we suddenly begin to realize that there
is a mythic precedent for Ursula's "liberated" response to Birkin's
male chauvinism. And if we observe in turn that it is the crucial episode of this myth which is iconographically evoked in the climactic
moment of the encounters between the other characters in the novel as
well, we begin to realize that Women in Love does indeed have an in-
forming myth.

The climactic episode in the myth occurs when Psyche, refusing
to be kept any longer in the dark concerning the identity of her lover,
holding a lamp in one hand and a sword in the other, approaches the
bed where Eros lies sleeping; and upon discovering that he is the god
of love himself she stands for a moment transfixed until, overwhelmed
with love, she stoops to embrace him. Similarly, in "Breadalby,"
Hermione holds aloft the ball of lapis lazuli as she stands over the
unsuspecting figure of Birkin in anticipation of a "voluptuous consummation" (p. 98); in "Death and Love" Gudrun springs up "to make a
light" when Gerald, "strange and luminous . . . inevitable as a supernatural being," comes in the dark to her bedroom (p. 335); and in
"Exeunt" Birkin bids adieu to Gerald: "He went in again, at evening
to look at Gerald between the candles. . . . Suddenly his heart con-
tracted, his own candle all but fell from his hand as, with a strange
whimpering cry the tears broke out. . . . Ursula stood aside and
watched the living man stare at the frozen face of the dead man. Both
faces were unmoved and unmoving. The candle-flames flickered in the
frozen air in the intense silence" (pp. 471-72).

Consequently, with something of a shock of recognition, we begin
to appreciate that Lawrence was not speaking abstractly when in his
"Foreword" to Women in Love he defended the novel in the name of the
"Eros of the sacred mysteries";[3] nor was he confusing the issue by

then going on to emphasize the individual's need to know and understand what is happening to him. For the essence of the myth of Eros and Psyche is the inextricable relationship between loving and knowing: love for Psyche is impossible without knowledge, but knowledge always operates for her as a function of her love, always takes the form of a "passionate struggle into conscious being" ("Foreword"). And it is this passionate element, as Erich Neumann points out in his "Commentary on the Tale by Apuleius," that distinguishes the myth of Eros and Psyche from other, and particularly "masculine," myths about the quest for knowledge, just as it is Psyche's active role that distinguishes her from other women who are in love with gods.[4] The myth of Eros and Psyche, in short, is the definitive myth of "woman becoming individual, self-responsible, taking her own initiative."[5]

Our concern now, in part, is simply to provide further evidence of the extent to which the myth of Eros and Psyche informs this novel and in the process gives this seemingly modernistic work its "universal significance" and makes the disparate strands "hang together in the deepest sense" (to paraphrase Birkin's musings on whether there is such a thing as an accident, p. 20). Before doing so, however, we should emphasize that our objective is in no way to suggest that Lawrence consciously structured Women in Love upon the myth or even that he had the myth in mind at all when he was writing the book. Instead our concern in observing the recurrence of mythical elements in Women in Love is to illustrate in this way that the experience which Lawrence is dramatizing is indeed archetypal.

Since, as Douglas Bush observes in Mythology and the Renaissance Tradition, "No myth has been retold in English more elaborately than the myth of Cupid and Psyche,"[6] and since, as Jean Hagstrum has recently demonstrated, an obsession with this myth is one of the hallmarks of the Romantic poets,[7] it seems unlikely that in the course of his education Lawrence was not somehow acquainted with the myth if not specifically with The Transformations of Lucius or The Golden Ass. Nor, as we have seen, does Lawrence's phrasing in his "Foreword" appear to be purely coincidental. Nevertheless, in view of the organic way in which the myth informs the novel, it would seem better to say that Lawrence's consciousness of the myth was something that emerged in the process of writing and that it is because he is concerned with dramatizing the very experience articulated in the story of Eros and Psyche that the mythic elements invariably manifest themselves.

That to put it this way is not to speak purely figuratively, furthermore, can be illustrated by pointing out that, without ever indicating any familiarity with Lawrence's novel, the phrase which Neumann repeatedly uses to describe Psyche is "woman in love" (pp. 81, ff). Similarly, just as Lawrence in his "Foreword" begins by explaining that the cultural crises of his time "may be taken for granted in the individuals," and concludes by focusing upon his own personal struggle to articulate, so Neumann ends his Commentary with a "Postscript" wherein he attempts to explain "how a man should have been able to produce the tale of Psyche, this central document of feminine psychology." And after observing the struggle between the matriarchy

and patriarchy which characterized the time of Apuleius he concludes:
"For Apuleius, as for many men of his time, this objective cultural
datum became subjective experience through his initiation into the
mysteries of Isis. . . . But another reason why with Apuleius the
experience of religious initiation became the personal experience of
the man is that he was one of those creative men who, like the feminine, must give birth" (p. 161). Moreover, just as Women in Love
has been seen to constitute an innovation in narrative, so Neumann
finds Apuleius' tale of Psyche to constitute a new phase in the
articulation of mythic motifs: "The most fascinating aspect of it is
that, along with its abundance of mythical traits and contexts, it
represents a development whose content is precisely the liberation
of the individual from the primordial mythical world, the freeing of
the psyche" (p. 153).

To turn directly now to the novel and the myth, we might begin
by observing that the initial motif in both is the "unmarriageable
daughter" and the challenge to the traditional concept of woman's
role in life which such a situation represents. In the myth, Psyche
is unmarriageable by virtue of her great beauty which engenders worship rather than desire, and which accordingly provokes the anger of
Aphrodite, who as the embodiment of purely sensuous and physical
attractiveness represents that lower kind of beauty which stimulates
sexual appetite and leads to reproduction. In Women in Love, though
the sisters are beautiful, it is mainly their sophistication that is
the problematic factor. But their effect on those around them is the
same as in the myth. As the sisters walk through Beldover, the working people stand back and the colliers' wives regard them with hostility: "Women, their arms folded over their coarse aprons . . .
stared after the Brangwen sisters with that long, unwearying stare
of aborigines" (p. 6).

Insofar as she is a goddess, however, Aphrodite is "above" Psyche,
and her outrage stems from the challenge to her superiority which the
worship of Psyche as a "new Aphrodite" predicates: "Behold, I the
first parent of created things; behold I, Venus, the kindly mother
of all the world, must share my honors with a mortal maid, and my
name that dwells in the heavens is dragged through earthly muck"
(p. 4). In this class-conscious respect, her role in the novel is
played by Hermione: "No one could put her down, no one could make
mock of her, because she stood among the first, and those that were
against her, were below her, either in rank, or in wealth, or in high
association of thought and progress and understanding" (p. 10).
Nevertheless Hermione, like Aphrodite, also feels that her status
has somehow been threatened: "Confident as she was that in every
respect she stood beyond all vulgar judgement . . . she suffered a
torture, under her confidence and her pride, feeling herself exposed
to wounds and to mockery and to despite" (p. 11).

Regarding Psyche's unwed condition as symptomatic of hubris,
Aphrodite determines to humble her by causing her to become consumed

with desire for the "vilest of men," for "one so broken that through
all the world his misery has no peer" (p. 5). It is not, however,
through any desire of her own that Psyche is unmarried, and this in
the logic of the myth is one reason why Aphrodite's plan for vengeance is abortive. In Women in Love, on the other hand, the sisters
do sound the hubristic note when they observe that the great temptation is "not to" get married, and their consciousness that this is
to invite the vengeance of the gods is nicely evoked in their reaction: "They both laughed, looking at each other. In their hearts
they were frightened" (p. 2). What makes the thought of marriage distasteful to Ursula, however, is something that the adulterous Aphrodite would understand--domesticity and subservience to a male--
whereas what makes marriage impossible for Gudrun is its reproductive
implications. Consequently, whereas Ursula, like Psyche, escapes
Aphrodite's vengeance, it is to a certain extent visited upon Gudrun
in terms of her sudden and inexplicable attraction to the "sinister"
aspects of the fratricidal Gerald, while, as retribution for her rejection of the very thought of physical motherhood, she is cursed
with having to act out the maternal role in her relationship with him.

In attempting to execute her revenge upon Psyche, Aphrodite does
not of course act alone or directly. Instead she enlists the aid of
her son, who as the "wanton god of love," we might now notice, functions as the mythic prototype for Lawrence's promiscuous male protagonists: "'He should have all the women he can,'" Gudrun observes
of Gerald; '--it is his nature. It is absurd to call him monogamous--
he is naturally promiscuous'" (p. 403). Although Birkin's promiscuity
takes a spiritual form, it amounts to the same thing insofar as woman
is concerned, as Ursula's response makes clear: "She wanted him to
herself, she hated the Salvator Mundi touch. It was something diffuse
and generalized about him, which she could not stand. He would behave
in the same way, say the same things, give himself as completely to
anybody who came along, anybody and everybody who liked to appeal to
him. It was despicable, a very insidious form of prostitution" (p. 121).

At the same time, it is mythically important that Eros should
take a "higher" form, since it symbolizes the fact that, wanton or
not, Eros is a divinity, and it is precisely on this basis--upon the
fact of their mutual superior status--that Aphrodite automatically
assumes the cooperation of her son in her attempt to punish a human
upstart. Similarly, as Ursula realizes, it is their shared aristocratic
background that constitutes such a powerful bond between Birkin and
Hermione: "It was strange how inviolable was the intimacy which
existed between him and Hermione. Ursula felt she was an outsider,
the very tea-cups and the old silver were a bond between Hermione and
Birkin. It seemed to belong to an old past world which they had in-
habited together, and in which Ursula was a foreigner. She was almost
a parvenue in their old cultured milieu" (p. 291).

Just as Aphrodite makes her final appeal to the sacredness and
priority of the mother-child relationship, furthermore--"I implore
you by all the bonds that bind you to her that bore you" (p. 5)--so
Hermione repeatedly refers to Birkin as her little boy, and rests her
case in his hands: "If only Birkin would form a close and abiding
connection with her, she would be safe during this fretful voyage of

life. He could make her sound and triumphant, triumphant over the
very angels of heaven. If only he would do it! . . . But this, this
conjunction with her, which was his highest fulfilment also, with the
perverseness of a wilful child he wanted to deny. With the wilfulness
of an obstinate child, he wanted to break the holy connection that was
between them" (pp. 11-12).

If, like Hermione, Aphrodite is thus the dominating maternal
spirit that would thwart any move toward independence, however, she
is also the principle which ensures that life will go on. And so in
the myth, after displaying her horrible fish-wife side, Aphrodite
returns to the place of her birth and concomitantly reveals both the
beautiful side of her character and the cyclicality of existence:
"Then she returned to the shore hard by, where the sea ebbs and flows,
and treading with rosy feet the topmost foam of the quivering waves,
plunged to the deep's dry floor" (p. 5). In the same way, in "Water-
Party," the discussion moves from Birkin's association of Aphrodite
with "universal dissolution" to Ursula's insistence that the "beginning comes out of the end" and her substitution of "roses of happiness" for his "fleurs du mal" (pp. 164-65). Perhaps the best evocation
of the Botticelli Aphrodite, however, is to be found in the description
of the arrival of the bride:

> In the opening of the doorway was a shower of fine foliage
> and flowers, a whiteness of satin and lace, and the sound of a
> gay voice saying:
> "How do I get out?"
> A ripple of satisfaction ran through the expectant people.
> They pressed near to receive her, looking with zest at the stoop-
> ing blonde head with its flower buds, and at the delicate, white,
> tentative foot that was reaching down to the step of the carriage.
> There was a sudden foaming rush, and the bride like a sudden surf-
> rush, floating all white beside her father in the morning shadow
> of trees, her veil flowing with laughter (pp. 12-13).

In the myth, with the withdrawal of Aphrodite to the seaside the
focus shifts back to the human level--particularly to Psyche's father's
consultation with the oracle, which provides the following advice.

> On some high crag, O king, set forth the maid,
> In all the pomp of funeral robes arrayed.
>
> Hope for no bridegroom born of mortal seed,
>
> But fierce and wild and of the dragon breed.
> He swoops all-conquering, borne on airy wing,
>
> With fire and sword he makes his harvesting;
>
> Trembles before him Jove, whom gods do dread,
> And quakes the darksome river of the dead (p. 7).

Taking into consideration her competition for Birkin the essence of
Hermione's advice to Ursula--delivered first "with rhapsodic intensity"

and then "as if the pythoness had uttered the oracle"--is to the same effect: "'I think you need a man--soldierly, strong-willed--. . . . You need a man physically strong, and virile in his will, not a sensitive man. . . . You would have to be prepared to suffer--dreadfully. . . . I feel it would be perfectly disastrous for you to marry him. . . . That which he affirms and loves one day--a little later he turns on in a fury of destruction. He is never constant, always this awful dreadful reaction. Always the change from good to bad, bad to good. And nothing is so devastating, nothing--'" (p. 287).

Psyche's father also interprets the words of the oracle to mean that his daughter's marriage will be a "devastating" thing for her, and consequently, though dressed as a bride, she is accompanied in funeral procession to the mountain crag and left to await the arrival of her deathly lover. Constituting what Neumann calls the "marriage of death" motif, the presence of this mythic element in Women in Love would seem to be too pervasive and self-evident to require much comment. One finds it dramatized in the deathly embrace of Diana Crich and her lover, in Gerald's coming--in "Love and Death"--from his father's grave to Gudrun's bed, and in all the numerous instances of murderous love. What this motif archetypally symbolizes, however, is the transition from maidenhood to womanhood--the end of girlhood and the entrance into a new phase of development; and since what characterizes Psyche's reaction at this point in the myth is her calm acceptance of her fate, where one finds the best evocation of the "marriage of death" is in Ursula's musings in "Sunday Evening" as she sits waiting for Birkin to come: "As the day wore on, the life-blood seemed to ebb away from Ursula. . . . Her passion seemed to bleed to death. . . . She realized how all her life she had been drawing nearer and nearer to this brink. . . . And one must fulfil one's development to the end, must carry the adventure to its conclusion. And the next step was over the border into death. So it was then! There was a certain peace in the knowledge" (p. 183).

In the myth, of course, the projected thanatogamous marriage does not take place--except in the symbolic sense; for, disobeying his mother, Eros himself takes the place of the wretch with whom he was commissioned to make Psyche fall in love. She, however, knows only that her husband is a wonderful lover, since the injunction that Eros places upon her the first night he comes to her is that she never seek to discover his identity. In much the same way, Birkin insists that he and Ursula meet on an impersonal plane--"'You are invisible to me, if you don't force me to be visually aware of you'" (p. 139)--just as this "paradise in the dark" motif, as Neumann calls it, is nicely evoked in Lawrence's opening description of Ursula: "She lived a good deal by herself, to herself, working, passing on from day to day, and always thinking, trying to lay hold on life, to grasp it in her own understanding. Her active living was suspended, but underneath, in the darkness, something was coming to pass. If only she could break through the last integuments! She seemed to try and put her hands out, like an infant in the womb, and she could not, not yet. Still she had a strange prescience, an intimation of something yet to come" (p. 3).

Every paradise has a serpent, however, and in this definitively feminine myth the serpent appears in the form of Psyche's two envious sisters, who by questioning her about her lover come to make her feel

uncomfortable. In Women in Love, both Gudrun and Hermione play this
role, but it is particularly in the conversation of Hermione and
Ursula in "Woman to Woman" that this phase of the myth is evoked:

> "I am so glad to see you," she said to Ursula, in her slow
> voice, that was like an incantation. "You and Rupert have become
> quite friends?"
> "Oh yes," said Ursula. "He is always somewhere in the back-
> ground."
> Hermione paused before she answered. She saw perfectly well
> the other woman's vaunt: it seemed truly vulgar.
> "Is he?" she said slowly, and with perfect equanimity. "And
> do you think you will marry?"
>
> . . . .
>
> Hermione watched her with slow, calm eyes. She noted this
> new expression of vaunting. How she envied Ursula a certain un-
> conscious positivity! even her vulgarity!
>
> . . . .
>
> "To what does he want you to submit?"
> "He says he wants me to accept him non-emotionally, and
> finally--I really don't know what he means. He says he wants
> the demon part of himself to be mated--physically--not the human
> being. You see, he says one thing one day, and another the next--
> and he always contradicts himself--"
> "And always thinks about himself, and his own dissatisfac-
> tion," said Hermione, slowly.
>
> . . . .
>
> "He wants me to sink myself," Ursula resumed, "not to have
> any being of my own--"
> "Then why doesn't he marry an odalisk?" said Hermione in
> her mild sing-song, "if it is that he wants." Her long face
> looked sardonic and amused (pp. 285-86).

The net result of such questioning, in the myth, is that Psyche dares
to disobey Eros' command; while he lies sleeping in her bedchamber,
she comes to him, carrying a lamp in one hand and in the other a sword--
to kill him should he be the monster that her sisters have insisted he
is. And here, as we have already suggested, it would at first seem that
it is Gudrun rather than Ursula who comes into focus as the Psyche
figure, since, whereas Gudrun makes a light, Ursula in "Excurse"
pointedly champions the darkness: "To speak, to see, was nothing. It
was a travesty to look and comprehend the man there" (p. 311). What
needs to be taken into consideration, however, is that what light
symbolizes in the myth is not what light has come to symbolize in the
modern world: in the myth light symbolizes a perception of the true
nature of things whereas light in the modern world symbolizes purely

cerebral knowledge and visual perception, as the first instance of
light-making in the novel--when Birkin visits Ursula's classroom--
makes clear:

> "It is so dark," he said. "Shall we have the light?"
> And moving aside, he switched on the strong electric
> lights. The class-room was distinct and hard, a strange
> place after the soft dim magic that filled it before he came
> (p. 29).

Thus, though Gudrun's act and posture do evoke the crucial scene
in the myth, her motives for making a light are not true to the spirit
of Psyche. Instead of being the means whereby she will be able truly
to see her lover, Gudrun's candle is really her weapon--her way of
warding off her lover and staying the moment when he will come to her
bed. Consequently, instead of being overwhelmed with love, Gudrun is
left lying "with dark, wide eyes looking into the darkness. She could
see so far, as far as eternity--yet she saw nothing. She was suspended
in perfect consciousness--and of what was she conscious?":

> She wanted to look at him, to see him.
> But she dared not make a light, because she knew he would
> wake, and she did not want to break his perfect sleep, that
> she knew he had got of her (p. 338).

And when he finally does awake and she lights the candle, what she
sees is not the naked splendor of a god but the "humiliating" spectacle of a man pulling on his pants: "'It is like a workman getting
up to go to work,'" thinks Gudrun (p. 341).

In contrast, by not trying to see "the man there," Ursula is
able to see the god, and she emerges as the true Psyche when she refuses to remain in the dark, metaphorically speaking: "'You want the
pardisal unknowing,' she said, turning round on him as he sat half
visible in the shadow. 'I know what that means, thank you. You want
me to be your thing, never to criticize you or to have anything to
say for myself'" (p. 243). Similarly, she reflects her awareness of
what Psyche's act symbolizes when she ridicules the canary who has
gone to sleep because a cloth has been placed over its cage: "'It
really thinks the night has come! How absurd! Really, how can one
have any respect for a creature that is so easily taken in!'" (p. 126).

Although the awakening of Eros to a knowledge of Psyche's dis-
obedience and his subsequent chastisement of her and return to his
mother's residence are in some ways best evoked in terms of Birkin's
parting words to Hermione and his return to "mother nature" after
Hermione has tried to kill him (and here one should note that if
Psyche does not try to kill her lover she does wound him when a drop
of oil from her lamp scalds his shoulder) and although the desolation
of Psyche after Eros has left is powerfully evoked in Gudrun's vigil--
"Ah, she could shriek with torment, he was so far off, and perfected,
in another world. . . . And here was she, left with all the anguish
of consciousness, whilst he was sunk deep into the other element of
mindless, remote, shadow-gleam. He was beautiful, far off, and perfected. They would never be together" (p. 339)--it is with respect

to Ursula that the two sides of the picture are brought together:
"After his illness Birkin went to the south of France for a time. He
did not write, nobody heard anything of him. Ursula, left alone, felt
as if everything were lapsing out. There seemed to be no hope in the
world. One was a tiny little rock with tide of nothingness rising
higher and higher" (p. 236). Also evoked by way of the water imagery
is Psyche's attempt to drown herself. And just as it is Pan who re-
vives her broken spirit, so it is in the "horses and cows in the field"
that Ursula finds a corrective to that which has occasioned her despair.

Specifically, Pan's advice to Psyche is that, instead of wearing
herself out in lamenting her loss, she seek to find and win back her
lover, and consequently the next phase of the myth involves Psyche's
direct confrontation with Aphrodite, since it is logically at his
mother's home that she can expect to find him. So Ursula too comes
face to face with the goddess in "Moony," and like Psyche experiences
her violence: as she walks toward Willey Water--where she will also
witness Birkin's attempt to stone the "accursed Syria Dea"--Ursula
notices something "like a great presence, watching her, dodging [sic]
her. She started violently. It was only the moon, risen through the
thin trees. But it seemed so mysterious, with its white and deathly
smile. And there was no avoiding it. Night or day, one could not escape
the sinister face, triumphant and radiant like this moon, with a high
smile. She hurried on, cowering from the white planet. . . . She
suffered from being exposed to it" (p. 237).

Unable to destroy Psyche in this way, Aphrodite next sets her
four tasks, all of which are seemingly impossible and progressively
death-dealing. And it is here, as Neumann observes, that "Psyche
becomes a feminine Hercules" at the same time that the difference
between masculine and feminine heroism is made dramatically clear
(p. 93).

The first task imposed upon Psyche is that she separate into their
proper piles a random heap of seeds, a task which in Women in Love
mainly takes the form of Ursula's sorting out the welter of theories
concerning the nature of life and love and marriage which are advanced
by the other characters in the novel, in particular Birkin. And just
as in the myth Psyche is aided by ants or the lowest orders, so Ursula
accomplishes this task by relying upon her instinct and by demanding
concrete evidence. Thus when Birkin becomes grandly philosophic about
the imminence of the end of the world, her response is "'And you and
me----?'" and when he goes on to argue that they are "flowers of dissolution," her protest is "'I don't feel as if I were'" (p. 164). It
is her ability to discriminate on the basis of what things really mean
to her, furthermore, which so distinguishes her from Gudrun who accepts
the conventional classifications and in masculine fashion insists upon
clear-cut distinctions, as the opening discussion of what marriage
means dramatizes so effectively.

The difference between the two sisters comes into even sharper
focus when one considers the second labor of Psyche: namely, that she
steal the fleece from a herd of savage cattle--a task which is designed
to test the courage of the female and accordingly to demonstrate that
her powers are equal to those of the male. Gudrun, as one recalls,
attempts to accomplish this task by direct confrontation, just as she

later strikes Gerald on the cheek to illustrate her defiance. In contrast, like Psyche who was aided by a reed, Ursula attempts to charm
the savage beasts by singing, and just as the advice of the reed was
to wait for nightfall so Ursula illustrates her courage by way of her
unsqueamish response to the cuttlefish lantern and her equality by
holding her own in the subsequent discussion of death.

Psyche's third task, to obtain a cup of water from a "hideous
stream" that pours down from "a rock of measureless height, rough,
slippery and inaccessible" and falls to bottomless depths, is strikingly evoked in Ursula's response to Birkin's body: "There were
strange fountains of his body, more mysterious and potent than any
she had imagined or known, more satisfying, ah, finally, mystically-
physically satisfying. She had thought there was no source deeper
than the phallic source. And now, behold, from the smitten rock of
the man's body, from the strange marvellous flanks and thighs, deeper,
further in mystery than the phallic source, came the floods of ineffable darkness and ineffable riches" (p. 306). That there should be
a homosexual dimension to this evocation, furthermore, is also prece-
dented in the myth, since the creature who aids Psyche in this task
is "the eagle of Ganymede," the eagle who carried off to Olympus
Zeus's young male paramour. In turn, the entire Birkin-Gerald relationship in Women in Love begins to fall into mythic place, for, as Neumann
explains with regard to the question of why homosexual love should
come to the aid of Psyche, "homoerotic and homosexual male pairs act
as 'strugglers,' taking up the war of liberation against the domination of the Great Mother" (p. 105).

If the overlying theme of the first three tasks is the ability of
woman to confront and incorporate masculine tendencies without losing
her femininity, the final task involves her ability to withstand those
feminine tendencies within her own self that would once more reduce
her to "typical woman" status. Thus Psyche is required to descend to
the underworld and to return with a casket filled with Persephone's
beauty ointment, a task which is designed to test her ability to face
up to the dark side of her own psyche. Both sisters are given this
opportunity in terms of their meeting with the repulsive Loerke, and
we now see the mythic rationale for Lawrence's characterization of
Loerke as the feminine figure in his homosexual relationship with
Leitner.

Though Loerke fascinates both sisters, Ursula does not come under
his power, and significantly it is chiefly by reason of her antagonism
to his concept of art. For what provided Psyche with guidance at the
outset of this task was a "tower," which, as the only inanimate and
man-made aid to Psyche, symbolizes culture. In turn, it is because,
like Psyche, she obeys the first instruction of the tower that Ursula
is able to rise above the sordidness of life whereas Gudrun is overcome with cynicism. This instruction is that when she is in the underworld Psyche must not show pity to a corpse, since what pity symbolizes
here is the indiscriminate all-embracing tendency of the female in the
same way that the corpse symbolizes the dead drag of the past and the
antilife principle. Accordingly, where Ursula best exemplifies this
ability to refrain from mothering death, from acting the Pietà, is in
her response to Birkin's illness in "Sunday Evening":

She saw him, how he was motionless and ageless, like some
crouching idol, some image of a deathly religion. He looked
round at her, and his face, very pale and unreal, seemed to
gleam with a whiteness almost phosphorescent.
"Don't you feel well?" she asked, in indefinable
repulsion.
"I hadn't thought about it."

. . . .

"Why don't you stay in bed when you are seedy? You look
perfectly ghastly."
"Offensively so?" he asked ironically.
"Yes, quite offensive. Quite repelling" (p. 188).

In contrast, as Gudrun finally admits to Gerald at the end of the
novel, and with respect to the night when he came from the grave to
her bed: "'When you first came to me. I had to take pity on you. But
it was never love'" (p. 433).

The tower also provides Psyche with a second instruction: namely,
that she must not open the casket, and here Psyche fails. In the interest of making herself irresistible to Eros, Psyche decides to steal
a little of the beauty ointment, but the effect of opening the casket
is that she falls into a deathly sleep. Now insofar as vanity is the
issue here, each of Lawrence's three female protagonists is a Psyche.
Thus Hermione agonizes over her appearance: "He would be there, surely
he would see how beautiful her dress was, surely he would see how she
had made herself beautiful for him" (p. 12). Similarly, Gudrun is
rarely to be seen without some reference to her beautiful attire, and
when Loerke asks for her "companionship in intelligence" she cannot
refrain from wondering, "Did he not think her good-looking, then?"
(p. 450). And Ursula would seem to be the most persistently vain of
the three:

"But don't you think me good-looking?" she persisted in
a mocking voice.
He looked at her, to see if he felt she was good-looking.
"I don't feel that you're good-looking," he said.
"Not even attractive?" she mocked, bitingly (p. 138).

What Psyche's act symbolizes, however, is not vanity in the conventional sense but rather the self-respect of the truly liberated
woman--the refusal to sacrifice femininity for the sake of achievement and the willingness to risk losing a lover in the interest of
being true to herself. As such, Psyche's vanity is a very different
thing than Hermione's, whose desire to be beautiful is indicative of
her total dependence upon the masculine for her own self-image, just
as it is very different from Gudrun's, whose "smart" appearance is
designed to make men feel that she is "one of the chaps." Only Ursula's
vanity is of the true Psyche variety as her response to Birkin's rejection of her "good looks," her "womanly feelings," her "thoughts
. . . opinions . . . ideas" as being mere "bagatelles" to him, makes

clear: "'You are very conceited, Monsieur,' she mocked. 'How do you
know what my womanly feelings are, or my thoughts or my ideas? You
don't even know what I think of you now'" (p. 139).

Consequently, whereas Hermione never awakens from the effects of
her violent attempt to make Birkin conscious of her, but rather moves
through the novel like a somnabulist, and whereas Gudrun is never able
to fall asleep because this would put her in a vulnerable position,
Ursula's failure to resist acting like a woman--as in the case of her
irrational outburst in the ring episode--has the effect of breaking
down Birkin's resistance. Just as the beauty of Psyche as she lies
on the path in her deathly sleep overpowers Eros and brings him back
to her, so it is the sight of the rings--which Ursula in her pride and
vanity had flung at him--that awakens Birkin to the extent of his love
for her: "He could not bear to see the rings lying in the pale mud of
the road. . . . They were the little tokens of the reality of beauty,
the reality of happiness in warm creation. . . . There was a darkness
over his mind. The terrible knot of consciousness that had persisted
like an obsession was broken, gone, his life was dissolved in darkness
over his limbs and body. But there was a point of anxiety in his heart
now. He wanted her to come back" (p. 301).

Reflected here, and then emphasized in terms of his subsequent
series of "yesses" to Ursula's questions about whether he "loves" her,
is the great change which has come over Birkin--he began, as one recalls, by arguing that the word "love" should be tabooed (p. 122).
And it is the similar change that has come over Eros, as Neumann explains, that makes this "sleeping beauty" phase of the myth so different from the fairy tale. There the princess must await the arrival
of her male rescuer; here she brings him to her, they rescue each
other. In the final analysis, therefore, it is the mutual development
of Eros and Psyche that makes this myth such a complete expression of
love and liberation--such a perfect dramatization of "star equilibrium."

Not only do all of the major motifs of the myth thus find expression in this modern novel, but so also do a number of the most famous
attempts to articulate or represent its meaning. In the description of
Ursula in "Sketch-Book," for example, Lawrence simultaneously evokes
both the ancient depiction of the emerging soul as a butterfly and
Canova's two sculptures--the one featuring the winged Eros embracing
Psyche, and the other in which the pair stand together gazing at a
butterfly: "Ursula was watching the butterflies, of which there were
dozens near the water, little blue ones suddenly snapping out of
nothingless into a jewel-life, a large black-and-red one standing
upon a flower and breathing with his soft wings, intoxicatingly,
breathing pure, ethereal sunshine: two white ones wrestling in the
low air; there was a halo about them" (p. 111). The second Canova
sculpture is also evoked in the description of Gudrun and Gerald as
they look at the "butterfly" lantern: "Gerald leaned near to her,
into her zone of light, as if to see. He came close to her, and stood
touching her, looking with her at the primrose-shining globe. And she
turned her face to his, that was faintly bright in the light of the
lantern, and they stood together in one luminous union, close together
and ringed round with light, all the rest excluded" (p. 166). Similarly,
there would seem to be an evocation of Keats' "Ode to Psyche," and
specifically his depiction of the lovers sleeping in the woods in

Lawrence's description of the Sherwood Forest consummation of Birkin and Ursula in "Excurse": "There were faint sounds from the wood, but no disturbance, the world was under a strange ban, a new mystery had supervened" (p. 312).

Most significant of all, however, may be Lawrence's introduction of "Flaxman and Blake and Fuseli" into the conversation between Gudrun and Loerke (p. 445). For what these three artists have in common is their depiction of the crucial discovery scene in the myth, and the point here is that for all their knowledge of art, Gudrun and Loerke are ignorant that the subject of these artists is the experience which they are living out. Thus the mentality they represent is the mentality which has tried to "explain myth away," as Lawrence puts it in his review of Carter's Dragon of the Apocalypse. But since myth, as Lawrence himself defined it, "is an attempt to narrate a whole human experience. . . . It describes a profound experience of the human body and soul, an experience which is never exhausted and never will be exhausted, for it is being felt and suffered now, and it will be suffered while man remains man," to attempt to explain myth away means only that "you go on suffering blindly, stupidly, 'in the unconscious,' instead of healthily and with the imaginative comprehension playing on the suffering."[8] And that this is the essence of Gudrun's plight is the point, significantly, of the first evocation of the myth in the novel. That is, at the beginning of Women in Love Gudrun envisions her future in terms of "jumping off a cliff," a fate which is reserved for Psyche's envious sisters just as the cliff is also the place where Psyche awaits her bridegroom. But while Gudrun emotionally apprehends the significance of her metaphor, her conscious response is, "'Ah! . . . What is it all but words!'" (p. 4).

The Textual Edition of
Lawrence's Letters

The Cambridge University Press Edition of Lawrence's Letters, Part 4

JAMES T. BOULTON

The case having been made for an edition, the manuscript and "technical" resources having been surveyed, and the "overall strategy" in the sense of the lay-out of the edition as a whole having been described, the focus is gradually narrowing to the text itself, and it falls to me to comment on how we shall present what D. H. Lawrence actually wrote in his multitudinous letters. This, of course, is the object of the edition: to present in readable, intelligible form Lawrence's _ipsissima_ _verba_. We shall not print every word as he wrote it: we shall not print postscripts in the margin or in other eccentric positions; we shall not show obscene words scribbled by Lawrence over Frieda's text; nor shall we reproduce one layer of Lawrence's text superimposed on another (as he wrote them occasionally on postcards). This is not a diplomatic edition, nor a facsimile; it is an edited text in the sense that editorial judgment plays a significant role in how Lawrence's words are presented and how they will be interpreted--but the text will be his. There will be no expurgations or bowdlerizations. Our "copy" is provided in most cases by Lawrence's autograph manuscript. There will obviously be some exceptions--some manuscripts have disappeared, and copies or printed versions alone remain--but they will be relatively few.

The scope of the edition will be coterminous with Lawrence's surviving letters: all will be included. Fortunately, though he wrote many postcards and some notes, he wrote few which are merely trivial, announcing the time of his arrival or accepting an invitation to tea-- or, at least, if he did, few survive. So the principle of inclusiveness will rarely create embarrassment. In any case there is invariably something distinctive even about messages which are, in essence, trivial.

The editors have, for their part, a major part to play and a great responsibility to fulfill. They must satisfy an international body of scholars as well as the well-read Lawrentian and what Dr. Johnson called "the common reader" (and he represents the majority).

The professional scholar expects to be informed and assured of the source from which a text is derived; the state of the manuscript; whether Lawrence made deletions or corrections; how we arrive at the date of a letter which Lawrence has not dated correctly--and if we do not believe his own dating, then why; if he quotes from a literary work, then has he quoted accurately; if he visits an exhibition, whether at the Royal Academy or in Munich, then what pictures is he likely to have seen; and so on. An editor responding to such demands is not merely a pedant catering to pedants. To feel it necessary to satisfy such expectations places the editor under an obligation to be accurate and thorough; it also makes valuable information available. Even Lawrence's deletions in the letters prove to be instructive and will be tactfully recorded. For example, when Louie Burrows asks him for a list of "great men" in February 1909, he includes in his list William the Silent, Martin Luther, Peter the Great, among others, but on second thoughts deleted Martin Luther.[1] One wonders why. Again, when the artist Ernest Collings first wrote to Lawrence he obviously adopted a very formal mode and addressed Lawrence as "Dear Sir"; in his reply Lawrence writes, "Dear Sir, Call me a lord if you will"; then, on second thoughts, he amends his manuscript to read, "Dear Mr Collings, Call me 'Sir' if you will."[2] Or again, it tells us something about the relationship between Lawrence and Louie Burrows when, writing to her in French, he does not find it natural to address her in the second person; he writes votre and then consciously deletes the word in order to substitute the tu appropriate to intimacy and affection.[3] Such information tucked away in footnotes makes a wide range of insights available to the reader to be used or ignored at his discretion. And when he finds the pictures Lawrence saw in the Winter Exhibition of 1908-1909 at the Royal Academy or at the Dulwich Art Gallery in March 1909 precisely identified in a note, one hopes that he will not regard that information as merely satisfying the scholar's addiction to footnotes: it exists to illuminate Lawrence's increasing artistic experience and his developing critical taste.

All readers, scholarly or not, want to have Lawrence's correspondents, friends, acquaintances, and people he casually mentions in his letters brought to life, given identity--in varying degrees to know their age, occupation, educational experience, cultural interests, etc. Only by such means will a reader be able to form a critical view and general understanding of the milieu in which Lawrence moved and had his being. Why, for example, did he find it so clearly rewarding to correspond with Ernest Collings, to the extent that the famous statement of Lawrence's "religion"--"My great religion is a belief in the blood, the flesh, as being wiser than the intellect"--is found in a letter to Collings (17 January 1913)? Why should he hold his student-friend Thomas Smith or his teaching colleague Arthur McLeod in such high regard? What was the significance for him of his uncle-by-marriage, Fritz Krenkow? Unless the editor first discovers and then communicates the answers to such questions, readers of Lawrence's letters will not bring to bear on their reading all the pertinent information which will aid their critical understanding. And since the writing and exchange of letters is necessarily and importantly a matter of

relationships between, and responses to, people, to individuals, the
Cambridge volumes will be illustrated by pictures of the men and women
who were significantly involved in his correspondence. We believe that
the visual images--of McLeod or Middleton Murry, Dorothy Brett, or
Rachel Annand Taylor--will help to transform mere names into people
who wrote to and received letters from Lawrence and contributed to
the formation of his distinctive genius.

The general intention governing all such editorial procedures is
to provide readers with a literary experience which approximates to
that enjoyed by the original recipients of Lawrence's letters. It cannot be the same. Though readers of the published texts are, in a certain sense, in a position comparable to that of the first recipient,
no reader becomes Bertrand Russell or Lady Ottoline Morrell or Koteliansky while reading. He cannot fully re-create the personality, the experiences, the prejudices, the range of knowledge, and so forth, which
coalesced in such individuals. Nor can he wholly apprehend the nature
and nuances of the relationship established between them and Lawrence.
To achieve the necessary insights which will permit an understanding
of, a "feel" for, that relationship, imagination is essential--but so
is information.

The responsibility of the editor at this point goes beyond the
first essential--the provision of a completely accurate text--and
requires that he render the text fully comprehensible. He must certainly avoid turning Lawrence's spontaneous, ebullient, or urgent
outbursts to his correspondents into lifeless archival records; he
must avoid the temptation to make his annotation into a monument to
his own scholarship; but equally he must ensure that his readers
understand what Lawrence is saying. Without understanding, there is
at best a restricted enjoyment. Unless the reader recognizes the range
of literary, Biblical, and classical allusions, the political or historical referents, the clash of personalities, or whatever is pertinent on particular occasions, he cannot be sensitive to Lawrence's
mental caliber, creative resourcefulness, and epistolary skill. Nor
can he estimate the sensitivity with which Lawrence discharges the
responsibility of a letter-writer to address every correspondent as
a unique individual. He can, of course, ignore the assistance offered
by an editor--the editor cannot escape the duty to provide it.

There are those who will dismiss this argument. Some will complain that footnotes in an edition of a near-contemporary will invariably tell them what they already know. Others will claim that spontaneity is the very essence of the "familiar" letter and it must be met
by immediate, unfettered response. Such readers will recall Pope's
view that in his letters a man expresses "thoughts just warm from the
brain without any polishing or dress, the very déshabille of the understanding."[4] Any distraction, however objectively helpful its purpose,
therefore destroys or at least diminishes the freshness of the read-
ing-experience.

To say that there is nothing in this assertion would be foolish,
but "freshness," "immediacy of response," can be bought at too high
a price. They may both be limited, muted by ignorance. Let us take a
specific example: a passage from a letter to Compton Mackenzie on
9 April 1920. (Mackenzie purports to print this letter in his Life

and <u>Times</u>.[5]) It is proper to observe that, when this letter is encountered in Volume 3 of the Cambridge Edition, its place in the chronological sequence will clarify some of the obscurities which appear when it
is read in isolation. The reader will know from preceding letters that
the person being described is the novelist Gilbert Cannan who had
recently returned from America, where he had organized some financial
assistance for Lawrence; that "Gwen" had been his mistress and "Mary"
(formerly the wife of James Barrie) his wife.

> He is tout americain--L'Americanisato--pocket book thick, fat,
> bulging with 1000 Lire notes--'these beastly hotels'--'Oh yes,
> picked up quite a lot of money over there'--'Oh yes, they seemed
> to take to me quite a lot'--'Yes, have promised a quantity of
> people I'll go back there this Fall.--'
>   Oh what a Fall was there!!
> However, we parted as friends who will <u>never</u> speak to each other
> again.
>   And Life is thorny, and Youth is vain
>   And to be wroth with one we love
>   Doth work like madness in the brain--
> Poor Gilbert--a soap pill. However, I've sent my check like
> lightning to the bank, to see if it'll be cashed safe and sound.
> Aspettiamo!--And today the filbert returns to Rome, to his deux
> Monds. --'Gwen is a wonderful and beautiful character--' --this
> to my nose. --Do you wonder I made a nose at it? 'Gwen's isn't
> a forgiving nature', says he. 'Neither is mine', reply I. Assez
> de ça. He's returned to his revue des deux Monds--and shortly
> the Mond, the Demi-Mond, and the Immond (to parody one of
> Mary's 'sayings')--return en trois to London. 'It has made no
> difference to <u>me</u>--' This from the filbert, regarding the mar-
> riage of Gwen. Ça parait, mon cher.

That this is spontaneous, vivid, witty, and makes an immediate
impact few will deny. But is it fully comprehensible? Since literary
pleasure depends on understanding, the passage will be limited in the
pleasure it offers at least to some--perhaps to most--readers. Some
will not be able to identify the third person in the trio Lawrence
mentions; others will wonder whether "revue des deux Monds" is an
example of his misspelling a foreign title; some may suspect that a
pun is involved but be unable to explain it; and still others will be
irritated because they cannot quite place all Lawrence's literary
quotations or allusions.

In a paragraph such as this Lawrence is manifestly relishing his
mastery of the epistolary genre but without some annotation the majority
of readers will be unable to savor the full extent of his skill. Their
experience would certainly not approximate to Mackenzie's when he first
read the letter. He, after all, would at once know the dramatis personae:
he would know that, during Cannan's absence in America, Gwen Wilson had
married Henry Mond (later 2nd Baron Melchett). This at least must be
made clear if Lawrence's later readers are to grasp the situation and
respond to his play on the title of the Parisian journal. Should an
editor go further? Should he elucidate the literary allusions in the

passage? I believe he should, in order to sharpen the reader's appreciation of Lawrence's ebullient, witty, creative flow. Only when we
acknowledge that the dramatic presentation of lived experience has
been focused and enriched by quotations from Julius Caesar, Coleridge's
Christabel, and a music-hall song ("Gilbert the filbert"), will the
creative achievement be within our comprehension. We then come closer
to a recognition of the diverse experiences, lived and literary, which
are fused by Lawrence's spirited creativity. Thus, with editorial
assistance, the whole scene has become fully accessible to his readers.
Or has it? Does everyone catch the precise nature of the contempt
conveyed in the description, "Poor Gilbert--a soap pill" (unfortunately
mistranscribed by Mackenzie as "soup frill")?

The charge that annotation dulls the response to the liveliness
and spirited creativity of the letters is a gross overstatement. What
is less often admitted is the irritation caused in an attentive reader
when he cannot understand the text with which he is presented. The
fact that Lawrence is a twentieth-century writer and remains peculiarly
a man of our time makes us less willing to admit the gulf which sepa-
rates us from him. The political and social context in which he lived
no longer exists; the culture he inherited has, in many respects, been
immeasurably eroded; the very language he uses, though it may seem
contemporary with our own, is sometimes markedly, sometimes subtly,
different. To claim, therefore, that we can get the full measure of
his sensitivity to the world about him, his critical intelligence, or
his complex personality without the guidance offered by tactful editing
is untrue.

His use of dialect is one obvious example: words such as "glegged,"
"frit," or "snied" would perplex most readers.[6] Or when he uses a term
which appears commonplace--"impressionist"--about Frank Brangwyn's
Orange Market, the majority of readers would not hesitate, believing
that the word connotes French Impressionism;[7] they would be wrong.
Again, the current generation of English readers would make no positive
response to Lawrence's remark, "Man's the animal baby 'who won't be
happy till he gets it--whatever he wants,'" or to his teasing of Blanche
Jennings, "You are a pale person--must be, since you swallow huge pink
pills."[8] His own contemporaries would translate these catchphrases
into the visual memory of placards advertising the virtues of Pear's
Soap and Parkinson's Pills.

Inevitably, then, the passing of time and our ignorance of the
quotidien affairs of Lawrence's correspondents must deaden the response
of present-day (and future) readers to a wide range of experiences
which he shared with his own contemporaries. Lawrence took a keen
interest in events reported in the press: this at once places us at a
disadvantage. So, to take a single example, having been on the south
coast at Rottingdean on a very windy day, he enlivens his account of
his visit by adding, "I thought I was going to be a second Miss
Charlesworth, and get blown over the cliff."[9] To Blanche Jennings the
allusion would be vivid; the modern reader would be left quite unmoved.
Without suitable annotation he cannot know of the minor cause célèbre
involving the "death" of May Charlesworth who wished people to believe
that she had fallen from a cliff near Llandudno; the press kept the
affair before the public for more than a year until the woman was

sentenced for fraud. A relevant footnote illuminates the fact, but
even more importantly it enables one to sense the "timbre" of Lawrence's
style at this point. Again, few readers would now comprehend Lawrence's
remark to Edward Garnett in November 1912: "I have . . . looked at the
Persian atrocity."[10] The indignation felt by radicals and left-wing
liberals at the aggressive behavior of Russia and England toward
Persia has long been forgotten; so has a pamphlet on the subject by
the Cambridge Professor of Arabic, Edward Granville Browne, an intimate
of the English Review fraternity; but this is what Lawrence had read.
The fact demands explanation but once more the reward is greater:
we derive further evidence of the shared values and political view-
point which Lawrence had established with the English Review circle.
And, to take a final example, it would be exasperating for a reader
not to have editorial assistance at the point where Lawrence remarks
to Arthur McLeod: "I've just had to sign an English Review protest
against the Spectator. . . . Galsworthy, Thomas Hardy and Yeats are
before me."[11] A reader can rightfully expect to learn that the Spectator had impugned the morality of the English Review, refusing (as
it expressed itself) to condone "garbage being dumped on the nation's
doorstep." Here, too, the facts require elucidation, but again added
insight follows. Not only did Galsworthy, Hardy, and Yeats precede
Lawrence's signature on the protest--so did ninety others. As he
addresses his former colleague still immured in the profession from
which he had freed himself, the pride of the young writer in associat-
ing himself with the "great" becomes all too plain.

The editor, then, is more than a compiler, a harmless drudge who
ferrets out hitherto unknown manuscripts and scraps of esoteric information. If he is sensitive both to the writer and to the reader,
to the uniqueness and achievement of the first and the needs--as he
conceives them--of the second, the editor acts as mediator between
the one and the other. To a considerable extent he exercises an inter-
pretative function for a heterogeneous audience over more than one
generation. This represents a challenge of some immensity: as an
editorial team we hope to meet it responsibly.

The Case for an Edition of the Letters of D. H. Lawrence

GERALD M. LACY

Since the death of D. H. Lawrence in 1930, there have been two principal editions of his letters which attempt to present a representative selection of his letters: The Letters of D. H. Lawrence, edited
by Aldous Huxley in 1932, and The Collected Letters of D. H. Lawrence,
two volumes, edited by Harry T. Moore in 1962. But as yet there is
still no complete edition of Lawrence's letters, no edition which
collects even a substantial portion of the total correspondence, nor
one which is consistently accurate in the texts of the letters it does
include.

A definitive edition of the letters is especially appropriate
for Lawrence because he is often cited as one of the best of English
letter writers, perhaps the best since Keats. The quality of Lawrence's
letters was recognized remarkably early. In The Savage Pilgrimage, one
of the more favorable of the many memoirs which appeared shortly after
his death, Catherine Carswell, a frequent recipient of letters from
Lawrence, gave this evaluation:

> Over the same period, his correspondence, whether measured by
> interest or by bulk, bids fair to rival the correspondence of
> our most communicative English men of letters. It is worth
> noting that from the very beginning most of Lawrence's corre-
> spondents have had the instinct to preserve what he wrote to
> them, and it may be safely predicted that his letters will be
> included with his more formal works in a particular sense that
> is faintly paralleled only in the case of Keats. They contain
> a free expression of his findings about life in the very
> accents he was accustomed to use in speech--accents that are
> fresh and inimitable.[1]

A more recent comment by Denis Donoghue points to several distinct qualities to be found in the letters, and I would like to quote him at length as a kind of summary statement on the multifaceted nature of Lawrence's correspondence. His statements are, I think, an accurate appraisal of the demands which the Lawrence letters make upon the reader.

> Lawrence's letters are objects of independent interest, they are
> not mere messages delivered to make up for the absence of a tele-
> phone. The interest they incur is consistent with a still greater
> interest in the art of his fiction: the letters are continuous
> with the fiction, they punctuate a life which is embodied in the
> novels and stories. It is hardly too much to say that they are
> more intimately related to his art than to the daily events
> upon which they appear to feed. . . . So the Collected Letters
> does not make an autobiography, any more than an autobiography
> makes a life: in both cases, we have to reckon with the diverse
> interventions of evasion, silence, form, and art. Reading the
> letters is a strenuous exercise because the reader cannot take
> them at face value, he must understand them as subject to many
> of the same forces which are at work in the fiction; he must
> interpret them, even when they appear to be merely offering them-
> selves as vehicles of information. . . . It is never enough if
> the reader merely takes the correspondence as a neutral context
> for the fiction, with an assumption that the correspondence is
> simple even when the fiction is complex. . . . The reader has
> to enter into a relation with the letters comparable, for ten-
> sion and interrogation, with his relation to "The Crown," the
> "Study of Thomas Hardy," and the novels themselves. He cannot
> take the letters as they appear to come, straight from the
> shoulder or the heart; their origin is more obscure than that.
> They are to be read, like Keats's letters, with a sense of
> their belonging to the creative work, even if there is a sense,
> too, that at a certain point a distinction between them and that
> work must be made. In both enterprises, the same forces are en-
> gaged; feeling, imagination, rhetoric, style, the symbolic act
> of language.[2]

As Donoghue says, "Lawrence's letters are among the most achieved letters in English literature." It could also be observed that the importance of the letters is well attested to by the frequency with which they have been utilized in critical commentaries during the course of this Conference.

Both from the standpoint of their literary quality and from the amazing quantity, Lawrence's letters deserve this reputation. In 1933, T. S. Eliot, for example, gave a lecture in New Haven on "English Letter Writers" which concentrated on Keats and Lawrence. Eliot said that "the best contemporary letters are as good in their way as those of any other time," and he referred to the letters of Lawrence, along with those of Virginia Woolf, as "masterpieces of the letter-writing art." The tenor of this appraisal is not unusual, but it should be especially significant since it comes from a critic who later passed rather severe judgments on Lawrence's fiction in After Strange Gods.[3]

Whatever one's opinion of Lawrence, as a literary figure or as a novelist, it would be difficult to deny the refreshing intimacy, the apparently spontaneous expressiveness, or the sheer power of conviction
that one quite often finds in Lawrence's correspondence. In short, one
has to be impressed with the presence of a creative energy similar to
that which distinguishes Lawrence's fiction and more formal prose.[4]
     Several of Lawrence's letters were published during his lifetime.
The first appeared in The Teacher in 1905 when the twenty-year-old
Lawrence wrote to the editor of this periodical and praised his journal for its usefulness to teachers. In 1924, Lawrence wrote an introduction for Maurice Magnus' Memoirs of the Foreign Legion, and shortly
thereafter, Norman Douglas took rather violent exception to some of
Lawrence's remarks and replied to him in D. H. Lawrence and Maurice
Magnus, A Plea for Better Manners. Lawrence belatedly answered Douglas'
attack in 1926 in a letter published in The New Statesman (Roberts
C138).
     Shortly after Lawrence's death in March 1930, letters began to
be published with regularity in periodicals and books. In August 1930,
Charles Lahr, apparently as an experiment to try out a new press,
published in an edition of six to twelve copies the "Letter to Charles
Lahr" (Roberts A55). Another letter was published in 1931 in an edi-
tion of five copies, "A Letter from Cornwall" (Roberts A59). Aside
from these rather special publications, the serious posthumous use of
Lawrence's letters began in 1932 with two radically different books,
Ada Lawrence Clarke's Young Lorenzo and Mabel Luhan's Lorenzo in Taos.
The use of the letters in numerous memoirs and reminiscences continued
through the publication of The Autobiography of Bertrand Russell in
1968.
     In 1932, Aldous Huxley edited what was the first real tool for
Lawrence scholarship, The Letters of D. H. Lawrence. Huxley does
not devote much space to an explanation of his editorial principles
in his admirable "Introduction," which was apparently intended as a
critical introduction to Lawrence rather than an introduction to the
letters. But with the publication of Huxley's own letters, it is
possible to see more clearly what direction Huxley the editor wished
his edition of the Lawrence letters to take.
     Lawrence died on 2 March 1930, and by 8 March, Huxley and Frieda
Lawrence were discussing the proper way to deal with Lawrence's letters.
Their decision was that it was "still too early to write of DHL" as it
should be done but that it would be desirable to publish an edition of
the letters. Huxley goes on in this letter to describe an edition which
"intersperses the letters with personal recollections of Lawrence by
various people who have known him at different epochs of his career."
It is one of the curious coincidences of literary history to notice
how surprisingly close this is to the idea which Edward Nehls so
successfully carried out twenty-five years later in his Composite
Biography. This idea, however, was abandoned; and by 7 May, Huxley was
writing Helen Corke, thanking her for her help with the letters. He
discussed "the rather indecent display of personalities which has become so unpleasantly common" and expressed his determination to avoid
this with Lawrence's letters. Huxley told Miss Corke that he was merely
collecting letters with the idea of publication to be "delayed for many

years." Huxley continued, telling her that if a selection came out in the near future it will be "only of the more impersonal letters," an idea which he repeated in a letter to Richard Aldington of 1 June. Huxley clearly intended to collect all the letters possible, and those that were not to be published in a selected edition "would remain in the general reservoir of letters" for the future, a "complete collection of letters for posterity to work on." In regard to the omission of unsavory comments, Huxley tells Mabel Dodge Luhan on 22 July that he will do his best "to insist on the exclusion of those personalities which Lawrence would have hated to have published." Huxley believed that this privacy should be respected "until the passage of time has rendered this curiosity impersonal."

Huxley makes one further comment which illuminates his important role as the first editor of the Lawrence letters. On 10 March 1931, Huxley wrote to Dorothy Brett that he was "cutting out feeling-hurting passages" but that he had decided to publish information which is repeated in several letters "because of the subtle variations introduced by Lawrence in varying his mood to different correspondents."[5]

It is obvious that some letters have been cut in Huxley's edition, but it has always concerned scholars that the omissions are not always indicated. Furthermore, Huxley was often wrong, as Moore and other Lawrence scholars have indicated, in his conjectural dating of the letters.

Harry T. Moore's edition of The Collected Letters of D. H. Lawrence appeared in 1962. Scholars were extremely glad to have the published texts of 1,257 letters in the two volumes. Moore republished 520 of the 790 letters in Huxley and added 737 new letters. Of these new letters, 296 had been previously published in sources other than Huxley, and 441 were published for the first time.

Moore's edition does not pretend to include every known Lawrence letter. The sources are Huxley's 1932 edition, other published sources, and some newly discovered and previously unpublished letters. In many cases original manuscripts were withheld from the editor's use, thus making it impossible for him to check the manuscript with the published texts. Harry T. Moore is to be praised for the magnitude of his work and his critical judgment in presenting an excellent selection of the letters, and he is in most cases clear in his statements of editorial principles. It is also clear that Moore was unable, because of many factors beyond his control, to produce a definitive edition containing all the letters. He was limited by the publisher to a commercially feasible edition with a minimum of scholarly explanation. In presenting a representative selection of the correspondence, The Collected Letters, with some limitations, serves the intention of its editor and gives the general reader a valuable addition to the Lawrence canon.

Since the last edition of the Lawrence letters in 1962, however, over 800 new letters have come to light in such volumes as Lawrence in Love: Letters from D. H. Lawrence to Louie Burrows (1968), The Quest for Rananim: D. H. Lawrence's Letters to S. S. Koteliansky, 1914-1930 (1979), Letters from D. H. Lawrence to Martin Secker, 1911-1930 (1970), and the Letters to Thomas and Adele Seltzer (1976). Of these four books, the first volume contains 165 letters which had never been published; the second contains 346 letters and only one-fourth of these had previously appeared; the Secker volume contains 196 letters, of which only sixteen had appeared before; and in the Seltzer volume only three of the letters had previously appeared. Thus in 1979 the case for a new, complete, and accurate edition of the Lawrence letters might be quantitatively supported by the following tabulation:

Number of known letters	5,500+
Number of letters published in sources appearing after the publication of CL	1,000
Number of letters presently unpublished	2,000+
Number of letters published with inaccurate texts	435
Number of inaccurate or incomplete letters in CL	98

These figures demonstrate: (1) that a large part of the known Lawrence correspondence remains unpublished; (2) that many letters (roughly 10 percent) are published in inaccurate texts; and (3) that scholars have one single source for only 80 percent of the letters presently published.

The Cambridge University Press edition of The Letters of D. H. Lawrence will, through its planning, its consistent editorial principles, and its commitment to provide a reliable text for every known letter within a single format, meet the need for a new edition of the letters of D. H. Lawrence.

Editing Lawrence's Letters: The Strategy of Volume Division

GEORGE J. ZYTARUK

The purpose of the Cambridge Edition of The Letters of D. H. Lawrence is to publish all of his available correspondence. Such an undertaking presents numerous editorial challenges. Two of the most fundamental ones are how many volumes should there be and where should the various volumes begin and end. I say "fundamental" because on these decisions so much of the edition's superstructure will depend. When Harry T. Moore was planning to bring out the Collected Letters,[1] he was restricted to two volumes. The consequences of that decision resulted in several very important limitations that have dogged the history of that particular edition. How many of us who have pored through those volumes have not wished that Moore's publisher had allowed him three volumes instead of two?

But, you may well ask: if you are planning to publish all the letters, what difference does the number of volumes make? Three, five, or ten? The correspondence will all be there! True, but in what form? How extensively annotated? Will an adequate index be included? And will the volumes be attractive and practical?

Much as we would have liked to have packed all of Lawrence's letters into one or two volumes, for the sake of convenience--and scholarly impressiveness--the editors of the Cambridge edition initially decided to bring out The Letters in six volumes. Almost immediately, it became apparent that six volumes would not be enough. Some previously unknown letters came to light, more accurate estimates of the size of each volume were made, and the decision to produce seven volumes was reached.

The task of volume division still remained to be tackled. Should each one be exactly the same size? What periods in Lawrence's life would various volumes try to span? Was it worthwhile to attempt to discover some unconscious artistry in the contents of any given volume?

Ought we to consider thematic titles for the volumes? "Son and Lover,"
for one perhaps; "Restless Italy," for another; "Boarding the Ship
of Death"--matter enough to challenge the keenest scholar's brain.
The temptation to label each volume in some such unforgettable phrase,
to carve in marble, as it were, seven epochs in the life of this
gifted writer, was fortunately overcome--and in the end, to use that
well-worn phrase, we shall let Lawrence speak for himself.

Nevertheless, the seven volumes will still have an individual
character, determined by our decisions regarding the beginning and
the end of each volume. In general, we anticipate that each volume
will be approximately 600 to 800 pages. Any variations in size will
arise from the number of letters included in each volume. The differences in the length of the letters and in the number of annotations
make it impossible to arrive at complete uniformity of size. But these
differences are not significant.

Each volume will present Lawrence's letters chronologically, and
each succeeding volume will pick up the correspondence where the previous volume ends. In one instance, letters written on the same day
will appear in two different volumes--a situation, which may arouse
some petty scholarly ire; however, there is adequate justification
for the case. The editors are, of course, fortunate to be working
with Lawrence's letters, since identifying some appropriate event or
moment to mark the end of a period in a writer's life is relatively
easy if the writer happens to be Lawrence. There are innumerable instances in his life when, having put behind him a part of his past,
he set out in a new direction. His decision to break with Jessie
Chambers and to become engaged to Louie Burrows, his resolve not to
write "quite so violently as Sons and Lovers any more,"[2] the banning
of The Rainbow, his abandonment of that ill-fated venture The Signature, his break with Bertrand Russell, his numerous attempts to start
the nucleus of a new society, his expulsion from Cornwall, his near-
fatal collapse in Mexico, the now much talked about failure in Brett's
bedroom,[3] or, to use a last example, his decision to issue the novel
Lady Chatterley's Lover by himself--any one of these events is of
sufficient moment to pause in the chronology of Lawrence's letters.

To provide you with all of the actual events that mark the begin-
nings and ends of the various volumes would not be appropriate at this
time; but a few examples are in order. To begin with Volume I. It spans
the period from July 1901 to 29 May 1913. The first known letter of
Lawrence is that written by him to Messrs. Haywood to whom he applied
for a position, which he subsequently obtained. The volume ends with
Lawrence's letter to Helen Corke, in which he sums up the events of
the last year--that part of his life which began with his leaving
England with Frieda Weekley in May 1912. Not strictly accurately, he
tells Helen Corke: "I have been married for this past year . . . You
would be surprised, how married I am." Almost prophetically he states:
"And this is the best I have known, or ever shall know." And he sums
up: "I seem to have had several lives, when I think back. This is all
so different from anything I have known before."[4] It seems that this
letter is a kind of "period"--one that pulls together all the strands
of Lawrence's life so far--and, taken in retrospect, brings to a close
a major phase of his life.

Volume II will begin with a letter written three days later, 1 June 1913. Previously unpublished, the letter informs Edward Garnett that Lawrence and Frieda are "balking" at the prospect of "coming to England," and we read: "You have no idea what an awful soul-effort it means--this coming to England." In the course of the letters in this volume Lawrence will return to England, leave, and return again. The outbreak of World War I will force him to stay in his homeland, and his marriage to Frieda will undergo a testing that few relationships can withstand. Added to that will be the fact that the major artistic achievement of the next three years, his novel The Rainbow, on which he placed such great hopes, will be publicly suppressed. Despite the turmoil of the war, his colossal failure in establishing Rananim, despite poverty and a serious breakdown in his personal relationships with several important people, Lawrence's artistic achievements during this period are considerable. Thus the letter which will mark the end of the second volume is one dated 31 October 1916, the day on which he dispatches to his agent James Brand Pinker his (these are Lawrence's words) "terrible and horrible and wonderful novel."[5] He writes, "I send you the conclusion of the novel Women in Love (which Mrs. Lawrence wants to be called Dies Irae)--all but the last chapter, which, being a sort of epilogue, I want to write later--when I get the typescript back from you."[6] Although Women in Love was not published until 9 November 1920--four years later--its virtual completion at this time is certainly the kind of event that can appropriately end the second volume of letters.

Whereas the letters of Volume II cover a period of three years and five months, the letters in Volume III (31 October 1916 to 3 June 1921) span four years and five months; Volume IV (4 June 1921 to 10 March 1924) and Volume V (12 March 1924 to 17 March 1927) cover about the same intervals of time, but Volume VI (18 March 1927 to 14 November 1928) are filled with letters written during a period of one year and eight months. Volume VII (17 November 1928 to 27 February 1930), which will bring the series to a close, covers an even shorter period, a year and three months. Considering the size of each volume it is obvious that readers will now have ready access to very detailed materials related to specific periods in his life, particularly those toward the end of his career, when he wrote a great number of letters during a relatively short time, letters which fortunately have been preserved.

In a multivolume edition, such as that being described here, it is necessary to provide the reader with individual volumes that are at once fairly self-contained and at the same time integrated with the other volumes in the series in an intelligible fashion. Toward accomplishing these ends, each volume will contain a separate "Introduction" to the letters, and sufficient annotations to guarantee a high level of comprehension to every reader of the letters in any particular volume. An index of basic items normally included in such a publication will be provided in each volume, but an analytical index with appropriate cross-references cannot logically be undertaken until all seven volumes have been completed.

In the meantime, however, the editors of each volume have undertaken to supply readers with essential cross-references to letters in

preceding volumes and to letters in forthcoming volumes, when such
references will assist the reader to a fuller understanding of the
letter under consideration. Let me cite a sample from Volume II. In
his letter to Edward Garnett dated 1 July 1914, Lawrence decides to
go to J. B. Pinker and sign the agreement with Methuen for the publication of The Rainbow. This event marks the break with Edward Garnett in the latter's role as literary mentor and Lawrence's acceptance
of Pinker as an agent. I think the reader at this point should know
(if he doesn't already know) that Lawrence was eventually to break
his agreement with Pinker in his letter to him dated 27 December 1919.
When the reader has the volume available, in which this letter appears,
he can turn to the letter and read: "I think there is not much point
in our remaining bound to one another. You told me when we made our
agreement that we might break it when either of us wished. I wish it
should be broken now."[7] These kinds of cross-references will be provided in the course of each volume, although references to letters
yet to be published pose more problems for the editor than references
to volumes already in print. An example of the latter, again from
Volume II, is found in the very first letter of that volume, in which
there are a number of references to members of Lawrence's family, all
of whom have been identified in substantial detail in Volume I. The
editor of the second volume will supply the reader with only the
barest of biographical details in the annotations to the letter and
refer the reader to the appropriate pages in Volume I, where more
detailed information is already available. To leave out these types
of cross-references completely, however, would seriously limit the
reader's over-all comprehension of the letters in any particular
volume. Editors of succeeding volumes will have to make sure that
they are not repeating information which has already been supplied
on a previous occasion. The assumption made is, of course, that all
the volumes will eventually be available to serious readers of the
letters.

What about the final volume? Seven as an adequate number to describe all the ages in the life of man may have served Shakespeare,
but the editors of Lawrence's letters could not stop with the number
"that ends this strange eventful history." Scholarly justice cries
out for an eighth volume. With over 5,500 letters, there is no doubt
that there is matter enough for a comprehensive index volume. If the
edition is to be the kind of scholarly tool that we believe it is,
then we must facilitate its use by scholars. How best to accomplish
this task is a moot question, for scholars are nothing if not anarchic
in their expectations. One may wish to consult the seven volumes for
every mention of "futurism," while another will expect to have indexed
for him all of Lawrence's references to his reading of Madame Blavatsky.
In Samuel Johnson's phrase, we shall endeavor to be "studious to please,
yet not ashamed to fail." Certainly some types of information are
mandatory. The names of all individuals (real and fictional) appearing
in the volumes will have to be indexed. All references to Lawrence's
creative works, published and unpublished, must be listed. A topical
index of his major ideas should be drawn up to facilitate scholarly
inquiry, and every title and author mentioned in the volumes should
be indexed. How much of this material should be assembled in convenient
form is open to question. Certainly, the eighth volume is not expected

to become the final authority on Lawrence on every subject, and the
editors anticipate that new discoveries in the letters will continue
to be made after their publication. Questions unanswered by the editors will in time, we hope, be answered by the host of commentaries
that will continue to appear. I, for one, will rejoice when the source
of Lawrence's allusion to swallowing a palm seed to make himself whole
is finally documented, or when we know, at last, who the man Gamba
was who told Lawrence "that the Latin nature is fundamentally geo-
metrical: its deepest aspiration is essential geometry--Form." Other
editors, I am sure, look forward to similar moments of heady rejoicing.

Because some of the items that are now unsolved may be solved by
the time Volume VIII is published, we intend to include all such new
information in the last volume, in the form of Appendices to the seven
volumes. Presently unlocated or unavailable letters will be included
in Volume VIII if such are located or are turned over to the editors
after the volume has been published in which these should have appeared originally. Nor do we plan to shy away from correcting errors
that we may commit along the way; as is the case in The Prose Works
of Jonathan Swift (Oxford: Basil Blackwell, 1969), a section of
"Errata and Corrigenda" will also appear in our last volume.

Having indexed Lawrence's references to as many subjects as the
editors think are significant and the publisher has agreed are finan-
cially feasible; having made note of every painting, piece of sculpture, essay, poem, drama and novel that appears in or is alluded to
in the letters; having taken note of all references to Scripture and
to profane works as well; having recorded Lawrence's first thoughts
and translated his excursions into languages other than English;
having hammered and nailed down as accurately as possible what Lawrence
wrote and tried to communicate to each of his correspondents; and,
finally, having tried to absolve ourselves of all our sins of commission and omission, we plan to tie up our boxes of index cards and
pronounce our task done. Only, you may be sure, to pick up the latest
issues of TLS or PMLA or MFS or RMS or SSF and read: "It is regret-
table that the editors of the Cambridge Edition of The Letters of
D. H. Lawrence failed to identify . . . misread . . . mistakenly
interpreted . . . committed an inexcusable blunder when they . . .
had the temerity to suggest that--." We shall read each such revelation to the end and learn that perhaps what we thought was a comma
after the word "rich" in Lawrence's letter to J. M. Murry written on
22 July 1913 was in fact a period; or that where Lawrence had written
"physic," he really had intended to write "psychic"; or that the
"Unidentified" person was obviously------. If anyone should happen
to be present on such an occasion, he should not be surprised to
hear one of us muttering under his breath something about Ruskin's
saying that "the thirst [for applause] if the last infirmity of
noble minds is also the first infirmity of weak ones."[8]

The Cambridge University Press Edition of *The Letters of D. H. Lawrence*: Sources for the Edition

DAVID FARMER

The resources available for the D. H. Lawrence Letters Project are vast--indeed, the copies of letters we have brought together at the editorial centers and have listed by computer number 5,620--a formidable body of correspondence to survive from an early twentieth-century figure who was moving constantly about the world and whose letter writing career lasted a scant twenty-nine years. The stories of assembling information on these letters are numerous, and many of them must wait for another occasion, for my purpose is to discuss briefly the nature of the resources for original material we have tapped, the role of computers in helping us, and the function of the Tulsa editorial center which was formerly at the Humanities Research Center at Austin.

The recent, systematic account of Lawrence's correspondence began with Gerald Lacy, whose dissertation under the direction of Warren Roberts grew into An Analytical Calendar of the Letters of D. H. Lawrence completed in 1971. Until Professor Lacy produced his Calendar we only knew that one could find significant but unspecified amounts of correspondence at, for instance, Texas, the Berg Collection at the New York Public Library, the University of Nottingham, the British Library, in private collections such as Bob Forster's and George Lazarus' in England, and in a number of other holdings. However, with the availability of Gerald's monumental effort we learned the exact whereabouts of 4,357 pieces of correspondence. Furthermore, Gerald was fortunate enough to have access to a young and developing Computation Center at Angelo State University where those rare individuals who carry on conversations with computers were anxious to demonstrate the application of their wonderous machines to an area of the humanities, thereby assuring additional support for their endeavors. The computer program written at ASU provided the first of numerous "printouts" listing Lawrence's letters by a unique number and organizing them in chronological order. When I consulted my copy of the "First San Angelo Edition" in preparing these remarks, I recalled vividly the expressions of delight at an early editorial meeting when we first saw the printout, realizing we then had the necessary bibliographical basis in terms of an easily updated account of the letter canon to launch the editorial work. I doubt we would be marking the issue of Volume I this year had not the Calendar and the later computerized updatings been produced, for it would have been extremely time-consuming to have depended upon hand-typed lists as the primary control of information on the thousands of letters which have come to our attention.

In 1973 it appeared that the Humanities Research Center (HRC) at Austin was in a position to build usefully on Gerald's computerized calendar, especially with the American editorial center established there, with Warren Roberts and myself there, with the support from HRC and several private endowment grants, and with the eventual hiring of Lin Vasey as our graduate assistant. Thus, we arranged with Gerald to transfer a computer tape from San Angelo to the Computation Center at Austin and set up the "Lawrence Shop" in an office just outside the HRC Director's offices. For years the HRC had been the center of all the major collection developments in the United States relating to Lawrence, and it was natural for an extension to take place. With coordination by Lin Vasey, we contacted systematically all known holders of letters to and from D. H. Lawrence even though such public and private holders had reported their materials to Gerald several years earlier. In addition, with the information that was then constantly reaching HRC (either via direct offers of sale or through the rare books grapevine) we tracked down yet more letters. Some we purchased for the permanent collections, others we attempted to direct to other institutions that were also collecting twentieth-century literary manuscripts. Regarding letters already in institutional hands, we corresponded patiently with curators whose more recent accounts differed from the reports they had given Gerald. Further careful tactics were observed in working with private collectors who were uncertain about allowing us to have hard copy (Xeroxes) from their precious originals.

We also made a systematic perusal of Book Prices Current, American Book Prices Current, catalogues from auction houses such as Sotheby's and Christies, and booksellers' catalogues since Lawrence's death in 1930. It is surprising to learn what materials have passed through the marketplace, and those items which were described in such sources were carefully tracked down. Thus, we were largely successful in gathering accurate information that added substantially to the printout.

When Northwestern University acquired Aldous Huxley's typescript for the 1932 edition of Lawrence's letters, we faced a slightly different task. It was necessary to work through the typescript to discover those letters which were transcribed but not included in his volume. Then, we checked our files to see if we had located a manuscript source for those letters ultimately not published by Huxley.

For a good number we did know of the location of the original manuscripts Huxley and Enid Hopkin Hilton made their transcriptions from;
however, for forty-seven others they transcribed but did not include
in the volume, the typescript at Northwestern provides the only known
source of the text because Lawrence's own manuscript letters in those
cases have been lost or destroyed.

There is an ongoing nature to keeping updated records on Lawrence's
letters, and this is where the editorial center at Tulsa provides
support. For example, the Christies sale of Arthur Houghton's and John
Baker, Jr.'s, letters by Lawrence will have to be followed to determine
where the originals came to rest. Although we already have file copies
in the form of Xeroxes, we will need to update our computer printout
so accurate information for location of originals and proper acknowledgement can be made in the published volumes. Such tracing following
a sale is delicate to pursue, for there is an understanding between
bookseller or auction room and the buyer that the nature of their
transaction is confidential. The people we have contacted in the book
trade, however, have all been helpful in forwarding inquiries to their
clients who may answer at their own discretion.

I have dwelt perhaps overlong on the background and procedure in
gathering information for the computer tape and printout now maintained at the University of Tulsa, but before closing I should describe briefly the nature of our master-list. All the known data on
Lawrence letters are maintained on a computer tape, and whenever we
feel it is time to generate another updated printout we can have one
practically overnight. The format of the printout is designed so quick
reference can be made by means of a unique number designating each
separate piece of correspondence in the data base. Since the letters
are listed in chronological order, the unique numbers are in a pro-
gressive sequence. Following the unique number is the date of the
letter, its place of writing, the person to whom it was written, the
location of the original manuscript, a note on its publication status,
and a symbol indicating languages other than English in which Lawrence
may have written. Also, the presence of Frieda's hand is noted. For
every letter entry in the printout we have a Xerox copy letter in the
editorial files at the University of Tulsa and the University of
Birmingham. Of course, computers are well-suited to generating various
types of listings, so we are able to have separate lists made of all
the letters Lawrence wrote to any given correspondent, all the letters
preserved in any given repository, or all the letters which remain
unpublished. Thus, while we all have a good idea of how D. H. Lawrence
himself may have reacted to the organization of his correspondence by
computation machines, the Cambridge University Press edition of The
Letters of D. H. Lawrence has been aided immeasurably by the use of
computers.

Some Conclusions

The Prose of D. H. Lawrence

HARRY T. MOORE

I

We are not always aware that prose continuously surrounds us; Molière emphasized this when he had his bourgeois gentlemen astonished to learn that he had been speaking prose all his life.

Literary prose is of course different from that of purely conversational prose, though it is often advantageous to have literary prose as near to the conversational as possible. Yet artistic prose can have a life of its own, with elements beyond the ordinary: rhythm, color, and image, for example, and these must of course help to illuminate meaning.

Various recent commentators, including T. S. Eliot, have followed Matthew Arnold in naming John Dryden, who died in 1700, as the pioneer of modern prose. After Dryden there were no more Sir Thomas Brownes with "the iniquity of oblivion blindly scattereth her poppy"; or the village dead who "rested quietly under the tramplings and drums of three conquests"; or a John Donne, a Robert Burton, or a Jeremy Taylor; not that Dryden wrote a prose that lacked force, and the same may be said of Swift and various others who followed. But English prose remained fairly restrained through the nineteenth century, even during the Romantic period; it broke loose, however, in a book published when D. H. Lawrence was an infant, a book which began with this sentence:

> A new voice hailed me of an old friend when, first returned from the Peninsula, I paced again in that long street of Damascus which is called Straight; and suddenly taking me wondering by the hand "Tell me (said he), since thou art here again in the peace and assurance of Ullah, and whilst we walk, as in the former years, toward the new blossoming orchards, full of the sweet spring as the garden of God, what moved thee, or how couldst thou take such journeys into the fanatic Arabia?"

And all of Charles Montague Doughty's Arabia Deserta, first published in 1888, is written in this fashion. As we all know, it greatly
influenced the man we call "the other Lawrence"--T. E. Lawrence ("of
Arabia"), but he didn't attempt such orchestral cadences--or couldn't.
In Doughty's nineteenth century, Ruskin wrote a mild prose with color
and a certain amount of cadence; but he too lacked the force of
Doughty. At times in Moby-Dick, Melville rose to dramatic ecstasy,
but this was rare among writers of the period. A prose of quite
another kind, which can be appreciated by those patient enough to
school themselves in it, is that of Henry James, whose excessively
complicated sentences, after one learns to read them, present not
only images, colors, and rhythms, but dramatic intensifications; and
if it seems at the farthest imaginable extreme from D. H. Lawrence's
writing, this helps to illustrate the range of prose that can be
shown to have quality.
     In the twentieth century, Joyce began coolly enough as a fiction
writer, though his prose always had color and images--then he developed a fascinating wildness too complicated to be treated in this
essay which deals with a writer of quite a different kind.
     But before considering D. H. Lawrence, let us look at still
another author, indeed the greatest of them all, Shakespeare, and
not with the purpose of attempting a comparison of quality, which
would be absurd, but merely to illustrate the use of a literary device which Lawrence often employs. Here are two lines from Hamlet:

     A' took my father grossly, full of bread,
     With all his crimes broad blown, as flush as May. . . .

     Admittedly, we are dealing with prose, and this last quotation
is poetry, but among other things it makes use of a technical device
which often helps to make prose distinctive. In the passage quoted,
we begin with "A' took my father grossly"--and how wonderfully that
word grossly comes in there--but after a moment's pause, Hamlet terribly expands the word's implications by adding full of bread; the
next line begins with only a mild vividness, "With all his crimes
broad blown," and after another brief stop spreads the implications
further with a striking simile, "as flush as May." This technique,
one phase or image growing out of another, is called Häefung by the
Germans, and the device is suggested by Henry James's expression,
"the law of successive Aspects"--whether he was referring to character
or language. In painting we have somewhat similar techniques, too
complicated to be discussed here, called simultaneism, used by the
futurists and cubists but, long before them, by such painters as
Bosch and the Brueghels.
     Now let us consider this aspect of presentation in a prose passage
of D. H. Lawrence, taken from the opening chapter of his travel book,
Sea and Sardinia. He is at a hilltop villa in Taormina, Sicily, early
one morning, planning to leave with his wife on a visit to Sardinia.
The long second paragraph of the book describes the Sicilian setting,
in one direction Southern Italy--or, in Lawrence's words, "the sunny
Ionian sea, the changing jewel of Calabria, like a fire-opal moved
in the light." Note "the law of successive Aspects" operating there,

each phrase followed by a vivid expansion. In the other direction
Lawrence can see the volcanic Mount Etna, which he calls "that wicked
witch, resting her thick white snow under heaven, and slowly, slowly
rolling her orange-coloured smoke."

He continues with further descriptions, which deserve quoting
if there were space, and he mentions that the ancient Greeks had
called Mount Etna the pillar of heaven or the pedestal of heaven. He
sees the villages and lemon groves below Etna, indicating that these
belong to "our world."

> But Etna herself, Etna of the snow and secret changing winds,
> she is beyond a crystal wall. When I look at her, low, white,
> witch-like under heaven, slowly rolling her orange smoke and
> giving sometimes a breath of rose-red flame, then I must look
> away from earth, into the ether, into the low empyrean. And
> there, in that remote region, Etna is alone. If you would see
> her, you must slowly take off your eyes from the world and go
> a naked seer to the strange chamber of the empyrean. Pedestal
> of heaven! The Greeks had a sense of the magic truth of things
> . . .

In that passage, picture follows picture and thought follows
thought, all of it a smooth-flowing rhythm intensified by developing
repetitions; note the reappearance of the "slowing rolling . . .
orange smoke," followed now by the occasional "rose-red flame."
Lawrence has often been criticized because his prose is repetitive,
but that was an organic part of his writing, as he explained in a
note apparently written in 1919, in relation to Women in Love: "In
point of style, fault is often found with the continual, slightly
modified repetition. The only answer is that it is natural to the
author; and that every natural crisis in emotion or understanding
comes from this frictional, to-and-fro which works up to culmination."

His views of Mount Etna were not merely those of a sightseer
emotionally impressed by a famous and beautiful landmark, a target
for tourists; no, he was seeing Etna as a part of life, as a living
entity. His emotion might not have the extreme of Hamlet's as Hamlet
reflected gruesomely on his father's death and was thinking about
killing his murderous uncle--but in this century we have few such
elements in our serious literature, which is for the main part either
psychological or sociological; we have no murders (or few) in such
writers as Joyce, Proust, Mann, Woolf, and authors of their stature:
our murders, however fascinating to read about, are largely confined
to our detective stories.

In Sea and Sardinia Lawrence was writing a travel book, but he
made it, like his other travel books, a prose masterpiece. It is not
shallow: it contains the reflections of a man deeply concerned with
human problems; but he is always aware of the presence of nature--
Mount Etna, which he calls "witch-like," is an exceedingly dangerous
volcano, whose last massive eruption had been in 1917, less than four
years before Lawrence was viewing it so awesomely. And his prose en-
traps the reader: he has written of Etna "slowly, slowly rolling her
orange-coloured smoke"; then a few passages later, we have this figure

again but, as noted earlier, he further vivifies it here when he
adds a phrase that strikes us deeply: Etna, he says, "slowly rolling her orange smoke [then the addition:] and giving sometimes a
breath of rose-red flame."

II

Lawrence wrote several kinds of prose, in some cases what we
might call a mixed prose. At all levels, it is certainly far above
the work of most of those who write novels in English today, in what
can be called a grocery-list prose (and usually the subject matter
is as mediocre as the text). Lawrence in his first youthful writings
sometimes manifested a certain crudeness, but even through that a
kind of power flashed. When Sons and Lovers, his third novel, came
out in 1913, many members of the literary world at once recognized
its excellence, and Lawrence had a mild public success--though never,
during his lifetime, more than that.

Most seasoned critics now consider him a giant, generally agreeing that The Rainbow of 1915 and Women in Love (first published in
1920 but completed several years before) are not only his two finest
novels, but also two of the finest in the English language (Lawrence's
Brangwensaga, as this writer was the first to call the two books). But
Lawrence's two other major novels must not be ignored: Lady Chatterley's Lover and Sons and Lovers. Lawrence completed Lady Chatterley
in 1928, two years before his death; it is now permitted to be published and is certainly this century's greatest romance, treating
love "as a serious and sacred theme" (as I have noted elsewhere).

Sons and Lovers is usually regarded as the greatest working-
class novel ever written, portraying Lawrence's childhood and youth
as a coalminer's son. There are scenes of gritty realism and a great
deal of Midlands dialect (known officially as "Derbyshire Broad"),
but there is also much lyricism, culminating in the last page of the
book, when the protagonist, Paul Morel, is grieving over the death
of his overloving and overloved mother, and walks through a field at
night:

> In the country, all was dead still. Little stars shone high up;
> little stars spread far away in the flood-waters, a firmament
> below. Everywhere the vastness and terror of the immense night
> which is roused and stirred for a brief while by the day, but
> which returns, and will be at last eternal, holding everything
> in its silence and its living gloom. There was no Time, only
> Space. Who could say his mother had lived and did not live?
> She had been in one place, and was in another, and that was all.
> And his soul could not leave her, wherever she was. Now she was
> gone abroad into the night, and he was with her still. They
> were together. But yet there was his body, his chest, that
> leaned against the stile, his hands on the wooden bar. They
> seemed something. Where was he?--one tiny upright speck of
> flesh, less than an ear of wheat lost in the field. He could
> not bear it. On every side the immense dark silence seemed
> pressing him, so tiny a spark, into extinction, and yet,

almost nothing, he could not be extinct. Night, in which everything was lost, went reaching out, beyond stars and sun. Stars
and sun, a few bright grains, went spinning round for terror,
and holding each other there in embrace, there in a darkness
that outpassed them all, and left them tiny and daunted. . . .

Note in that passage, not quoted in full, how all the elements
change and grow. Paul first sees the night as a thing of terror,
which continually comes back and will finally remain forever. Then
he thinks of life and death, and of his mother in death, yet there
is his own body, whose living concreteness is emphasized by his contact with the wood of the stile. Then again we have the sky, the
planets spinning in terror--almost a projection of the great Van Gogh
painting, <u>Starry Night</u>, with its luminous objects that whirl about
flaring against the bluish dark sky. Paul Morel, the tiny human speck
in the great landscape and skyscape will not follow his mother into
the darkness of death: "Turning sharply, he walked towards the city's
gold phosphorescence. . . . He walked towards the faintly humming,
glowing town, quickly."
And that <u>quickly</u>, preceded by a comma, rather unusually ends the
book with an adverb, but an adverb rich with meaning, for Lawrence
used the word <u>quickly</u> in the Biblical sense, suggesting the vibrancy
of life. He makes this clear in an essay called "The Novel," in which
he really gives away what might be called, in the familiar phrase,
the secret of his trade.
Oddly enough, one of Lawrence's greatest contemporaries, William
Butler Yeats, had a philosophy of writing that was not too different
from Lawrence's sense of the quick. It will probably be not too offensive a divagation to examine briefly Yeats's somewhat similar idea,
as he expressed it in his too-little-known essay of 1897, "The Celtic
Element in Literature," which for its ideas draws somewhat upon Ernest
Renan, but more upon Matthew Arnold. Like Arnold, Yeats finds a Celtic
strain in the finest of English literature, in such writers as Shakespeare and Keats; and Yeats also draws upon many other primitive litera-
tures to be seen as influences; all of which certainly applies to
Lawrence, whose prose was often partly Biblical and whose vision was
often inspired by the primitive: he early read such authors as Frazer
and Frobenius, and during his 1917-18 residence in Cornwall, he often
referred to his awareness of the Celtic spirit.
Yeats agrees with Arnold that, besides the magic-seeming Celtic
way of writing, there is literature which may be great of its kind
but does not have the essential radiance which Lawrence called "quick":
Arnold spoke of "the Greek way of writing" and "the faithful way of
writing," in contrast to the Celtic bursts of magic. Yeats offered
a quotation from Keats, "in the Greek way," which he says "adds lightness and brightness to nature":

> What little town, by river or sea-shore,
> Or mountain-built with quiet citadel,
> Is emptied of its folk this pious morn?--

and Yeats also quotes two lines from Shakespeare, also in what Yeats
and Arnold call "the Greek way":

> I know a bank whereon the wild thyme blows,
> Where oxlips and the nodding violet grows,

and Yeats noted that on these occasions the poets were looking "at
nature without ecstasy, but with the affection a man feels for the
garden where he has walked daily and thought pleasant thoughts. They
looked at nature in the modern way, the way of people who are poeti-
cal, but are more interested in one another than in a nature which
has faded to be but friendly and pleasant, the way of people who have
forgotten the ancient religion."

But Yeats also provides other quotations from Keats and Shakespeare, which he seems to find more exciting, as cited by Arnold as
examples of "the Celtic way": "Keats's 'magic casements opening on
the foam of perilous seas in faery lands forlorn'; in his 'moving
waters at their priestlike task of pure ablution round earth's human
shores'; in Shakespeare's 'floor of heaven,' 'inlaid with patens of
bright gold'; and in his Dido standing 'upon the wild sea banks,'
'a willow in her hand' and, in the ritual of the old worship of Nature
and the spirits of Nature, waving 'her love to come again to Carthage.'"

Yeats finds "delight and wonder" in these and other passages he
quotes, and it is necessary to add that, when some years later he
went from his almost purely mythological phase into what is often
called his "intellectual period," he didn't forsake the essential
Celtic spirit of his vision; he merely combined it with his deveoping
ideas, as all his great later poetry shows.

As for Lawrence, he was not of course following Yeats into the
Celtic mode: the important point is that his idea of the quick was
close to it in execution, actually more so in his prose than in
most of his poems; and, as we have seen, Lawrence was aware of the
Celtic, though not necessarily from Yeats's essay. Lawrence's idea
of the quick applied not only to descriptive material, but also to
fictional characters in their relation to life. At one place in his
1925 essay, "The Novel," he writes:

> We have to choose between the quick and the dead. The quick is
> God-flame, in everything. And the dead is the dead. In this
> room where I write, there is a little table that is dead: it
> doesn't even weakly exist. And there is a ridiculous little
> iron stove, which for some unknown reason is quick. And there
> is an iron wardrobe truck, which for some more mysterious reason
> is quick. And there are several books whose mere corpus is dead,
> utterly dead and non-existent. And there is a sleeping cat,
> very quick. And a glass lamp, alas, is dead.

Lawrence applies these standards to other novelists, their
stories and their characters--the then current bestsellers, but also
some of the books which have survived from a farther past. In another
essay, "Why The Novel Matters," whose date of composition is uncertain, Lawrence says that, "being a novelist, I consider myself

superior to the saint, the scientist, the philosopher, and the poet, who are all great masters of different bits of man alive, but never get the whole." For "The novel is the one bright book of life. Books are not life. They are only tremulations on the other. But the novel as a tremulation can make the whole man alive tremble. Which is more than poetry, philosophy, or any other book-tremulation can do," for "the novel is the book of life."

Some passages soon to be quoted from Lawrence's novels will demonstrate why he had the audacity to make such statements. The prose in these recent quotations is, noticeably, a lively prose, fairly straight and with only a minimum of the colloquial or the slangy (such as "the whole hog"). He could write amusingly slangy prose, but he didn't always do so. For example, in his superb critical volume, Studies in Classic American Literature, he writes a fairly straight, though always lively, prose, as in the two chapters about Fenimore Cooper, which contain such paragraphs as:

> Perhaps my taste is childish, but these scenes in Pioneers seem to me marvellously beautiful. The raw village street, with wood-fires blinking through the unglazed window-chinks, on a winter's night. The inn, with the rough woodsman and the drunken Indian John; the church with the snowy congregation crowding to the fire. Then the lavish abundance of Christmas cheer, and turkey-shooting in the snow. Spring coming, forests all green, maple-sugar taken from the trees: the clouds of pigeons, flying from the south, shot in heaps; and night-fishing on the teeming, virgin lake; and deer-hunting.

That is not typical of Lawrence's prose because it is not straight from his original vision; it is, rather, an attempt at an impression of Cooper (and, we may note, an improvement). Only a few pages later, Lawrence begins his essay on Poe with two genuinely funny colloquial-slangy sentences which have amused many readers: "Poe had no truck with Indians or Nature. He makes no bones about Red Brothers and wigwams."

III

Even in what must be called his poorer novels, Lawrence wrote brilliantly. There are for example the three "leadership" novels of the early and middle 1920s: Aaron's Rod, Kangaroo, and The Plumed Serpent. The point of Aaron's Rod is not quite comprehensible, if not downright silly, but there are some compelling descriptions of Florence and other parts of Italy. Kangaroo, set in Australia, is a far better book; Lawrence's description of different parts of the continent includes some of the finest passages in English prose, as in his other novel about Australia, The Boy in the Bush, written in collaboration with an Australian woman whose original text he exten-sively altered. The Boy in the Bush is a fine adventure novel and could be made into an excellent film, but the leadership book, Kangaroo, is less commendable, though it has many good points, in-cluding the long chapter of autobiographical reminiscence about the hideous experiences, in wartime England, of Lawrence and his German-baroness wife, Frieda. And Kangaroo is further interesting because it presents the dilemma of a man wooed on one side by conventional socialists and on the other by native fascists; but, in spite of his unpleasant experiences in the realm of democracy, he chooses to leave for America.

The third leadership novel, The Plumed Serpent, contains the finest descriptions of Mexico in English prose. Consider these few brief passages, which may be fairly familiar: "The morning was clear and hot, the pale brown lake quite still, like a phantom. People were moving on the beach, in the distance tiny, like dots of white: white dots of men following the faint dust of donkeys." Or: "The lake was quite black, like a great pit. The wind suddenly blew with violence, with a strange ripping sound in the mango-trees, as if some membrane in the air were being ripped." Or: "She could see Sahula; white-fluted twin towers of the church, obelisk shaped above the pepper-trees; beyond, a mound of hill standing alone, dotted with dry bushes, distinct and Japanese looking; beyond this, the corrugated, blue-ribbed, flat-flanked mountains of Mexico." And the quotations could go on. The two chapters on the changes of season, with the arrival of the smashing rains, are particularly vivid.

But prose, for all its virtues, can never be enough in imaginative works; mere prose must have a meaning--and the meaning is not always necessarily "good." In one of Lawrence's great earlier novels, The Rainbow, he dealt with three generations of a family, and in Women in Love he focused on the further experiences of the two older girls of the third generation in their efforts, often humanly mistaken, to find fulfillment. But in The Plumed Serpent, the story of a forty-year-old Irishwoman trying in her peculiar way to find fulfillment in Mexico, we have a book that can only be called vicious and brutal. The prose can be admired but, as T. S. Eliot once wisely remarked, you can appreciate a man's gift of writing without agreeing with his ideas--and in The Plumed Serpent the ideas, to affirm it once again, are vicious and brutal.

The Irishwoman, Kate, is not aware of the behavior of her lover, Cipriano, who has adopted the pre-Columbian name Huitzolopochtli, when he is leading his men in quest of bandits in the country: "He stripped his captives and tied them up. But if it seemed a brave man, he would swear him in. If it seemed a knave, a treacherous cur, he stabbed him to the heart, saying, "I am the red Huitzolopochtli of the knife"--(Chap. XXII)--a passage whose ridiculous final words don't mitigate the horror of the execution of a man Cipriano simply dislikes. In the following chapter, Cipriano and his friend, the other self-appointed god, Don Ramón, carry out the ritual murders of three men in front of a despoiled church: mystic and unjustified murder.

Lawrence had idiotically thought he was writing a great book; to his credit, he later repudiated it. Lawrence has often been called a fascist or at least a protofascist, but it has often been shown that these terms did not apply to most phases of his life; and when he was completing The Plumed Serpent in Mexico in 1925 he was working under the shadow of a nearly fatal illness that left him virtually a

skeleton for the remaining five years of his life. He continued to
turn out fine prose, not always of his highest reach, but he wrote
some very great poetry at this time, though he was never again stupid
enough to write anything so depraved as The Plumed Serpent.

The Biblical element occasionally suggested in Lawrence's prose
is particularly noticeable in the opening chapter of The Rainbow,
too long (and perhaps too well known) to be quoted here. Lawrence
in his youth broke away from orthodox religion and created a pre-
dominantly mystic religion of his own, with what he called his "dark
gods"; yet he never quite broke away from Christianity. The essay
written toward the end of his days, "Hymns in a Man's Life," indicated how the songs sung in the Congregational chapel he attended
as a child influenced him throughout his life. And in one of his
last pieces of fiction, his novella, The Escaped Cock (which various
publishers after his death timidly renamed The Man Who Died), the
opening paragraph shows the Biblical influence upon the rhythms of
his prose, though the prose itself is distinctly modern, and indeed
this is one of the outstanding passages in modern prose, describing
the place where the virgin priestess of Isis is to meet the prophet
(unnamed) who has been resurrected after his crucifixion:

> The wind came cold and strong from inland, from the invisible
> snows of Lebanon. But the temple, facing south and west,
> towards Egypt, faced the splendid sun of winter as he curved
> down towards the sea, the warmth and radiance flooded in
> between the pillars of painted wood. But the sea was in-
> visible, though its dashing sounded among the hum of pines.
> The air was turning golden to afternoon. The woman who served
> Isis stood in her yellow robe, and looked up at the steep
> slopes coming down to the sea, where the olive-trees silvered
> under the wind like water splashing.

This is only half the paragraph, but it easily shows how superior
Lawrence is to the grocery-list prose of today's novelists: consider
merely how the sea's "dashing sounded among the hum of pines," and
how "the olive-trees silvered under the wind like water splashing."
(And think of Irving Wallace, Gore Vidal, Barbara Cartland, and the
others of their ilk. Their books, in grocery-list prose, are not of
the kind that such different important critics as Henry James, T. S.
Eliot, and Edmund Wilson spoke of as "written.")

In his fading last years, Lawrence often turned out a prose
without color, though often vitally sharp, as in the satiric sketches,
"The Lovely Lady" and "Mother and Daughter"; but he could still write
now and then with a suggestion of his old power, as the passage quoted
from The Escaped Cock demonstrates. Many of Lawrence's short stories
and novellas which are also powerfully written have not been drawn
upon here, for reasons of space, and this essay will conclude with
discussions of parts of Lawrence's novels, two of which, as noted
earlier, critics generally regard as Lawrence's greatest imaginative
achievements: The Rainbow and Women in Love.

Once again, in such considerations, we must remember that good
prose is made up not only of rhythm, color and image, but also of

meaning, with all these elements integrated. Studies along these
lines must be partly subjective, and can be ruined if they are too
mathematical. An example of that occurs in a book on modern British
style published in 1978; in dealing with Lawrence and other authors,
the volume provides a series of tables which are formulistically
mathematical; in relation to two of Lawrence's books, tables tell us,
for example, how many final sentences in paragraphs end in ten words
or less, how many doubled conjunctions appear in headwords, how many
times only occurs as a headword, how many anterior appositives appear,
how many noun formations end in "-ness" and "-ity," and how many
"Déja Vu" items make their appearance. Is all this an expression of
regret that Lawrence didn't figure out all these matters in advance?
If he had done so, we would not have had The Rainbow and Women in
Love.

Yet, despite the flame of inspiration that burned in him, Lawrence
was a more deliberate writer, was in most cases a more careful writer
and even rewriter, than he is usually credited with being. Certainly
all the leitmotifs (theme chords if you prefer) in Women in Love were
not altogether accidental, though when an imaginative author is working at high pitch, his artistic sensibilities provide him with his
essential material, but his intellect is also illuminated by the
effort and plays an important part in the act of creativity. We can
find more than twenty leitmotifs in Women in Love if we count symbol-
istic images that are used at least five times, not always in a precisely repetitive way, but with variations.

One of the most common can be called the ice-corruption motif,
usually associated with Gerald Crich. An example of this occurs early
in the first chapter, with Gudrun Brangwen's first view of Gerald:
"There was something northern about him that magnetized her. In his
clear northern flesh and his fair hair was a glisten like sunshine
refracted through crystals of ice"--and so the passage goes on.
Throughout the book, we have this arctic theme which Gerald's friend
Rupert Birkin prophetically comes to see as a figure of "ice-corruption," which will destroy him. An example of this occurs in Chapter XIX: "Birkin thought of Gerald. He was one of those strange wonderful demons from the north, fulfilled in the destructive frost
mystery. And was he fated to pass away in this knowledge, this one
process of frost-knowledge, death by perfect cold? Was he a messen-
ger, an omen of universal dissolution into whiteness and snow?"

The destruction of Gerald in a fatal chilliness after a mountain
fall is forecast even earlier, in Chapter XIV, when he keeps diving
into the cold waters of the lake in search of the bodies of his sister and the young doctor who had been with her in the boat which
turns over at the "water party"; Gerald's search is futile. After
he has given up the attempt, of diving and diving into the fatal
waters, he tells Gudrun, "And do you know, when you are down there,
it is so cold, actually, and so endless, so different really from
what it is on top, so endless--you wonder why it is so many are
alive, why we're up here." In Chapter XX, the arctic whiteness of
Gerald is emphasized again when Birkin tells him, "You have a northern kind of beauty, like light refracted from snow. . . ." In Chapter XXIX, "Gerald looked shining like the sun on frost." Other

suggestions can be found throughout, emphasizing Gerald's gleaming whiteness and often intimating his terrible death in a frozen corner of the Tyrolese Alps.

The concept of will is an important factor in Women in Love: Lawrence is as always fighting against compulsive will, and personifies it in the character of Hermione Roddice; many leitmotifs suggesting the operation of will occur throughout the book. But the most important of all the thematic modes is that of balanced stars. This is used again and again by Birkin, particularly after Ursula tells him that he wants her to be a satellite. He violently denies this in various ways during the book, using the star symbol, as in Chapter XIII: "One must commit oneself to a conjunction with the other--for ever. But it is not selfless--it is a maintaining of the self in mystic balance and integrity--like a star balanced with another star." And this recurrent motif (Birkin speaks of "star-equalibrium," of two people as "balanced stars," again and again). The book has many incomparably excellent scenes, from the satire of the people at Hermione's country house to the comic encounter of Birkin and Ursula in the Nottingham marketplace (one of the greatest comic episodes in modern literature), from the confrontation of Hermione and Birkin, when she tries to kill him, to the terrible climax in the Tyrolese Alps.

But, great as Women in Love is, it really doesn't stand above the book so closely related to it--The Rainbow. We can close by quoting two passages from that novel, passages which are of particular interest because each of them shows a pair of lovers from each of two generations undergoing a somewhat similar experience, but oh, how differently! And the contrast is not only one of generation (tied strongly into the plot), but the difference of later-period attitudes and naturally of the characters themselves. There is further contrast in the prose treatment of the passages.

In the first of them (from Chapter IV, called "The Girlhood of Anna Brangwen"), Will and Anna, apparently early in the second half of the nineteenth century, are stacking wheat sheaves in the moonlight:

> "We will put up some sheaves," said Anna. So they could remain there in the broad, open place.
> They went across the stubble to where the long rows of upreared shocks ended. Curiously populous that part of the field looked, where the shocks rode erect; the rest was open and prostrate.
> The air was all hoary silver. She looked around her. Trees stood vaguely at their distance, as if waiting, like heralds, for the signal to approach. In this space of vague crystal her heart seemed like a bell ringing. She was afraid lest the sound should be heard.
> "You take this row," she said to the youth, and passing on, she stooped in the next row of lying sheaves, grasping her hands in the tresses of the oats, lifting the heavy corn in either hand, carrying it, as it hung heavily against her, to the cleared space, where she set the two sheaves sharply down,

bringing them together with a faint, keen clash. Her two bulks
stood leaning together. He was coming, walking shadowily with
the gossamer dusk, carrying his two sheaves. She waited near
by. He set his sheaves with a keen, faint clash, next to her
sheaves. They rode unsteadily. He tangled the tresses of corn.
It hissed like a fountain. He looked up and laughed. . . .
    They stooped, grasped the wet, soft hair of the corn,
lifted the heavy bundles, and returned. She was always first.
She set down her sheaves, making a pent house with those others.
He was coming shadowy across the stubble, carrying his bundles.
She turned away, hearing only the sharp hiss of his mingling
corn. She walked between the moon and his shadowy figure.
    She took her new two sheaves and walked towards him, as
he rose from stooping over the earth. He was coming out of the
near distance. She set down her sheaves to make a new stook.
They were unsure. Her hands fluttered. Yet she broke away, and
turned to the moon, which laid bare her bosom, so she felt as
if her bosom were heaving and painting with moonlight. And he
had to put up her two sheaves, which had fallen down. He worked
in silence. The rhythm of the work carried him away again, as
she was coming near.
    They worked together, coming and going, in a rhythm, which
carried their feet and their bodies in tune. She stooped, she
lifted the burden of sheaves, she turned her face to the dimness where he was, and went with her burden over the stubble.
She hesitated, set down her sheaves, there was a swish and
hiss of mingling oats, he was drawing near, and she must turn
again. And there was the flaring moon laying bare her bosom
again, making her drift and ebb like a wave. . . .
    And the work went on. The moon grew brighter, clearer,
the corn glistened. He bent over the prostrate bundles, there
was a hiss as the sheaves felt the ground, a trailing of heavy
bodies against him, a dazzle of moonlight on his eyes. And then
he was setting the corn together at the stook. And she was
coming near.
    He waited for her, he fumbled at the stook. She came. But
she stood back till he drew away. He saw her in shadow, a dark
column, and spoke to her, and she answered. She saw the moonlight flash question on his face. But there was a space between
them, and he went away, the work carried them, rhythmic. . . .
    Into the rhythm of his work there came a pulse and a
steadied purpose. He stopped, he lifted the weight, he heaved
it towards her, setting it as in her, under the moonlight space.
And he went back for more. Ever with increasing closeness he
lifted the sheaves and swung striding to the centre with them,
ever he drove her more nearly to the meeting, ever he did his
share, and drew towards her, overtaking her. There was only
the moving to and fro in the moonlight, engrossed, the swinging in the silence, that was marked only by the spash of sheaves,
and silence, and a spash of sheaves. And ever the spash of his
sheaves broke swifter, bearing up to hers, and ever the splash
of sheaves recurred monotonously, unchanging, and ever the
splash of his sheaves beat nearer.

Till at last, they met at the shock, facing each other,
sheaves in hand. And he was silvery with moonlight, and with
a moonlit, shadowy face that frightened her. She waited for him.

That extremely long passage covers only about half the episode,
which ends in passionate kissing and, eventually, a decision to be
married.
The daughter of Will and Anna, the Ursula Brangwen who is also
to function importantly in The Rainbow, undergoes that other so different love scene in Chapter XI, entitled "First Love." In this case
the man is a distant Polish cousin, Anton Skrebensky, a fundamentally
weak character. When, under the force of Ursula's passion, he feels
his heart begin "to fuse like a bead," and "he knew he would die,"
it is not physical death he is thinking of, but annihilation of his
essential self by Ursula, whom Lawrence has made one of the free-
minded "new Women" his contemporaries Bernard Shaw and H. G. Wells
were also writing about. In the passage about to be quoted, we again
have a wheat field in one of those intense Van Gogh nights:

They went towards the stackyard. There he saw, with something like terror, the great new stacks of corn glistening and
gleaming transfigured, silvery and present under the night-blue
sky, throwing dark, substantial shadows, but themselves majestic and dimly present. She, like glimmering gossamer, seemed
to burn among them, as they rose like cold fires to the silvery-
bluish air. All was intangible, a burning of cold, glimmering,
whitish-steely fires. He was afraid of the great moon-confla-
gration of the cornstacks rising above him. His heart grew
smaller, it began to fuse like a bead. He knew he would die.
She stood for some moments out in the overwhelming lumi-
nosity of the moon. She seemed a beam of gleaming power. She
was afraid of what she was. Looking at him, at his shadowy,
unreal, wavering presence a sudden lust seized her, to lay hold
of him and tear him and make him into nothing. Her hands and
wrists felt immeasurably hard and strong, like blades. He
waited there beside her like a shadow which she wanted to
dissipate, destroy as the moonlight destroys a darkness,
annihilate, have done with. She looked at him and her face
gleamed bright and inspired. She tempted him.

As in the preceding passage, much more is to follow; but perhaps
an idea of Lawrence's power has been suggested, as well as the dif-
ference--the different way in which Lawrence dealt with a rather
repetitive situation, in a strikingly new kind of prose; the first
passage was in some ways Biblical in rhythm, and had also the effect
of a rather stately ballet worked out against a night such as Van
Gogh's, though more quietly than in the second passage, whose first
paragraph is the most fiercely effective of the two.
A collection of critical writings about Lawrence, edited by
Andor Gomme, which was published in London and New York in 1978,
contained an opening essay on Lawrence's prose which ended by saying
that it was so great that its effect upon writing in English may not
be fully appreciated until a thousand years have past.
Well, maybe some of us won't have to wait that long.

Beyond D. H. Lawrence

KEITH SAGAR

Lawrence has been dead for half a century; I have been working on
Lawrence for a quarter of a century; it is perhaps an appropriate
moment to stand back from both the works and the life, and ask some
large questions about Lawrence and the way we teach him and write
about him. I sense a generation gap opening up, a certain resistance
to Lawrence in our students and younger readers; or is it simply a
resistance to the way we teach him and the assumptions we make about
him? Why should we expect Lawrence to mean the same to young readers
in the late seventies and eighties that he meant to us in those far-
off fifties? Are we going to go on telling them that we cannot put
them onto any other writer who can more adequately interpret their
world, more appropriately voice their own aspirations, hopes, fears,
needs, than one who was of the same generation as their great-grand-
fathers?

The excitement generated by Lawrence in his lifetime and for two
generations of readers since has been something more than the recognition of great literary talent. For his own generation Lawrence was
a prophet, obscure and erratic, but felt to be in touch, as no one
else at that time seemed to be, with the sources of vitality and hence
able to see more clearly than anyone else the sickness of his society.
Every generation needs such a prophet.

The next generation, whose consciousness and conscience he might
have helped to shape, was too preoccupied with the turbulent politics
of the thirties and the horrors of the forties to listen to Lawrence or
to such voices in the wilderness as F. R. Leavis and Harry T. Moore.

Thanks largely to Penguin books, which published all his major
works in 1950, the next generation, my generation, discovered Lawrence
afresh in the fifties, adopted him as its spokesman, and attempted to
shape itself in his image. It is not easy now to remember just what it
was in Lawrence that we latched onto so avidly. He asked us the necessary questions, the questions St. Mawr asks Lou: what is real? are you
alive? He stood for "the maximum of fearless adult consciousness, that
has the courage even to submit to the unconsciousness of itself."

In a world given over entirely to liberal rational humanism
(that was how it looked at Cambridge), we felt that liberal values
had not stood the test of recent history, that rationalism was false
and sterile insofar as it claimed to be able, in time, to explain
everything and jettisoned so many other human faculties, and that
humanism made arrogant assumptions no more tenable than the medieval
theory that the earth must be the center of the universe because we
live on it. We were all living under the mushroom cloud which we
felt to be symbolic of the total divorce between man and nature and
the irresponsibility of science. Germ warfare was being developed.
A horrible, obscene disease, myxomatosis, was deliberately spread in
an attempt to wipe out the rabbit population of England. DDT almost
wiped out the birds. Industry was pouring pollution unchecked into
our air and waters. Living communities were being razed and replaced
by vertical slums in the name of progress. The education system was
a process of elimination designed to produce an elite for government,
management, and the professions.

Of course political solutions were being propounded for some of
these problems, and Marxism was thriving in the universities up to
1956, but most of us felt that the search for political solutions
was merely tinkering, or, in the case of Marxism, a belief that the
great machine would work better if it were turned upside down. Mate-
rialism was the enemy. We wanted to redefine the term "standard of
living."

Also we wanted to be rid of all that cant and hypocrisy, especially in sexual and religious matters, which was beginning to re-
assert itself after the war. Lawrence opened all the doors. He offered
not only a damning analysis of what was false in society, but a new
orientation, a whole new system of values whereby everything could be
judged according to whether or not it is life-enhancing. There would
be a bloodless revolution, for when a sufficient number of people
came to make Lawrentian demands on their own lives and on society,
society would have to change to accommodate them.

In some ways, to some extent, this has happened. Some of Lawrence's
battles have been won. There is now less cant and hypocrisy. The education system is more open and child-oriented. Lawrence took women
more seriously as independent beings, free souls, than any earlier
English novelist and made a tremendous contribution to their emanci-
pation (though precious little thanks he has had for it). But his
most spectacular success was in the effect he had on our attitudes
to sex ("a making free and healthy of this sex"). Perhaps younger
readers need to be reminded of what it was like in the fifties. Here
is the beginning of Philip Larkin's poem "Annus Mirabilis":

> Sexual intercourse began
> In nineteen sixty-three
> (Which was rather late for me)--
> Between the end of the Chatterley ban
> And the Beatles' first LP.
>
> Up till then there'd only been
> A sort of bargaining,

        A wrangle for a ring,
        A shame that started at sixteen
        And spread to everything.[1]

    Other battles have been lost. Our society is even more material-
istic and mechanized. Life is even more thoroughly secularized. Alternative societies have nearly all degenerated or fallen into the
hands of frauds and fanatics. On other fronts the fight continues,
but Lawrence's weapons and strategy have become outmoded, though he
can still inspire the troops.
    Lawrence was shaped by his time, region, and class. He directed
his efforts to changing the world, especially England. The England
of 1980 is completely different from the England of 1910 or even 1930.
He did not live to see fascism rampant, the death camps, nuclear war,
the dismantling of the British Empire, the Welfare State, the rise
of the unions, the industrialization of the third world, worldwide
terrorism, the breakdown of law and order at home, the decline of
religion and marriage, permissive sexual morality, the contraceptive
pill, the legalized slaughter of the unborn, feminism, the pop scene,
television, space exploration, biological engineering, the control
of many diseases, including tuberculosis--the list is endless. No
writer dead half a century can be a spokesman for people born into
this world. He can be a continuing source of standards and inspiration, a fund of life, but so can all great writers of the past.
    A writer's value to his contemporaries is bound to be rather
different from his value to posterity. For his contemporaries the
surface of his work will be directly applicable to their lives and
time. The received values are being challenged in very specific ways.
The way we live is wrong here and here and here. This has obvious
advantages in terms of relevance and urgency, but there is the disadvantage of the temptation, both for the reader and for the writer
himself, to turn the vision into a political program or a cult, and
to deal with symptoms rather than root causes. This is why it is often
necessary to wait some decades to be sure how great a writer is, to
wait until that part of his achievement which can date has dated, so
that we can see clearly what remains.
    The primary and unique discipline for the imaginative writer is
to find metaphors for his own nature. The Waste Land is a great poem
not because it is a clever analysis of Western civilization, but
because, in drawing from the world around him metaphors for his own
nature, his own psychic problems, Eliot was able to communicate an
authenticated vision of alienation which, because it derived from
those depths of the psyche at which all men are alike, was immediately
recognized as expressing a common sense of alienation, and therefore
as an "objective" account.
    Kafka found metaphors for his own very peculiar nature, his
psychic disturbances; they revealed and embodied, in an extreme and
very pure form, common anxieties.
    If metaphors are really authentic and dredged from the depths,
they translate the local and temporal experience into terms equally
applicable to human experience at any time and any place. They fan
outwards into vast perspectives of permanent realities, including

those of the nonhuman world. Thus we go to Shakespeare to find out
what it was like to live through that particular watershed of English
history, but at the same time find outselves journeying into ourselves,
being changed, and seeing our distinctive twentieth-century situation
rather differently.

All great writers are disturbed. Their inner conflicts are the
source of their creative energies. Lawrence's favorite metaphors are
generated by the stress between the opposing claims of his parents;
between the male and female elements in his sexual make-up; between
his puritanism and anti-puritanism; his need for rootedness and for
freedom, for continuity and change. All these stresses and many others
he was able to cope with by objectifying them as metaphors (in the
large sense that a whole novel may be a metaphor). This process is of
great value not only to the writer himself as auto-therapy; he is
like the shaman who makes the dangerous journey into the spirit world
again and again for the sake of his people, or the haruspex who exam-
ines the entrails of animals and birds for revelations. But the other
world the writer enters is his own unconscious; the entrails he exam-
ines are his own. His metaphors are the clues he brings back of what
he has found there. A conscious examination of himself and his experience would not take him far without such clues, nor could his find-
ings be validated and communicated without them.

The imagination attends to both seen and unseen, strives to bring
more and more of life into consciousness and to reach an inclusive
vision within which the warring dualities of existence can be atoned.
It has all other human faculties at its service, and so leaves behind
all other disciplines in the pursuit of the deepest, most permanent
truths. The vision of life, as inclusive as the writer can make it,
and the provisional orientation towards life he takes up on the strength
of it, Lawrence called his metaphysic. Every great writer must have a
metaphysic; and every major new work is a new attempt to extend and
test and substantiate it. The ultimate test of greatness in a writer
is the adequacy of his metaphysic.

The most taxing challenge for the literary critic is the task of
evaluating a great writer's metaphysic. "Give me a lever and I will
move the world." There are no fixed criteria. Belief in fixed cri-
terion--Marxist, Christian, or whatever--seems to me to disqualify
a critic. Some critics have offered an absolute standard we are all
supposed to find unquestionable. Leavis based all his criticism on
Lawrence's own aphorism "Art for life's sake." But "life" is not an
unquestionable good. Nietzsche tells of the wood-sprite Silenus who,
if caught, had to answer any question truthfully. On one occasion he
was caught and asked, "What is man's greatest good?" He replied,
"Ephemeral wretch, begotten by accident and toil, why do you force me
to tell you what it would be your greatest boon not to hear? What
would be best for you is quite beyond your reach: not to have been
born, not to be, to be nothing. But the second best is to die soon."[2]
What right have we to rule out in advance such a metaphysic? It has
got to be "Art for truth's sake."

We can test a writer's "reality" against our own sense of it,
but this is very dangerous. It may prevent us from making that imaginative leap into another man's world which must precede any judgment.

It may simply give us the opportunity to rationalize our inertia or discomfort at finding some of our cherished habits of thought and feeling under assault. We must bring the writer's reality into the closest possible contact with our own, but to take our own as a standard would be arrogant in the extreme, since the great writer is by definition larger than we are.

We can test a writer's metaphysic against what we take to be common human experience. But what if the writer believes everybody's understanding of what common human experience is to be a huge misunderstanding or a conspiracy to believe things because we believe everyone else believes them?

One of Lawrence's own favorite methods was to pit his own metaphysic against that of some other great writer, Hardy, for example, at the beginning of his career, Tolstoi and Dostoevski toward the end. Always he accuses the other writer of distortion, of putting his thumb in the balance. Hardy's form, he says, is "execrable in the extreme," "for nothing in his work is so pitiable as his clumsy efforts to push events into line with his theory of being, and to make calamity fall on those who represent the principle of Love."[3] We can see the distortion very clearly in this well-known passage from Tess of the D'Urbervilles:

> The call seldom produces the comer, the man to love rarely coincides with the hour for loving. Nature does not often reply 'Here!' to a body's cry of 'Where?' till the hide-and-seek has become an irksome, outworn game.
> In the present case, as in millions, it was not the two halves of a perfect whole that confronted each other at the perfect moment; a missing counterpart wandered independently about the earth, waiting in crass obtuseness till the late time came. Out of which maladroit delay spring anxieties, disappointments, shocks, catastrophes, and passing-strange destinies.[4]

This is not the place to argue the justice of Lawrence's criticism of Hardy. The point I want to make is that, if it is cheating in a novelist thus to make things work out badly to fit a pre-existing pessimistic metaphysic, is it not equally cheating to make things work out well to fit a pre-existing optimistic metaphysic? In Lawrence the call always produces the comer (in the form of a Polish widow, a Ministry Inspector, an Italian circus-rider, a Mexican general, a gipsy, a gamekeeper, a Priestess of Isis) . . . and Nature is always right on cue.

Lawrence would argue that he had proved that life can be great. He had known suffering and frustration, but in his moment of greatest need fate had given him Frieda, and everything which had gone before fell into place as a necessary prelude. From this he generalized that life actively concerns itself with the fulfillment of those who have the courage to submit wholly to it. But Hardy was not pessimistic out of sheer perversity. The prevalence in his work of betrayal and frustration, the succession of wasted lives, the close association of misery and marriage, testifies to a life which must have enforced such generalizations. This is what he had experienced, seen in his friends, heard in village gossip, and read in newspapers.

Lawrence says of Hardy's protagonists: "They have not the necessary strength: the question of their unfortunate end is begged in the beginning."[5] But Lawrence's decision to give his characters the necessary strength is equally question-begging. If we apply the thumb-in-the-balance test to Anna Karenina and Lady Chatterley's Lover (a comparison Lawrence himself invites), it is not Tolstoy who is pushing harder.

Putting one's thumb in the balance is only one way of cheating, favoring one's own preconceived interpretation of reality. What is in the other pan is, or ought to be, reality itself, raw, uninterpreted, complete—the inescapable facts. A more insidious, less easily detectable form of cheating is leaving certain facts out of account. Lawrence was well aware that he was leaving a great deal out of account, and had his defense:

> Realism is just one of the arbitrary views man takes of man.
> It sees us all as little ant-like creatures toiling against
> the odds of circumstance, and doomed to misery. It is a kind
> of aeroplane view. It became the popular view, and so today
> we actually are, millions of us, little ant-like creatures
> toiling against the odds of circumstance, and doomed to
> misery; until we take a different view of ourselves. For
> man always becomes what he passionately thinks he is; since
> he is capable of becoming almost anything.[6]

Ursula "believed more in her desire and its fulfillment than in the obvious facts of life." So did Lawrence. His impatience with Hardy, Bennett, Chekhov, Mann, Tolstoi, and many other major writers was because they did not. They insisted on writing about men and women who do not despise life and yet are denied it. There is in Lawrence remarkably little undeserved suffering, loneliness, frustration, breakdown, loss, which is not merely a prelude to a resolution or resurrection. His metaphysic excludes a large part of what has traditionally been regarded as tragic experience.

Lawrence's vision was essentially utopian; it was almost idealistic. The usual distinction between the ideal and the real seems to me to blur an essential distinction. There are really three possibilities for the artist: to write of what is, what should be, or what could be. To write exclusively about what is Lawrence rightly saw to be a dead realism, a capitulation, a "giving in before you start." To write about what should be does not seem to me to be a particularly interesting or valuable or even adult activity; there can be no checks on the writer's self-indulgence, escapism, wish-fulfillment, if he is not obliged to pay any debts to reality.

That Lawrence thought of himself as writing of what could be is evidenced by the many attempts he made to translate his vision into life as well as art. Most of them were fiascos. He asked too much of his early girl-friends, and all those relationships were painful fiascos. He asked too much of his marriage, and was bitterly disillusioned. He asked too much of his friends, and found them all Judases. He asked too much of humanity, and had to write it off as an evolutionary dead end. There was the fiasco of the visit to Cambridge in 1915; of the proposed lecture-tour with Russell; of The Signature and Rainbow Books and Music; the whole series of fiascos resulting from his attempts to set up Rananim, culminating in the sick farce at the Café Royal in 1923. Only the long-dead Etruscans did not let him down, and the natural world, though he was very careful what aspects of that he looked at.

His works had to compensate for all these failures. He had a natural tendency to turn his back on aspects of reality he could not stomach and drift toward his desired image. He did not resist this tendency, but rationalized it: "When one is shaken to the very depths, one finds reality in the unreal world. At present my real world is the world of my inner soul, which reflects on to the novel I write. The outer world is there to be endured, it is not real--neither is the outer life."[7] By this means any facts he could not face could be easily disposed of, consigned to an "unreal" world of madness or nightmare. According to this reasoning, the war, for example, "never happened": "Not to me or to any man, in his own self. It took place in the automatic sphere, as dreams do. But the actual man in every man was just absent--asleep--or drugged--inert--dream-logged."[8] The job of the artist is to bring inner and outer realities together, not to escape from one into the other.

The testing of one man's metaphysic against another's can be extended in what I find to be a useful way by taking literally the metaphor I have used of orientation toward experience. Let us imagine all possible orientations toward life to be points on a compass. The bleak North is nihilism, the belief that life is unredeemable. Let us appoint Beckett as its literary representative. The opposite, the warm South, is Lawrence's position, the belief that life is not in need of redemption. In the East let us put the meliorists, who say that life can be reformed, improved by purely secular reorganization; Brecht can stand here. And in the West stands religion, the belief that life can be redeemed from outside itself, by transcendental means; the later Eliot can stand for this. Now we can test the relative adequacy of each position by subjecting it to the heaviest possible bombardment from the other three, and seeing what is left when the smoke clears.

There would not be much left of Lady Chatterley after prolonged exposure to Beckett's laser beams; not much left of Lawrence's infantile politics after exposure to Brecht; not much of his pseudo-religious terminology after exposure to Eliot. But Beckett, Brecht, and Eliot might well suffer even more from Lawrence's fire, might well be shown to leave even more than he does out of account, as if that were the price of their special insights.

Is there, then, any modern writer whose metaphysic can be set against Lawrence's who is genuinely more inclusive, who neither puts his thumb in the balance nor leaves a great deal out of account, who stands, as it were, in the center of the circle, drawing together and attempting to reconcile what is irreducible in all the visions on the circumference (for he has been there too)? The writer who seems to me to have come nearest to achieving this is Ted Hughes.

At one end of the spectrum Hughes is very Lawrentian: in his opposition to rationalism, humanism, and certain aspects of science;

in his insistence on the sacredness, miraculousness of Nature; in
his belief in the need for an ego-death and a resurrection in individuals; and in his belief in the ability of two people to recon-
stitute each other in marriage. At the other end of the spectrum he
looks unflinchingly, especially through the eyes of his persona
Crow,[9] at all those aspects of Nature and human experience Lawrence
turned a blind eye to.

Lawrence, dazzled by the glamor of the universe, failed to
notice a great deal of the evidence, evidence meticulously noted by
Crow. For example, Crow quickly recognized war as a characteristic
human activity:

> And when the smoke cleared it became clear
> This had happened too often before
> And was going to happen too often in the future
> And happened too easily
> Bones were too like lath and twigs
> Blood was too like water
> Cries were too like silence
> The most terrible grimaces too like footprints in mud
> And shooting somebody through the midriff
> Was too like striking a match
> Too like potting a snooker ball
> Too like tearing up a bill
> Blasting the whole world to bits
> Was too like slamming a door
> Too like dropping in a chair
> Exhausted with rage
> Too like being blown to bits yourself
> Which happened too easily
> With too like no consequence.[10]

Crow's own characteristic activity is predation, a central activity
of Nature which Lawrence chose to pay little attention to.

In their ruthless quest for personal fulfillment Lawrence's
protagonists refuse to be distracted by the death-cries of others.
Lawrence is callous in his insistence on the total existential freedom of every individual. Even Frieda compared him to the little boy
who said, "I'll teach you to be a toad!" as he stamped on the toad.
Against this we can set Hughes' "Existential Song":

> Once upon a time
> There was a person
> Running for his life.
> This was his fate.
> It was a hard fate.
> But Fate is Fate.
> He had to keep running.
>
> He began to wonder about Fate
> And running for dear life.
> Who? Why?

And was he nothing
But some dummy hare on a recetrack?

At last he made up his mind,
He was nobody's fool.
It would take guts
But yes he could do it.
Yes yes he could stop.
Agony! Agony!
Was the wrenching
Of himself from his running.
Vast! And sudden
The stillness
In the empty middle of the desert.

There he stood--stopped.
And since he couldn't see anybody
To North or to West or to East or to South
He raised his fists
Laughing in awful joy
And shook them at the Universe

And his fists fell off
And his hands fell off
He staggered and his legs fell off
It was too late for him to realize
That this was the dogs tearing him to pieces
That he was, in fact, nothing
But a dummy hare on a racetrack.

And life was being lived only by the dogs.[11]

Hughes does not pay for these insights, as so many modern writers do, by losing his grip on the essential Lawrentian positives. In the epilogue to Gaudete[12] he performs the incredible feat of holding together in a single all-embracing vision the bleak realities and black negatives of Crow and the joyful affirmations of Season Songs.[13]

Lawrence achieved far more than we have any right to ask of any man in a full lifetime, let alone half a lifetime. For almost half a century he has stood alone as a beacon of sanity. But we do him no service to claim that he had all the answers or that all the answers he had to the wants of his day are as relevant now as they were then. His life and thought-adventure took him deep into new continents, but there is still infinite darkness beyond his farthest vision to be explored. He believed he was participating in a process of evolving human consciousness, and that future explorers would go much farther. He would have wished us to strive to go beyond those frontiers where he reached the limit of his vision, to try to construct a metaphysic adequate to our world, with the help of the greatest writers of our own time--"for brave men are for ever born, and nothing else is worth having."

Notes

Index

Notes

TEDLOCK, Lawrence's Voice

1. Stephen Crane, The Red Badge of Courage, eds. Sculley Bradley, Richmond Beatty, and E. Hudson Long (New York: Norton, 1976), pp. 42-43.

2. David Garnett, "Review of Phoenix: The Posthumous Papers of D. H. Lawrence," in Critics on Lawrence, ed. W. T. Andrews (London: Allen and Unwin, 1971), p. 46.

3. W. H. Auden, "Some Notes on D. H. Lawrence," in ibid., p. 47.

4. Virginia Woolf, "Sons and Lovers," in ibid., pp. 37-39.

5. Frank Glover Smith, D. H. Lawrence: The Rainbow (London: Edward Arnold, 1971), p. 71.

6. Ian Robinson, "D. H. Lawrence and English Prose," in D. H. Lawrence: A Critical Study of the Major Novels and Other Writings, ed. A. H. Gomme (New York: Harvester Press, 1978), pp. 14-28.

7. D. Kenneth M. Mackenzie, "Ennui and Energy in England, My England," in ibid., p. 126.

8. Keith Alldritt, The Visual Imagination of D. H. Lawrence (Evanston: Northwestern University Press, 1971), ch. 6.

9. John Remsbury and Ann Remsbury, "Lawrence and Art," in Gomme, p. 216.

CUSHMAN, The Achievement of England, My England
and Other Stories

1. Leo Gurko, "D. H. Lawrence's Greatest Collection of Short Stories--What Holds It Together," Modern Fiction Studies 18 (Summer 1972), 173-82.

2. Kingsley Widmer's analysis of the stories is scattered through The Art of Perversity: D. H. Lawrence's Shorter Fictions (Seattle: University of Washington Press, 1962). D. Kenneth M. Mackenzie's "Ennui and Energy in England, My England," in D. H. Lawrence: A Critical Study of the Major Novels and Other Writings, ed. A. H. Gomme (New York: Barnes & Noble, 1978), pp. 120-41, discusses the stories in terms of ennui and energy to very little effect.

3. Gilbert uses this concept in her essay "D. H. Lawrence's Uncommon Prayers," found on pp. 73-93 of this volume.

4. The Collected Letters of D. H. Lawrence, 2 vols., ed. Harry T. Moore (New York: Viking, 1962)1:204.

5. The Ladybird, in D. H. Lawrence, Four Short Novels (New York: Viking Compass, 1965), pp. 43-44.

6. The CSS abbreviation supplies the page references in The Complete Short Stories of D. H. Lawrence, vol. 2 (New York: Viking Compass, 1961).

7. E. W. Tedlock, Jr., D. H. Lawrence, Artist and Rebel: A Study of Lawrence's Fiction (Albuquerque: University of New Mexico Press, 1963), p. 106.

8. George H. Ford, Double Measure: A Study of the Novels and Stories of D. H. Lawrence (New York: Holt, 1965), p. 31.

9. John B. Vickery, The Literary Impact of "The Golden Bough" (Princeton: Princeton University Press, 1973), p. 306.

10. Foreword to Fantasia of the Unconscious, in Psychoanalysis and the Unconscious and Fantasia of the Unconscious (New York: Viking Compass, 1960), p. 57.

11. Mark Spilka, "Ritual Form in 'The Blind Man,'" in D. H. Lawrence: A Collection of Critical Essays, ed. Mark Spilka (Englewood Cliffs, N. J.: Prentice-Hall, 1963), p. 115, and Tedlock, D. H. Lawrence, Artist and Rebel, p. 110.

12. The Collected Letters, p. 566.

13. Clyde de L. Ryals, "D. H. Lawrence's 'The Horse Dealer's Daughter': An Interpretation," Literature and Psychology 12 (Spring 1962): 39.

14. Widmer, The Art of Perversity, p. 149.

15. The Collected Letters, p. 670.

16. Widmer, The Art of Perversity, p. 110.

17. Unsigned review in the New York Times Book Review, 19 November 1922, reprinted in D. H. Lawrence: The Critical Heritage, ed. R. P. Draper (New York: Barnes & Noble, 1970), p. 189.

POYNTER, The Early Short Stories of Lawrence

1. The Collected Letters of D. H. Lawrence, ed. Harry T. Moore (London: Heinemann, 1962), 1:270.

2. *Selected* *Letters* *of* *D.* *H.* *Lawrence*, ed. Richard Aldington (Harmondsworth, Middlesex, England: Penguin, 1976), p. 53.

3. Ibid., p. 55.

MACNIVEN, D. H. Lawrence's Indian Summer

1. D. H. Lawrence, "Accumulated Mail," *Phoenix*, ed. Edward D. McDonald (New York: Viking, 1936), p. 803.

2. *The* *Collected* *Letters* *of* *D.* *H.* *Lawrence*, ed. Harry T. Moore (New York: Viking, 1962), 2:703. Subsequent quotations from Lawrence's letters are from this edition and will be identified in context by date alone.

3. D. H. Lawrence, *St.* *Mawr* *and* *The* *Man* *Who* *Died* (New York: Random House, [1959]), p. 201.

4. D. H. Lawrence, *The* *Complete* *Short* *Stories* (New York: Viking, 1961), 2:546. Subsequent quotations from Lawrence's short stories are from this edition.

SQUIRES, Editing *Lady* Chatterley's *Lover*

1. My forthcoming study, *The* *Creation* *of* "*Lady* Chatterley's *Lover*," offers the evidence for this date.

2. Unpublished, Yale University. Permission to publish this extract has been granted by Yale, Cambridge University Press, Laurence Pollinger Ltd., and the estate of the late Mrs. Frieda Lawrence Ravagli.

3. Unlike nearly all of the surviving typescript, page 216 of Ts-I is a page of ribbon copy in purple ink, its wording much different from the wording of the manuscript or of the Florence Edition. But Lawrence himself almost certainly retyped this page.

4. *Principles* *of* *Textual* *Criticism* (San Marino, California: Huntington Library, 1972), pp. 165, 193.

5. "Multiple Authority: New Problems and Concepts of Copy-Text" (1972), in Fredson Bowers, *Essays* *in* *Bibliography,* *Text,* *and* *Editing* (Charlottesville: University Press of Virginia, 1975), p. 463. In his edition of *The* *Red* *Badge* *of* *Courage*, for example, Bowers regularizes the accidentals at 42:7 and 90:1-2.

6. "Regularizing Accidentals: The Latest Form of Infidelity," *Proof* 3 (1973), 15, 19. Parker's remarks largely apply to works of nineteenth-century American literature, for which printers allowed some irregularity in accidentals.

7. Stephen Crane's *The* *Red* *Badge* *of* *Courage* is very similar in its textual history and requires that an editor create an eclectic text, drawing readings from two authorities--manuscript and first edition.

8. Frederick Anderson, Review of Jane Millgate's *Editing* *Nineteenth-Century* *Fiction*, in *Nineteenth* *Century* *Fiction*, 34 (1979), 75.

GILBERT, D. H. Lawrence's Uncommon Prayers

1. T. S. Eliot, After Strange Gods: A Primer of Modern Heresy (London: Faber and Faber, 1934), p. 20.

2. Ibid., p. 39.

3. Ibid., p. 58.

4. Ibid., p. 56.

5. Eugene Goodheart, The Utopian Vision of D. H. Lawrence (Chicago: University of Chicago Press, 1963), pp. 5-7. For other useful discussions of Lawrentian "diabolism," see also George H. Ford, Double Measure: A Study of the Novels and Stories of D. H. Lawrence (New York: Holt, 1965), and James C. Cowan, D. H. Lawrence's American Journey: A Study in Literature and Myth (Cleveland: Case Western Reserve University Press, 1970).

6. See my Acts of Attention: The Poems of D. H. Lawrence (Ithaca, N. Y.: Cornell University Press, 1973), pp. 316-17.

7. Karl Shapiro, "The First White Aboriginal," reprinted in The Poetry Wreck, Selected Essays: 1950-1970 (New York: Random House, 1975), p. 160.

8. Ibid., p. 156.

9. William Carlos Williams, Selected Poems (New York: New Directions, 1963), pp. 95-99.

10. William Carlos Williams, Kora in Hell: Improvisations (San Francisco: City Lights Books, 1967), p. 55.

11. Denise Levertov, The Poet in the World (New York: New Directions, 1973), p. 178.

12. Ibid., p. 85.

13. Gary Snyder, Earth House Hold (New York: New Directions, 1969), p. 122.

14. Joyce Carol Oates, New Heaven, New Earth: The Visionary Experience in Literature (New York: Fawcett, 1974), pp. 50, 52. ("The Hostile Sun," Oates's study of Lawrence's poetry, was also published separately by Black Sparrow Press, Santa Barbara, California, in 1973.)

15. Robert Bly, ed. and trans., Friends, You Drank Some Darkness, Three Swedish Poets: Martinson, Ekelof, and Transtromer (Boston: Seventies Press / Beacon Press, 1975), p. 3.

16. Robert Bly, ed., Neruda and Vallejo: Selected Poems (Boston: Seventies Press / Beacon Press, 1971), pp. 14-15.

17. Ted Hughes, Gaudete (New York: Harper & Row, 1977), p. 8.

18. Ted Hughes, "Pike," in Selected Poems: 1957-1967 (New York: Harper & Row, 1972), p. 51.

19. Adrienne Rich, "Three Conversations" (with Barbara Gelpi), in Adrienne Rich's Poetry, ed. Barbara Charlesworth Gelpi and Albert Gelpi (New York: Norton, 1975), p. 112.

20. Stephen Spender and J. L. Gili, trans., and Francisco Garcia Lorca and Donald M. Allen, eds., The Selected Poems of Federico Garcia Lorca (New York: New Directions, 1955), p. 135.

21. Portions of the discussion below were originally delivered at the 1978 Modern Language Association Conference in New York as a paper entitled "Hell on Earth: Birds, Beasts and Flowers as Subversive Narrative" and have subsequently appeared as an essay with the same title in The D. H. Lawrence Review. I am grateful to James Cowan, editor of the Review, for encouraging my work on that paper and for permitting me to reprint portions of it here.

22. The Complete Poems of D. H. Lawrence, ed. Vivian de Sola Pinto and Warren Roberts (New York: Viking, 1964), p. 191. All references to Lawrence's poems (included hereafter in the text) will be to this edition.

23. Kenneth Rexroth, Introduction to D. H. Lawrence, Selected Poems (New York: Viking, 1959), p. 14; Tom Marshall, Psychic Mariner: A Reading of the Poems of D. H. Lawrence (New York: Viking, 1970), p. 116.

24. See "The Living Cosmos: Varieties of Otherness," in my Acts of Attention, pp. 162-89.

25. Rexroth, p. 14.

26. See Marshall, p. 117.

27. D. H. Lawrence, The Lost Girl (London: Heinemann, 1920), p. 347.

28. Paradise Lost, IX, 782.

29. See W. B. Yeats, Collected Poems (New York: Macmillan, 1955), "The Rose," pp. 31-49.

30. Samson Agonistes, II, 99-102.

31. Ibid., I, 41.

32. See John Donne, "Good Friday. Riding Westward."

33. D. H. Lawrence, The Escaped Cock, ed. Gerald M. Lacy (Santa Barbara, California: Black Sparrow, 1978), p. 43.

34. D. H. Lawrence, Apocalypse, with an introduction by Richard Aldington (New York: Viking Compass, 1966), p. 39.

35. Denise Levertov, The Sorrow Dance (New York: New Directions, 1967), p. 30.

36. D. H. Lawrence, Studies in Classic American Literature (New York: Viking, 1924), p. 191.

COWAN, D. H. Lawrence and the Resurrection
of the Body

This paper is an expanded form of a paper originally written for "The Healing Arts: A Dialogue Between Literature and Medicine," which met under the auspices of the

Institute on Human Values in Medicine, 1975-76. It will be included in the forthcoming proceedings of this dialogue group. Grateful acknowledgment is made to the chairperson of the dialogue group, Professor Joanne Trautmann, and to the Institute on Human Values in Medicine.

1. Lawrence's works are cited parenthetically in my text by abbreviated title and page numbers as follows:

CP   The Complete Poems of D. H. Lawrence, eds. Vivian de Sola Pinto and Warren Roberts (New York: Viking, 1971).

EP   Etruscan Places (New York: Viking, Compass, 1968).

FU   Fantasia of the Unconscious, in Psychoanalysis and the Unconscious and Fantasia of the Unconscious (New York: Viking, Compass, 1960).

K   Kangaroo (Melbourne, London, Toronto: Heinemann, 1955).

LCL   Lady Chatterley's Lover (New York: Grove, 1959).

MEH   Movements in European History (Oxford: Oxford University Press, Humphrey Milford, 1925).

MWD   St. Mawr and The Man Who Died (New York: Vintage Books, n.d.).

P   Phoenix: The Posthumous Papers of D. H. Lawrence, ed. Edward D. McDonald (New York: Viking, 1968).

P II Phoenix II: Uncollected, Unpublished, and Other Prose Works by D. H. Lawrence, ed. Warren Roberts and Harry T. Moore (New York: Viking, 1968).

PU   Psychoanalysis and the Unconscious, in Psychoanalysis and the Unconscious and Fantasia of the Unconscious (New York: Viking, Compass, 1960).

2. T. S. Eliot, The Complete Poems and Plays, 1909-1950 (New York: Harcourt, 1958), p. 3.

3. Stephen Spender, "D. H. Lawrence" (audio-tape) (Cincinnati: Sound Seminars, McGraw-Hill 75910, n.d.).

4. See Kate Millett, Sexual Politics (Garden City, N. Y.: Doubleday, 1970, pp. 240, 243-44.

SPILKA, Lawrence Versus Peeperkorn
on Abdiction

1. "Thomas Mann," Selected Literary Criticism, ed. Anthony Beal (New York: Viking, 1966), p. 265.

2. See Lionel Trilling's account of Mill's position in The Liberal Imagination (New York: Doubleday, 1950), p. viii.

3. The Magic Mountain (New York: Modern Library, 1955), p. 549. Page references to this edition in the text will follow the initials MM.

4. *Letters* *of* *Thomas* *Mann,* *1889-1955*, eds. Richard and Clara Winston (New York: Knopf, 1971), p. 213. Page references to this edition in the text will follow the initial *L*.

5. "Surgery for the Novel--or a Bomb," *Selected* *Literary* *Criticism*, p. 115.

6. *The* *Complete* *Poems* (London: Heinemann, 1957), 2:178. Page references to vols. 2 and 3 of this edition will appear in the text after the initials *CP*.

7. A. O. J. Cockshut, *Man* *and* *Woman:* *A* *Study* *of* *Love* *and* *the* *Novel,* *1740-1940* (London: Collins, 1977), p. 160.

8. Lawrence's hatred of the confinement of invalidism is amply documented. Just before his death, however, he was forced to spend the month of February 1930 in the Ad Astra sanatorium at Vence, which he likened to a mountain hotel (and which Harry Moore would later liken to *The* *Magic* *Mountain*). Not wanting to die there, he insisted on being moved in March to a villa in the village below. As he told Frieda's daughter that winter, "The nights are so awful. . . . At two in the morning, if I had a pistol I would shoot myself." On these final days, see Barbara Weekley Barr, "Memoir of D. H. Lawrence," in *D.* *H.* *Lawrence:* *Novelist,* *Poet,* *Prophet*, ed. Stephen Spender (New York: Harper & Row, 1973), pp. 32-35; and Harry T. Moore, *The* *Priest* *of* *Love* (New York: Farrar, 1974), pp. 496-504.

9. *The* *Captain's* *Doll*, in *Four* *Short* *Novels* *of* *D.* *H.* *Lawrence* (New York: Viking, 1965), p. 242. Note also in this tale the Peeper-kornish nature of the Herr Regierungsrat, the Austrian boyfriend of Hepburn's mistress Hannele (pp. 229-32); and the poisonous monkshood growing on the mountainside whose "laughing-snake gorgeousness" so intrigues Hepburn (pp. 244-45). And see also Gerald Crich's death in the Austrian Tyrol in *Women* *in* *Love*.

10. In *CP* II, see "Blank," "Desire Is Dead," "Man Reaches a Point," "Grasshopper," "Basta," "Nullus," "Dies Irae," "Dies Illa," "The Death of Our Era," "The New Word," "Sun in Me," and "Be Still," on pp. 233, 236, 240-47. Especially appropriate here are the lines: "Desire may be dead / and still a man can be / a meeting place for sun and rain, / wonder outwaiting pain / as in a wintry tree."

11. In a letter to me dated 6 January 1979.

12. *The* *Intelligent* *Heart:* *The* *Story* *of* *D.* *H.* *Lawrence* (New York: Grove, 1962), p. 477; *Richard* *Aldington:* *An* *Intimate* *Portrait*, eds. Alister Kershaw and Frédéric-Jacques Temple (Carbondale: Southern Illinois University Press, 1965), p. 85. See also *The* *Priest* *of* *Love*, p. 455.

13. *Frieda* *Lawrence:* *The* *Story* *of* *Frieda* *von* *Richthofen* *and* *D.* *H.* *Lawrence* (New York: Viking, 1973), pp. 238, 243. The original German edition appeared in 1972. Lucas, who probably draws on Moore's precedent, gives no reference for Frieda's revelation.

14. In the letter to me cited above, where Moore also remarks that Frieda had "*volunteered* a denial that Lawrence was impotent" on one of his many later visits to Taos to interview her--possibly to

protect Lawrence from that public charge. So much for oral and epistolary testimony!

15. See Dorothy Brett, Lawrence and Brett: A Friendship
(Santa Fe: Sunstone Press, 1974; Philadelphia and New York: Lippincott, 1933); and Emily Hahn, Lorenzo: D. H. Lawrence and the Women
Who Loved Him (Philadelphia and New York: Lippincott, 1975), pp. 309-
10. Harry Moore also includes this testimony in the British Penguin
edition of The Priest of Love and in the corrigenda for the paperback edition published by Southern Illinois University Press. Other
Lawrence scholars have already questioned the validity of the word
"boobs" as part of Lawrence's vocabulary. This seems to me a verbal
quibble, not unlike Lawrence's, over the wrong appendages. Whatever
its verbal inaccuracies, the new reminiscence rings true in tenor
and substance.

16. "A Propos of Lady Chatterley's Lover," in Sex, Literature
and Censorship, ed. Harry T. Moore (New York: Twayne, 1953), p. 120.
Page references to this edition in the text follow the initials AP.

17. David Garnett, "Frieda and Lawrence," in D. H. Lawrence:
Novelist, Poet, Prophet, p. 39.

18. See Lucas, Frieda Lawrence, pp. 200-203, 243-53, 255; and
Moore, The Priest of Love, pp. 378, 415, 455, 507.

19. See Barbara Weekley Barr, in Spender, p. 30.

20. Mark Spilka, The Love Ethic of D. H. Lawrence (Bloomington:
Indiana University Press, 1955), pp. 194-98.

21. Lady Chatterley's Lover (New York: Grove, 1962), p. 346.
Quotations in the text identified by chapter only are from this
edition.

22. The Priest of Love, p. 428.

23. Selected Letters of James Joyce, ed. Richard Ellmann (London:
Faber and Faber, 1975), p. 190.

24. "'Mentalized Sex' in D. H. Lawrence," Novel: A Forum on
Fiction 8 (Winter 1975):114-16, 122.

25. "Character and Consciousness: D. H. Lawrence, Wilhelm
Reich, and Jean-Paul Sartre," University of Toronto Quarterly 43
(Summer 1974):330. See also Adamowski's "Being Perfect: Lawrence,
Sartre, and Women in Love," Critical Inquiry 2 (Winter 1975):
367-68.

CLARK, Immediacy and Recollection

1. D. H. Lawrence, Women in Love (New York: Viking, 1960),
p. viii.

2. Atheneum, 25 February 1911, p. 217.

3. D. H. Lawrence, Sons and Lovers (New York: Viking, 1958),
p. 152.

4. _Phoenix: The Posthumous Papers of D. H. Lawrence_ (London: Heinemann, 1936), pp. 580-81.

5. D. H. Lawrence, _Etruscan Places_ in _Mornings in Mexico and Etruscan Places_ (London: Heinemann, 1956), p. 72.

6. D. H. Lawrence, _The Rainbow_ (London: Heinemann, 1955), p. 2.

7. _The Collected Letters of D. H. Lawrence_, 2 vols., ed. Harry T. Moore (New York: Viking, 1962), 1:364.

8. _Phoenix_, p. 85; Passage IA.

9. D. H. Lawrence, _Twilight in Italy_ (London: Heinemann, 1956), p. 13; Passage IB.

10. Ibid., p. 14; Passage IB.

11. _Women in Love_, p. 465; Passage IC.

12. _The Collected Letters_, p. 151; Passage IIA.

13. Ibid., p. 150; Passage IIA.

14. Ibid., pp. 150-51; Passage IIA.

15. Ibid., p. 151; Passage IIA.

16. _English Review_ (September 1913), pp. 219-20; Passage IIB.

17. _Twilight in Italy_, pp. 51-52; Passage IIC.

18. Ibid., p. 53; Passage IIC.

19. _The Collected Letters_, p. 227; Passage IIIA.

20. Ibid., p. 241; Passage IIIC.

21. Ibid., p. 241; Passage IIID.

22. D. H. Lawrence, _The Escaped Cock_, ed. Gerald M. Lacy (Los Angeles: Black Sparrow Press, 1973), p. 35; Passage IIIE.

23. D. H. Lawrence, _Sea and Sardinia_ (London: Heinemann, 1956), p. 52; Passage IVA.

24. _Phoenix II: Uncollected, Unpublished and Other Prose Works by D. H. Lawrence_, ed. Warren Roberts and Harry T. Moore (London: Heinemann, 1968), p. 600.

25. Ibid., p. 597.

26. D. H. Lawrence, _The Princess and Other Stories_, ed. Keith Sagar (London: Penguin, 1971).

27. _Phoenix_, p. 829; Passage IVB.

28. Hebrews 13:14.

29. D. H. Lawrence, _The Symbolic Meaning: The Uncollected Versions of "Studies in Classic American Literature,"_ ed. Armin Arnold, with Preface by Harry T. Moore (Fontwell, Arundel: Centaur Press, 1962), p. 94.

30. Ibid., p. 97.

31. Ibid.

32. Phoenix, p. 94.

33. D. H. Lawrence, St. Mawr and The Man Who Died (New York: Random House, 1959), p. 149.

34. The Collected Letters, pp. 794-95; Passage VA.

35. Phoenix, p. 24; Passage VB.

36. St. Mawr, p. 152.

37. Ibid., p. 146; Passage VC.

38. Ibid.

39. Ibid., pp. 145-46; Passage VC.

40. Ibid., p. 134.

41. Ibid., p. 135.

42. Ibid., p. 140.

43. Ibid., p. 159.

44. Ibid., p. 146; Passage VC.

45. Mornings in Mexico, pp. 80-81; Passage VD.

46. Ibid., p. 82; Passage VD.

BALBERT, The Loving of Lady Chatterley

1. Lady Chatterley's Lover (New York: Grove, 1959), p. 291. All subsequent references are to this edition and will include the abbreviation LCL and the page number.

2. My initial, more comprehensive statement of the significance of "the phallic imagination" is in my essay on how Lawrence derived the concept in Sons and Lovers, in "Forging and Feminism: Sons and Lovers and the Phallic Imagination," The D. H. Lawrence Review 2 (Summer 1978), 83-113. Lawrence, of course, describes the correlative processes of "singling out" and "star-equilibrium" throughout Psychoanalysis and the Unconscious and Fantasia of the Unconscious (New York: Viking, Compass, 1960).

3. Near the end of his life, in a discussion with his friend, Earl Brewster--reported by Harry T. Moore, in his biography of Lawrence--Lawrence explained the significance of the symbolism in his "pictures," and implicitly commented on his intentions in Lady Chatterley's Lover:

"I try," Lawrence told his Buddhistic friend, "to keep the Middle of me harmonious to the Middle of the universe. Outwardly I know I'm in a bad temper, and let it go at that." But he stuck to his beliefs "and put a phallus, a lingam you call it, in each one of my pictures somewhere. And I paint no picture that won't shock people's castrated social spirituality." But this man's motive was never obscenity: "I do this out of positive belief that the phallus is a great sacred image: it represents a deep, deep life which has been

denied in us, and still is denied. Women deny it horribly,
with a grinning travesty of sex. But pazienza! pazienza!
One can still believe. And with the lingam, and the mystery
behind it, goes beauty" (The Priest of Love: A Life of D. H.
Lawrence, rev. ed. [New York: Farrar, 1974], p. 328).

In a letter to S. S. Koteliansky on 23 December 1927, Lawrence is
quite explicit about his intentions in Lady Chatterley's Lover: "It's
the most important novel ever written and as Jehovah you would probably find it sheer pornography. But it isn't. It's a declaration of
the phallic reality" (The Collected Letters of D. H. Lawrence, ed.
Harry T. Moore, 2 vols. [New York: Viking, 1962], 2:1028).

4. Both Lawrence's anger at society and his related prophetic
impulse for the creation of Lady Chatterley's Lover are reflected
in a letter about the novel, sent to G. R. G. Conway on 15 March 1928:

> It is--in the latter half at least--a phallic novel, but tender
> and delicate. You know I believe in the phallic reality, and
> the phallic consciousness: as distinct from our irritable
> cerebral consciousness of today. That's why I do the book--
> and it's not just sex. Sex alas is one of the worst phenomena
> of today: all cerebral reaction, the whole thing worked from
> mental processes and itch, and not a bit of the real phallic
> insouciance and spontaneity. But in my novel there is (The
> Priest of Love, p. 424).

5. "In Our Time: A Review." From Phoenix (New York: Viking,
1936), p. 366.

6. Ibid., p. 535.

7. Women in Love (New York: Viking, 1960), p. viii.

8. My explanation here of Lawrence's use of rhythm and repetition
is a slightly reworded version of my original discussion in D. H.
Lawrence and the Psychology of Rhythm (The Hague: Mouton, 1974).

9. The Collected Letters, p. 251.

10. "Pornography and Obscenity," which appeared in 1929, is re-
printed in Sex, Literature and Censorship, ed. Harry T. Moore (New
York: Viking Compass, 1959), pp. 64-81. Snodgrass's essay, "A Rocking-
Horse: The Symbol, the Pattern, the Way to Live," is from The Hudson
Review 11 (Summer 1958):191-200, and is reprinted in D. H. Lawrence:
A Collection of Critical Essays, ed. Mark Spilka (Englewood Cliffs,
N. J.: Prentice-Hall, 1963), pp. 117-26.

11. See Mark Spilka's excellent discussion of both the issue of
what he calls "bourgeois life" vs. "organic life" in Lady Chatterley's
Lover, and the necessity for the symbol and fact of Clifford's paralysis, in his study, The Love Ethic of D. H. Lawrence (Bloomington:
Indiana University Press, 1955), pp. 177-204.

12. The Prisoner of Sex (New York: Signet, New American Library,
1971), p. 97.

13. Sons and Lovers (New York: Viking Compass, 1958), p. 317.

14. _Armies of the Night_ (New York: Signet, New American Library, 1968), p. 36.

15. _The Prisoner of Sex_, p. 107.

16. Two of the most publicized and unfortunate examples of the dangers of feminist criticism of Lawrence are in Kate Millett's _Sexual Politics_ (Garden City, N. Y.: Doubleday, 1970), and Carolyn Heilbrun's _Towards a Recognition of Androgyny_ (New York: Harper Colophon, 1974). I assume that Mailer's pertinent request, in _The Prisoner of Sex_ (p. 105), for Millett to take off her business suit is sufficient rejoinder to her insensitive summary of the first sexual scene in _Lady Chatterley's Lover_, as Millett maintains that "Mellors concedes one kiss on the navel and then gets to business" (p. 243). Heilbrun remains content with an odd assertion that _Lady Chatterley's Lover_ is distasteful because of "its demeaning of the female figure" (p. 101)-- no doubt the last charge that Lawrence would have expected about his worshipful novel.

17. _The Rainbow_ (New York: Viking Compass, 1961), p. 180.

SANDERS, D. H. Lawrence and the Sacralization
of Nature

1. _Sons and Lovers_ (New York: Viking, 1958), pp. 353-54.

2. _John Thomas and Lady Jane_ (New York: Viking, 1973), p. 130.

3. _The Plumed Serpent_ (New York: Knopf, 1966), p. 54.

4. I have explored these misgivings about language within a larger context in my essay, "The Lefthandedness of Modern Literature," _Twentieth-Century Literature_ 23, no. 4 (December 1977):417-36

5. _The Rainbow_ (New York: Viking, 1961), p. 213.

6. _Women in Love_ (New York: Viking, 1960), p. 65.

7. Ibid., p. 399.

8. _John Thomas and Lady Jane_, p. 84.

9. _The Rainbow_, p. 141.

10. Ibid., pp. 125-26.

11. _Women in Love_, pp. 220-21.

12. _Phoenix_ (New York: Viking, 1936), p. 419.

13. _The Rainbow_, p. 437.

14. _Women in Love_, pp. 469-70.

ROSS, Homoerotic Feeling in _Women in Love_

I thank Stephen Gill, Cecil Lang, Robert Langbaum, Kenny Marotta, Leo Rockas, and Alex Zwerdling for suggesting improvements in substance and style.

1. D. H. Lawrence, "Prologue to _Women in Love_," ed. George Ford, _Texas Quarterly_ 6, no. 1 (1963), 98-111.

2. It would be invidious to mention names since the charge is almost universal.

3. Charles L. Ross, The Composition of "The Rainbow" and "Women in Love": A History (Charlottesville: University Press of Virginia, 1979), pp. 126-30.

4. David Cavitch, D. H. Lawrence and the New World (New York: Oxford University Press, 1969), p. 67.

5. Jeffrey Meyers, "Lawrence and Homosexuality," London Magazine 13, no. 4 (1973), 71, 78. The first phrase was originally John Middleton Murry's; Meyer endorses it without qualification.

6. Ibid., p. 86.

7. For a discussion of the distinction between author's intentions and enacted intentions, see Dorothea Krook, "Intentions and Intentions: The Problem of Intention and Henry James's The Turn of the Screw," in The Theory of the Novel, ed. John Halperin (New York: Oxford University Press, 1974), pp. 353-55.

8. Ross, pp. 97-123.

9. The last two drafts of the novel are listed as E441 d and e in Warren Roberts, A Bibliography of D. H. Lawrence (London: Rupert Hart-Davis, 1963), p. 353. I shall cite the penultimate draft (or E441d) as roman numeral I, and the final draft (E441e) as II.

10. Prologue, pp. 107-8.

11. Timothy d'Arch Smith, Love in Earnest: Some Notes on the Lives and Writings of English "Uranian" Poets from 1889 to 1930 (London: Routledge & Kegan Paul, 1970), pp. 191-93.

12. Prologue, p. 101.

13. Prologue, p. 103.

14. Meyers, p. 81.

15. d'Arch Smith, p. 187.

16. S. F. Damon, Amy Lowell: A Chronicle (Boston: Houghton Mifflin, 1935), p. 369.

17. The new dialogue occupies all of page 64 in the Modern Library edition. D. H. Lawrence, Women in Love (New York: Random House, n.d.).

18. This inspiration required the insertation of an extra, handwritten page, II:330a, which runs from page 234, line 37, to page 235, line 38, in the Modern Library edition.

19. After a visit from David Garnett and Francis Birrell he wrote: "These horrible little frowsty people, men lovers of men, they give me such a sense of corruption. . . ." Lawrence to S. S. Koteliansky, 20 April 1915, in The Collected Letters of D. H. Lawrence, ed. Harry T. Moore (London: Heinemann, 1962), p. 333.

20. These are Keynes's own words, in D. H. Lawrence: A Composite Biography, ed. Edward Nehls (Madison: University of Wisconsin Press, 1957), I, 288.

21. Scott Sanders, D. H. Lawrence: The World of the Five Novels (New York: Viking, 1973), pp. 127-28.

22. D. H. Lawrence, "We Need One Another," Phoenix, ed. E. D. McDonald (New York: Viking, 1936; rept., 1968), p. 193.

23. It is chapter 16 out of 31, so there are precisely fifteen on either side.

ROSSMAN, The Boy in the Bush in the Lawrence Canon

For permission to examine the copy of The Boy in the Bush marked by M. L. Skinner, and for permission to examine the typescript of the novel, the author thanks the Humanities Research Center at the University of Texas at Austin.

1. In addition to Moore's account of these materials, there exists a 56-page thesis, unpublished, by Rose Anne Serar Lee, "The Boy in the Bush: A Study of the Collaboration of D. H. Lawrence and M. L. Skinner" (University of Texas, 1967), which Moore cites. My citations to The Boy in the Bush will be made in parentheses within the text to the first English edition (London: Martin Secker, 1924). The American reprint edited by Harry T. Moore is identical in content and pagination.

2. My account of the collaboration draws upon numerous readily available materials, in addition to the accounts by Moore and Lee. For general background, I have learned from Marjorie Ree's "Mollie Skinner and D. H. Lawrence," published in the Australian journal Westerly (March 1964). More important for specific matters have been the articles by M. L. Skinner herself and her friend Katherine Susannah Prichard, which appeared, respectively, in the Australian publications Southerly (13, no. 4, 1952) and Meanjin, no. 4 (Summer 1950). Skinner and Prichard are reprinted in Edward Nehls' D. H. Lawrence: A Composite Biography, vol. II (Madison: University of Wisconsin Press, 1958), cited in my text as Nehls II. Citations to Lawrence's letters are to The Collected Letters of D. H. Lawrence, vol. II, ed. Harry T. Moore (New York: Viking, 1962), cited parenthetically as CL II; and to The Letters of D. H. Lawrence, ed. Aldous Huxley (London: Heinemann, 1932), cited parenthetically as AH. Lawrence's preface to Skinner's Black Swans can be found in Phoenix II, eds. Warren Roberts and Harry T. Moore (New York: Viking, 1968), cited as P II.

3. Skinner runs a continuous marginal line from p. 330 to p. 341, where she adds the words "To end DHL." Then a new marginal line runs from p. 342 to p. 345. Numerous typescript changes were also made by Lawrence on this chapter.

ARNOLD, D. H. Lawrence in Ascona?

1. See the report about the Berlin exhibition by Wieland Schmied in Die Zeit (Overseas Edition), 14 April 1979, p. 16.

2. See Robert Lucas, Frieda von Richthofen (Munich: Kindler, 1972); and Martin Green, The von Richthofen Sisters (London:

Weidenfelt and Nicholson, 1974). Emanuel Hurwitz, who wrote the
chapter on Otto Gross in the exhibition catalogue, is the author of
the first book on Gross, Otto Gross (Frankfurt am Main: Suhrkamp,
1979).

3. Her real name was Frieda. To distinguish her from Frieda
Lawrence, I shall use the name by which she was called by her
friends: Friedel.

4. For a detailed description of Lawrence's itinerary, see Armin
Arnold, "D. H. Lawrence in der Schweiz," Neue Zürcher Zeitung,
Morgenausgabe, 21 May 1957; and Armin Arnold, "In the Footsteps of
D. H. Lawrence in Switzerland," Texas Studies in Language and Litera-
ture, 3 (1961), 184-88.

5. The Collected Letters of D. H. Lawrence, ed., Harry T. Moore
(London: Heinemann, 1962), 1:227.

6. D. H. Lawrence, Twilight in Italy (London: Heinemann, 1956),
p. 145, cited hereafter in the text as T.i.I.

7. Frieda Lawrence, The Memoirs and Correspondence, ed. E. W.
Tedlock (London: Heinemann, Ltd., 1961), pp. 73-74.

8. Green, p. 60.

9. In fact, Gross was in Berlin at the time, but Lawrence could
have found out only after his arrival in Ascona.

BLANCHARD, The "Real Quartet" of
Women in Love

1. See Nina Auerbach's fine study of this tradition, Communities
of Women: An Idea in Fiction (Cambridge, Mass.: Harvard University
Press, 1978), pp. 3-5.

2. Among the exceptions is L. D. Clark. In "The Contravened
Knot" (Approaches to the Twentieth-Century Novel, ed. John Unterecker
[New York: Thomas Y. Crowell, 1965]), Clark writes, "Relationships
between the two men and between the two women are important but subordinate" (p. 57). Although Clark believes the importance of women-
together in the novel is "far from negligible" (p. 76), even he
concludes that Lawrence is more interested in "the question of sympathy . . . between man and man" (p. 75).

3. Ford, "An Introductory Note to D. H. Lawrence's Prologue to
Women in Love," The Texas Quarterly, 6, no. 1, p. 94.

4. Delavenay, D. H. Lawrence and Edward Carpenter: A Study in
Edwardian Transition (New York: Taplinger, 1971) and Delany, D. H.
Lawrence's Nightmare: The Writer and His Circle in the Years of the
Great War (New York: Basic Books, 1978).

5. See, for example, Edmund Bergler, M.D., "D. H. Lawrence's
The Fox and the Psychoanalytic Theory on Lesbianism," A D. H. Lawrence
Miscellany, ed. Harry T. Moore (Carbondale: Southern Illinois University Press, 1959). Bergler argues that "The Fox" contains "a series
of observations and between-the-lines allusions [about lesbianism]

which are clinically correct. Mingled with these are inaccuracies"
(p. 52).

6. Millett, Sexual Politics (New York: Avon Books, 1969, 1971),
p. 266. A few critics, however, had made similar arguments earlier
than the past decade; Katherine Anne Porter, for example, complained
that in Lady Chatterley's Lover Lawrence shows that "women must be
kept apart, for they contaminate each other." See "A Wreath for the
Gamekeeper," Encounter (February 1960), p. 70.

7. Howe, "Feminism and Literature," in Images of Women in Fic-
tion: Feminist Perspectives, ed. Susan Koppelman Cornillon (Bowling
Green, Ohio: Bowling Green University Popular Press, 1972), p. 266.
Core, "'The Closed Door': Love Between Women in the Works of D. H.
Lawrence," The D. H. Lawrence Review 11, no. 2, p. 120. Harris,
"D. H. Lawrence and Kate Millett," The Massachusetts Review 15,
no. 3, p. 527.

8. T. E. Apter, "Let's Hear What the Male Chauvinist is Saying:
The Plumed Serpent," Lawrence and Women, ed. Anne Smith (London:
Vision Press, 1978).

9. Ford, "An Introductory Note," p. 97.

10. The Collected Letters of D. H. Lawrence, ed. Harry T. Moore
(New York: Viking, 1962), 1:441.

11. Collected Letters, 1:565. This is the letter in which
Lawrence also writes Mansfield, "I do think a woman must yield some
sort of precedence to a man, and he must take this precedence."

12. Millett, pp. 265–66.

13. Keith Sagar, "The Genesis of The Rainbow and Women in Love,"
The D. H. Lawrence Review 1, no. 3, p. 196.

14. Even the precise nature of Lawrence's relationship with
William Henry Hocking remains speculative.

15. The Collected Letters, I, 273.

16. Charles Ross (in "The Composition of Women in Love: A History, 1913–1919," The D. H. Lawrence Review, 8, no. 2, p. 207) cites
an unpublished letter from Lawrence to Thomas Seltzer, dated
7 September 1919, in the Humanities Research Library, University of
Texas at Austin: "And which title do you prefer, 'Women in Love,'
or 'The Sisters.'" Also see The Collected Letters, I, 615. Lawrence,
of course, also considered other titles (The Wedding Ring, The
Latter Days, Dies Irae, Noah's Ark), but none, apparently, that
emphasized brotherhood.

17. D. H. Lawrence, The Rainbow (New York: Viking, 1961), p. 217.
Subsequent references are in text notes.

18. The Quest for Rananim: D. H. Lawrence's Letters to S. S.
Koteliansky, ed. George J. Zytaruk (Montreal: McGill-Queen's University Press, 1970), p. 39.

19. D. H. Lawrence, Women in Love (New York: Viking, 1960), pp. 418-19. Subsequent references are in text notes.

20. Ford, "An Introductory Note," p. 96.

21. Ibid. Also see Eldon S. Branda, "Textual Changes in Women in Love," Texas Studies in Literature and Language, 6, no. 3. Branda also argues, "Always, where changes are made, Lawrence seemed to be making Birkin less concrete in his association with other men; this becomes more significant when we see that he was becoming more positive in describing Birkin's association with women" (p. 312).

22. Auerbach, Communities of Women, p. 9.

23. Howe, "Feminism and Literature," p. 266.

24. See Auerbach's discussion, Communities of Women, p. 9.

25. The Collected Letters, 1:324.

HINZ and TEUNISSEN, Women in Love and the Myth of
Eros and Psyche

1. Phoenix II, Uncollected, Unpublished and Other Prose Works by D. H. Lawrence, eds. Warren Roberts and Harry T. Moore (London: Heinemann, 1968), pp. 539-42.

2. Women in Love (New York: Viking, 1960), p. 142. Subsequent references will be to this edition and will be incorporated in the text.

3. Our rationale for using the name "Eros" rather than "Cupid" derives partly from Lawrence's usage here and partly from the fact that "Cupid" has connotations which, if they are true to the initial characterization of the god, are not true to the final depiction of him in the myth.

4. Erich Neumann, Amor and Psyche: The Psychic Development of the Feminine: A Commentary on the Tale by Apuleius, trans. from the German by Ralph Manheim (Princeton: Princeton University Press, 1956). Included in Neumann's book is also H. E. Butler's translation of Apuleius' tale, and since there is no way of knowing which translation Lawrence could have read, for the purpose of convenience subsequent quotations from the myth will refer to this translation.

5. The Collected Letters of D. H. Lawrence, ed. Harry T. Moore (New York: Viking, 1962), 2:615.

6. Douglas Bush, Mythology and the Renaissance Tradition in English Poetry (New York: Norton, 1963), p. 241.

7. Jean Hagstrum, "Eros and Psyche: Some Versions of Romantic Love and Delicacy," Critical Inquiry, 3 (Spring 1977):521-42.

8. See Phoenix: The Posthumous Papers of D. H. Lawrence, ed. Edward D. McDonald (New York: Viking, 1968), p. 296.

BOULTON, The Cambridge University Press Edition
of Lawrence's Letters, Part 4

1. The Letters of D. H. Lawrence, ed. James T. Boulton (Cambridge: Cambridge University Press, 1979), 1:114; hereafter cited in the text and notes as Letters.

2. Ibid., 1:471.

3. Ibid., 1:289.

4. Correspondence of Alexander Pope, ed. George Sherburn (Oxford: Oxford University Press, 1956), 1:160.

5. Compton Mackenzie, My Life and Times: Octave Five (London: Chatto & Windus, 1966), pp. 177-78.

6. Letters, 1:343, 364, 371.

7. Ibid., 1:196.

8. Ibid., 1:252, 119.

9. Ibid., 1:127.

10. Ibid., 1:469.

11. Ibid., 1:277.

LACY, The Case for an Edition of the Letters
of D. H. Lawrence

1. Catherine Carswell, The Savage Pilgrimage: A Narrative of D. H. Lawrence (London: Martin Secker, 1932), pp. vii-viii.

2. Denis Donoghue, "Till the Fight is Finished: D. H. Lawrence in His Letters," in D. H. Lawrence, Novelist, Poet, Prophet, ed. Stephen Spender (New York: Harper & Row, 1973), pp. 198-99.

3. From a report of this lecture in "Contemporary Letters Are As Good As Any, Says Eliot," Yale News, 24 February 1933. For reference to this lecture see Donald Gallup, A Bibliography of T. S. Eliot (London: Faber and Faber, 1969), p. 227 C341. In the only other reference to the lecture, F. O. Matthiessen quotes from it in The Achievement of T. S. Eliot (New York: Oxford University Press, 1959 reprint of 1935 edition), p. 90. Mrs. Eliot, in a letter of 18 June 1970, informs me that no manuscript of this lecture has been preserved.

4. It is worth pointing out that even Lawrence's letters have had their influence on at least one of the major novels of the twentieth century. In the Selected Letters of Malcolm Lowry (New York: Capricorn, 1969), Lowry acknowledges to his editor, Albert Erskine, in a letter of 30 June 1946, that Under the Volcano contains several "echoes" of phrases found in Lawrence's letters.

5. Letters of Aldous Huxley, ed. Grover Smith (New York: Harper & Row, 1969), pp. 331-32, 335-39, 340.

ZYTARUK, Editing Lawrence's Letters: The Strategy of
Volume Division

1. Harry T. Moore, ed., The Collected Letters of D. H. Lawrence
(New York: Viking, 1962).

2. Aldous Huxley, ed., The Letters of D. H. Lawrence (London:
Heinemann, 1932), p. 174.

3. See the "Epilogue" in Dorothy Brett, Lawrence and Brett: A
Friendship, with an Introduction, Prologue, and Epilogue by John
Manchester (Santa Fe: Sunstone Press, 1974), p. III

4. James T. Boulton, ed., The Letters of D. H. Lawrence (Cambridge: Cambridge University Press, 1979), 1:551.

5. The Collected Letters, 1:480

6. Ibid.

7. Ibid., p. 602.

8. John Ruskin, "Of Kings' Treasuries," Sesame and Lilies (1865),
Sec. 3.

SAGAR, Beyond D. H. Lawrence

1. Philip Larkin, High Windows (London: Faber and Faber, 1974),
p. 34.

2. Friedrich Nietzsche, The Birth of Tragedy (Garden City, N. Y.:
Doubleday, 1956), p. 29.

3. D. H. Lawrence, Phoenix (London: Heinemann, 1936), p. 480.

4. Thomas Hardy, Tess of the D'Urbervilles (London: Macmillan,
1950), p. 49.

5. Lawrence, p. 439.

6. D. H. Lawrence, Phoenix II (London: Heinemann, 1968), p. 281.

7. Harry T. Moore, ed., Collected Letters of D. H. Lawrence
(London: Heinemann, 1962), 1:453.

8. D. H. Lawrence, Aaron's Rod (Harmondsworth: Penguin Books,
1950), p. 144.

9. Ted Hughes, Crow (London: Faber and Faber, 1970).

10. Ibid., p. 22.

11. Keith Sagar, The Art of Ted Hughes (Cambridge: Cambridge
University Press, 1978), p. 132. Reprinted by kind permission of
Olwyn Hughes.

12. Hughes, Gaudete (London: Faber and Faber, 1977).

13. Hughes, Season Songs (London: Faber and Faber, 1976).

Index